BATTLEGROUND
PRAYERS
& DECREES

THE INSTITUTE OF SPIRITUAL WARFARE'S PRAYER GUIDE AND COMPENDIUM

Prayer M. Madueke

BEST-SELLING AUTHOR OF MONITORING SPIRITS
& PRAYING WITH THE BLOOD OF JESUS

ISBN: 978-1-964584-03-4

Published by Prayer Publications.
Printed in the United States of America.

4 Free Ebooks

In order to say a 'Thank You' for purchasing *Battleground Prayers and Decrees*, I offer these books to you in appreciation. Click or type **madueke.com/free-gift** in your browser.

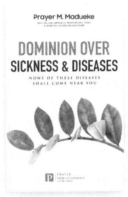
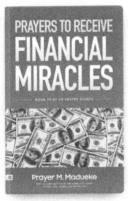

Message from the Author

I want to see you succeed, grow, and break free from negativity and obstacles. My hope is for you to thrive, unaffected by negative influences and challenging situations. Because of that, please permit me to introduce two courses that I believe passionately will help you:

1. To break the evil altars and powers of your father's house, The role of altars in the realm of existence is very key because altars are meeting places between the physical and the spiritual, between the visible and the invisible.

    Unless a man cuts off the evil flow from the power of his father's house, he will not fulfil his destiny. **Click here** to learn more about **my course** on how to tear down unholy altars and close the enemy's entryways into your life!

2. To help you seamlessly break iron-like problems, illness, delayed marriage, poverty, or any long-standing battle.

    Discover **the transformative power of Christian fasting and prayer**. Remember, Matthew 17:21 teaches us, *"But this kind of demon does not go out except by prayer and fasting."* Ready to overcome your struggles? **Click here** to learn more about this course.

Embrace the journey ahead with faith, for through prayer, fasting, and the dismantling of evil altars, you shall unlock the doors to spiritual liberation and divine breakthrough. May your path be illuminated by His grace as you walk towards a life free from bondage.

If you're seeing this from the physical copy, type the link: **madueke.com/courses** in your browser to view all the courses on my website.

Christian Counselling

We were created for a greater purpose than only survival and God wants us to live a full life.

If you need prayer or counselling, or if you have any other inquiries, please visit the counselling page on my website to know when I will be available for a phone call.

Click or type **links.madueke.com/counselling** in your browser.

Let's Connect on Youtube ▶

Join me on my YouTube channel, "Prayer M. Madueke," where I share powerful insights, guidance, and prayers for spiritual breakthroughs.

Subscribe today to unlock the secrets of the Kingdom and embrace an abundant life. Let's grow together!

Click or type links.madueke.com/youtube in your browser.

TABLE OF CONTENTS

ONE

UNDERSTANDING SPIRITUAL WARFARE

DECREE-1

(Ephesians 6:12; Galatians 5:17; 1 Peter 5:7-9, Luke 22:31, Matthew 13:19, 24-30; Luke 11:24-26, Luke 22:31, Joshua 7:21, Genesis 3:1-6., Exodus 14:26-31, Exodus 12:29, 30, Exodus 9:25-26)

Day 1

Expectations:

1. The destruction of every principality behind your problems.
2. The destruction of every evil power militating against your life and destiny.
3. The destruction of every evil program going on against your life.
4. Complete deliverance from the activities of spiritual wickedness.
5. The destruction of everything that is blocking your way to freedom.

YOUR DECREE:

Any principality behind my problems; your time is up, be frustrated by the power of God, in the mighty name of Jesus. I command every evil power militating against my destiny to fail woefully, in the name of Jesus. Let the rulers of darkness blocking my way to freedom scatter and be disengaged, in the name of Jesus. Almighty God, arise and deliver me from the powers of sin and its consequences, in the name of Jesus. Father Lord, deliver me from the activities of spiritual wickedness in the high places, in the name of Jesus. Any evil force weakening my strength in the Lord, I break your backbone, in the name of Jesus.

> For we do not wrestle against flesh and blood, but against the rulers, against the authorities, against the cosmic powers over this present darkness, against the spiritual forces of evil in the heavenly places.
>
> — EPHESIANS 6:12

> For the desires of the flesh are against the Spirit, and the desires of the Spirit are against the flesh, for these are opposed to each other, to keep you from doing the things you want to do.
>
> — GALATIANS 5:17

Every satanic agreement and evil movement taking place to draw me away from God, fail woefully, in the name of Jesus. Let the might of God sustain me from every evil action against my faith in Christ, in the name of Jesus. Blood of Jesus, speak me out of every work of the devil and his agents, in the name of Jesus. Every evil program going on against my life, be terminated by the speaking blood of Jesus, in the name of Jesus. Almighty God, deliver and empower me to rise and stand against the wiles of the devil, in the name of Jesus. I command the strength of the devil in my life to be destroyed by divine might, in the name of Jesus. Every enemy of my sound health, be destroyed by the anointing from God, in the name of Jesus. Father Lord, command my blessing to manifest in my life from above, in the name of Jesus. I command everything in me to rise against the works of the devil and his agents in my life, in the name of Jesus. Every demonic accomplishment against my life, be destroyed in a moment, in the name of Jesus.

Day 2

Expectations:

1. Receiving the grace to overcome every evil going on against you.
2. Receiving the power to rise and stand against all the wiles of the devil.
3. Commanding promotion from above to begin to manifest in every area of your life.
4. The weakening of every adversary in the battle field of your life
5. The termination of every war going on against your health and settlement in life

YOUR DECREE:

Almighty God, release your grace upon me and help me to overcome every evil that is going on against my destiny, in the name of Jesus. Let the glory of God begin to manifest in my life against every satanic movement, in the name of Jesus. Father Lord, empower me to rise and stand against the wiles of the devil, in the name of Jesus.

Casting all your anxieties on him, because he cares for you. Be sober-minded; be watchful. Your adversary the devil prowls around like a roaring lion, seeking someone to devour. Resist him, firm in your faith, knowing that the same kinds of suffering are being experienced by your brotherhood throughout the world.

— 1 PETER 5:7-9

"Simon, Simon, behold, Satan demanded to have you, that he might sift you like wheat

— LUKE 22:31

I humble myself under the mighty hand of God before, during and after the time of battle, in the name of Jesus. Promotion from above, begin to manifest in every area of my life, in the name of Jesus. Let the power of God to cast all my cares upon God without getting worried come upon me, in the name of Jesus. Almighty God, help me to patiently wait to be promoted in due time according to your plan, in the name of Jesus. Let the caring strength of God begin to manifest in my life without obstructions, in the name of Jesus. Anointing and divine grace to be sober and vigilant, fall upon me, in the name of Jesus. I command every adversary in the battle field of my life to be weakened unto death, in the name of Jesus. Every demonic and satanic possessed agent, seeking to devour me, be frustrated, in the mighty name of Jesus. By the power of the anointing of God, I resist every evil force militating against my destiny, in the name of Jesus. Any satanic weapon resisting my faith in Christ, be rendered impotent, in the name of Jesus. Any affliction going on against my life, be terminated by the spoken word of God, in the name of Jesus. Any war going on against my health and settlement in life, end to my favor, in the name of Jesus. By the power of God, I take unto my life the whole armor of God, in the mighty name of Jesus. Let my faith in Christ Jesus frustrate every satanic strength militating against my destiny, in the name of Jesus.

Day 3

Expectations:

1. **Receiving the anointing to withstand every satanic uprising against your life and destiny.**

2. **The destruction of every evil, apportioned to the remaining days of your life.**

3. **The destruction of every satanic plantation in your heart, body, life and destiny**

4. **The removal of every demonic stone in your heart**

5. **The destruction of everything that has been assigned to weaken the word of God in your heart, life and destiny.**

YOUR DECREE:

Anointing to withstand every satanic uprising against my life, fall upon me, in the name of Jesus. Any evil apportioned to the remaining days of my life, receive destruction without success, in the name of Jesus. Almighty God, increase my strength and wisdom against the devil and his determined agents, in the name of Jesus. Almighty God, fix the breastplate of righteousness into my life and let it be permanent, in the name of Jesus.

When anyone hears the word of the kingdom and does not understand it, the evil one comes and snatches away what has been sown in his heart. This is what was sown along the path. He put another parable before them, saying, "The kingdom of heaven may be compared to a man who sowed good seed in his field, but while his men were sleeping, his enemy came and sowed weeds among the wheat and went away. So when the plants came up and bore grain, then the weeds appeared also. And the servants of the master of the house came and said to him, 'Master, did you not sow good seed in your field? How then does it have weeds?' He said to them, 'An enemy has done this.' So the servants said to him, 'Then do you want us to go and gather them?' But he said, No, lest in gathering the weeds you root up the wheat along with them. Let both grow together until the harvest, and at harvest time I will tell the reapers, "Gather the weeds first and bind them in bundles to be burned, but gather the wheat into my barn."

— MATTHEW 13:19, 24-30.

Almighty God, by your power, I destroy every satanic plantation in my heart, in the name of Jesus. By divine intervention, I remove every demonic stone in my heart, in the name of Jesus. Anointing to hear God's word and put them into practice, fall upon me, in the name of Jesus. Father Lord, increase and retain your joy, peace and your word in my heart, in the name of Jesus. Let the word of God be permanently fixed into my heart and be used against the works of the devil at the right time, in the name of Jesus. Any tribulation or persecution assigned to weaken the word of God in me, be frustrated, in the name of Jesus. Every satanic thorn planted in my life against the manifestation of the word of God, be uprooted, in the name of Jesus. Almighty God, deliver me from the things of this world, in the name of Jesus. Every satanic desire to have me and sift me as wheat, be frustrated by the power of God. Let the prayers of Jesus and his wishes for the saints begin to manifest in my life, in the name of Jesus. Every arrow of weakness in faith, fired against me, I return you back to your sender, in the name of Jesus. By the power of divine strength, I receive the strength to be strong to strengthen all believers around me, in the name of Jesus.

Day 4

Expectations:

1. **The destruction of every evil spirit that has been anointed to kill you.**

2. **The destruction of every negative word ever released against your destiny.**

3. **Receiving the grace to supplicate and persevere in prayers.**

4. **The destruction of every evil spirit assigned to steal the word of God from your heart.**

5. **Frustrating the aborting power of the devil against any aspect of your life and destiny.**

YOUR DECREE:

Any evil spirit, anointed to kill me, fail woefully and be disappointed, in the name of Jesus. I put on the shield of faith and the supernatural ability to be able to quench all the fiery darts of the wicked fighting against my life, in the name of Jesus. Any demonic helmet in my head, visible or invisible, be replaced with the helmet of salvation, in the name of Jesus. Let the sword of the Spirit, the word of God destroy to death every negative word released against my destiny, in the name of Jesus. Father Lord, increase my perseverance and supplication for all saints, in the name of Jesus. Anointing to pray always with all prayer and supplications in the Spirit, fall upon me, in the name of Jesus.

> "When the unclean spirit has gone out of a person, it passes through waterless places seeking rest, and finding none it says, 'I will return to my house from which I came.' And when it comes, it finds the house swept and put in order. Then it goes and brings seven other spirits more evil than itself, and they enter and dwell there. And the last state of that person is worse than the first."
>
> — LUKE 11:24-26.

Any evil spirit assigned to steal the word of God from me, I bind and cast you out, in the mighty name of Jesus. Anointing to retain the word of God and use them in times needed, fall upon me, in the name of Jesus. Let the stealing power of the devil and his agents fail woefully in my life, in the name of Jesus. Let the aborting power of the devil against me be frustrated in every area of my life, in the name of Jesus. Anointing and God's grace to understand the word of God and apply them rightly, come upon me, in the name of Jesus. Every plan of the wicked ones to deny me of the knowledge of God and the right way to apply them, be frustrated, in the name of Jesus. Every satanic network against the right application of God's word in the time of battle, scatter, in the name of Jesus.

Day 5

Expectations:

1. **The destruction of every evil hand planting negativity in your life**

2. **Commanding every area of your life to be turned to good ground by the power of God**

3. **The destruction of every enemy of the fruitfulness that comes from God's word assigned against you.**

4. **The destruction of every serpent in the garden of your life, fighting against the manifestation of God's word in your life.**

5. **Commanding the field of your life to bear fruits without delay.**

YOUR DECREE:

Any evil hand planting negativity into my life, wither and dry up, in the name of Jesus. Any seed of the devil and memory failure planted into my life against God's word, die, in the name of Jesus.

"Simon, Simon, behold, Satan demanded to have you, that he might sift you like wheat

— LUKE 22:31

Almighty God, make every area of my life to be a good ground to grow the word of God to the peak, in the name of Jesus. I break and loose myself from the deceitfulness of riches that choke God's word, in the name of Jesus. Every enemy of the fruitfulness that comes from God's word, be terminated, in the name of Jesus. Divine ability to understand and apply the word of God in my life in times of battle, possess me forever, in the name of Jesus. Almighty God, empower your word to bear fruits in my life in season and out of season, in the name of Jesus. Every word of God I ever heard, read or study, bring positive fruits into my life up to hundredfold, in the name of Jesus. Every serpent in the garden of my life, fighting against the manifestations of God's word in my life, I cut you to pieces, in the name of Jesus. Father Lord, sow your word into every area of my life and cause it to bear fruits to a hundredfold, in the name of Jesus. I command the field of my life to bear fruits without any break, in the name of Jesus. Any seed and tares sowed by the devil and his agents into my life while I sleep or awake, die, in the name of Jesus. Any blades of sickness, sin of all kinds with their consequences in my life, wither and dry up from your root, in the name of Jesus. Let the appearance of tares and all kinds of problem in my life die without negotiations, in the name of Jesus. By the power of God, I command divine reapers to bring me to heaven, in the mighty name of Jesus. Father Lord, reward me by the power in the speaking blood of Jesus, in the name of Jesus. Every enemy in the battle field of my life, your time is up, be frustrated unto death, in the name of Jesus. Let the glowing power of the devil and his agents against me die in my life without escape, in the name of Jesus.

Day 6

Expectations:

1. **Commanding heavenly reapers to gather every tare in your life and burn them to ashes**

2. **Scattering every enemy of divine plantation in the garden of your life**

3. **Breaking yourself loose from the lies of the devil**

4. **Complete deliverance from every bondage that makes you transgress against God**

5. **The destruction of every demonic movement against your life**

6. **The destruction of every satanic structure and demonic stronghold against your life**

YOUR DECREE:

Almighty God, remember me in the time of harvest, in the mighty name of Jesus. Let the heavenly reapers gather every tare in my life, bind them in bundles and burn them to ashes now, in the name of Jesus.

> When I saw among the spoil a beautiful cloak from Shinar, and 200 shekels of silver, and a bar of gold weighing 50 shekels, then I coveted them and took them. And see, they are hidden in the earth inside my tent, with the silver underneath."
>
> — JOSHUA 7:21

Every enemy of divine plantation in the garden of my life, be exposed and be disgraced, in the name of Jesus. Any unclean spirit occupying any part of my life, I bind and cast you out, in the name of Jesus. Let the returning power of the devil and his agents in my life be frustrated unto death, in the name of Jesus. I command every satanic ability to come back to my life to fail woefully and be frustrated, in the name of Jesus. Every satanic knock or force at the entrance door of my life, be frustrated unto death, in the name of Jesus. I command all demon and their problems never to return back into my life, in the name of Jesus. Every evil spirit ever cast out of my life, be crippled and forbidden from coming back, in the name of Jesus. Almighty God, close my eyes against satanic prosperity, corrupt wealth, defiled riches and contaminated breakthroughs, in the name of Jesus. Any evil spirit, energized to bring me back to sin, I bind and cast you out, in the name of Jesus. Almighty God, deliver me from the bondage of transgression and trespassing against your word, in the name of Jesus. Anointing to hate and abhor anything that is cursed, fall upon me, in the name of Jesus. Let the anger of God against my life be destroyed by God's mercy, in the name of Jesus. Almighty God, close my eyes against sin and covetousness, in the name of Jesus.

Now the serpent was more crafty than any other beast of the field that the Lord God had made. He said to the woman, "Did God actually say, 'You shall not eat of any tree in the garden'?" And the woman said to the serpent, "We may eat of the fruit of the trees in the garden, but God said, you shall not eat of the fruit of the tree that is in the midst of the garden, neither shall you touch it, lest you die.'" But the serpent said to the woman, "You will not surely die. For God knows that when you eat of it your eyes will be opened, and you will be like God, knowing good and evil." So when the woman saw that the tree was good for food, and that it was a delight to the eyes, and that the tree was to be desired to make one wise, she took of its fruit and ate, and she also gave some to her husband who was with her, and he ate.

— GENESIS 3:1-6.

Let my eyes be removed from seeing and coveting evil, in the name of Jesus. I break and loose myself from the lies of the devil, in the name of Jesus. Every satanic beast in the battle field of my life, die without mercy, in the name of Jesus. Everything forbidden by God, I reject you and draw away from you, in the name of Jesus. Every tree planted in the garden of my life, whither and dry up from your root, in the name of Jesus. Anointing to reject the lies of the devil, fall upon me, in the name of Jesus. I break and loose myself from any discussion, relationship and agreement with the devil, in the name of Jesus. I withdraw my hand and every organ of my body from touching, admiring or wanting anything from the devil, in the name of Jesus. Every demonic movement anywhere against me, be destroyed perfectly, in the mighty name of Jesus. Any satanic structure, demonic stronghold in my life, be uprooted, in the name of Jesus. I command every sin energized to bring me to bondage to be frustrated, in the name of Jesus. Let the eyes of the devil, sin and its consequences be blinded before me, in the name of Jesus. I command every part of my life that is alive to sin to receive deliverance, in the name of Jesus. I break and loose myself from every evil movement motivated by Satan, in the name of Jesus. Almighty God, fill every area of my life with your word, in the name of Jesus. Anointing to retain God's word and to use it in times of need, possess me, in the name of Jesus. I break and loose myself from the program of Satan, sin and its consequences, in the name of Jesus. Any satanic master key, built to open my life to sin, melt by fire, in the name of Jesus. Let the living place of the devil and his problem in my life be destroyed and replaced with divine habitations, in the name of Jesus. Any warring demon trained and assigned to fight against the will of God for my life, be frustrated, in the name of Jesus. I command every wicked spirit assigned to destroy my life to be bound and cast out, in the name of Jesus.

Then the Lord said to Moses, "Stretch out your hand over the sea, that the water may come back upon the Egyptians, upon their chariots, and upon their horsemen." So Moses stretched out his hand over the sea, and the sea returned to its normal course when the morning appeared. And as the Egyptians fled into it, the Lord threw the Egyptians into the midst of the sea. The waters returned and covered the chariots and the horsemen; of all the host of Pharaoh that had followed them into the sea, not one of them remained. But the people of Israel walked on dry ground through the sea, the waters being a wall to them on their right hand and on their left. Thus the Lord saved Israel that day from the hand of the Egyptians, and Israel saw the Egyptians dead on the seashore. Israel saw the great power that the Lord used against the Egyptians, so the people feared the Lord, and they believed in the Lord and in his servant Moses.

— EXODUS 14:26-31.

Every judgment of death passed against me because of my past sins, be reversed by the speaking blood of Jesus. Let the words of the serpent into my ears be rendered impotent, in the name of Jesus. Any civilization assigned to destroy my relationship with God, I reject you, in the name of Jesus. Any demonic knowledge against God in my life, I reject you forever, in the name of Jesus. Any unprofitable information from satanic kingdom to destroy my faith in Christ, I reject you, in the name of Jesus. Any arrow of confusion fired against my relationship with God, I return you back to your sender, in the name of Jesus.

Day 7

Expectations:

1. **Complete deliverance from every food and drink assigned to destroy you.**

2. **Commanding the withdrawal of your desires from everything that is bad but pleasant to the flesh.**

3. **The frustration of every evil force that has ever been mobilized against you.**

4. **Complete deliverance from every prison yard, evil detention locking you and pegging you.**

5. **The destruction of every mountain standing against your moving to your promise land.**

6. **The scattering of every uprising from the water and from any other creature against your life**

YOUR DECREE:

Almighty God, deliver me from food and drinks assigned to destroy me, in the name of Jesus. Any good thing that is corrupt and defiled, I reject you forever, in the name of Jesus. Anointing and wisdom to say no to evil and be steadfast in it, fall upon me, in the name of Jesus. I withdraw my desires from everything that is bad and pleasant to the flesh, in the name of Jesus. I close and remove my eyes, thoughts and imaginations from everything forbidden by God, in the name of Jesus. Anointing to despise the things of the world, possess me, in the name of Jesus.

At midnight the Lord struck down all the firstborn in the land of Egypt, from the firstborn of Pharaoh who sat on his throne to the firstborn of the captive who was in the dungeon, and all the firstborn of the livestock. And Pharaoh rose up in the night, he and all his servants and all the Egyptians. And there was a great cry in Egypt, for there was not a house where someone was not dead.

— EXODUS 12:29, 30.

I cover the remaining days of my life in this world with the speaking blood of Jesus. Every evil force that will ever be mobilized against me in this life, be frustrated before me, in the name of Jesus. Let the remaining nights of my unrepentant enemies, now and forever be filled with mourning, sorrow and deaths, in the name of Jesus. Let the killing power of God rise against every demonic plan against my life, in the name of Jesus. I release the remaining days of my life from satanic activity, in the name of Jesus. Any mountain standing against my moving to my promised land, be removed by force, in the name of Jesus. Almighty God, send your angels into every prison yard, evil detention houses, spiritually and physically to deliver every part of me locked up by the devil, in the name of Jesus. I cover every member of my family from satanic attack from henceforth, in the name of Jesus. Let the cries and the pains of my unrepentant enemies increased without a stop, in the name of Jesus. Any evil spirit, blocking my way to heaven at the appointed time, be removed by heavenly force, in the name of Jesus. I stretch my hand against every water of death that has been assigned to draw me to death, in the name of Jesus. Let the powers of darkness and the waters of destructions from the heavenlies bow before me, in the name of Jesus. I command the whole creation to rise and fight for me without a stop, in the name of Jesus. Every evil movement against me in the waters and in the heavenly places, be demobilized, in the name of Jesus. I command the troubles in the waters to trouble my unrepentant enemies, in the name of Jesus. Let the uprisings against me from the waters and among other creatures be frustrated, in the name of Jesus. Every satanic embargo placed against my destiny, be removed by heavenly forces, in the name of Jesus. By the power of the almighty

God, I destroy everything put in place to destroy me, in the name of Jesus. Anything or person that must perish for my life to move forward, perish now, in the name of Jesus. Almighty God, deliver me from wrong eating and drinking habits, in the name of Jesus. Any food or drink prepared to defile me, to make me sick or to kill me, I reject you, in the name of Jesus. Almighty God, deliver me from every form of temptation, in the name of Jesus. Let every evil personality that has been attached to my life, be exposed and be disgraced, in the name of Jesus.

> The hail struck down everything that was in the field in all the land of Egypt, both man and beast. And the hail struck down every plant of the field and broke every tree of the field. Only in the land of Goshen, where the people of Israel were, was there no hail.
>
> — EXODUS 9:25-26.

Let the hail from heaven begin to smite every enemy of my peace, settlement and establishment, in the name of Jesus. Let all of my positions, occupied by the devil and his agents all over the world, be recovered, in the name of Jesus. Let my land and my place in life be cleared-off of every demonic habitation, in the name of Jesus. Every demonic achievement in my life, be destroyed and be replaced with divine achievement, in the name of Jesus. Every evil plantation in the garden of my life and destiny, be uprooted, in the name of Jesus. Almighty God, arise and spare my family in times of mass destruction and any form of problem, past, present and future, in the name of Jesus. Almighty God, permanently retain the candle of my life to burn with your light, in the name of Jesus. Every enemy of God's continuous righteousness in my life, be exposed and be disgraced, in the name of Jesus. Every wicked movement against me and my family, be terminated by death, in the name of Jesus. Let the fire of God enter into the whole creation and burn to ashes, every work of the devil in my life, in the name of Jesus.

Thunder of God from the third heaven, arise and visit the camp of my unrepentant enemies, in the name of Jesus. Anything that belonged to me under the captivity of the devil and his agents, I recover you now, in the name of Jesus. O Lord arise, empower me and assist me to take over the wealth and the riches of the heathen, in the name of Jesus. Anything in my life under satanic servitude be released by force, now, in the name of Jesus. Anointing for divine immediate and total freedom, manifest in my life, in the name of Jesus. Every demonic strength in the sea and other creatures, militating against my life, be weakened to death, in the name of Jesus.

Every satanic vision against my life, receive death, in the name of Jesus. I command failure, defeat and death to minister to my unrepentant enemies, in the name of Jesus. I command the morning and night of my stubborn enemies to be removed from peace, in the name of Jesus. Every joy apportioned to my unrepentant enemies, disappear and be replaced with sorrows, in the name of Jesus. I command the angels of God to use the weapons of mass destruction against all my unrepentant enemies that has vowed to destroy me, in the name of Jesus. I command the weapons that angel Michael and other holy angels used against the devil and his royal angels to descend upon the devil and demons against my life, in the name of Jesus. O Lord, arise and protect me from every satanic weapon, in the name of Jesus. I command every satanic military zone among the creations to avoid me and destroy my problems, in the name of Jesus. Let the soldiers of the devil that are after my life begin to destroy each other without a stop, in the name of Jesus. Any evil agreement against my destiny, fail woefully, in the name of Jesus. I command the waters of death and affliction to avoid me and return to the camp of my enemies, in the name of Jesus. Any demonic army, mobilized against me, turn around and destroy your senders, in the name of Jesus. Let the host of satanic soldiers mobilized against me and my family scatter, in the name of Jesus. Almighty God, empower me to walk out from every danger and satanic domain without being touched, in the name of Jesus. Let the salvation power of God save me from every destruction, in the name of Jesus. Let the delivering power of God deliver me from every satanic activity, program, in the name of Jesus. I command every demonic fear to depart from my life forever and be replaced with the fear of God, in the name of Jesus. Let the believing power of God invade my life and take full control of my life forever, in the name of Jesus. Every demon mobilized against me, both now and in the future, be crippled on their way, in the name of Jesus.

TWO

THE WEAPONS OF OUR WARFARE

DECREE-1

(Ephesians 1:16-20, 2 Corinthians 10:3-5, 1 Corinthians 15:30-32, Ephesians 6:12; 4:18., Jeremiah 17:9, Romans 7:18, 1 Timothy 6:12, 1 Corinthians 9:25-27, Ephesians 6:10, 11, 13, Colossians 3:9-14., Zechariah 4:6, James 4:6-7, 2 Corinthians 12:9., Ephesians 6:13-18, Luke 8:12, 2 Corinthians 4:3-4., 1 Thessalonians 2:18, 1 Timothy 3:6, 7)

Day 1

Expectations:

1. Commanding the ceasing power of God to cease all the powers of darkness working against your life and destiny

2. The complete destruction of all demonic ceasing power working against your life and destiny.

3. The destruction of every evil power assigned to close your mouth.

4. The destruction of every demonic authority causing you to stand in jeopardy before any problem.

5. Quenching every strange fire kindled against your life and destiny.

YOUR DECREE:

Ancient of days, increase my faith in Christ to rise above every evil weapon prepared against me, in the name of Jesus. Let the ceasing power of God cease the powers of darkness assigned to weaken my destiny, in the name of Jesus. Almighty God, energize me spiritually to stand in warfare against every satanic power working against my life, in the name of Jesus. Any strange fire kindled to burn against my destiny, day and night, be quenched by the fire of the Holy Ghost, in the name of Jesus.

> I do not cease to give thanks for you, remembering you in my prayers, that the God of our Lord Jesus Christ, the Father of glory, may give you the Spirit of wisdom and of revelation in the knowledge of him, having the eyes of your hearts enlightened, that you may know what is the hope to which he has called you, what are the riches of his glorious inheritance in the saints, and what is the immeasurable greatness of his power toward us who believe, according to the working of his great might that he worked in Christ when he raised him from the dead and seated him at his right hand in the heavenly places.
>
> — EPHESIANS 1:16-20

Any evil force, watering-down my prayer life, wherever you are, scatter in shame, in the name of Jesus. I command every satanic ceasing power against my prayer life to be destroyed, in the name of Jesus. Anointing to pray the right prayers without ceasing, fall upon me, in the name of Jesus. Almighty God, empower me to give you thanks under every situation all the days of my life, in the name of Jesus. Every evil power, assigned to close my mouth spiritually or physically, be disengaged unto death, in the name of Jesus. Let the mobility of the devil and his agents towards my life be terminated, in the name of Jesus. Every problem in my life, attacking my prayer life, receive divine solution and die, in the name of Jesus.

> For though we walk in the flesh, we are not waging war according to the flesh. For the weapons of our warfare are not of the flesh but have divine power to destroy strongholds. We destroy arguments and every lofty opinion raised against the knowledge of God, and take every thought captive to obey Christ.

— 2 CORINTHIANS 10:3-5

Every yoke of carnality in my life, break to pieces, in the name of Jesus. Any evil spirit attached to my flesh, be detached by the crying blood of Jesus, in the name of Jesus. Any war going on against my flesh, be terminated by heavenly soldiers, in the name of Jesus. I confront and conquer every demonic soldier with heavenly weapons, in the name of Jesus. Blood of Jesus, cry me out of every impossibility, in the name of Jesus. Every satanic weapon from the camp of the devil, I render you impotent, in the name of Jesus. Almighty God, increase your might in my life and use me to destroy every satanic establishment, in the name of Jesus. Let the secrets of the devil, known and unknown evil structure, built against my destiny be pulled down, in the name of Jesus. I command the strength of witches and wizard against my life to be wasted, in the name of Jesus. Let the memory of the devil and his agents about my life be made irrelevant, in the name of Jesus. Almighty God, inspire me to pray directly against evil spirits in operation, in the name of Jesus. Let the God of our Lord Jesus stand for me all the days of my life without withdrawing, in the name of Jesus. By the anointing of the father of glory, I destroy every satanic investment in every area of my life, in the name of Jesus. Father Lord, empower me with your Spirit of wisdom and revelation, in the name of Jesus. Every good thing willed to me by the blessed Holy Trinity, manifest before me now, in the name of Jesus. Let the knowledge of God increase and multiply in my life without a break, in the name of Jesus. Father Lord, separate the eyes of my understanding from every evil practice, in the name of Jesus. By the power of the enlightening of the Almighty God, I open my eyes to every divine understanding, in the name of Jesus. Every spirit of hopelessness in my life, I bind and cast you out, in the name of Jesus. Father Lord, enrich me with your riches without corruption, pollutions or demonic defilement, in the name of Jesus. Any evil personality, sitting upon my inheritance, be unseated by force, in the name of Jesus.

> Why are we in danger every hour? I protest, brothers, by my pride in you, which I have in Christ Jesus our Lord, I die every day! What do I gain if, humanly speaking, I fought with beasts at Ephesus? If the dead are not raised, "Let us eat and drink, for tomorrow we die.
>
> — 1 CORINTHIANS 15:30-32

Any demonic authority causing me to stand in jeopardy before any problem, I bind and cast you out, in the name of Jesus. Anointing to take charge over the devil and his agents in every part of my life, possess me, in the name of Jesus. Let the joy I have in Christ increase without measure, in the name of Jesus. Let my protesting power against demonic activity increase, in the name of Jesus.

Day 2

Expectations:

1. The rejection of every death prepared against your life, family and destiny.

2. The destruction of every arrow of deceit fired against you and your destiny

3. The destruction of every beast like demon and his agents attacking your life

4. Destroying every resisting and standing power of the enemies against your life.

5. The complete dethroning of the might of the devil and his agents

YOUR DECREE:

Father Lord, empower me never to agree with the devil and his agents, in the name of Jesus. I command the word of the devil and his agents to bow and surrender forever before the unchangeable word of God, in the name of Jesus. By the power of my prayers, I protest against the activities of the devil and his agents everywhere on earth, in the name of Jesus. Every death prepared against my life, go back to your sender and come back no more to me, in the name of Jesus. Almighty God, by your mercy, increase your presence in my life forever, in the name of Jesus. Every evil march against my relationship with God, be demobilized to death, in the name of Jesus. Every beast like demon and his agents in the battle field of my life, be destroyed by heavenly soldiers, in the name of Jesus. Deaths that will kill my problems and spare me alive without death, manifest in my life, in the name of Jesus. Every arrow of deceit fired against my destiny, I fire you back, in the mighty name of Jesus. Let the forces of darkness assigned to deny me of my rights, benefits and entitlement be put to shame forever, in the name of Jesus. Let the exceeding greatness of God's power and blessings begin to manifest in my life every day, in the name of Jesus. By the anointing in the working power of God, I command every creature to start working to my favor, in the name of Jesus. I receive in full the benefits of the sacrifice of Jesus in the cross of Calvary, in the name of Jesus. Any evil force contending with my glory, scatter and perish, in the name of Jesus.

> For we do not wrestle against flesh and blood, but against the rulers, against the authorities, against the cosmic powers over this present darkness, against the spiritual forces of evil in the heavenly places.
>
> They are darkened in their understanding, alienated from the life of God because of the ignorance that is in them, due to their hardness of heart.
>
> — EPHESIANS 6:12; 4:18.

I command the strength of my enemies to finish and die without renewal, in the name of Jesus. Almighty God, put your word of death into my prayer life to kill every problem in my life, in the name of Jesus. I command my prayers to be filled with divine weapon against every organized enemy in the battle field of my life, in the name of Jesus. Let the resisting and the standing powers of my enemies collapse and rise no more, in the name of Jesus. I command the strength of my enemies in the beginning of the battle to finish and fail them, in the name of Jesus. Let the multiplying power of the devil and his agents disappear before me, in the name of Jesus. I command the aborting anointing of the devil against me to cease from operation in every area of my life, in the name of Jesus. Let my standing up, sitting down and moving from place to place be filled with divine presence, in the name of Jesus. Almighty God, by your power that raised Jesus Christ from death, I command all my buried and arrested blessings in the kingdom of darkness to be released, in the name of Jesus. Father Lord, by your mercy, take me from where I am now to where I supposed to be, in the name of Jesus. Any of my blessing hanging in the heavenly places, come down to me by heavenly force, in the name of Jesus. Almighty God, by your promotional power, promote me to sit in the heavenly places with you and Christ forever and ever, in the name of Jesus. Let the might of the devil and his agents be dethroned and brought to nothing before me, in the name of Jesus. Any evil spirit dominating my life, I bind and cast you out, in the name of Jesus. I command every name in my life contending against the name of Jesus to be destroyed without mercy, in the name of Jesus. Let the rising power of the devil and his agents over my life be brought down to the dust, in the name of Jesus. Any power attached to this world and in the coming world, assigned against the power of Christ in my life, die, in the name of Jesus. I command the whole creature to fight for me and to bring every activity of the devil and his agents to nothing in my life, in the name of Jesus. Every evil head rising against me from the pit of hell and among the whole creature, I cut you off, in the name of Jesus.

> The heart is deceitful above all things, and desperately sick; who can understand it?
>
> — JEREMIAH 17:9

> For I know that nothing good dwells in me, that is, in my flesh. For I have the desire to do what is right, but not the ability to carry it out.
>
> — ROMANS 7:18

Let the disappointing power of God disappoint every enemy of my relationship with Christ, in the name of Jesus. Let every satanic deposit in my life, catch fire and burn to ashes, in the name of Jesus. Almighty God, be exalted above the heavenlies without any rival in my life, forever and ever, in the name of Jesus. Let every evil knowledge that is contending with divine knowledge in my life, be dethroned, in the name of Jesus. Let every blessing attached to my life under satanic captivity, be released by force, in the name of Jesus. Every disobedient demon fighting against the plan of God for my life, be dethroned and messed up, in the name of Jesus. Satan, whether you like it or not, I bring you down to nothing in every area of my life, in the name of Jesus. I cast down every evil spirit that has risen over me, in the mighty name of Jesus. By the power in the name of Jesus, I cast down every problem that has risen over my life.

Fight the good fight of the faith. Take hold of the eternal life to which you were called and about which you made the good confession in the presence of many witnesses.

— 1 TIMOTHY 6:12

Every athlete exercises self-control in all things. They do it to receive a perishable wreath, but we an imperishable. So I do not run aimlessly; I do not box as one beating the air. But I discipline my body and keep it under control, lest after preaching to others I myself should be disqualified.

— 1 CORINTHIANS 9:25-27

I break every yoke of ungodliness in my life to pieces, in the name of Jesus. Almighty God, deliver me from the pursuits of ungodly gains and defiled happiness, in the name of Jesus. Let everything in my life that is holding me down in sin, loose hold over my life, in the name of Jesus. I remove by force, every satanic container and property in my life, in the name of Jesus. Almighty God, deliver me from every temptation that has been designed to deny me of heaven, in the name of Jesus. I break and loose myself from every satanic snare, in the name of Jesus. Any spirit of the love of money in my life, I bind and cast you out, in the name of Jesus. Almighty God, deliver me from the spirit of covetousness and greed, in the name of Jesus. Anointing to flee from the lusts of the flesh, fall upon me, in the name of Jesus. Let the fighting Spirit of God fight my battles forever, in the name of Jesus. Anointing to fight for eternal life in Christ without sin, fall upon me, in the name of Jesus. Every evil mouth speaking evil and problems into my life, close up forever and ever, in the name of Jesus. By the power of the ascending anointing of God, I rise above my problems without struggle, in the name of Jesus.

Day 3

Expectation:

1. **The destruction of every demon attacking your mind**

2. **The destruction of every yoke of corruption in your life**

3. **The destruction of every satanic embargo placed upon your life and destiny**

4. **The termination of the reign of the devil, sin and its consequences in your life**

5. **The destruction of every instrument of unrighteousness in your life**

YOUR DECREE:

Father Lord, empower me with your gifts to destroy every satanic gift and talents, in the name of Jesus. Every demon attacking my mind, eyes and every other organ in my body, I bind and cast you out, in the name of Jesus. Every satanic darkroom in any area of my life, be replaced with divine light, in the name of Jesus. Father Lord, deliver my understanding from evil spirits, in the name of Jesus. Any strange fire and evil sacrifice ever offered against me, expire with your demons attached, in the name of Jesus. Any good thing from God lacking in my life, come back and settle forever, in the name of Jesus. Every yoke of ignorance, lack of divine knowledge upon my life, break to pieces, in the name of Jesus. Any spiritual blindness in any area of my life, be destroyed by the speaking blood of Jesus. Every evil crown on my head, drop, catch fire, burn to ashes and be replaced with the incorruptible crown of God, in the name of Jesus. Let every evil arrangement against my destiny in the physical and in the spirit realm, be scattered, in the name of Jesus. Ancient of days, empower me to run my heavenly race with the yoke of godliness without sin, in the name of Jesus. Father Lord, encourage me never to give up in pleasing you under any circumstance, in the name of Jesus. Anointing to run heavenly race without compromise, and to receive divine honor, fall upon me, in the name of Jesus. I command every demon contending against my faith to bow without resistance, in the name of Jesus. Father Lord, help me to be temperate in all things to enable me receive a high price at the end of my race to heaven, in the name of Jesus. Any yoke of corruption in my life, visible or invisible, break to pieces, in the name of Jesus.

> Finally, be strong in the Lord and in the strength of his might. Put on the whole armor of God, that you may be able to stand against the schemes of the devil. Therefore, take up the whole armor of God, that you may be able to withstand in the evil day, and having done all, to stand firm.
>
> — EPHESIANS 6:10, 11, 13

I command every organ of my body to rise against every evil nature, sinful character in every area of my life, in the name of Jesus. Let divine whirlwind blow away every evil deposit in every area of my life, in the name of Jesus. I command the reign of the devil, sin and its consequences in my life to be terminated, in the name of Jesus. I command my mortal body to be delivered completely from every demonic arrest, in the name of Jesus. Every instrument of unrighteousness in my life, catch fire and burn to ashes, in the name of Jesus. Let the life of Jesus Christ take over every area of my life forever, in the name of Jesus. Almighty God, manifest your dominion over every area of my life with your power of righteousness, in the name of Jesus. Every spirit of death in my life, die by the death of Jesus in the cross of Calvary, in the name of Jesus. Blood of Jesus, terminate the ministry of every death from the devil in my life, in the name of Jesus. Any death from satanic kingdom militating against the death of Jesus Christ in the cross of Calvary in my life, die, in the name of Jesus. Let the life that

Jesus Christ brought through his death begin to manifest in my life, in the name of Jesus. I command every iota of death from hell living inside me to be replaced with the life of Christ, in the name of Jesus. By the power of God, let every wrong thing in my life be stopped by force, in the name of Jesus. Heavenly father, empower me to bring my body to the subjection to obey you with perfect obedience, in the name of Jesus. By the grace and combined mercies of God, I receive divine power to make heaven after my services to God here on earth, in the name of Jesus. I refuse to miss any divine opportunity to please God and displease the devil every day of my life, in the name of Jesus. Father Lord, forbid me by your power and the crying blood of Jesus to be a cast away after serving you here on earth, in the name of Jesus.

> Do not lie to one another, seeing that you have put off the old self with its practices and have put on the new self, which is being renewed in knowledge after the image of its creator. Here there is not Greek and Jew, circumcised and uncircumcised, barbarian, Scythian, slave, free; but Christ is all, and in all. Put on then, as God's chosen ones, holy and beloved, compassionate hearts, kindness, humility, meekness, and patience, bearing with one another and, if one has a complaint against another, forgiving each other; as the Lord has forgiven you, so you also must forgive. And above all these put on love, which binds everything together in perfect harmony.
>
> — COLOSSIANS 3:9-14.

I command every organ of my body to rise in righteousness and power together with Christ, in the name of Jesus. Father Lord, help me to seek things of the above, in the name of Jesus. I withdraw my affection from every evil thing on earth, and I direct them towards the things above, in the name of Jesus. I command my life to be hidden in Christ, in the name of Jesus. Let the appearing power of the Lord Jesus command every good thing I need to appear in my life, in the name of Jesus. Holy Ghost power, arise in your power and mortify my body, soul and spirit on earth, in the name of Jesus. Let every link to idolatry in every area of my life be cut off by the speaking blood of Jesus. Let the wrath of God fall upon every enemy of my relationship with God, in the name of Jesus. Every evil leg, walking about for my sake, break to pieces, in the name of Jesus. By the power of God's anger, I command every work of the devil and his agents in my life to be destroyed, in the name of Jesus. Every spirit of lying, assigned to separate me from God, I bind and cast you out, in the name of Jesus. By the anointing of the Holy Ghost, I put off every evil deed out of my life forever, in the name of Jesus. Let the renewing power of God renew the life of Christ in my life, in the name of Jesus. Every demonic wisdom, knowledge and understanding against God in my life, receive destruction, in the name of Jesus. Any demonic power attacking me with evil nature, receive destruction, in the name of Jesus. Every satanic embargo placed upon my life and destiny, be lifted, in the name of Jesus. I break and loose myself from the manipulations of witches and wizards, in the name of Jesus.

> Then he said to me, "This is the word of the Lord to Zerubbabel: Not by might, nor by power, but by my Spirit, says the Lord of hosts.
>
> — ZECHARIAH 4:6

> But he gives more grace. Therefore, it says, "God opposes the proud but gives grace to the humble." Submit yourselves therefore to God. Resist the devil, and he will flee from you.
>
> — JAMES 4:6-7

Any evil host militating against my destiny, scatter in shame, in the name of Jesus. Every evil mountain, standing against my destiny, disappear by the presence of God, in the name of Jesus. Let the headstone of hindrance on my way to greatness be removed by the wind of God, in the name of Jesus. Every evil cry against my life from the witchcraft kingdom, be silenced by the speaking blood of Jesus, in the name of Jesus. Let the power in God's grace and mercy bring the whole creature to fight for my sake, in the name of Jesus. Almighty God, empower me to finish every good thing that I have started to your own glory, in the name of Jesus. By the power of divine might, I receive victory over the power of the devil and his agents, in the name of Jesus. Spirit of the living God, arise in your power and fight my battles, in the mighty name of Jesus. Blood of Jesus, flow into my foundation, at the depth of my heart and circumcise me in and out, in the name of Jesus. Every demonic bondage in my life, break to pieces, in the name of Jesus. Spirit of holiness, bowel of mercy, divine kindness, humbleness of mind, meekness and longsuffering, take over every area of my life, in the name of Jesus. Anointing and God's grace to approach matters rightly without sin, possess me, in the name of Jesus. Almighty God, put in me the garment of charity, which is the bond of perfection, in the name of Jesus.

But he said to me, "My grace is sufficient for you, for my power is made perfect in weakness." Therefore, I will boast all the more gladly of my weaknesses, so that the power of Christ may rest upon me.

— 2 CORINTHIANS 12:9.

Therefore, take up the whole armor of God, that you may be able to withstand in the evil day, and having done all, to stand firm. Stand therefore, having fastened on the belt of truth, and having put on the breastplate of righteousness, and, as shoes for your feet, having put on the readiness given by the gospel of peace. In all circumstances take up the shield of faith, with which you can extinguish all the flaming darts of the evil one; and take the helmet of salvation, and the sword of the Spirit, which is the word of God, praying at all times in the Spirit, with all prayer and supplication. To that end, keep alert with all perseverance, making supplication for all the saints.

— EPHESIANS 6:13-18

By the power of the sufficient grace of God in my life, I command every work of the devil in my life to expire, in the name of Jesus. Let the grace and the strength of God in my life be made perfect, in the name of Jesus. Every weakness in any area of my life, your time is up, be destroyed by the power of God, in the name of Jesus. Father Lord, empower me to understand what to do in every situation and move me to do them well, in the name of Jesus. Let the exaltations of the devil in my life be brought down to the dust, in the name of Jesus. Almighty God, increase your joy in my life, no matter the situation of things around me, in the name of Jesus. Every evil organization assigned to disgrace me, fail woefully and be publicly disgraced, in the name of Jesus. Anointing to start well and finish well, fall upon me, in the name of Jesus. Every evil host assigned to waste my efforts in life, scatter and be put to shame, in the mighty name of Jesus. Let the destroying power of God destroy all my problems, in the name of Jesus. I command the mouth and tongue of my heart to open and swallow God's righteousness, in the name of Jesus. Let the peace of God reign supreme in my life forever and ever, in the name of Jesus. Almighty God, arise by the power of your mercy and rule over every area of my life, in the name of Jesus. Every yoke of infirmity in my life, break to pieces, in the name of Jesus. Let the power of Christ rest upon every impossibility in my life, in the name of Jesus. Let the distressing power of God distress every distress in my life to death, in the name of Jesus.

The ones along the path are those who have heard; then the devil comes and takes away the word from their hearts, so that they may not believe and be saved.

— LUKE 8:12

> And even if our gospel is veiled, it is veiled to those who are perishing. In their case the god of this world has blinded the minds of the unbelievers, to keep them from seeing the light of the gospel of the glory of Christ, who is the image of God.
>
> — 2 CORINTHIANS 4:3-4.

Father Lord, take me away from the way side to my ordained place in life, in the name of Jesus. Let the listening ear of God hear my prayers and come to my rescue immediately, in the name of Jesus. I command everything in me to draw near to God and abide in his word forever, in the name of Jesus. Father Lord, by your mercy, add more grace into my life and empower me not to receive your grace in vain, in the name of Jesus. Every spirit of pride in my life, your time is up, I bind and cast you out, in the name of Jesus. ==Anointing to submit to God and obey Him at all times, fall upon me, in the name of Jesus.== Let the power of God that resisted the devil and pushed him out from the heavenlies begin to manifest in my life, in the name of Jesus. Let every evil spirit avoid me and flee forever from my presence, in the name of Jesus.

> because we wanted to come to you—I, Paul, again and again—but Satan hindered us.
>
> — 1 THESSALONIANS 2:18

> He must not be a recent convert, or he may become puffed up with conceit and fall into the condemnation of the devil. Moreover, he must be well thought of by outsiders, so that he may not fall into disgrace, into a snare of the devil.
>
> — 1 TIMOTHY 3:6, 7

Any fainting spirit assigned to destroy my strength, I bind and cast you out, in the name of Jesus. Let the strengthening grace of God be multiplied in my life without delay, in the name of Jesus. Father Lord, by the power of your sustaining grace, keep me alive to fulfil my destiny with divine and sound health, in the name of Jesus. I command everything in me to renounce every hidden thing of dishonesty, in the name of Jesus. Any spirit of craftiness, handling the word of God in deceit, I bind and cast you out, in the name of Jesus. Almighty God, purge my conscience and make it holy before you, in the name of Jesus. I command my ministry to receive God's grace to fulfil divine purpose here on earth, in the name of Jesus. Every spiritual blindness in my life, your time is up, be cleared by the flowing blood of Jesus, in the name of Jesus. Every spirit of corruption, defilement and mind pollution in my life, I bind and destroy your activities out of my life, in the name of Jesus. Let the light of the glorious gospel of Christ shine all over my life forever, in the name of Jesus. Elemental powers of darkness assigned to rule and reign over me, I bind and cast you out to destruction, in the name of Jesus. I break and loose myself from every satanic hindrance assigned to stop my ministry, in the name of Jesus. I break and loose every part of my life from satanic snares, in the name of Jesus. Every arrow of ignorance and timidity, fired to destroy me, go back to your sender, in the name of Jesus. I break and loose myself from the condemnation of the devil and his agents, in the name of Jesus. Every negative report prepared against me, I reject you, return back to your sender, in the name of Jesus. Any evil force, pushing me to the pit of shame, reproach, disgrace, failures and defeats, scatter and fail woefully, in the name of Jesus. Every demonic judgment against me, designed to waste my life, I reverse you, in the name of Jesus.

THREE

DIVINE ABILITY, THE OVERCOMERS SECRET

DECREE-1

(1 Peter 1:3-9, 2 Peter 1:10-11, 2 Timothy 2:3-4, 1 Timothy 6:10-12., 1 Peter 2:11, 1 Corinthians 10:13., Hebrews 2:18, Psalms 34:19, Isaiah 43:1-2)

Day 1

Expectations:

1. The destruction of every blockage against the manifestation of God's blessings in your life.
2. The breaking of the yoke of manifold temptation projected against your life.
3. Commanding every good thing that is fading away from your life and family to receive divine renewal.
4. Commanding the ending power of God to end every evil occurrence in your life, family and destiny.

Blessings from God the father of our Lord Jesus Christ, wherever you are, begin to manifest in my life without a break, in the name of Jesus. Let the abundant mercy of God begin to rain heavily in every part of my life, in the name of Jesus. By the power in the word of God, I command the lively hope that comes by the resurrection of Jesus Christ to manifest in my life from today and forever, in the name of Jesus. Father Lord, release your undefiled and incorruptible inheritance into my life, in the name of Jesus. Every blockage to the manifestations of God's blessing into my life be removed without delay, in the name of Jesus. Anointing to be blessed beyond measure, fall upon my life, in the name of Jesus. Any good thing that is fading away in my life, receive divine renewal, in the name of Jesus.

> Blessed be the God and Father of our Lord Jesus Christ! According to his great mercy, he has caused us to be born again to a living hope through the resurrection of Jesus Christ from the dead, to an inheritance that is imperishable, undefiled, and unfading, kept in heaven for you, who by God's power are being guarded through faith for a salvation ready to be revealed in the last time. In this you rejoice, though now for a little while, if necessary, you have been grieved by various trials, so that the tested genuineness of your faith—more precious than gold that perishes though it is tested by fire—may be found to result in praise and glory and honor at the revelation of Jesus Christ. Though you have not seen him, you love him. Though you do not now see him, you believe in him and rejoice with joy that is inexpressible and filled with glory, obtaining the outcome of your faith, the salvation of your souls.
>
> — 1 PETER 1:3-9

Every good thing reserved for me by God from the day of creation, begin to manifest in my life, in the name of Jesus. I command my portion of God's power for every saved soul to be released unto me, in the mighty name of Jesus. By the power of God's revelational anointing, I command every satanic kingdom to release my blessings from their kingdom by force, in the name of Jesus. Let my joy and happiness under satanic arrest be released by heavenly force, in the name of Jesus. Let the rejoicing power of God invade my life from the third heaven, in the name of Jesus. Almighty God, by your mercies, bless me in season and out of season, in the name of Jesus. Every yoke of manifold temptations in my life, break to pieces, in the name of Jesus. Every trial of my faith and satanic motivated temptations assigned to waste my life, be destroyed, in the name of Jesus. Blood of Jesus, make me an overcomer and bless me with overcomers blessings, in the name of Jesus. I command the destroying power of the devil and his agents to rise and destroy their investments in my life, in the name of Jesus. Almighty God, invade my life with blessings that will cause me to burst into endless praise and joy, in the name of Jesus. Let the appearing power of Jesus provoke the appearance of every good thing in my life to manifest, in the name of Jesus. Every enemy of seeing good things from manifesting in my life, be frustrated, in the name of Jesus.

Therefore, brothers, be all the more diligent to confirm your calling and election, for if you practice these qualities you will never fall. For in this way there will be richly provided for you an entrance into the eternal kingdom of our Lord and Savior Jesus Christ.

— 2 PETER 1:10-11

Share in suffering as a good soldier of Christ Jesus. No soldier gets entangled in civilian pursuits, since his aim is to please the one who enlisted him.

— 2 TIMOTHY 2:3-4

I command the fullness of God's glory to manifest in my life by the mercies of God Almighty, in the name of Jesus. Let the overcoming power of God enter into my life and make me an overcomer in every area of my life, in the name of Jesus. I command every enemy of the manifestations of God's glory in my life to be destroyed without delay, in the name of Jesus. Let the fire of God burn to pieces every evil manifestation in my life, in the name of Jesus. Let the ending power of God end every evil occurrence in my life, in the name of Jesus.

> For the love of money is a root of all kinds of evils. It is through this craving that some have wandered away from the faith and pierced themselves with many pangs. Fight the Good Fight of Faith But as for you, O man of God, flee these things. Pursue righteousness, godliness, faith, love, steadfastness, gentleness. Fight the good fight of the faith. Take hold of the eternal life to which you were called and about which you made the good confession in the presence of many witnesses.
>
> — 1 TIMOTHY 6:10-12.

Father Lord, empower me, by your mercy, to be a good soldier of Christ by your special grace, in the name of Jesus. Father Lord, empower me to give more diligence to make my calling and election sure, in the name of Jesus.

Day 2

Expectations:

1. **The destruction of every demonic entanglement affecting any area of your life.**
2. **The uprooting of every root of evil, planted in any area of your life.**
3. **Complete deliverance from every temptation assigned to disgrace you publicly.**
4. **The breaking of the afflicting power of the devil over your life, family and destiny.**
5. **Commanding the rescuing power of God to rescue you from every temptation.**

Every demonic falling spirit, militating against my destiny, I bind and cast you out of my life, in the name of Jesus. Almighty God, give me divine entrance into every good thing that will assist me to be an overcomer, in the name of Jesus. Anointing and righteousness that will help me to enter into an everlasting kingdom at the end with Christ fall upon me, in the name of Jesus.

> Beloved, I urge you as sojourners and exiles to abstain from the passions of the flesh, which wage war against your soul.
>
> — 1 PETER 2:11

> No temptation has overtaken you that is not common to man. God is faithful, and he will not let you be tempted beyond your ability, but with the temptation he will also provide the way of escape, that you may be able to endure it.
>
> — 1 CORINTHIANS 10:13.

Every demonic entanglement in every area of my life, be roasted by fire, in the mighty name of Jesus. I break and loose myself from every worldly attachment, in the mighty name of Jesus. Anointing to please God without sin, possess me, in the name of Jesus. Almighty God, deliver me from the yoke of covetousness and the spirit of the love of money, in the name of Jesus. Every root of evil, planted in my life, be uprooted by the hand of God, in the name of Jesus. I break and loose myself from the spirit of mistakes and errors, in the name of Jesus. Every evil plantation of sorrow in any area of my life, I bind and cast you out, in the mighty name of Jesus. Father Lord, help me to flee from every appearance of evil, in the name of Jesus. Any temptation, climbing the ladder of my life, I pull you down, in the mighty name of Jesus. Let the escaping door from every temptation be opened for me, in the name of Jesus.

> For because he himself has suffered when tempted, he is able to help those who are being tempted.
>
> — HEBREWS 2:18

> Many are the afflictions of the righteous, but the LORD delivers him out of them all.
>
> — PSALMS 34:19

Let the rescuing power in the name of Jesus rescue me from every temptation, hardship and suffering, in the name of Jesus. Every satanic yoke of affliction in my life, break to pieces, in the name of Jesus. Let the afflicting power of the devil and his agents in my life be terminated by God Almighty, in the name of Jesus.

Almighty God, empower me to keep my integrity and maintain a holy walk with you forever, in the name of Jesus. Heavenly father, empower me to follow after righteousness, godliness, faith, love, patience and meekness, in the name of Jesus. Every evil spirit fighting my faith in Christ, I bind and cast you out, in the name of Jesus. Every evil force fighting my faith in Christ, be destroyed, in the name of Jesus. I command everything in my life to lay hold on eternal life with Christ, in the name of Jesus. I command my profession of faith to be steady without compromise, in the name of Jesus. I charge everything within and outside me to refuse to cooperate with sin and its consequences, in the name of Jesus. Let the quickening power that is in the resurrection power quicken every weak and dead thing in my life for righteousness, in the name of Jesus. Every demonic spot in any part of my life, receive cleansing by the speaking blood of Jesus.

> But now thus says the Lord, he who created you, O Jacob, he who formed you, O Israel: "Fear not, for I have redeemed you; I have called you by name, you are mine. When you pass through the waters, I will be with you; and through the rivers, they shall not overwhelm you; when you walk through fire you shall not be burned, and the flame shall not consume you.
>
> — ISAIAH 43:1-2

Every satanic fear in any area of my life, be replaced with the fear of God without delay, in the name of Jesus. Let the fear of God in me destroy every arrow of fear fired against my life, in the name of Jesus. By the power of the redeeming anointing of God, I command every part of my life to be redeemed, in the name of Jesus. Let the name of Christ enter into my life to destroy every evil name fighting against my destiny, in the name of Jesus. Any evil river flowing into my life, dry up, in the mighty name of Jesus. Any marine spirit attack going on against my destiny, be terminated, in the name of Jesus. Every lie and evil witness ever told against my life, be exposed, in the name of Jesus. I break and loose myself from the company of evil doers, in the name of Jesus. Spirit of truth and honesty, take control over my life forever, in the name of Jesus.

I command every part of my life to lay aside all malice, hypocrisy and envy to serve God without sin, in the name of Jesus. Let all sinful lifestyle be destroyed in every area of my life forever, in the name of Jesus. You my life, I command you to abstain from lust, in the name of Jesus. I command my body, soul and spirit to frustrate every appearance of sin and its consequences, in the name of Jesus. Blood of Jesus, purify my conversation and relationship with people, especially with the opposite sex, in the name of Jesus. Father Lord, deliver me from every temptation assigned to disgrace me publicly, in the mighty name of Jesus. Let the deliverance power of God deliver me from every form of temptation, in the name of Jesus.

FOUR

WAITING UPON GOD THROUGH PRAYER AND FASTING

DECREE-1

(Isaiah 40:28-31, Matthew 4:1-2, 10, 11, Matthew 17:21, Esther 4:16., Acts 27:33, Exodus 8:10, 15:11., Psalm 89:6., Exodus 10:21-23., Job 38:12, 13., Acts 16:16, 19., Romans 8:19. , Exodus 3:13, Genesis 32:9, 29., Genesis 4:2-4., Genesis 12:1., Joshua 21:43-45, Genesis 13:1-4., Exodus 20:3-5, 22, 23)

Day 1

Expectations:

1. **Receiving the spirit of God, so as to be able to pray and fast**
2. **The destruction of the yoke of prayerlessness**
3. **The frustration of all the spirit that brings weariness, tiredness and hunger during your prayer and fasting period**

Almighty God put your Spirit in me in order to enable me to fast and wait upon you, in the name of Jesus. Heavenly father, deliver me from every sin and qualify me to be spiritually and physically fit to fast and pray with results, in the name of Jesus. Every enemy of my prayer and fasting be destroyed, in the name of Jesus. Let my knowledge about God increase to enable me pray and fast with great results, in the name of Jesus. Let the everlasting strength of God to pray and fast manifest in my life, in the mighty name of Jesus.

Have you not known? Have you not heard? The Lord is the everlasting God,

the Creator of the ends of the earth. He does not faint or grow weary;

his understanding is unsearchable. He gives power to the faint, and to him who has no might he increases strength. Even youths shall faint and be weary, and young men shall fall exhausted;

but they who wait for the Lord shall renew their strength; they shall mount up with wings like eagles;

they shall run and not be weary; they shall walk and not faint.

> — ISAIAH 40:28-31

Spirit of praying and fasting according to God's will, possess me, in the name of Jesus. Every yoke of prayerlessness in my life, break to pieces, in the name of Jesus. Let the ending power of God end the activities of the devil, assigned to frustrate my prayer and fasting engagements, in the name of Jesus. I command the seed of prayerlessness in my life to be destroyed without delay, in the name of Jesus. I bind and cast out every weakness and fainting spirit in my prayer and fasting life, in the name of Jesus. Every sickness, programed into my life to work against my prayer and fasting life, I bind and cast you out, in the name of Jesus. Almighty God, by your creative power, create in me the spirit of prayer and fasting without measure, in the name of Jesus. Let the spirit that brings weariness, tiredness and hunger during my prayer and fasting be frustrated out of my life and ministry, in the name of Jesus. Almighty God, give me a perfect understanding in my prayer and fasting exploits, in the name of Jesus.

> Then Jesus was led up by the Spirit into the wilderness to be tempted by the devil. And after fasting forty days and forty nights, he was hungry. Then Jesus said to him, "Be gone, Satan! For it is written, "'You shall worship the Lord your God and him only shall you serve". Then the devil left him, and behold, angels came and were ministering to him.
>
> — MATTHEW 4:1-2, 10, 11

Spirit of the living God, lead me into a prayer and fasting that will cripple every demonic activity hindering my divine promotion, prosperity and breakthrough, in the name of Jesus. Every temptation, assigned to cripple my faith in Christ, during my fasting period, be frustrated, in the name of Jesus. Every satanic embargo placed on my prayer and fasting life, be lifted, in the name of Jesus. Every demonic offer, shown unto me during and after my fasting, I reject you, in the name of Jesus.

Every spirit of fainting and discouragement in times of prayer and fasting, I bind and cast you out, in the name of Jesus. Let the might of God come upon me in times of prayer and fasting, in the name of Jesus. Let my strength increase more and more in times of prayer and fasting, in the name of Jesus. Almighty God, renew my strength to pray and fast with immediate results, in the name of Jesus. Let my life mount up with the wings of eagles during and after prayer and fasting, in the name of Jesus. I command all problems to bow forever during and after my prayer and fasting, in the name of Jesus. Let my spiritual speed to run, walk and fly to any level in life increase through my life of prayer and fasting, in the name of Jesus.

> He said to them, "Because of your little faith. For truly, I say to you, if you have faith like a grain of mustard seed, you will say to this mountain, 'Move from here to there,' and it will move, and nothing will be impossible for you."
>
> — MATTHEW 17:21

I command the devil to get behind me and be weakened in every area of my life forever and ever, in the name of Jesus. Every demonic demand from me before, during and after fasting, I reject you, in the name of Jesus. Every yoke of impossibility in my life, break to pieces as I pray and fast in this program, in the mighty name of Jesus. Almighty God, lead me to prayer and fasting period that will destroy the demons behind all level of problems in this life, in the name of Jesus.

> "Go, gather all the Jews to be found in Susa, and hold a fast on my behalf, and do not eat or drink for three days, night or day. I and my young women will also fast as you do. Then I will go to the king, though it is against the law, and if I perish, I perish."
>
> — ESTHER 4:16.

As day was about to dawn, Paul urged them all to take some food, saying, "Today is the fourteenth day that you have continued in suspense and without food, having taken nothing.

— ACTS 27:33

Any destructive letter ever written against me by the devil and his agent, be reversed to my favor, in the name of Jesus. Every demonic decree, evil agreement assigned to bring me and my people to mourning, weeping and wailing, be reversed, in the name of Jesus.

Day 2

Expectations:

1. **The destruction of every evil meeting convened to plan against you.**
2. **The frustration of every evil gang up against your life and destiny**
3. **Commanding all your good records that have been replaced with lies and wrong information to manifest for your promotion**
4. **The destruction of every weapon of death prepared against you**

Almighty God raise people, true believers to pray and fast against evil plans all over the world, in the name of Jesus. Any evil meeting ever convened to plan against me and my people, scatter in disappointment, in the name of Jesus. Anointing to pray and fast until something positive happens, manifest in my life, in the name of Jesus. Let the plans of my unrepentant enemies against me and my people fail woefully, in the name of Jesus. Any evil gang up against my life and destiny, be frustrated, in the name of Jesus. Let the gallows prepared for me be used against my enemies, in the mighty name of Jesus. I command my helpers to have sleepless nights until they help me according to God's plan, in the name of Jesus. Every good record about me, replaced with lies and wrong information, manifest for my promotion, in the name of Jesus. I withdraw every demonic file, written against me from the office of my destiny helpers, and I replace it with the right information concerning me, in the name of Jesus. Any weapon of death prepared against me, be reversed, in the name of Jesus. Let my enemies begin to make mistakes that will promote me and reward them with demotions, in the name of Jesus. Anything that must happen in my prayer and fasting program for my life to move forward, begin to happen, in the name of Jesus.

Every evil plot against me, my family and my loved ones, be crippled during my prayer and fasting period, in the name of Jesus. Any man, woman or power sitting upon my promotion, be unseated during my prayer and fasting period, in the name of Jesus. Every demonic conspiracy against my destiny and people, be crippled during my prayer and fasting period, in the name of Jesus. I command all strongmen demanding honor that are meant for God alone to be humbled and publicly disgraced as I go into prayer and fasting, in the name of Jesus. As I go into prayer and fasting, every problem that has refused to let me go must be destroyed, in the name of Jesus. In this my prayer and fasting period, no unrepentant enemy will stand on my way alive, in the name of Jesus. No yoke of bondage shall survive in my life during and after my prayer and fasting, in the name of Jesus. Let the evil plans of my enemy be frustrated as I go into prayer and fasting, in the name of Jesus. Every organized darkness assigned to waste my life and that of my people, be destroyed, in the name of Jesus.

And he said, "Tomorrow." Moses said, "Be it as you say, so that you may know that there is no one like the Lord our God. "Who is like you, O Lord, among the gods?

Who is like you, majestic in holiness, awesome in glorious deeds, doing wonders?

— EXODUS 8:10, 15:11.

For who in the skies can be compared to the LORD? Who among the heavenly beings is like the LORD.

— PSALM 89:6.

In this prayer and fasting program, let my serpent swallow the serpents of my enemies, in the name of Jesus. I command the waters in the bodies of my determined enemies to be defiled, polluted and contaminated with destructive demons, in the name of Jesus. Every demonic frog outside the premises of my unrepentant enemies, invade their residence and refuse to leave until they repent or perish, in the name of Jesus. Let every destructive lice of plagues from the pit of hell, trained to destroy enter into the foundational lives of my enemies until they repent or perish, in the name of Jesus. I command swarms of flies to invade the camp of my enemies for destruction and refuse to leave until they repent or perish, in the name of Jesus. I command everything that gives my enemies joy and peace to die until they repent or perish, in the name of Jesus. Let every good thing in the lives of my enemies begin to leave until they repent or perish, in the name of Jesus.

Day 3

Expectations:

1. **The destruction of all determined and unrepentant witches and wizards against your life.**

2. **The destruction of all the investments of the enemies of God within and around you.**

3. **The breaking of any demonic presence within and around you.**

4. **Commanding the flood of heavenly soldiers to enter into your life and into all that concern you, to torment and frustrate every demonic personality disturbing you.**

Every determined witch or wizard in the battlefield against my life and destiny, be invaded with swarms of flies and the plagues of boils, in the name of Jesus. Let the secret parts of the bodies of my stubborn enemies be defiled with destructive boils, in the name of Jesus. Let blains accompany evil boils from satanic altars to torment my unrepentant enemies, in the name of Jesus. Let the plagues of hail and fire enter into my enemy's domain until they repent or perish, in the name of Jesus.

> Then the Lord said to Moses, "Stretch out your hand toward heaven, that there may be darkness over the land of Egypt, a darkness to be felt." So Moses stretched out his hand toward heaven, and there was pitch darkness in all the land of Egypt three days. They did not see one another, nor did anyone rise from his place for three days, but all the people of Israel had light where they lived.
>
> — EXODUS 10:21-23.

I release the locust of destruction into all the investment of the enemies of God within and around me, in the name of Jesus. Let the strength of darkness overpower every light my enemies are using against me, in the name of Jesus. Father Lord, in this prayer and fasting program, take me to a journey of my Passover to my promised land, in the name of Jesus. I smite the borders of the strongman, all witches and wizards plotting evil against me and I command problems to invade their lives, in the name of Jesus. Let flow of destructive destructions enter into my enemy's camp and waste their hopes to deaths, in the name of Jesus. I command the rivers and all places in life to send problems into the camp of my enemies without a break, in the name of Jesus. Every demonic presence in my house, office and presence, be destroyed without break, in the name of Jesus. Every evil presence within and around me, be destroyed by the creatures, in the name of Jesus. Let flood of heavenly soldiers enter into my life, my house and my presence to torment every demonic personality that refused to let me rest, in the name of Jesus. Demons in my bedchamber, my bed, house and office, I bind and cast you out, in the name of Jesus. Let the angels of destruction, every wild creature, visible and invisible arise and enter everywhere to locate my problems and waste them, in the name of Jesus.

Have you commanded the morning since your days began, and caused the dawn to know its place, that it might take hold of the skirts of the earth, and the wicked be shaken out of it?

— JOB 38:12, 13.

Let the whole creature release destructions against my determined problems, powers behind them and waste them, in the name of Jesus. I release destructions in abundance into the residence, bedchambers, the covens, altars and into the kneading-troughs of my unrepentant enemies. Almighty God, by your mercies; sever my life, place of abode, my place of work and my presence from satanic attacks, in the name of Jesus. Almighty God, by your mercies put division between me and demons forever, in the name of Jesus. Let the grievous swarms of problems assigned to waste my life return back to the senders and avoid me forever, in the name of Jesus. I break and loose myself from the demons that corrupts, defile and pollute the mind, body, soul and spirit, in the name of Jesus. Let the hand of the LORD remove the strength, prosperity of the witches and wizards assigned against my life, in the name of Jesus.

> As we were going to the place of prayer, we were met by a slave girl who had a spirit of divination and brought her owners much gain by fortune-telling. But when her owners saw that their hope of gain was gone, they seized Paul and Silas and dragged them into the marketplace before the rulers.
>
> — ACTS 16:16, 19.

I command their fields of evil business to be invaded by destructive angels, in the name of Jesus. Let the appointed time for the judgment of the wicked against me come immediately, in the name of Jesus. I command the ashes of furnace to be sprinkled everywhere I go, against my problems and the powers behind them, in the name of Jesus. Let the breath of the witches and wizards against my life be defiled, polluted and corrupted by deaths, in the name of Jesus. Let the breath of my unrepentant enemies, demons behind them be polluted with boils and blains, in the name of Jesus. I command helpers of my unrepentant enemies to withdraw or be attacked from all side among the creatures, in the name of Jesus.

> But when her owners saw that their hope of gain was gone, they seized Paul and Silas and dragged them into the marketplace before the rulers.
>
> — ROMANS 8:19.

Let the land of evil ones, their domains be filled with darkness without light, in the name of Jesus. Let the mornings, days and nights of every witch or wizards in the battle field against me afflict them until they repent or perish, in the name of Jesus. I command the heavens of all witches and wizards against me to close with divine key until they repent or perish, in the name of Jesus. Let thunder and hail, fire and rain of affliction descend upon every evil personality with determination to bring me into bondage and keep me suffering, in the name of Jesus. Almighty God, deliver my destiny from the control of evil ones, in the name of Jesus. Father Lord, by your mercies, deliver all the wicked ones ready to repent and surrender to Jesus, in the mighty name of Jesus.

> Then Moses said to God, "If I come to the people of Israel and say to them, 'The God of your fathers has sent me to you,' and they ask me, 'What is his name?' what shall I say to them?"
>
> — EXODUS 3:13

> And Jacob said, "O God of my father Abraham and God of my father Isaac, O Lord who said to me, 'Return to your country and to your kindred, that I may do you good.

— GENESIS 32:9, 29.

Let the name of God manifest in all land and deliver the repentant sinner, in the name of Jesus. By the name God of Abraham, Isaac and Jacob, I deliver sinners from all the nations of the world, in the name of Jesus. Let the face of God manifest among the heathens and deliver people in mass, in the name of Jesus.

PRAYERS AGAINST EVIL SACRIFICE

Day 4

Expectations:

1. The silencing of every evil sacrifice going on against you.
2. The silencing of every evil voice speaking against you, your family and destiny
3. The destruction of every enemy of your service to God.
4. Commanding the destruction of any occult man, woman or kingdom that has vowed to destroy you.
5. The destruction of every instrument of death prepared against you.
6. The destruction of every satanic embargo placed on your life.

Let the blood sacrifice of the Lord Jesus Christ cry for me before God to silence every evil sacrifice ever offered against my destiny, in the name of Jesus. Any evil sacrifice going on against my life in any evil altar be silence by the crying blood of Jesus. Every enchantment and divination by any witch or wizard against my life, back fire, in the name of Jesus. Every enemy of my services to God, be exposed and be disgraced, in the name of Jesus. Any occult man or woman that has vowed to destroy my life, turn around and destroy yourself, in the name of Jesus. Every instrument of death prepared against my life, I render you impotent, in the mighty name of Jesus. Let the sorceries of the witches and wizards against my destiny be destroyed before me, in the name of Jesus. Wherever they will call my name for evil, blood of Jesus, answer for me, in the name of Jesus. Every satanic embargo placed upon my life through evil sacrifice, be lifted, in the name of Jesus.

> And again, she bore his brother Abel. Now Abel was a keeper of sheep, and Cain a worker of the ground. In the course of time Cain brought to the Lord an offering of the fruit of the ground, and Abel also brought of the firstborn of his flock and of their fat portions. And the Lord had regard for Abel and his offering
>
> — GENESIS 4:2-4.

Any evil sacrifice ever offered against my life by anyone living or dead, expire, in the name of Jesus. Almighty God, arise in your power and respect the sacrifice of the blood of Jesus in my life, in the name of Jesus. Any evil mouth from any evil altar calling my name for evil, close in shame and disgrace, in the name of Jesus. Any instrument of death, raised against me in any evil altar, destroy your owners, in the name of Jesus. Almighty God, reject any evil sacrifice going on here on earth by any idolatrous person, in the name of Jesus. Let the wrath of God confront and conquer any battle going on against me from any evil altar, in the name of Jesus.

Almighty God, arise in your power and prosper my sacrifice through the blood of Jesus. Every good door closed against my life from evil altar, open by the speaking blood of Jesus, in the name of Jesus. I break and loose myself from every sin and its consequences, in the name of Jesus. Any evil reign organized against me from any evil altar, be terminated, in the mighty name of Jesus. I break and loose myself from any demonic influence militating against my destiny, in the name of Jesus. I break and loose myself from any satanic attack from evil altars, in the name of Jesus.

> Now the Lord said to Abram, "Go from your country and your kindred and your father's house to the land that I will show you.
>
> — GENESIS 12:1.

Let the rising of Cain, any occult man or woman from anywhere against my destiny be brought to nothing, in the name of Jesus. Powers of darkness, assigned to mess my life up through witchcraft attacks, be frustrated, in the name of Jesus. Let the blood of Jesus cry to heaven and attract the presence of God for my sake here on earth, in the name of Jesus.

> Thus the Lord gave to Israel all the land that he swore to give to their fathers. And they took possession of it, and they settled there. And the Lord gave them rest on every side just as he had sworn to their fathers. Not one of all their enemies had withstood them, for the Lord had given all their enemies into their hands. Not one word of all the good promises that the Lord had made to the house of Israel had failed; all came to pass.
>
> — JOSHUA 21:43-45

Any evil voice speaking against my life from any evil altar, be silenced by the speaking voice of the blood of Jesus, in the name of Jesus. Any human blood sacrifice crying against my destiny, close your mouth for my sake, in the name of Jesus. Any evil sacrifice ever done among the creation militating against my life, break and expire, in the name of Jesus. I break and loose myself from the bondage of fugitive and vagabond, in the name of Jesus. Any evil covenant and curse frustrating my efforts in life, break and expire, in the name of Jesus.

Day 5

Expectations:

1. Commanding the earth to yield to your efforts
2. The destruction of every evil force moving you away from your divine call and place in life
3. The termination of every demonic motivated strife in your land of promise
4. The destruction of everything hindering or affecting the manifestation of God's blessing in your life, family and destiny
5. Commanding the voice of God to outcry every negative voice speaking against you.
6. The silencing of every blood sacrifice crying against you from any evil altar

Almighty God, prosper my handwork by the blood sacrifice of the Lord Jesus, in the mighty name of Jesus. Let the yielding power of the earth yield into my efforts in life with divine strength, in the name of Jesus.

> So Abram went up from Egypt, he and his wife and all that he had, and Lot with him, into the Negeb. Now Abram was very rich in livestock, in silver, and in gold. And he journeyed on from the Negeb as far as Bethel to the place where his tent had been at the beginning, between Bethel and Ai, to the place where he had made an altar at the first. And there Abram called upon the name of the Lord.
>
> — GENESIS 13:1-4.

Any evil force moving me out from divine call and my place in life, be frustrated, in the name of Jesus. Almighty God, take me to my promise land, settle me down and establish me, in the name of Jesus. Let that power that moved Abraham out of his country, his kindred and from his father's house to a land God prepared for him, begin to move me, in the name of Jesus. Let the landing power of God take me and land me in my place of prosperity, in the name of Jesus. Any demonic motivated strife in my land of promise be terminated by divine peace, in the name of Jesus.

Let the voice of God outcry every evil voice speaking from satanic kingdom against me, in the name of Jesus. Almighty God, help me to hear your voice and obey your commands and empower me to ignore every evil voice, in the name of Jesus. Let the blessings of God for my answers to divine call begin to manifest in my life, in the name of Jesus. Any evil voice calling me from evil altars, I reject you, in the mighty name of Jesus. Every hindrance to the manifestations of God's blessings in my life, be removed, in the name of Jesus. Let the removing power from God remove me from every bondage of poverty, in the name of Jesus. Any evil presence in my life from the kingdom of darkness, be replaced with divine presence, in the name of Jesus. Any spirit in my life respecting or practicing religion without Christ and his righteousness, I bind and cast you out, in the name of Jesus. Any power moving me to bow to false gods, be frustrated out of my life, in the name of Jesus. Any spirit of idolatry, living inside me, I bind and cast you out, in the name of Jesus.

Almighty God, deliver me from abomination, vanity, foolishness and blood sacrifice, in the name of Jesus. I break and loose myself from every unprofitable relationship, spiritually and physically, in the name of Jesus. Any demonic influence causing me to bow down to images, worship or sacrifice to false gods, be frustrated, in the name of Jesus. Father Lord, deliver me from the consequences of idolatry and every negative action I had ever taken, in the name of Jesus.

> You shall have no other gods before me. "You shall not make for yourself a carved image, or any likeness of anything that is in heaven above, or that is in the earth beneath, or that is in the water under the earth. You shall not bow down to them or serve them, for I the Lord your God am a jealous God, visiting the iniquity of the fathers on the children to the third and the fourth generation of those who hate me, And the Lord said to Moses, "Thus you shall say to the people of Israel: 'You have seen for yourselves that I have talked with you from heaven. You shall not make gods of silver to be with me, nor shall you make for yourselves gods of gold.
>
> — EXODUS 20:3-5, 22, 23.

Any evil gang up against me by occult men and women, scatter and fail woefully, in the name of Jesus. Let fire from God come down and burn to ashes every property of the devil prepared against me, in the name of Jesus. Anointing to bow down to only one true God, fall upon me, in the name of Jesus. Any evil movement from any evil altar against my destiny, be stopped and be paralyzed, in the name of Jesus. Any blood animal sacrifice crying against me in any evil altar, be silenced unto death, in the name of Jesus.

FIVE

THE LORD GOD OF ABRAHAM, ISAAC AND JACOB

DECREE-1

(Exodus 3:15; 6:3., Genesis 3:6-8, Ephesians 2:19-20., Galatians 1:1., Psalms 91:1., Matthew 4:23-25; 8:1-4., Matthew 8:16-17, 23-24, 26., Luke 6:6, 10)

Day 1

Expectations:

1. The destruction of every yoke in your life that is from the witchcraft kingdom.
2. Liberating yourself and all the areas of your life from demonic captivity.
3. Commanding divinely motivated blessings to locate you.
4. The destruction of every movement of Pharaoh and his taskmasters against you and your destiny.
5. The destruction of every satanic taskmaster set to monitor your life and destiny.

Every evil yoke in my life from witchcraft kingdom, I challenge you with the name of the God of Abraham, Isaac and Jacob, in the name of Jesus. I break and loose myself from any evil covenant, known and unknown, in the name of Jesus. Any area of my life under the captivity of the devil, receive deliverance by the power in the name of Abraham, Isaac and Jacob, in the name of Jesus. Almighty God, increase the number of my destiny helpers, in the name of Jesus. Any evil law passed against my relationship with God, be revoked, in the name of Jesus. Let the multiplication power of God multiply my life with the best things of life, in the name of Jesus. Let God's goodness multiply exceedingly in every area of my life, in the name of Jesus. I command divine motivated blessings to locate me from every part of the world, in the name of Jesus. Almighty God, fill your containers in my life with your blessings, in the name of Jesus. Any satanic agent that has risen in rank to torment my destiny, be disgraced, in the name of Jesus.

> God also said to Moses, "Say this to the people of Israel: 'The Lord, the God of your fathers, the God of Abraham, the God of Isaac, and the God of Jacob, has sent me to you.' This is my name forever, and thus I am to be remembered throughout all generations.
>
> I appeared to Abraham, to Isaac, and to Jacob, as God Almighty, but by my name the Lord I did not make myself known to them.
>
> — EXODUS 3:15; 6:3.

By the power in the name God Almighty, I destroy every satanic investment in my life, family and ministry, in the name of Jesus. Let the unknown names of God manifest in the battle field to fight for me, in the name of Jesus. Every movement of Pharaoh and his taskmasters against my destiny, be demobilized, in the name of Jesus. By the power in God's strong hand, I command every evil voice speaking against me to be terminated, in the name of Jesus. I break and loose myself from every evil covenant and curses militating against my life, in the name of Jesus. Almighty God, hear my groaning, weeping, cries and deliver me from demonic suffering, in the name of Jesus. Any evil plan to reduce divine might in my life by the devil and his agents, fail woefully, in the name of Jesus. Almighty God, arise and deliver me from every satanic plan against my destiny, in the name of Jesus. Any satanic taskmaster set to monitor my life anywhere, be frustrated, in the name of Jesus. Almighty God, deliver me from any affliction targeted to waste my life, in the name of Jesus. I break and loose myself from the bondage and the burdens of my enemy, in the name of Jesus. Let the fighting power of my enemies be reduced to nothing, in the name of Jesus. Every demonic rigorous assignment assigned to destroy me, be frustrated, in the name of Jesus. Father Lord, deliver me from bitter life and hard bondage, in mortar and with brick, in the name of Jesus.

> So when the woman saw that the tree was good for food, and that it was a delight to the eyes, and that the tree was to be desired to make one wise, she took of its fruit and ate, and she also gave some to her husband who was with her, and he ate. Then the eyes of both were opened, and they knew that they were naked. And they sewed fig leaves together and made themselves loincloths.
> And they heard the sound of the Lord God walking in the garden in the cool of the day, and the man and his wife hid themselves from the presence of the Lord God among the trees of the garden.
>
> — GENESIS 3:6-8

> So then you are no longer strangers and aliens, but you are fellow citizens with the saints and members of the household of God, built on the foundation of the apostles and prophets, Christ Jesus himself being the cornerstone.
>
> — EPHESIANS 2:19-20.

Any evil force opening my eyes to forbidden things, I bind and cast you out of my presence, in the name of Jesus. Any evil tree planted in the garden of my life, be uprooted by thunder, in the name of Jesus. Almighty God, deliver me from the food and drinks assigned to waste my life, in the name of Jesus. Any satanic appeal to my tastes, I reject you, in the name of Jesus. I receive power to close my eyes from everything forbidden by God, no matter how badly I need them, in the name of Jesus. Let the roots and the leaves of the evil trees in my life dry up, in the name of Jesus. Any sin designed to stripe me naked, be destroyed forever in my life, in the name of Jesus. Any evil voice of serpent speaking in the garden of my life, be silenced unto death, in the name of Jesus. Father Lord, empower me to give birth to a breakthrough that will destroy every evil plan against my life, in the name of Jesus. Any manner of service designed to frustrate my destiny, I reject you, in the name of Jesus. Any evil decree signed to kill my young ones and the good things in my life, be reversed, in the name of Jesus. Almighty God, empower me to conceive good things and deliver them at the right time, in the name of Jesus. Any evil spirit sent to monitor me and abort divine plans and visions in my life, I bind and cast you out, in the name of Jesus. Every satanic commandment against the plans of God for my life, be frustrated, in the name of Jesus. Any evil river that is flowing into my life, dry up, in the name of Jesus.

Day 2

Expectations:

1. **The breaking of the backbone of all your stubborn enemies.**

2. **The termination of all satanic oppression going on against your life and destiny.**

3. **Commanding divine circumcision on all the uncircumcised areas of your life**

4. **The destruction of every evil personality, sitting upon your right, benefit and entitlement.**

5. **The destruction of any inherited generational bondage that is affecting you.**

Ancient of days, empower me to keep your commandment in every situation, in the name of Jesus. I command the backbone of my stubborn enemies to break to pieces, in the name of Jesus. Father Lord, send your angel of deliverance to deliver me from every satanic prison, physically and spiritually, in the name of Jesus. I confront and conquer any organized witch or wizard with a vow to destroy me, in the name of Jesus. Let my cries for deliverance reach God and provoke Him to deliver me from strong enemies, in the name of Jesus. Every satanic oppression going on against my life, be terminated by the name of the God of Abraham, Isaac and Jacob, in the name of Jesus. Every Pharaoh in the battle field of my life, be defeated by the God of Abraham, Isaac and Jacob, in the name of Jesus. By the names of the God of the fathers of Israel, I bring every enemy of my life to nothing, in the name of Jesus.

Paul, an apostle—not from men nor through man, but through Jesus Christ and God the Father, who raised him from the dead.

> He who dwells in the shelter of the Most High will abide in the shadow of the Almighty.

I bring together everything about my life under the shadow of the Almighty God, in the name of Jesus. Every uncircumcised part of my life, receive divine circumcision, in the name of Jesus. Every evil character separating me from God's presence and mercy, be destroyed by the speaking blood of Jesus. Let the power in the death of Jesus destroy every sin in my life and bring me closer to God, in the name of Jesus. Every enemy of my peace with God, be exposed and be disgraced, in the name of Jesus. I receive my full portion from the common wealth of God through the death of Jesus in the cross of Calvary, in the name of Jesus. Blood of Jesus, link me up to the covenant of promise and hope in God through Christ, in the name of Jesus. Let the speaking blood of Jesus bring me near to God's kingdom and take away every problem in my life, in the name of Jesus. I command the middle wall of partition between me and Christ's blessings to be broken to pieces, in the name of Jesus. Every satanic law or evil tradition, holding me in bondage, be destroyed by the speaking blood of Jesus, in the name of Jesus. Every wicked ordinance militating against the love of God in my life, be abolished by the power in the blood of Jesus. I command the plantations of fear in my life from any witchcraft coven to be replaced with divine boldness, in the name of Jesus. Let the LORD God of Israel, the God of Abraham, Isaac and Jacob arise in anger and judge all my unrepentant enemies, in the name of Jesus. Every evil personality, sitting upon my right, benefit and entitlement, repent and be unseated, in the name of Jesus. I break and loose myself from every inherited generational bondage, in the name of Jesus. Every evil authority that has ganged up against my life, scatter and be disappointed, in the name of Jesus. Any evil spirit in covenant with my enemies to torment my life, I bind and cast you out, in the name of Jesus.

And he went throughout all Galilee, teaching in their synagogues and proclaiming the gospel of the kingdom and healing every disease and every affliction among the people. So his fame spread throughout all Syria, and they brought him all the sick, those afflicted with various diseases and pains, those oppressed by demons, those having seizures, and paralytics, and he healed them. And great crowds followed him from Galilee and the Decapolis, and from Jerusalem and Judea, and from beyond the Jordan.

When he came down from the mountain, great crowds followed him. And behold, a leper came to him and knelt before him, saying, "Lord, if you will, you can make me clean." And Jesus stretched out his hand and touched him, saying, "I will; be clean." And immediately his leprosy was cleansed. And Jesus said to him, "See that you say nothing to anyone, but go, show yourself to the priest and offer the gift that Moses commanded, for a proof to them."

— MATTHEW 4:23-25; 8:1-4.

Spirit of the living God, enter into my foundation and deliver me from every satanic work, in the name of Jesus. Let the anointing in the teaching of the word of God bring my body, soul and spirit to perfect deliverance, in the name of Jesus. Every demonic work, sickness and disease in any part of my life, receive destructions, in the name of Jesus. I command every part of my life that has been possessed by demons to be discharged by the power in the stripes of Jesus. I command every satanic torment in my life to stop and be destroyed, in the name of Jesus. Anointing to follow Christ to the end, possess me, in the name of Jesus. Every satanic achievement in my life, be destroyed, in the mighty name of Jesus.

By the power of the God of the beginning, I command every negative thing in my life to be terminated by death, in the name of Jesus. By the power in the God of every beginning, I command the earth to rise against all my problems among the creations, in the name of Jesus. Every strange fire from the altars of darkness burning in my life, be quenched by the speaking blood of Jesus. Heavenly father, mobilize your angels to visit me and to destroy every demonic presence in my life, in the name of Jesus. Every evil plan to stop me from serving God, fail woefully, in the name of Jesus. Almighty God, arise in your power and take me with ease to my promised land, in the name of Jesus. Every evil mouth speaking against the plans of God in my life, be closed by the blood of Jesus. Any mountain standing between me and God, disappear, in the name of Jesus.

> That evening they brought to him many who were oppressed by demons, and he cast out the spirits with a word and healed all who were sick. This was to fulfil what was spoken by the prophet Isaiah: "He took our illnesses and bore our diseases."
>
> And when he got into the boat, his disciples followed him. And behold, there arose a great storm on the sea, so that the boat was being swamped by the waves; but he was asleep. And he said to them, "Why are you afraid, O you of little faith?" Then he rose and rebuked the winds and the sea, and there was a great calm.
>
> — MATTHEW 8:16-17, 23-24, 26.

I command every demon in charge of my suffering and hardship to be bound and cast out, in the name of Jesus. Every evil seed that was planted into my life while I was asleep, die, in the name of Jesus. By the power in God's word, I bind and cast out every demon militating against my destiny, in the name of Jesus. Let the healing power in the stripes of Jesus minister healing into every part of my life, in the name of Jesus. Almighty God, arise by your mercy and end my wilderness experience with testimonies, in the name of Jesus. I dethrone every evil king and queen that wants to rule over my life, in the name of Jesus. Every evil hand, raised against me by witches and wizards, wither, in the name of Jesus. Let the conspiracy of Pharaoh and his taskmasters against me back fire, in the name of Jesus. Almighty God, increase my faith to conquer every evil movement among the creation, in the name of Jesus. Let the covering power in the blood of Jesus cover me from every problem assigned to expose me to danger, in the name of Jesus. Any evil wave from the marine kingdom, raised against my life, be terminated by the divine presence in my life, in the name of Jesus. Let the power of Christ enter into my life and calm every satanic violence that is taking away my peace, in the name of Jesus. Every evil tempest in my life, be terminated by divine presence, in the name of Jesus.

> On another Sabbath, he entered the synagogue and was teaching, and a man was there whose right hand was withered.
>
> And after looking around at them all he said to him, "Stretch out your hand." And he did so, and his hand was restored.
>
> — LUKE 6:6, 10.

Lord Jesus, enter into the dark room of my life and occupy every space with your light, in the name of Jesus. Every darkness militating against my destiny, be removed and replaced with divine light, in the name of Jesus. Let the teaching ministry of Christ manifest positively in my life, in the name of Jesus. Let the restoration power of God restore every good thing I have ever lost, in the name of Jesus. Father Lord, bless my hand and prosper everything I touch in life, in the name of Jesus. O God arise and bless the works of my hands, in the name of Jesus. Almighty God, single me out from the multitude and deliver me from every trouble, in the name of Jesus. Every spirit of leprosy, scaring my helpers away from me, be cleansed by the cleansing power in the blood of Jesus. Every evil word that has been spoken to torment my life, expire, in the name of Jesus. Let the hand of Christ, by his mercy, be stretched to touch me for deliverance, in the name of Jesus. Let the cleansing power in the blood of Jesus flow into my foundation and wash me clean, in the name of Jesus. Every yoke of hatred and rejection in my life, visible and invisible, break to pieces, in the name of Jesus. Every power, driving good people and good things away from my life, be frustrated, in the name of Jesus. Father Lord, empower me to start meeting good people and good things from today, in the name of Jesus.

SIX

DEMONS IN HUMAN BODY AND IN YOUR PRESENCE

DECREE-1

(James 4:7., John 5:14., 1 Samuel 16:14-15., 1 Peter 5:8-9., Ephesians 4:27, Matthew 12:43-45., Romans 8:11., Mark 16:17-18., Luke 10:19; 9:1, John 14:12-14., Matthew 18:18, 19, Acts 3:6-8)

Day 1

Expectations:

1. **Total deliverance from every form of satanic arrest.**
2. **Deliverance from every enticement and invitation to sin.**
3. **Complete freedom from every inherited sin.**
4. **Paralyzing the contending power of all evil kingdoms against your life.**

By the power in the speaking blood of Jesus, I break away from every satanic arrest and I cleanse my body, soul and spirit from every sin, in the name of Jesus. Every invitation, given to sin and its consequences into my body, soul and spirit, I withdraw them now, in the name of Jesus. I break and loose myself from every law of sin and demonic dominance, in the name of Jesus. Almighty God, deliver me from every inherited sin, conscious and unconscious sin, in the name of Jesus. Blood of Jesus, deliver me and speak me out of every captivity of sin, in the name of Jesus (Romans 7:7-24). I command my spirit man to be liberated from the law of sin immediately, in the name of Jesus.

> Submit yourselves therefore to God. Resist the devil, and he will flee from you.
>
> — JAMES 4:7.

> Afterward Jesus found him in the temple and said to him, "See, you are well! Sin no more, that nothing worse may happen to you."
>
> — JOHN 5:14.

By the power of God's healing strength, I receive divine healing all over my body, soul and spirit by the power in the blood of Jesus. Almighty God, break every law and protocol, to deliver me wherever I need deliverance, in the name of Jesus. I command every part of my body, soul and spirit to be made whole by the power in the voice of Christ, in the name of Jesus. Let the contending power of evil kingdoms over my life be paralyzed to death, in the name of Jesus. Every satanic limitation, confinement and evil roadblock in my life, be violently removed, in the name of Jesus. Let the seeing power of Christ find me and take me away from every bondage, in the name of Jesus. Powers of darkness that brings back sin, that repeats sin in human life, your time has expired in my life, avoid me forever, in the name of Jesus. Almighty God, improve my prayer life and give me the strength to say no to the against the devil and his agents, in the name of Jesus. Almighty God, empower me with your resisting power that drove the devil and all dark angels from the third heaven, in the name of Jesus. By the power of the LORD that giveth more grace, I receive more grace to resist the devil and his agents, in the name of Jesus.

Any spirit of pride in any area of my life, be resisted unto death forever, in the name of Jesus. Father Lord, give me a humble spirit and let it be permanent in my life, in the name of Jesus. Anointing to submit to God and win battles, possess me, in the name of Jesus. I command the devil, sin and its consequences to flee away from me and never look back forever and ever, in the name of Jesus. Heavenly chains of righteousness, made with the blood of Jesus and every heavenly material, draw me near to God, in the name of Jesus. Let the power of God take me away from all evil and bring me close to the blessed Holy Trinity, forever and ever, in the name of Jesus. I command everything in me to cease communication, agreement and compromise with Satan and his agents, in the name of Jesus.

Day 2

Expectations:

1. The destruction of every yoke of sin and iniquity over you.
2. The destruction of every form of satanic revival around your life and destiny.
3. Commanding every part of your life to come under God's control
4. The destruction of every form of demonic darkness harboring sin in your life.
5. Liberating every part of your life previously captured by sin, Satan and sickness.
6. The breaking of every yoke of spiritual and physical ignorance upon your life

Every yoke of sin in my life, your time is up, break to pieces, in the name of Jesus. Any satanic revival of sin in my life, be destroyed and terminated forever, in the name of Jesus. Blood of Jesus, flow into my foundation and kill every trace of sin in my life, in the name of Jesus. Every instrument of sin assigned to deceive me, be frustrated, in the name of Jesus.

> Now the Spirit of the Lord departed from Saul, and a harmful spirit from the Lord tormented him. And Saul's servants said to him, "Behold now, a harmful spirit from God is tormenting you.
>
> — 1 SAMUEL 16:14-15.

Be sober-minded; be watchful. Your adversary the devil prowls around like a roaring lion, seeking someone to devour. Resist him, firm in your faith, knowing that the same kinds of suffering are being experienced by your brotherhood throughout the world.

— 1 PETER 5:8-9.

Almighty God, by your mercy, don't allow your Spirit to depart from me, in the name of Jesus. By the power in the word of God, I cast all my care upon God, in the mighty name of Jesus. Father Lord, empower me to be sober and vigilant against the devil and all his schemes, all the days of my life, in the name of Jesus. Let the grace and mercy of God keep me active in fulfilling my purpose, here on earth, in the name of Jesus. Blood of Jesus, block Satan against every entrance door of my life, in the name of Jesus. I command every demonic spirit in charge of troubles to avoid my life and destiny forever, in the name of Jesus. I humble every part of my life to be under the mighty hand of God for permanent control, in the name of Jesus. Anything inside and outside me, under demonic motivation to rebel or exalt itself against God, receive deliverance and power to submit to God forever, in the name of Jesus. Every sword of sin getting ready to slay me and bring me into bondage, I render you powerless, in the name of Jesus. Anything in me, among the creatures, causing me to appear sinful, receive destruction, in the name of Jesus. Every satanic work manifesting in any area of my life, I cut you off from my life forever, in the name of Jesus. Every demonic darkness, harboring sin in my life, be exposed by divine light from above, in the name of Jesus.

Every part of my life, captured in sin, your time is up, receive immediate deliverance, in the name of Jesus. I break the steadfast power of every enemy of my zeal to serve God and fulfill my divine given destiny, in the name of Jesus.

Every attack against my faith in Christ Jesus, be terminated in failure and defeat, in the name of Jesus. Every demonic accomplishment in my life, be reversed, in the name of Jesus. I command every creature to mobilize forces against sin and problems in my life, in the name of Jesus.

and give no opportunity to the devil.

— EPHESIANS 4:27

"When the unclean spirit has gone out of a person, it passes through waterless places seeking rest, but finds none. Then it says, 'I will return to my house from which I came.' And when it comes, it finds the house empty, swept, and put in order. Then it goes and brings with it seven other spirits more evil than itself, and they enter and dwell there, and the last state of that person is worse than the first. So also will it be with this evil generation."

— MATTHEW 12:43-45.

Father Lord, deliver me from all kind of ignorance assigned against my destiny fulfilment, in the name of Jesus. Any past sin, present and future, assigned to return and defeat me, you are a liar, be crippled by the speaking power in the precious blood of Jesus. I break and loose myself from every demonic knowledge and wisdom designed to waste my life, in the name of Jesus. I break and loose myself from every unprofitable learning, in the name of Jesus. Every defiled conversation and relationship, I disengage myself from you forever, in the name of Jesus. Every yoke of spiritual and physical ignorance upon my life, break to pieces, in the name of Jesus.

Day 3

Expectation:

1. **Complete deliverance from all manner of deceit, corruption and defilement affecting you**
2. **The destruction of every negative testimony against your life**
3. **The destruction of every darkness that is hindering your progress**
4. **The destruction of every yoke of carnality affecting you**
5. **The termination of every form of satanic presence in your life, family and destiny**
6. **The destruction of all determined enemies against your life, family and destiny**

Almighty God, deliver me from all manner of deceit, corruption and defilement, in the name of Jesus. Let the renewing power of the devil and his agents fail woefully in my life, in the name of Jesus. I put myself back to the new man who God has created in righteousness and holiness, in the name of Jesus. I command every part of my life, body, soul and spirit to put away lying and every other work of the devil, in the name of Jesus. Every negative testimony against my life, be reversed by the speaking blood of Jesus, in the name of Jesus. Every evil force with a vow and determination to walk me out of divine presence, scatter in shame, in the name of Jesus. Every darkness, hindering my progress in life, your time is up, be replaced with the divine light of God, in the name of Jesus. Let the separating power of God separate me from every form of iniquity, in the name of Jesus. Let the returning power of Satan and his agents into my life be incapacitated, in the name of Jesus. I command the strength of the enemy, over my heavenly candidacy, to be destroyed without remedy, in the name of Jesus. Almighty God, apply your cleansing, washing and purifying power into my heart and sanctify me, in the name of Jesus. I command the afflicting and oppressing ability of the devil, his agents, sin and every problem attached in my life to be weakened unto death, in the name of Jesus. Father Lord, do something that will cripple every problem in my life forever, in the name of Jesus. Every yoke of carnality upon my life, break to pieces, in the mighty name of Jesus. Every evil force with the yoke of carnality to sell me to a particular sin, scatter in defeat, in the name of Jesus. Almighty God, deliver my will power from the captivity of the devil, evil character and sinful lifestyle, in the name of Jesus. Every permission, allowance, place and opportunity given to Satan and sin into my life, be withdrawn by heavenly forces, in the name of Jesus. Blood of Jesus, purge my conscience of every sin and all evil domination, in the name of Jesus. Let the returning power of every unclean spirit back into my life be crippled forever, in the name of Jesus. Let the word of God occupy every empty space in my body, soul and spirit forever, in the name of Jesus. Let the walking back of demons and their problems into my life be crippled and demobilized, in the name of Jesus. Father Lord, by your power, I command Satan and his agents never to find rest, comfort and peace in my life, in the name of Jesus. I command every part of my life, body, soul and spirit to trouble every satanic presence out of my life, in the name of Jesus. Let the troubling power of God trouble the devil and his troubles out of my life, in the name of Jesus.

Day 4

Expectations:

1. **Blocking demons from entering your life**
2. **Clearly separating yourself from sin, Satan and demonic connection**
3. **Separating yourself from the wickedness going on in this generation and its consequence**
4. **Commanding the power of God to make your life better**
5. **Revoking every evil exchange that has ever taken place in your life and recovering all that you ever lost**
6. **Destroying every satanic residence or place of operation in your life**

Blood of Jesus, stripes of Jesus Christ and all heavenly soldier that drove the devil and his dark angels, demons out of heaven, block every entrance into my life against them, in the name of Jesus.

> If the Spirit of him who raised Jesus from the dead dwells in you, he who raised Christ Jesus from the dead will also give life to your mortal bodies through his Spirit who dwells in you.
>
> — ROMANS 8:11.

> And these signs will accompany those who believe: in my name they will cast out demons; they will speak in new tongues; they will pick up serpents with their hands; and if they drink any deadly poison, it will not hurt them; they will lay their hands on the sick, and they will recover."
>
> — MARK 16:17-18.

Let the entering power of the devil, his agents, sin and lives troubles be paralyzed and forbidden from reentering me for any reason, in the name of Jesus. Let the righteousness of Jesus Christ protect my life from every satanic inversion, in the name of Jesus. Let the coming back of the devil, sin and every evil work find Christ's blood, his name and righteousness in every entrance of my life, in the name of Jesus. By the power of God's rebuking anointing, I rebuke the devil and everything that connects me with him, in the name of Jesus. You my body, soul and spirit; you will not be found empty, swept and garnished by the devil, in the name of Jesus. Opportunity to invite wicked spirits into my life after deliverance prayers, be destroyed by the destroying power of God, in the name of Jesus. I command the demons that worsen human conditions to avoid me forever, in the name of Jesus. Let the power of God make my life better with every day that passes, in the name of Jesus. Every wickedness going on in this generation, my life is not your candidate, avoid me and die forever, in the name of Jesus. Let the doings of the devil and all his agents in my life be undone without compromise, in the name of Jesus. Anointing to hate what God hates and love what God loves without compromise, fall upon me, in the name of Jesus. Anything in me given consent to the devil, his agents and sin, I command you to receive deliverance, in the name of Jesus. Anointing to do what is right, good in the sight of God without thinking twice, possess me, in the name of Jesus. Father Lord, take all the places given to Satan and his agents forever, in the name of Jesus. Every evil exchange that has taken place in my life, spiritually or physically, be reversed, in the name of Jesus. Every satanic residence, place of operation in my life, be replaced by the blessed Holy Trinity, in the name of Jesus. I reverse every satanic affair in my life and destiny, without renewal, in the name of Jesus. Let the performing places of the devil and his agents in my life be withdrawn forever, in the name of Jesus.

Behold, I have given you authority to tread on serpents and scorpions, and over all the power of the enemy, and nothing shall hurt you.

And he called the twelve together and gave them power and authority over all demons and to cure diseases

— LUKE 10:19; 9:1

"Truly, truly, I say to you, whoever believes in me will also do the works that I do; and greater works than these will he do, because I am going to the Father. Whatever you ask in my name, this I will do, that the Father may be glorified in the Son. If you ask me anything in my name, I will do it.

— JOHN 14:12-14.

By the power of God given unto me in His word, I tread upon every serpentine-like problem and trouble of life, in the name of Jesus. Let the scorpion-like problems in my life, be destroyed with its venom in my life, in the name of Jesus. Every satanic poison injected into my life, dry up, in the name of Jesus. Let the powers of the enemies of my life be incapacitated and brought to nothing before me, everywhere in this life, in the name of Jesus. I command the hurting power of God to hurt my problems and every enemy of my life to death, in the name of Jesus. Every demonic hurting power, be crippled before me forever and ever, in the name of Jesus. By the power in the word of God, I receive power and authority over all devils to cure all diseases, in the name of Jesus. Let the authority and power given to me by Jesus begin to operate against all satanic power and authority until they bow and surrender before me everywhere in life, in the name of Jesus. Let the calling power of Christ fall upon me to answer and destroy every demonic activity, in the name of Jesus. I receive power and divine grace to believe and act according to God's word without any doubt, in the name of Jesus.

Day 5

Expectations:

1. **Receiving the power to work for God without stopping.**
2. **Destroying everything that wants to affect or hinder your work with God.**
3. **Upgrading your brain by the power of the Almighty God**
4. **Destroying every satanic structure in any area of your life**
5. **Destroying every hindrance to answers to your prayers and commanding your answers to manifest**
6. **Commanding every impossible situation in your life to become possible by the power of God.**

Almighty God, empower me to work for you without a stop forever and ever, in the name of Jesus. Anointing to increase my work for God and walk with Him, increase in me without a break, in the name of Jesus. Every hindrance to my work for God, be removed forever, in the name of Jesus. Oh Lord, give me the zeal to seek for your presence in all the days of my life, in the name of Jesus. Father Lord, upgrade my brain and thinking ability; thought energy and power to marshal out facts to find and discover new things that will move the world forward, positively, in the name of Jesus. Every satanic structure in any area of my life, catch fire, burn to ashes, in the name of Jesus. Every good thing, godliness and the nine fruits of the Spirit of God stolen from me, I recover you by force, in the name of Jesus. Sin inside of me, outside of me, come out against yourselves and avoid me forever, in the name of Jesus.

> Truly, I say to you, whatever you bind on earth shall be bound in heaven, and whatever you loose on earth shall be loosed in heaven. Again I say to you, if two of you agree on earth about anything they ask, it will be done for them by my Father in heaven.
>
> — MATTHEW 18:18, 19

> But Peter said, "I have no silver and gold, but what I do have I give to you. In the name of Jesus Christ of Nazareth, rise up and walk!" And he took him by the right hand and raised him up, and immediately his feet and ankles were made strong. And leaping up, he stood and began to walk, and entered the temple with them, walking and leaping and praising God.
>
> — ACTS 3:6-8.

You the manifestations of the answers to my prayers, show yourself in every area of my life, in the name of Jesus. Every delay to the manifestation of all good prayers in the past, be terminated, in the name of Jesus. Every past prayer, asking, seeking and knocking under delay, begin to manifest without delay, in the name of Jesus. You my answered prayers of agreement in the past, receive immediate manifestation, physically and now, in the name of Jesus. Heavenly father, arise in your mercy and release all answer to my prayers, both asking, seeking, knocking and in agreement, in the name of Jesus. Let my past prayers, plus the good ones prayed for me by others, begin to receive answers to manifestations, in the name of Jesus. By the power attached to prayers by God, I command every impossibility to become possible through my past, present and future prayers, in the name of Jesus. Any challenge in this life, disgrace and impossible situation that defiled every solution, even silver and gold; bow before my prayers now, in the name of Jesus. By the strength in the name of Jesus, I decree against every work of the devil, put together to die before me everywhere in life, in the name of Jesus. Let the lifting power of God enter my words of prayer and lift me from demonic cast downs, in the name of Jesus. Every inherited bondage from the day of Adam and Eve in my life, till now, break to pieces, in the name of Jesus. I command the long-time problems and troubles of my life to die, in the name of Jesus. Every garment of poverty, suffering, famine and ugly situations in my life, catch fire and burn to ashes, in the name of Jesus. Let the multiplying power of God multiply God's answers to my past, present and future prayers, in the name of Jesus. Any mountain standing against me in this program, disappear forever, in the name of Jesus. I command the feet of my testimonies and answer to my prayers to receive divine motivated strength, and walk out from bondage, in the name of Jesus. Anointing to walk out from every degree of problem and power to walk back to divine presence, fall upon me, in the name of Jesus. I command everything that must happen for me to enter into unceasing praises to God here on earth to happen now, in the name of Jesus. Blessed Holy Spirit, release all answers you have ever prayed for me by your mercy, in the name of Jesus. Almighty God, destroy every satanic achievement in my life without any remain, in the name of Jesus. Anything that will glorify God and put the devil and his works down, begin to manifest in my life every day, in the name of Jesus. Let the doing power of God do in my life everything that will perfect my life and show forth divine praise, in the name of Jesus. I command the presence of Satan and all problems in my life to disappear from me forever, in the name of Jesus. I command my inner man and everything about me to hate the devil every dark angel, in the name of Jesus. Any war that Satan and his agents are engaged in or will ever be engaged in against my relationship with Christ, end to my favor, in the name of Jesus. Every evil captivity against my mind, your time has expired, be terminated, in the mighty name of Jesus. Every demonic investment, evil organized activity of impossibility in my life, be terminated by the speaking blood of Jesus, in the name of Jesus.

SEVEN

THE POWER OF I AM THAT I AM

DECREE-1

(Exodus 3:14; 6:3., Revelation 1:4., Hebrews 1:10-12, Psalms 90:2., Psalm 102:24-27, Malachi 3:6, Exodus 3:7-8, Genesis 50:18-21, Exodus 12:30-33, Isaiah 60:1)

Day 1

Expectations:

1. The destruction of every evil personality holding you in bondage
2. The destruction of every strange power ministering against your life
3. The frustration of every satanic decision against your life
4. Complete deliverance from every activity of the evil ones
5. The destruction of every spiritual and physical taskmaster raised against you
6. Complete deliverance from every form of captivity.

By the power of I AM THAT I AM, I command every evil personality holding me in bondage to release me by force, in the name of Jesus. Every yoke of captivity in any area of my life, break to pieces, in the name of Jesus. Any strange power ministering against my life, I command you to give up your ghost, in the name of Jesus. Let the satanic flames of fire burning in any area of my life be quenched by the speaking blood of Jesus, in the name of Jesus. Every satanic decision against my life, be frustrated, in the name of Jesus. Let the God of the fathers of Israel come to my rescue and deliver me from all troubles, in the name of Jesus. Almighty God, increase your determination to set me free from every activity of the evil ones against me, in the name of Jesus. Every spiritual and physical taskmaster, raised against me, scatter, in the name of Jesus.

> God said to Moses, "I am who I am." And he said, "Say this to the people of Israel: 'I am has sent me to you.
>
> I appeared to Abraham, to Isaac, and to Jacob, as God Almighty, but by my name the Lord I did not make myself known to them.
>
> — EXODUS 3:14; 6:3.

> John to the seven churches that are in Asia: Grace to you and peace from him who is and who was and who is to come, and from the seven spirits who are before his throne
>
> — REVELATION 1:4.

Almighty God, by your name of Him which is, and which was, and which is to come, arise for my sake and destroy all my past, present and future problems, in the name of Jesus. Let the seven Spirit of God deliver me from every evil spirit militating against my life, in the name of Jesus. Every satanic throne of darkness attacking my life, be frustrated, in the name of Jesus. Every evil witness against my life, be reversed to my favor, in the name of Jesus. Every evil prince here on earth and the demons behind their attacks in my life, be judged by the Spirit of God, in the name of Jesus. Let the speaking blood of Jesus speak me out of every danger, in the name of Jesus. Father Lord, deliver me by your mercy from the remaining problems of this life, in the name of Jesus. By the power in the name of the Lord, I AM THAT I AM, I command every organized darkness in my life to be disorganized, in the name of Jesus. Let the ability in God's name frustrate every demonic activity going on in my life, in the name of Jesus. Any evil voice, calling me from any evil altar, receive judgment from The LORD God of the fathers of Abraham, Isaac and Jacob, in the name of Jesus. Every demonic settlement in my life, catch fire and burn to ashes, in the name of Jesus. Any evil strength in my life, be destroyed by divine strength, in the name of Jesus. Let the driving force of the devil, his agents and problems be terminated by divine names in my life, in the name of Jesus. Any evil tongue speaking against my life, be silence by the word of God, in the name of Jesus. Almighty God, appear in the battle field of my life and disengage every satanic military personnel assigned against me, in the name of Jesus. Let the bombarding power of God bomb the camp of my enemies, in the name of Jesus.

Day 2

Expectations:

1. **The frustration of every evil movement against your life**
2. **The termination of every affliction and oppression against your life**
3. **The destruction of every weapon of war raised against you by your enemies.**
4. **The termination of every negative and discouraging word ever spoken against you by evil people and satanic kingdoms**
5. **The destruction of every garment of suffering, hardship and poverty in your life**

Let the name of the God Almighty frustrate every evil movement against my life, in the name of Jesus. Let the afflictions and the oppressions of the wicked against my life be terminated, in the name of Jesus. Let the hearing ears of my determined enemies stocked with lies against me be opened by divine truth, in the name of Jesus. Every weapon of war raised against me by my enemy, I render you impotent, in the name of Jesus. Any discouraging word from every satanic kingdom against me, perish, in the name of Jesus.

> And, "You, Lord, laid the foundation of the earth in the beginning and the heavens are the work of your hands; they will perish, but you remain; they will all wear out like a garment, like a robe you will roll them up, like a garment they will be changed. But you are the same, and your years will have no end."
>
> — HEBREWS 1:10-12

Before the mountains were brought forth, or ever you had formed the earth and the   world, from everlasting to everlasting you are God.

— PSALMS 90:2.

I command the beginning and the end of my problems to die without harm in my life, in the name of Jesus. Any faulty foundation in my life, be destroyed by the crying blood of Jesus. Every satanic material in the foundation of my life, catch fire and burn to ashes, in the name of Jesus. I command the powers that inhabit the heaven and earth to rise against every unrepentant enemy of my life, in the name of Jesus. Let the perishing power in the word of God put an end to every work of the devil in my life, in the name of Jesus. Any evil force forcing good things and good people out of my life, receive termination, in the name of Jesus. Every garment of suffering, hardship and poverty in my life, be roasted by fire, in the name of Jesus. I command every demonic spirit in my life to be bound and cast out, in the name of Jesus. I break and loose myself from every satanic lifestyle, in the name of Jesus. I command the work of the devil in my life to wax old and die without extension, in the name of Jesus. Let the folding and the rolling power of God roll away by divine folding every work of the devil in my life unto destructions and death, in the name of Jesus. By the power in the changing anointing of God, I change every bad thing in my life to good, better and best to the glory of God Almighty, in the name of Jesus. Father Lord, release your ministering angels to minister into my life without a stop, in the name of Jesus. I plead for the aborting power in the word of God to abort every evil plantation in my life, in the name of Jesus. By the strength in the name, I AM THAT I AM, I command every evil power attached to my problems to be diminished to nothing, in the name of Jesus. Let the destroying power in the name of God, the I AM THAT I AM destroy every satanic establishment in my life, in the name of Jesus. By the power in the sending anointing of God, I send destructive power of God against every problem in my life, in the name of Jesus. Every enemy of the manifestation of the power attached to the name, I AM THAT I AM, in my life, be demolished, in the name of Jesus. Every satanic boasting against my destiny, fail woefully, in the name of Jesus. Almighty God, show your Almightiness in every area of my life, in the name of Jesus. Any evil call contending with the call of God in my life, receive death, in the name of Jesus. Every generational problem in my life that has refused to let me go, be terminated by heavenly forces, in the name of Jesus.

"O my God," I say, "take me not away in the midst of my days, you whose years endure

throughout all generations!" Of old you laid the foundation of the earth, and the heavens are the work of your hands. They will perish, but you will remain; they will all wear out like a garment. You will change them like a robe, and they will pass away, but you are the same, and your years have no end.

— PSALM 102:24-27.

By the power in the generating power of God, let my life be filled with every good thing that will end my weakness and lack of everything that is from God, in the name of Jesus. Every yoke of untimely death of good things and life in my life, break to pieces, in the name of Jesus. Let my years on earth be filled with divine presence and manifestation of God's power, in the name of Jesus. Every witchcraft embargo placed upon my life, be lifted, in the name of Jesus. By the power that laid the foundation of heaven and earth, I command the strength of the earth to favor me forever, in the name of Jesus.

Day 3

Expectations:

1. **Receiving the nature, likeness and image of God**
2. **Commanding every good thing to be welcomed into your life by the welcoming power of God**
3. **Commanding every good thing to continue to manifest in your life**
4. **Commanding the forming power of God's word to format your life and rearrange everything**
5. **Commanding the mercy of God to take you to your place in life (your promise land).**
6. **The destruction of every evil messenger, agent and servant sent against you**

Almighty God, impart your nature, divine image, likeness and divine strength into every part of my life, in the name of Jesus. Let the welcoming power of God welcome every good thing into my life, in the name of Jesus. I command every power of darkness to avoid me forever, in the name of Jesus. Almighty God, use me to distribute your blessings everywhere, here on earth, in the name of Jesus. By the power of God's continuity in life, I command the good things of life to continue to manifest in every area of my life, in the name of Jesus. Let the forming power in the word of God format my life and rearrange everything in me to perfection to the glory of God, in the name of Jesus. Let the oppressing power of the devil and his agents bow before the power in the name, I AM THAT I AM, in every area of my life, in the name of Jesus. Any evil force questioning the strength of the name, I AM THAT I AM, in my life, be broken to pieces, in the name of Jesus. Every yoke of impossibility, holding me captive, I confront and conquer you by the power in the name of God, I AM THAT I AM, in the name of Jesus. Every evil plantation in my life from the headquarters of Satan, your time is up, be destroyed by the power in the name of God, I AM THAT I AM, in the name of Jesus.

> "For I the Lord do not change; therefore you, O children of Jacob, are not consumed.
>
> — MALACHI 3:6

> Then the Lord said, "I have surely seen the affliction of my people who are in Egypt and have heard their cry because of their taskmasters. I know their sufferings, and I have come down to deliver them out of the hand of the Egyptians and to bring them up out of that land to a good and broad land, a land flowing with milk and honey, to the place of the Canaanites, the Hittites, the Amorites, the Perizzites, the Hivites, and the Jebusites.
>
> — EXODUS 3:7-8

Let the seeing eye of God see my afflictions and every bad thing in me and destroy them, in the name of Jesus. Every demonic personality, evil taskmaster in my life, be exposed and be disgraced, in the name of Jesus. Every messenger of sorrow in my life, I reject you and your message forever, in the name of Jesus. By the anointing that are in the deliverance power of God, I receive my total deliverance, in the name of Jesus. Father Lord, by your mercy, take me to my place in life, my promised land, in the name of Jesus. Every evil messenger sent against me from the evil kingdom, I reject you and your message; go back to your sender, in the name of Jesus. Any evil spirit in the temple of my life, I bind and cast you out, in the name of Jesus. Almighty God, strengthen my covenant with you and invoke your blessings into my life, in the name of Jesus. Let the light of God in Christ shine all over my life without a stop, in the name of Jesus. Let the power that binds God the Father, God the Son, and God the Holy Spirit bind me to the righteousness of Christ, in the name of Jesus. By the power of the refining fire of God, I command every part of my life to be refined by God's fire, in the name of Jesus. Any evil voice, speaking against the plans of God for my life, be silenced by the speaking power in the name of God, I AM THAT I AM, in the name of Jesus. Almighty God, by your name, the God of the Hebrews, frustrate every name given to any problem in my life by medical science, in the name of Jesus. Every evil change in my life, be frustrated and be reversed by divine change, in the name of Jesus. I command every satanic fire burning in any part of my life to be put off, in the name of Jesus. Let the contending power of the devil and his agents be destroyed by the name of God, in the name of Jesus. Any evil journey, embarked to challenge my relationship with God, be terminated in sorrow, in the name of Jesus.

His brothers also came and fell down before him and said, "Behold, we are your servants." But Joseph said to them, "Do not fear, for am I in the place of God? As for you, you meant evil against me, but God meant it for good, to bring it about that many people should be kept alive, as they are today. So do not fear; I will provide for you and your little ones." Thus he comforted them and spoke kindly to them.

— GENESIS 50:18-21

Almighty God, empower my dreams in life to come true without delay, in the name of Jesus. Every yoke of sin and Satan in my life, break to pieces, in the name of Jesus. I command all my enemies to come before me and bow down to me before my God, in the name of Jesus. Let the humiliating power of God humiliate my enemies and promote me before them, in the name of Jesus. Every good thing that has forgotten me, begin to remember me and come back, in the name of Jesus. Almighty God, cause my enemies to be afraid of me, to your own glory, in the name of Jesus. Father Lord, promote and prosper me before my masters and my enemies, in the name of Jesus. Every evil thought against me from the devil and his agents, back fire, in the name of Jesus. Almighty God, empower me and bless me to help the helpless and the needy all over the world, in the name of Jesus. Any satanic blockage to my destiny, be removed violently by the powers attached to God's names, in the name of Jesus. Any satanic dark room in any area of my life, receive light from the names of God, in the name of Jesus. Any satanic habitation in my life, be cleansed by the speaking blood of Jesus, in the name of Jesus. Any evil sacrifice ever offered against my life, by anyone living or dead, expire by the power attached to the name of God, the I AM THAT I AM, in the name of Jesus. Almighty God, take away every satanic burden in my life and exchange it with the yoke of Christ, in the name of Jesus. Father Lord, increase your love in my life and use it to destroy every satanic hatred, in the name of Jesus. Let the honor of God bring every kind of honor without sin, in my life, in the name of Jesus. I break and loose myself from every agent of pollution and defilement, in the name of Jesus.

And Pharaoh rose up in the night, he and all his servants and all the Egyptians. And there was a great cry in Egypt, for there was not a house where someone was not dead. Then he summoned Moses and Aaron by night and said, "Up, go out from among my people, both you and the people of Israel; and go, serve the Lord, as you have said. Take your flocks and your herds, as you have said, and be gone, and bless me also!" The Exodus, the Egyptians were urgent with the people to send them out of the land in haste. For they said, "We shall all be dead.

— EXODUS 12:30-33

Arise, shine, for your light has come, and the glory of the Lord has risen upon you.

— ISAIAH 60:1.

Almighty God, give me prosperity that will end every problem in my life, spiritually and physically, in the name of Jesus. I command the congregation of witches and wizards against my life to scatter and be put to shame, in the name of Jesus. Let weapons of the household enemies against my life back fire, in the name of Jesus. Any evil personality, ordained to destroy me, fail woefully and destroy yourself, in the name of Jesus. Any evil sacrifice offered against my destiny, by anyone, living or dead, expire, in the name of Jesus. Almighty God, make me a wonder in the midst of my enemies and people that wrote me off, in the name of Jesus. Any witchcraft door, gate locking any good thing that belonged to me, open by force and release them, in the name of Jesus. Almighty God, deliver me from the battles of the day and night staged against me, in the name of Jesus. Let the rising up of my enemies be put down without movement again, in the name of Jesus. I command the agents of sorrow, weeping and crying prepared against my family to back fire, in the name of Jesus. Let the habitations of my stubborn and unrepentant enemies, spiritually and physically be invaded by angels of death, in the name of Jesus. Every satanic movement against my destiny, among the creations, be terminated in defeat by the power attached to God's name, in the name of Jesus. I command the whole universe to rise in defense to the name of God in my life, in the name of Jesus. I command the problems in my life to gather together for destruction by the powers of God attached to the name of God; the I AM THAT I AM, in the name of Jesus.

EIGHT

GOD'S REDEMPTIVE NAMES

DECREE-1

(Genesis 22:13-14; 12:10-13, 18., Genesis 21:1-3., John 4:10; 3:16, Judges 6:23-24, Isaiah 53:5, Colossians 1:20., Jeremiah 23:6, 1 Corinthians 1:30, Exodus 15:26, 23-25., Isaiah 53:4-5, Matthew 8:16-17., 1 Peter 2:24., Exodus 17:15., 1 Corinthians 15:57, Numbers 21:1-3, Joshua 6:20-2i., Ezekiel 48:35., Matthew 28:20., Matthew 18:19., Exodus 23:17)

Day 1

Expectations:

1. **Putting an end to every lack, famine and poverty in your life**
2. **The destruction of every organized poverty from the satanic kingdom affecting you**
3. **The destruction of every evil sacrifice and inherited sin, promoting famine in your life**

By the power of God's redemptive name Jehovah-Jireh, I command every lack, famine and poverty in my life to disappear, in the name of Jesus. Almighty God, manifest in my life as Jehovah-Jireh and supply all my needs without exception, in the name of Jesus. Every organized poverty from the satanic kingdom in any area of my life, be disorganized unto failure, in the name of Jesus. Every evil sacrifice and inherited sin, promoting famine in my life, be destroyed by the mercy of God, in the name of Jesus. Almighty God, replace poverty with abundance in every area of my life, in the name of Jesus. Father Lord, arise in your power and deliver me from hardship, suffering and pain, in the name of Jesus.

And Abraham lifted up his eyes and looked, and behold, behind him was a ram, caught in a thicket by his horns. And Abraham went and took the ram and offered it up as a burnt offering instead of his son. So Abraham called the name of that place, "The Lord will provide"; as it is said to this day, "On the mount of the Lord it shall be provided.

Now there was a famine in the land. So Abram went down to Egypt to sojourn there, for the famine was severe in the land. When he was about to enter Egypt, he said to Sarai his wife, "I know that you are a woman beautiful in appearance, and when the Egyptians see you, they will say, 'This is his wife.' Then they will kill me, but they will let you live. Say you are my sister, that it may go well with me because of you, and that my life may be spared for your sake." When Abram entered Egypt, the Egyptians saw that the woman was very beautiful. So Pharaoh called Abram and said, "What is this you have done to me? Why did you not tell me that she was your wife?

— GENESIS 22:13-14; 12:10-13, 18.

Every demonic motivated famine, designed to displace me in life, receive the manifestation of the name of God Jehovah-Jireh, in the name of Jesus. Any evil force, moving me to go down to Egypt to beg for bread, I command you to scatter and fail before me, in the name of Jesus. Father Lord, increase my faith and help me to pray and believe in you to provide in times of famine, in the name of Jesus. Every satanic attack against my handwork, be frustrated, in the name of Jesus. Every sin targeting my life to separate me from God, fail woefully in my life, in the name of Jesus. Any suggestion from the devil to succeed outside God, I reject you, in the name of Jesus.

Day 2

Expectations:

1. **Complete deliverance from fear and sin.**
2. **The destruction of every curse militating against your life and destiny.**
3. **The exposure and destruction of every Judas attached to your life**

Almighty God, deliver me from the fear and sin attached to every famine in my life, in the name of Jesus. Anointing to obey God in or outside Egypt, possess me, in the name of Jesus. Every blessing attached to the name of God Jehovah-Jireh, I receive them double, in the name of Jesus. Almighty God, by the power in your name Jehovah-Jireh, make me a great nation and bless me beyond human imagination, in the name of Jesus. Let the blessing and greatness that accompany the name of God, Jehovah-Jireh, begin to manifest in every area of my life, in the name of Jesus. Every curse militating against my life and destiny, be destroyed by the power in the name of God, Jehovah-Jireh, in the name of Jesus. Anointing that empowered Abraham to leave his country, kindred and father's house to answer the divine call, fall upon me, in the name of Jesus. Almighty God, by your name Jehovah-Jireh, bless them that bless me and through me, bless all the nations of the world, in the name of Jesus. Every evil journey, embarked to harm me and distract my move with God, be terminated in sorrow, in the name of Jesus. Let the power in the name of God, Jehovah-Jireh, empower me with skills, talents and spiritual gifts that will move the world forward for good, in the name of Jesus. Almighty God, through the works of my hands, bless the entire universe and cause them to serve you all the days of their life, in the name of Jesus. Father Lord, raise men and women that will support me and help me to fulfil divine destiny, in the name of Jesus. Let the people planted by the devil to frustrate divine vision for my life be separated from me, in the name of Jesus. Any Judas, attached to my life to betray me, your time is up; be exposed to shame, in the name of Jesus.

Day 3

Expectations:

1. **Receiving the power to prosper without a break**
2. **The destruction of every mountain of poverty standing on your way**
3. **Commanding every area of your life to conceive and birth things that will increase your joy and happiness**

Almighty God, sanctify me and make me your altar, a dwelling place forever, in the name of Jesus. Anointing to pray, fast when the needs arise and to call upon you at all times, fall upon me, in the name of Jesus. By the power of the calling power of God, I receive power to answer the call of God for my life, in the name of Jesus. By your name Jehovah-Jireh, I receive the power to prosper without a break from henceforth, in the name of Jesus. Every mountain of poverty standing on my way to prosperity, disappear without delay, in the name of Jesus.

The Lord visited Sarah as he had said, and the Lord did to Sarah as he had promised. And Sarah conceived and bore Abraham a son in his old age at the time of which God had spoken to him. Abraham called the name of his son who was born to him, whom Sarah bore him, Isaac.

— GENESIS 21:1-3.

Almighty God, command every part of my life to conceive and give birth to things that will increase my joy and happiness forever, in the name of Jesus. Every blessing I missed at my youth, wherever you are, I command you to manifest with joy and happiness, in the name of Jesus. Almighty God, sanctify me and circumcise my heart by the power in the blood of Jesus. Let my growth attract every good thing in life by the power in the name of God Jehovah-Jireh, in the name of Jesus. By the power in the sacrifice of Jesus in the cross of Calvary, I receive divine presence in every area of my life, in the name of Jesus. By the provisional power in the name of God, I bring back everything good I ever lost, in the name of Jesus.

Day 4

Expectations:

1. **The destruction of any evil force preventing the birth of good things in your life**
2. **Commanding the blood of Jesus to speak you out of every lack**
3. **The destruction of every fire of sickness and disease burning in your life**

Any evil force preventing the birth of good things in my life and family, I bind and cast you out, in the name of Jesus. Blood of Jesus, speak me out of every demonic lack that has been assigned to torment my life, in the name of Jesus. Any fire of sickness and disease burning in my life, I put you off by the stripes of Jesus, in the name of Jesus. Any evil deposited in my life, be destroyed by the presence of Jehovah-Jireh, in the name of Jesus. O Lord arise in your mercy and provide my needs without delay, in the name of Jesus. Any trial and test before me from the Lord, end to my favor, in the name of Jesus.

> Jesus answered her, "If you knew the gift of God, and who it is that is saying to you, 'Give me a drink,' you would have asked him, and he would have given you living water."
>
> "For God so loved the world, that he gave his only Son, that whoever believes in him should not perish but have eternal life.
>
> — JOHN 4:10; 3:16.

By the power in the name of God, Jehovah-Jireh, I receive in abundance into my life the water of life, in the name of Jesus. Almighty God, take me to the source of your living water and empower me to get drunk, in the name of Jesus. Anointing to cooperate with Jesus Christ in every area of my life, fall upon me, in the name of Jesus. I command every obstacle preventing me from receiving the blessings of God be frustrated, in the name of Jesus. Let the provisional power in the name of God Jehovah-Jireh come upon me, in the name of Jesus. Power of God that retains God's blessings, arrest me and keep me far away from lack and famine, in the name of Jesus. Let the linking and connecting power in the blood of Jesus link and connect me to everything about God, in the name of Jesus.

Day 5

Expectations:

1. **The destruction of every satanic armed robber assigned to steal from you.**
2. **Commanding the wind of God to blow away every evil presence from you.**
3. **Commanding every problem in your life to end**

Father Lord, take me to the well of waters from heaven and water me with living water, in the name of Jesus. I disengage myself from every satanic armed robber assigned to steal from me, in the name of Jesus. I command every opening in my life to discharge every demonic material from them, in the name of Jesus. Let the love of God that brought Jesus Christ into this world command all blessings from above to invade my life, in the name of Jesus. Wind of God from heaven, focus on me and blow away every evil presence in my life, in the name of Jesus. By the power in the giving ability of God, I receive everything from God that will keep me far away from the devil, his agents, sin and its consequences, in the name of Jesus. I command every problem in my life to perish and remain perished, forever and ever, in the name of Jesus. Omnipotent God, through your boundless capacity to provide every good thing, bestow upon me your unceasing blessings, in the name of Jesus. Let the restoration power of God restore every good thing my ancestors lost to the devil, his agents and sin, in the name of Jesus. Every condemnation from the devil, his agents and sin in my life, be destroyed by the speaking blood of Jesus. I command every part of my life to refuse to accept defeat, condemnation, curses and failures, in the name of Jesus. Every fake light in any area of my life, be replaced with the light of God, the Lord Jesus, in the name of Jesus. I break and loose myself from every darkness reigning over my life and destiny, in the name of Jesus. Every evil ever done in my life, be undone by the power in the speaking blood of Jesus, in the name of Jesus. Almighty God, command your truth, your word to rule and reign over my life, in the name of Jesus. Let the manifesting anointing of the Holy Ghost command all good things from God to manifest in my life without a break, in the name of Jesus.

Day 6

Expectations:

1. **The destruction of every satanic roadblock standing between you and God**
2. **Commanding every area of your life to be available for God without delay**
3. **The destruction of every satanic deposit in your life hindering the manifestation of God**

Every demonic roadblock between me and God, be cleared away by divine whirlwind, in the name of Jesus. Let the finding power of God find me whenever I am needed by God without struggle, in the name of Jesus. I command every area of my life to be available for God without delay, in the name of Jesus. Almighty God, perfect my relationship with you and give me your type of understanding to heed your counsel, in the name of Jesus. Father Lord, empower me to give you my best whenever you need them, in the name of Jesus. Any satanic deposit in me, hindering the manifestation of God in my life, be removed without negotiation, in the name of Jesus. I command every part of my life to begin to please God with joy and happiness, in the name of Jesus. Let my rising early every morning be accompanied with the power to please God, in the name of Jesus. I decree that as I retire to bed every night, I'll draw forth divine presence and peace, in the name of Jesus. Blood of Jesus, speak death to every sin and problem that wish to rise with me every morning, in the name of Jesus. Almighty God, empower me in the remaining nights of my life to embrace the righteousness of Christ without sin, in the name of Jesus.

But the Lord said to him, "Peace be to you. Do not fear; you shall not die." Then Gideon built an altar there to the Lord and called it, The Lord Is Peace. To this day it still stands at Ophrah, which belongs to the Abiezrites.

— JUDGES 6:23-24

But he was pierced for our transgressions; he was crushed for our iniquities; upon him was the chastisement that brought us peace, and with his wounds we are healed.

— ISAIAH 53:5

Almighty God, speak your peace to manifest in every area of my life, in the name of Jesus. Let the fear of the devil, his agents and their activities depart forever from my life, in the name of Jesus. Every judgment passed against me from satanic department of death, be reversed, in the name of Jesus. Almighty God, command your type of life to take over my life forever, in the name of Jesus. Any evil altar ministering against my life, catch fire and burn to ashes, in the name of Jesus. I withdraw everything about my life from the captivity of every satanic altar, in the name of Jesus. By the power of God's name Jehovah-Shalom, I bring divine presence into my life forever, in the name of Jesus.

Day 7

Expectations:

1. **Commanding every negative report concerning you to be transformed into positive report**
2. **The frustration of every evil personality or agent of darkness despising your relationship with God**
3. **Complete healing for every physical and spiritual wound in your life**

Let every negative report concerning my life be transformed into positivity for the glory of God, in the name of Jesus. Let the revelation that will take me away from every satanic activity begin to manifest, in the name of Jesus. Father Lord, cloth me with your beauty, in and out, in the name of Jesus. Any evil personality, agent of darkness despising my relationship with God, be frustrated in shame, in the name of Jesus. Let every spiritual and physical wound in my life, receive healing by the stripes of Jesus. Father Lord, heal me from every witchcraft inflicted bruise, in the name of Jesus. Oh Lord, let your corrective discipline remove me from every form of satanic punishment, in the name of Jesus. I command the oppressors of my life and destiny to cease and die, in the name of Jesus. Every door of affliction opened against my life, be closed forever, in the name of Jesus. I command the promoters of evil in my life to be frustrated unto death, in the name of Jesus. Every demonic presence in my life, wherever you are, depart and come back no more, in the name of Jesus. Every evil personality occupying my space in life to deny me of my blessings, be removed in shame, in the name of Jesus. I command my detained blessings and denied promotions to be released by heavenly force, in the name of Jesus. Every evil spirit in the battle field of my life crying against my destiny, be silenced by the crying blood of Jesus.

Any evil plantation in my life from the witchcraft world, be uprooted, in the name of Jesus. Any problem emanating from my foundation, be squeezed unto death, in the name of Jesus. I break and loose myself from every evil and unprofitable relationship, in the name of Jesus.

Day 8

Expectations:

1. The destruction of every demonic stronghold built against your life
2. The scattering of every evil soldier (both physical and spiritual) encamped against you
3. The destruction of every aggressive witch or wizard assigned to destroy and waste you

Every demonic stronghold built against the manifestations of my progress and joy, be pulled down, in the name of Jesus. Any evil soldier, spiritually or physically encamped against me, scatter and fail, in the name of Jesus. Almighty God, let your sustaining power sustain my purity and relationship with you forever, in the name of Jesus. All satanic grasshoppers eating me alive, your time is up, die, in the name of Jesus. I command all the impoverishing demons in every area of my life to die without negotiation, in the name of Jesus. I command the problems that woke up with me today and the ones that want to follow me to sleep to die, in the name of Jesus. Let the cleansing power that is in the blood of Jesus cleanse me from every sin and its consequences, in the name of Jesus. Every aggressive witch and wizard assigned to destroy me, be frustrated without success, in the name of Jesus. Let the destroying power of God destroy every work of the devil and his agents over my life, in the name of Jesus.

and through him to reconcile to himself all things, whether on earth or in heaven, making peace by the blood of his cross.

— COLOSSIANS 1:20.

In his days Judah will be saved, and Israel will dwell securely. And this is the name by which he will be called: The Lord is our righteousness.'

— JEREMIAH 23:6

And because of him you are in Christ Jesus, who became to us wisdom from God, righteousness and sanctification and redemption

— 1 CORINTHIANS 1:30

Almighty God, command your strengthening and sustaining grace to come upon me without measure, in the name of Jesus. Father Lord, make me worthy to receive your knowledge and every spiritual support to enable me win every war ahead of me, in the name of Jesus. Let the peace that comes through the blood of Jesus begin to manifest in my life, in the name of Jesus. Let the reconciling power of God reconcile me with God the father, God the son and God the Holy Ghost, in the name of Jesus. Father Lord, send your saving power into the battle field of my life to save me from every satanic attack, in the name of Jesus.

Day 9

Expectations:

1. **Commanding the angels of God to take you and everything about you to a place of safety.**
2. **The destruction of every form of unrighteousness in your life and destiny.**
3. **Receiving the anointing from God for promotion, the same way Joseph was promoted.**

Angels of the living God, I command you to take me and everything about me to a place of safety, in the name of Jesus. By the power of God's righteousness in Christ, I command every unrighteousness in my life to be destroyed, in the name of Jesus. By the power of God Almighty, I receive the grace to be made righteous, wise, redeemed and purified for God's use, in the name of Jesus. Almighty God, frustrate every part of my body, soul and spirit from committing sin or cooperating with the devil, in the name of Jesus. Let the miscarrying power of God enter into my life to miscarry every sin and its consequences in my life, in the name of Jesus. Anointing from God that promoted Joseph in Egypt, fall upon me and promote me, in the name of Jesus. Let the gracious power of God help me to remain with Him all the days of my life, in the name of Jesus. Any evil sword prepared to cut me off from divine mercy, be rendered impotent and powerless, in the name of Jesus. Almighty God, empower me to differentiate your voice from satanic voices, in the name of Jesus. Every enemy of the manifestations of God's character in my life, be frustrated unto death, in the name of Jesus.

saying, "If you will diligently listen to the voice of the Lord your God, and do that which is right in his eyes, and give ear to his commandments and keep all his statutes, I will put none of the diseases on you that I put on the Egyptians, for I am the Lord, your healer."

When they came to Marah, they could not drink the water of Marah because it was bitter; therefore, it was named Marah. And the people grumbled against Moses, saying, "What shall we drink?" And he cried to the Lord, and the Lord showed him a log, and he threw it into the water, and the water became sweet. There the Lord made for them a statute and a rule, and there he tested them.

— EXODUS 15:26, 23-25.

Almighty God, grant me the empowerment to diligently, discipline, and steadfastly seek your voice, and to promptly obey you, in the name of Jesus. Pour forth your anointing, oh Lord, and mend my past through your redeeming power, in the name of Jesus. Father Lord, let your anointing guide me to walk righteously for the duration of my existence on earth, in the name of Jesus. Every force opposing the word of God in my spirit and every facet of my life, be completely brought to death, in the name of Jesus. Heavenly Father, strengthen me to uphold your commandments and faithfully follow them till eternity, in the name of Jesus.

Day 10

Expectations:

1. **The destruction of every evil spirit, assuming animal forms, assigned to attack you**
2. **The destruction of every evil spirit in any creature, monitoring your life to attack you**
3. **The termination of every demonic attack to misuse your tongue**

By the healing power of the stripes of Jesus, I terminate all diseases and health conditions in my life, in the name of Jesus. I command every obstruction on my path to divide and make way, just as the Red Sea parted before the Israelites, in the name of Jesus. Any evil spirit, assuming animal forms, assigned to attack me in the wilderness, my dwelling, or workplace, be brought to an end, in the name of Jesus. Any evil spirit in any creature, monitoring my life to attack me, I bind and cast you out, in the name of Jesus. Father Lord, water every part of my life with the living water and satisfy all my needs in life, present and future, in the name of Jesus. Every root of bitterness planted in any area of my life, be uprooted, in the name of Jesus. Every demonic attack to misuse my tongue in life, fail woefully, in the name of Jesus. Let the crying of the wicked and their activity over my life be silenced by the crying blood of Jesus, in the name of Jesus. Almighty God, open my eyes and show me where to cast my nets, in the name of Jesus. Let the seeing eyes of the devil, his agents and sin be blinded before me, in the name of Jesus. I decree that my presence will destroy every evil presence, block their movements spiritually and physically, in the name of Jesus. Blood of Jesus, enter into my eyes and destroy every sin of lust and covetousness, in the name of Jesus.

Every dream of failure and defeat assigned to keep me in bondage, be reversed, in the name of Jesus.

Day 11

Expectations:

1. **The destruction of every evil altar built to destroy your life**
2. **The destruction of every satanic structure raised against your life**
3. **Putting an end to every affliction affecting your life and destiny**

Every evil altar built to destroy my life, catch fire, burn to ashes, in the name of Jesus. Every satanic structure in any part of my life, be destroyed forever, in the name of Jesus. Almighty God, stretch forth your hand and take me away from satanic presence, in the name of Jesus.

> Surely he has borne our griefs and carried our sorrows; yet we esteemed him stricken,
> smitten by God, and afflicted. But he was pierced for our transgressions; he was crushed for our iniquities; upon him was the chastisement that brought us   peace,
> and with his wounds we are healed.
>
> —   ISAIAH 53:4-5

> This was to fulfil what was spoken by the prophet Isaiah: "He took our illnesses and bore our diseases."
>
> —   MATTHEW 8:16-17.

By the anointing power of Christ Jesus that borne my griefs and carried away my sorrows in the cross of Calvary, I drop all my problem in the cross, in the name of Jesus. I command my problems and every negative thing in my life to appear before the cross and die, in the name of Jesus. Every negative action going on openly or secretly against my life, I bring you to the cross, in the name of Jesus. You the works of the devil, his agents and the powers of sin and its consequences, appear and be judged before the cross, in the name of Jesus. Any affliction in my life, hear the word of God, you must not rise the second time, therefore, die forever, in the name of Jesus. I replace every insult, wound, bruise, grief, sorrow with peace from Christ through his death, in the name of Jesus.

Day 12

Expectations:

1. **The destruction of every dark angel assigned against you**
2. **The destruction of every evil deposit in your life and the ones that came through evil hands that ever touched you**
3. **Complete deliverance for any part of your life, body, soul and spirit that is under satanic attack**

Let the fear of God dominate and overtake every satanic fear in my life, in the name of Jesus. As I lift up my eyes in faith today let my eyes see divine provision in every area of my life, in the name of Jesus. Any dark angel assigned to follow me around to waste my efforts in life, I bind and cast you out of my sight, in the name of Jesus. Any evil deposit through the evil hands that ever touched me in life from birth, be cleared by the power in the blood of Jesus. Lord Jesus, I bring before you every sickness and disease in my life for complete deliverance, in the name of Jesus. Any part of my life, body, soul and spirit under satanic attack, receive deliverance, in the name of Jesus. I bind and cast out any evil spirit behind every problem in my life, in the name of Jesus. Let the healing power in the stripes of Jesus run through my life for perfect healing of my soul, body and spirit, in the name of Jesus. Every yoke of infirmity in my life, your time is up, break to pieces, in the name of Jesus. By the power in the stripes of Jesus, I command every sickness in my life spiritually or physically to bow, in the name of Jesus.

He himself bore our sins in his body on the tree, that we might die to sin and live to righteousness. By his wounds you have been healed.

— 1 PETER 2:24.

And Moses built an altar and called the name of it, The Lord Is My Banner

— EXODUS 17:15.

But thanks be to God, who gives us the victory through our Lord Jesus Christ.

— 1 CORINTHIANS 15:57.

Anything among the creatures that will move me to thank God without a break, begin to manifest, in the name of Jesus. Every hindrance to God's praise in my life, your time is up, show up immediately and die, in the name of Jesus. I command the victory that will swallow defeats of the past, present and future to manifest now, in the name of Jesus. Everything that is good and comes through Jesus Christ our Lord, locate me everywhere I go, in the name of Jesus. Dear Father, because Jesus took away my sins on the cross, I tell every issue in my life to go away and never return to me, in Jesus' name.

Day 13

Expectations:

1. **The destruction of every strength of sin and disease in your body, soul and spirit**
2. **The termination of every war going on against your life**
3. **The destruction of every enemy in the battle of your life**

Every strength of sin and disease in my body, soul and spirit, be destroyed, in the name of Jesus. I command every organ of my body to be dead to sin and all its consequences, in the name of Jesus. Any war going on against my life, end to my favor by the name of God, Jehovah-Nissi, in the name of Jesus. Every enemy in the battle field of my life, be defeated by the power in the name, Jehovah-Nissi, in the name of Jesus. Let the arresting power of God arrest blessings that are outside my life and bring them into my life by divine mercy, in the name of Jesus. Almighty God, open my eyes to see the answers to my prayers, in the name of Jesus. I command the long-time problems in my life to vanish out of my sight forever and ever, in the name of Jesus. Let the name of God Jehovah-Jireh replace every satanic name in my life, in the name of Jesus. I command my closed heaven to open to hear the voice of God for the manifestations of my blessings, in the name of Jesus. Let the determining power of God manifest in my life to provide all my needs without delay, in the name of Jesus.

When the Canaanite, the king of Arad, who lived in the Negeb, heard that Israel was coming by the way of Atharim, he fought against Israel, and took some of them captive. And Israel vowed a vow to the Lord and said, "If you will indeed give this people into my hand, then I will devote their cities to destruction." And the Lord heeded the voice of Israel and gave over the Canaanites, and they devoted them and their cities to destruction. So the name of the place was called Hormah.

— NUMBERS 21:1-3

So the people shouted, and the trumpets were blown. As soon as the people heard the sound of the trumpet, the people shouted a great shout, and the wall fell down flat, so that the people went up into the city, every man straight before him, and they captured the city. Then they devoted all in the city to destruction, both men and women, young and old, oxen, sheep, and donkeys, with the edge of the sword.

— JOSHUA 6:20-2I.

Command the eyes of all evil spies monitoring my life to be blinded, in the name of Jesus. Any fight in the spirit realm going on against my life, be terminated to my favor, in the name of Jesus. Every stone of hindrance placed before me to trap me down, be removed by heavenly force, in the name of Jesus. Any part of my life in satanic prison, be released by force, in the name of Jesus. I break and loose myself from every vow holding me down in bondage, in the name of Jesus. I command the evil altars where the devil is being worshipped to catch fire and be burnt down to ashes, in the name of Jesus.

Day 14

Expectations:

1. **Commanding the hearing ears of the devil and his agents to be stopped by God's power**
2. **Commanding the miracles that will take you to your promise land to begin to manifest**
3. **The destruction of the enemy of your full and complete deliverance**
4. **Commanding the silencing power of God to silence every evil voice and tongue against you**

Let the hearing ears of the devil and his agents against me be stopped, in the name of Jesus. I command my blessings in the hand of my enemies and strangers to be released by the power of God, in the name of Jesus. Oh heaven, empower me to do anything on Earth through Christ to the glory of God, in Jesus' name. Any miracle that will take me to my promised land, wherever you are, begin to manifest, in the name of Jesus. Let the name and presence of God forever be known in my life as salvation from sin, present in deliverance from the consequence of sin and perfection by the cleansing power in the blood of Jesus.

The circumference of the city shall be 18,000 cubits. And the name of the city from that time on shall be, The Lord Is There."

— EZEKIEL 48:35.

teaching them to observe all that I have commanded you. And behold, I am with you always, to the end of the age."

— MATTHEW 28:20.

Every enemy of my full deliverance and the manifestations of God's blessing, be frustrated, in the name of Jesus. Let the teaching power of the Holy Ghost come upon me and use me to teach others, in the name of Jesus. Father Lord, empower me with the gift of teaching, in the name of Jesus. Anointing and obedience to observe God's word, possess me and spread all over the world through me, in the name of Jesus. Let the presence of Jesus Christ occupy every part of my life, body, soul and spirit forever, in the name of Jesus. Let the starting power of God help me to start and finish well in every divine assignment, in the name of Jesus. I receive the auction of the Holy Ghost to make heaven together with uncountable others, in the name of Jesus. Every enemy of God in my life, be frustrated, in the name of Jesus. Let the name of God's presence never depart from my life forever and ever, in the name of Jesus. Blood of Jesus, speak divine presence at all times in every area of my life without a stop, all the days of my life, in the name of Jesus. Blessed Holy Spirit, cease not from teaching me the mysteries of life with the power to obey you all the days of my life, in the name of Jesus. Let the silencing power of God silence every evil voice speaking against me from witchcraft covens, in the name of Jesus. By the anointing attached to the name of God, Jehovah-Jireh, I receive in abundance, everything that will make me fulfil destiny, in the name of Jesus. I command the breakthrough that will single me out and take me out of every problem to manifest now, in the name of Jesus. Let the trumpet of victory be sound from heaven for my sake, in the name of Jesus. Almighty God, command your heavenly angels to blow horns of prosperity on my behalf, in the name of Jesus. I terminate every sound of witchcraft against my destiny by divine silence, in the name of Jesus. Let the compassing soldiers of God compass the camp of my enemies and set them ablaze, in the name of Jesus. Every spiritual or physical wall built to block me from entering into my blessings, collapse and fall flat, in the name of Jesus. Let the angels of God from the third heaven invade the camp of my enemies without notice, in the name of Jesus. I cast out every accursed thing in my life, in the name of Jesus. Let the wisdom and masterplan of the devil and his agents fail woefully before me, in the name of Jesus. Any silver and gold brought to defile my financial strength, be detected and removed, in the name of Jesus. I command the whole creation to open their mouth and shout a shout of victory for my sake, in the name of Jesus. Every negative word ever spoken against me to torment me, expire, in the name of Jesus. Every satanic armed soldier prepared against me, destroy yourselves, in the name of Jesus. By the crying blood of Jesus, I silence every evil noise in my residence, in the name of Jesus. I take back forcefully all the good things I lost since the time of Adam and Eve from the kingdom of darkness, using the name of Jesus. Every satanic soldier, coming against me from any evil kingdom, I cripple your movement, in the name of Jesus. Father Lord, surround me with your guiding angels, in the name of Jesus. Any evil priest offering sacrifices against my life, be frustrated with painful errors, in the name of Jesus.

> Again I say to you, if two of you agree on earth about anything they ask, it will be done for them by my Father in heaven.
>
> — MATTHEW 18:19.

> Three times in the year shall all your males appear before the Lord God.
>
> — EXODUS 23:17

Every curse of poverty in my life, your time is up, expire by the name, Jehovah-Jireh, in the name of Jesus. By the power of God invested in the name of God, Jehovah-Jireh, I receive every good thing my ancestors handed over to the devil and his agents, in the name of Jesus. Let the transferring power of God through his name Jehovah-Jireh transfer the wealth of the Gentiles to me, in the name of Jesus.

NINE

WARFARE WITH GOD'S ATTRIBUTES

DECREE-1

(Psalms 139:7-12; 9:2, Revelation 4:8, 11., Ezekiel 1:5, 10, 13, 14; 10:12, 14, 15, 20, Revelation 5:9-14, Revelation 7:9-12., Revelation 11:16, 17, Psalms 104:24, Proverbs 3:19, Daniel 2:20-21, Romans 11:33, Colossians 2:23, James 1:5, Genesis 1:1, Exodus 15:17, Deuteronomy 3:24, 1 Chronicles 16:25, Job 40:2; 42:2, 2 Samuel 21:15-21, 1 Chronicles 18:11, 2 Samuel 2:5-7 , 2 Samuel 5:1-4 , Psalms 84:10, 2 Samuel 2:1, Isaiah 40:12-15, Jeremiah 32:17, Daniel 4:35, Matthew 19:26, Genesis 28:15,16, Joshua 2:11, Psalms 139:7-12, Psalms 147:4; 94:9-11 , Luke 16:15, Hebrews 4:13, John 4:25, 28-30, 42, Exodus 3:14, Hebrews 1:12, Psalms 90:2, Psalms 102:24-27, Malachi 3:6, John 1:17, Psalms 19:7, James 1:25, Ezekiel 12:25, Romans 3:4, 1 Corinthians 1:9, Deuteronomy 2:17-19, Numbers 22:10-11, 1 Corinthians 1:9, 1 Thessalonians 5:24, Hebrews 6:18, 2 Timothy 2:13, Joshua 21:43-45)

Day 1

Expectations:

1. **The destruction of every satanic hideout in your life.**
2. **The frustration of all the witches and wizards against your life.**
3. **The destruction of the thoughts and plans of the evil ones against your life and destiny.**

By the searching power of the Holy Spirit, I locate every satanic hide out in my life for immediate destruction, in the name of Jesus. I command the down-sitting and the uprising of witches and wizards in my life to be frustrated, in the name of Jesus. Every part of my life that is concealing the glory of God, release it now, in the name of Jesus. Every evil thought of the devil and his agents against my life, be exposed and be disgraced, in the name of Jesus. Father Lord, take me far away from the reach of the devil and his agents, in the mighty name of Jesus. Let the ability of witches and wizards against my family members be rendered impotent, in the name of Jesus. For what you have done to me O Lord, I will rejoice forever, praise and sing to your glory. Every enemy of divine blessings in my life, be frustrated, in the name of Jesus. I command every marvelous work of God to increase in manifestation in every area of my life, in the name of Jesus. Almighty God, make me a singing container in this generation, in the name of Jesus.

Where shall I go from your Spirit? Or where shall I flee from your presence?
If I ascend to heaven, you are there! If I make my bed in Sheol, you are there!
If I take the wings of the morning and dwell in the uttermost parts of the sea,
even there your hand shall lead me, and your right hand shall hold me.

> If I say, "Surely the darkness shall cover me, and the light about me be night," even the darkness is not dark to you; the night is bright as the day, for darkness is as light with you. I will be glad and exult in you; I will sing praise to your name, O Most High.
>
> — PSALMS 139:7-12; 9:2

Almighty God, compass my path, my going out, my coming in and my lying down and take over every activity in my life, in the name of Jesus. Let my ways be under the perfect control of the Holy Spirit, in the name of Jesus. I command my thoughts, my words, and my actions to be under divine guidance, in the name of Jesus.

Day 2

Expectation:

1. The destruction of all the enemies against your settlement and establishment

2. Commanding all the enemies of your life and destiny to surrender and bow

3. The destruction of every fake crown in your life (both physically and spiritually).

And the four living creatures, each of them with six wings, are full of eyes all around and within, and day and night they never cease to say, "Holy, holy, holy, is the Lord God Almighty, who was and is and is to come!" "Worthy are you, our Lord and God, to receive glory and honor and power, for you created all things, and by your will they existed and were created."

— REVELATION 4:8, 11.

By the power of the Almighty of God, I command every enemy of my destiny to surrender and bow, in the name of Jesus. In the name of Jesus, I receive the power to enter every good door that God has opened for me. By the power of the worthiness of God, I command every part of my life to be worthy to receive divine blessings, in the name of Jesus. Almighty God, inject your holy character into me, in the name of Jesus. In the name of Jesus, let every ungodly character within me be removed and replaced with the character of God. Let God the creator of all things be honored in my life forever and ever, in the name of Jesus. Anything in me that doesn't give God glory, your time is up, begin to honor God without a break, in the name of Jesus. Lord Jesus, stand in the sea of my life and take over my life without a rival, in the name of Jesus. Every fake crown in my life, spiritually and physically, catch fire and burn to ashes, in the name of Jesus. By the power of the Holy Spirit, I protect my front and back from every satanic attack, in the name of Jesus. I command every part of my life, body, soul and spirit to be sanctified and completely freed from Satan, sin and every problem in life, in the name of Jesus. Let the hand of God rest upon me to frustrate the manifestations of the devil and his agents in my life, in the name of Jesus.

And from the midst of it came the likeness of four living creatures. And this was their appearance: they had a human likeness as for the likeness of their faces, each had a human face. The four had the face of a lion on the right side, the four had the face of an ox on the left side, and the four had the face of an eagle. As for the likeness of the living creatures, their appearance was like burning coals of fire, like the appearance of torches moving to and fro among the living creatures. And the fire was bright, and out of the fire went forth lightning. And the living creatures darted to and fro, like the appearance of a flash of lightning. And their whole body, their rims, and their spokes, their wings, and the wheels were full of eyes all around—the wheels that the four of them had. And everyone had four faces: the first face was the face of the cherub, and the second face was a human face, and the third the face of a lion, and the fourth the face of an eagle. And the cherubim mounted up. These were the living creatures that I saw by the Chebar canal. These were the living creatures that I saw underneath the God of Israel by the Chebar canal; and I knew that they were cherubim.

— EZEKIEL 1:5, 10, 13, 14; 10:12, 14, 15, 20.

Let the burning coals of fire from above burn to ashes every problem in my life, in the name of Jesus. Almighty God, shine your lamp into my life to drive away every darkness, in the name of Jesus. Father Lord, send your lightening into every evil kingdom to destroy their base of attack against my life, in the name of Jesus. In the name of Jesus, I decree that every living and non-living creature shall provide abundant support to my life for the glory of God. With the mighty power of divine lightning from heaven, I declare that every demonic activity working against my destiny shall be revealed, all in the name of Jesus. Every demonic prophesy and vision against my life, be terminated, in the name of Jesus.

Day 3

Expectations:

1. **Complete protection from all demonic attacks**
2. **Commanding all creatures to minister total deliverance to you without delay**
3. **Commanding the face of Christ to manifest in your life like a Lion and equally destroy every evil presence in your life**

Dear Almighty God, I ask for your protection on every side of my life—front, back, and all around—shield me from every demonic attack, In Jesus' name, I pray. Let the wing of the Lord fly me away from every danger, in the name of Jesus. Let the eyes of the Lord surround my life from every side, in the name of Jesus. By the power in the wheel of God, I command my life to be wheeled away from every evil presence, in the name of Jesus. Father Lord, show your face in the battle field of my life and cause the evil powers to be crippled, in the name of Jesus. Almighty God, command the whole creature to minister total freedom into my life without delay, in the name of Jesus. Let the cherubim's and the wheel of the Almighty move me to my promised land where the enemies of my life will be frustrated, in the name of Jesus. Almighty God, open my eyes to see you fighting for me all the time, in the name of Jesus. Dear Heavenly Father, with the power of your life-giving spirit, guide and direct every of my existence to embrace and embody the way of living that reflects your divine nature, in the name of Jesus. May the presence of Christ, manifest in my life and begin its transformative work within me, all in the name of Jesus. Amen. Let the face of Christ manifest in my life like a Lion and destroy every evil presence in my life, in the name of Jesu. By the power in the wonderful knowledge of God upon my life, I frustrate the plans of the devil and his agents over my life, in the name of Jesus. Almighty God, empower me to attain to your knowledge, wisdom and understanding, in the name of Jesus. Father Lord, take me to a height higher than the devil and his agents, here in this world, in the name of Jesus. I command every part of my life to appear before the Spirit of God for perfect deliverance from every demonic activity, in the name of Jesus. Let my life, body, soul and spirit flee from every appearance of evil, in the name of Jesus. Every evil presence in my life, disappear and be destroyed by divine presence, in the name of Jesus.

And they sang a new song, saying, "Worthy are you to take the scroll and to open its seals, for you were slain, and by your blood you ransomed people for God from every tribe and language and people and nation, and you have made them a kingdom and priests to our God, and they shall reign on the earth." Then I looked, and I heard around the throne and the living creatures and the elders the voice of many angels, numbering myriads of myriads and thousands of thousands, saying with a loud voice, "Worthy is the Lamb who was slain, to receive power and wealth and wisdom and might and honor and glory and blessing! "And I heard every creature in heaven and on earth and under the earth and in the sea, and all that is in them, saying, "To him who sits on the throne and to the Lamb be blessing and honor and glory and might forever and ever! "And the four living creatures said, "Amen!" and the elders fell down and worshiped.

— REVELATION 5:9-14.

By God's boundless mercy, I receive the grace to behold the throne of God and witness the divine seating arrangement in heaven, all in the name of Jesus. Let the leadership style of Jesus be imparted into my life, in the name of Jesus. Let God's handwriting concerning my life, begin to manifest immediately without hindrance, in the name of Jesus. Anointing to hear the voice of angels speaking to me, possess me, in the name of Jesus. I command every part of my life to hear and obey divine proclamation, in the name of Jesus. Any satanic spot or wrinkle in my life, be cleansed by the cleansing power in the blood of Jesus, in the name of Jesus.

Day 4

Expectations:

1. **The destruction of every satanic chain in any area or part of your life.**
2. **The destruction of every evil seal on your life.**
3. **The destruction of every evil root in your life.**

Father Lord, make me worthy to honor you and to make it to heaven at last, in the name of Jesus. Any satanic chains in any area of my life, visible or invisible, break to pieces, in the name of Jesus. Any evil seal in any area of my life, be loosed by the crying blood of Jesus, in the name of Jesus. Almighty God, empower me to do good and please you till the last moment of my life here on earth, in the name of Jesus. Lion of the Tribe of Judah, wherever you are, appear by your mercy in the battle field of my life and deliver me, in the name of Jesus. Any evil root in my life, be destroyed and be replaced with the root of David, in the name of Jesus. Every satanic seal of bondage in my life, break to pieces, in the name of Jesus. Let the prevailing power of Jesus Christ arise for my sake and prevail over my life, family and ministry, in the name of Jesus. Any evil blood sacrifice crying against my life from every satanic kingdom, be silenced by the crying blood of Jesus, in the name of Jesus. By the power of the seven Spirit of God, I bind and cast out any evil spirit fighting against my life, in the name of Jesus. Almighty God, walk me into your kingdom and perfect my deliverance, in the name of Jesus. Let the sound of harps and golden vials, filled with heavenly fragrances, carry my prayers and present them before God, and lead to the swift manifestation of my answers, in the name of Jesus. Miracles, signs and wonders that will move me to start singing a new song forever, manifest in my life, in the name of Jesus. Let the worthiness of Christ be linked to my life for divine purification, in the name of Jesus. I command the killers of good things to avoid my life forever, in the name of Jesus. Let the redeeming power of God redeem me from every satanic bondage, in the name of Jesus. Blood of Jesus, start your full work in my life from every side and command your deliverance power to manifest in my life, in the name of Jesus. I command every creature to rise and fight for me, in the mighty name of Jesus. Let the risen Christ rise with everything that will make me happy and heavenly minded forever, in the name of Jesus. I receive from the slain lamb, power, riches, wisdom, strength, honor, glory and blessings undefiled, in the name of Jesus. I command every part of my life to embrace the Kingship of Christ without delay, in the name of Jesus. I command every area of my life to surrender to the kingship of Christ forever, in the name of Jesus. Let every part of my life begin to hear the voice of Jesus Christ without a minus, in the name of Jesus. I command the angels of God to minister to my needs with all manner of blessings in place, in the name of Jesus.

Day 5

Expectations:

1. **The destruction of every throne of darkness ministering against you.**
2. **The destruction of every living problem in your life hindering your progress.**
3. **The destruction of every demonic achievement or breakthrough in your life and the total recovery of all that you lost**

Let every throne of darkness ministering to me, collapse before the throne of God, in the name of Jesus. Every living problem in my life, hindering my progress, die with the slain lamb of God and rise no more, in the name of Jesus. I command heaven and earth to combine forces to destroy the works of the devil and his agents in my life, in the name of Jesus. Let the breakthrough and every demonic achievement in my life be destroyed by the Spirit of God in me, in the name of Jesus.

After this I looked, and behold, a great multitude that no one could number, from every nation, from all tribes and peoples and languages, standing before the throne and before the Lamb, clothed in white robes, with palm branches in their hands, and crying out with a loud voice, "Salvation belongs to our God who sits on the throne, and to the Lamb!" And all the angels were standing around the throne and around the elders and the four living creatures, and they fell on their faces before the throne and worshiped God, saying, "Amen! Blessing and glory and wisdom and thanksgiving and honor and power and might be to our God forever and ever! Amen."

— REVELATION 7:9-12.

Almighty God, with your power that calmed the winds, I beseech you to command an end to every problem in my life, all in the name of Jesus. Every polluted wind here on earth and among every creature, avoid my life, in the name of Jesus. I command the carriers of poison, charm and every satanic weapon to be rendered impotent before me, in the name of Jesus. I command the tree of my life to bear good fruits from every branch globally, in the name of Jesus. Almighty God, through your divine power, I nullify the influence of evil forces in my life, in the name of Jesus. Father Lord, seal me with your seal that will empower me to live holy and make heaven, in the name of Jesus. Mercy of God, write my names in the book of life and empower me to make heaven by your ability without negotiation, in the name of Jesus. Father Lord, through my ministry, cause numberless people from all nations, kindreds, tongues to make heaven, in the name of Jesus. Blood of Jesus, with your ink of authority, by the special mercy of God, write my name among the saints that will forever worship you in heaven, in the name of Jesus. Empower me to render unto you forever, an unending thanksgiving, honor, power and might, in the name of Jesus.

Day 6

Expectations:

1. **Receiving God's fleeing power to be able to flee from all appearance of evil and the works of the devil**
2. **Receiving the anointing to remain under divine presence**
3. **Commanding the restoration of all the blessings that you ever lost**

Oh Lord, let my amen to all your commandments resound eternally in righteousness, in the name of Jesus. Almighty God, impart in me the fleeing power from above to flee from all appearance of evil, poverty and all the works of the devil, in the name of Jesus. Anointing to remain under divine presence, fall upon me, in the name of Jesus. May the same divine power that elevated Jesus Christ from earth to heaven lift me away from every designated demonic stage in my life, in the name of Jesus. Father Lord, help me to be conscious of your presence everywhere I go, in the name of Jesus. I decree the restoration of my blessings, taken by the devil and his agents to be returned to me, in the name of Jesus. Let the promotion of God in my life be confirmed on earth, under the earth, in the sea, and among every creature to the glory of God, in the name of Jesus. I command blessings, honor, glory and power unto the Lord Jesus in my life forever and ever, in the name of Jesus. I command every creature to agree with my relationship with God forever and ever, in the name of Jesus.

> And the twenty-four elders who sit on their thrones before God fell on their faces and worshiped God, saying, "We give thanks to you, Lord God Almighty, who is and who was, for you have taken your great power and begun to reign.
>
> — REVELATION 11:16, 17.

Father Lord, start my holiness and righteousness from my heart, the root of my life and spread it to all the branch without exception, in the name of Jesus. I command every area of my life, in and out to embrace divine approved purity without spot or wrinkle, in the name of Jesus. Let the purification power in the blood of Jesus Christ penetrate into my life and perfect my holiness, in the name of Jesus. Every trace of the work of the devil and his agents in my life, be destroyed by the crying blood of Jesus.

Day 7

Expectations:

1. **Commanding an end to every warfare going on against your destiny.**
2. **Commanding the strength of your mornings to destabilize every satanic program against your life.**
3. **The destruction of every satanic embargo placed upon your life and destiny.**

By divine presence, I command every warfare going on against my destiny to end to my favor, in the name of Jesus. I command the strength of the remaining mornings in my life to destabilize every satanic program against my life and destiny, in the name of Jesus. Every satanic embargo placed upon my life, be destroyed by the strength of God, in the name of Jesus. I command the waking up and the sleeping of the devil, his agents and sin in my life to be destroyed, in the name of Jesus.

> O LORD, how manifold are your works! In wisdom have you made them all; the earth is full of your creatures.
>
> — PSALMS 104:24.

> The Lord by wisdom founded the earth; by understanding he established the heavens;
>
> — PROVERBS 3:19.

Let the manifold of God's work in wisdom bring every good thing into existence in my life, in the name of Jesus. I command the whole earth to bring into my life the fullness of God's riches, in the name of Jesus. Almighty God, cover me with your light, in the name of Jesus. Almighty God, stretch out into my life every good thing like a curtain, in the name of Jesus. Let the heaven of heavens respond to my needs without delay, in the name of Jesus. Father Lord, furnish my life with your beauty and lay the beams of my life with heavenly strength, in the name of Jesus. Carry me to my promised land with the wings of the wind without harm, in the name of Jesus. Make me a flaming fire that will consume every work of the devil everywhere among the creation, in the name of Jesus. I command the powers that holds the foundation of the earth to minister to me, in the name of Jesus. I command my testimonies to emanate from everywhere, the deep of the waters, top of the mountains and from the third heaven, in the name of Jesus. Let the reproof of the Lord remove all forms of evil from my life, invoking the name of Jesus. Amen. By the power in God's thunderous voice, I put fear into the camp of my enemies, in the name of Jesus. Any valley among the creations holding-down my blessings, release them, in the name of Jesus.

Day 8

Expectations:

1. Commanding the hills of creation to minister deliverance and blessing to your life
2. Commanding every good thing on earth to bear fruit into your life.
3. The destruction of every witchcraft creature assigned against you.
4. Receiving the wine of God that gives joy and everlasting peace.

By the power in the blood of Jesus, I set bound between me and every satanic work, in the name of Jesus. Let the hills of the creations minister deliverance and blessings into my life without a break, in the name of Jesus. I command the habitations of the heaven and the earth to cooperate with God's will for my life, in the name of Jesus. Let the good things from God satisfy my life with all goodies, in the name of Jesus. I command every good thing on earth to bear fruits into my life in abundance, in the name of Jesus. Let the wine of God that gives joy and everlasting peace be filled in my life for divine intoxication, in the name of Jesus. Let the oil of God that makes face to shine and the bread that gives strength begin to minister into my life, in the name of Jesus. Any witchcraft animal among the creature assigned against me, I command them to die, in the name of Jesus. Every plantation of the devil in my life, be uprooted, in the name of Jesus. By the power of God apportioned to this day, I cripple every demonic strength assigned against my destiny, in the name of Jesus. Satan, you are a thief, I command you to release all the power you have stolen from God to torment people here on earth, in the name of Jesus. I forbid the devil and his agents from operating against me this day, in the name of Jesus. Every weapon the devil and his agents are using against me, I turn them against his kingdom, in the name of Jesus. I command the operational base of the devil to be set ablaze, in the name of Jesus. Let the founding power in God's wisdom gather every best thing here on earth and in heaven and bring them into my life, in the name of Jesus. Almighty God, fill me with your wisdom to discover great things that are known and unknown, in the name of Jesus. Let the understanding of God that established the heavens settle me and establish me in every good thing, in the name of Jesus. Almighty God, increase your understanding in me and help me to use them to your own glory, in the name of Jesus. Let the impartation of God's knowledge manifest in my life to the glory of God, in the name of Jesus. Father Lord, drop all your attribute into my life and use them to the best for mankind, in the name of Jesus. Father Lord, keep me in sound wisdom, understanding, knowledge and power, in the name of Jesus.

Day 9

Expectations:

1. **Receiving God's kind of health, strength and capacity to operate against the devil.**
2. **Commanding the goodness of God to penetrate into your foundation and into all the areas of your life.**
3. **The dethroning of any man, woman or power around you, using silver, gold, power and authority to serve the devil.**

Let the honoring power of God bring honor into my life, in the name of Jesus. By divine discretion, I command the works of the devil here on earth to be destroyed, in the name of Jesus. Father Lord, give me your kind of health, strength and capacity to operate against the devil here on earth, in the name of Jesus. Let the goodness of God penetrate into my foundation, health, marrow and bones for divine purpose, in the name of Jesus.

> Daniel answered and said: "Blessed be the name of God forever and ever, to whom belong wisdom and might. He changes times and seasons; he removes kings and sets up kings; he gives wisdom to the wise and knowledge to those who have understanding;
>
> — DANIEL 2:20-21

> Oh, the depth of the riches and wisdom and knowledge of God! How unsearchable are his judgments and how inscrutable his ways!
>
> — ROMANS 11:33.

Any man, woman or power using silver, gold, power and authority to serve the devil, be dethroned, in the name of Jesus. Every good thing around evil men and women, begin to leave, in the name of Jesus. Father Lord, raise godly men and women that will replace evil leaders, in the name of Jesus. Let the devil and his agents around me, in the cities begin to make mistakes that will remove them from power, in the name of Jesus.

Day 10

Expectations:

1. **Commanding the backbone of evil leaders in your community and nation to be broken**
2. **Commanding the wisdom and might from above to arrest and function in every area of your life**
3. **Commanding the God that changes times and seasons to change your life**

Almighty God, arise and position me to rule over the wicked and not the other way round, in the name of Jesus. Backbone of evil leaders in my community, city and nation, be broken to pieces, in the name of Jesus. Wisdom and might from above, arrest every area of my life and use them to honor God forever, in the name of Jesus. O Lord that changes times and seasons, change my situation and better my life to perfection, in the name of Jesus. Let the evil powers that be, within and around me be changed by the God of heaven, in the name of Jesus. Every evil king reigning among men, be removed in shame, in the name of Jesus. Every witch or wizard assigned to fight Christianity, be disgraced from office, in the name of Jesus. Any idolatrous person working against me, be frustrated, in the name of Jesus. I command all occult people, wicked satanic agents to lose their wealth to me and other believers around, in the name of Jesus. Changes that will destroy evil kingdom, begin to take place, in the name of Jesus. By the power of God's Spirit, I disengage every demonic spirit assigned to spoil my day, in the name of Jesus. I command the powers of darkness in the uttermost part of the earth, sea, air and land assigned against me to be frustrated, in the name of Jesus. Let the light of God's power enter into my reins and take over every satanic darkroom in my life, in the name of Jesus. Let the shining power of God's light shine into my life forever, in the name of Jesus. Any darkness in any area of my life trying to hide from divine light, be located and be destroyed, in the name of Jesus. Manipulation of the devil and his agents over my life, be terminated without success, in the name of Jesus. Let the leading power of God deliver me out of every danger, in the name of Jesus.

Day 11

Expectations:

1. Complete deliverance from the evil control of the devil and his agents
2. The destruction of every darkness covering you
3. Commanding the light of God to take over you
4. The destruction of every gang up against your life
5. The termination of every problem that has entered your life from your mother's womb.

Almighty God, hold me by your right hand and deliver me from the evil control of the devil and his agents, in the name of Jesus. I command the coverings of darkness in my life to be destroyed by the manifestation of the light of God, in the name of Jesus. Let the light of God take over my life, morning, day and night forever, in the name of Jesus

.

> "Which things have indeed a shew of wisdom in will worship, and humility, and neglecting of the body; not in any honour to the satisfying of the flesh."
>
> — COLOSSIANS 2:23

> "If any of you lack wisdom, let him ask of God, that giveth to all men liberally, and upbraideth not; and it shall be given him."
>
> — JAMES 1:5

> "In the beginning God created the heaven and the earth."

— GENESIS 1:1

By your wisdom O Lord, show me your wisdom and power in a great measure without a lack of them, in the name of Jesus. Let the giving power of God begin to manifest in my life on daily bases, in the name of Jesus. Anointing to keep asking from God, increase in my life, in the name of Jesus. Every good thing that God started from the beginning of this world, begin to show yourself in my life, in the name of Jesus. Almighty God, launch me into the depth of your wisdom, knowledge and help me to declare your unsearchable judgment here on earth, in the name of Jesus. Father Lord, empower me to find your ways known and unknown to men, in the name of Jesus. Ancient of days, upgrade my brain above every human here on earth, in the name of Jesus. By the power in the fear of God, I intimidate every demonic fear in my life, in the name of Jesus. Every work done by the devil in my life, be destroyed by the speaking blood of Jesus, in the name of Jesus. I command the foundation that holds the earth to rise in torment against the devil, his agents and all the problem in my life, in the name of Jesus. Let the eyes of the enemy looking at me be closed and weakened towards me, in the name of Jesus. By the power of God's increase, I increase every good thing in my life to multitudes, in the name of Jesus. Let the diminishing power of God from above empty me of every satanic investment, in the name of Jesus. I command the gang up of the devil and his agent against my life to be put to nothing, in the name of Jesus. Every problem that entered into my life from my mother's womb, I destroy your strength, come out and enter no more, in the name of Jesus.

Day 12

Expectations:

1. **The crippling of every strength of the devil in your life**
2. **Commanding the establishing power of God to establish you in God's will**
3. **The frustration of every evil arrow fired against you from satanic kingdom**

Almighty God, bless me with a breakthrough that will empower me to praise you forever, in the name of Jesus. Let the crippling power of God cripple every strength of the devil in my life, in the name of Jesus.

> "Thou shalt bring them in, and plant them in the mountain of thine inheritance, in the place, O LORD, which thou hast made for thee to dwell in, in the sanctuary, O LORD, which thy hands have established."
>
> — EXODUS 15:17

> "O Lord GOD, thou hast begun to shew thy servant thy greatness, and thy mighty hand: for what God is there in heaven or in earth, that can do according to thy works, and according to thy might?"
>
> — DEUTERONOMY 3:24

Father Lord, bring me out from wrong places and plant me in the mountain of abundance without lack, in the name of Jesus. Father Lord, bring me to serve and worship in your sanctuary with clean hands and heart every day, in the name of Jesus. Let the establishing power of God establish me in God's will forever, in the name of Jesus. Any evil arrow fired against my life from satanic kingdom, I fire you back, in the name of Jesus. I break and loose myself from every satanic program, in the name of Jesus. Let the manipulations of the witches and wizards against my life be terminated, in the name of Jesus. Everything that God has written concerning me, begin to manifest without distractions, in the name of Jesus. Any bad thing fashioned against my life, fail woefully, in the name of Jesus. I command the sum total of God's plan and thoughts for my life to begin to manifest without distractions, in the name of Jesus. Let the sand in the waters of the earth rise in defense for my sake against marine kingdom warring against me, in the name of Jesus. Anything that must die among the creatures for the perfect plan of God for my life, die, in the name of Jesus. By your mercy O Lord, show me your greatness without a break and keep me holy for a continuous relationship, in the name of Jesus.

Day 13

Expectations:

1. Receiving the anointing to hate idolatry and idolatrous worship
2. Commanding the strength of God's presence to overcome you and take you away from every weakness.
3. The killing of every serpent of darkness in the garden of your life and destiny.

Let your mighty hand be upon me forever with performance of signs and wonders, in the name of Jesus.

> "For great is the LORD, and greatly to be praised: He also is to be feared above all gods."
>
> — 1 CHRONICLES 16:25

> ""I know that thou canst do everything, and that no thought can be withholden from thee."
>
> Shall he that contendeth with the Almighty instruct him? He that reproveth God, let him answer it."
>
> — JOB 40:2; 42:2

Father Lord, empower me to praise you with all my heart in a great way without stopping, in the name of Jesus. Let the fear of God in me increase until the whole creature feels it, in the name of Jesus. Anointing to hate idolatry the same way

God hates it, fall upon me, in the name of Jesus. Anointing to fear God, serve Him and worship Him forever, fall upon me, in the name of Jesus. Let the strength of God's presence overcome me and take me away from every weakness, in the name of Jesus. Let the joy of the Lord in my life be strengthened to the highest level, in the name of Jesus. Let the waking and the killing power of God weaken every evil action against my life unto death, in the name of Jesus. Almighty God, kill every serpent of darkness in the garden of my life, in the name of Jesus. Anointing to worship God in the beauty of holiness, fall upon me, in the name of Jesus. Anything here on earth contending with God in my life, receive destruction, in the name of Jesus. Let the reign of Christ in my life prevail over every demonic power, in the name of Jesus. Every unanswered prayer in my life, your time is up, be answered, in the name of Jesus. Let the blessings of God be numerous and more countable than the sands of the sea, in the name of Jesus. Every evil force standing against the manifestations of God's plan and purpose for my life, scatter, in the name of Jesus. I invoke the whole creature to rise and fight every evil power hindering the manifestation of God's plan for my life, in the name of Jesus. Every spirit of hatred and rejection against my life, I bind and cast you out, in the name of Jesus. Almighty God, empower me to hate the devil and his works and the presence of sin with perfect hatred, in the name of Jesus. Almighty God, wake me up from spiritual slumber, in the name of Jesus. Every unrepentant demon assigned to fight the will of God for my life, be frustrated, in the name of Jesus. Any evil sacrifice ever offered against me, expire, in the name of Jesus.

Day 14

Expectations:

1. **The destruction of every power fighting against your divine assignment**
2. **The destruction of every enemy of God's leadership, over your life and destiny**
3. **Commanding the best things in this life to rush into your life**
4. **The dethroning of every witch and wizard in the position of authority in your community**

Any man, woman or power, fighting against my divine assignment in life, fail woefully, in the name of Jesus. By the power of God that can do all things, let all my heart desires according to the will of God be manifested, in the name of Jesus. Every enemy of the leadership of God in my life, be exposed and be disgraced, in the name of Jesus. Let the withholding power of the devil and his agents bow before the manifestations of every good thing in my life, in the name of Jesus. I command the best things of life to rush into my life among the creation, in the name of Jesus.

> "Moreover the Philistines had yet war again with Israel; and David went down, and his servants with him, and fought against the Philistines: and David waxed faint. And Ishbi-benob, which was of the sons of the giant, the weight of whose spear weighed three hundred shekels of brass in weight, he being girded with a new sword, thought to have slain David. But Abishai the son of Zeruiah succoured him, and smote the Philistine, and killed him. Then the men of David sware unto him, saying, thou shalt go no more out with us to battle, that thou quench not the light of Israel. And it came to pass after this, that there was again a battle with the Philistines at Gob: then Sibbechai the Hushathite slew Saph, which was of the sons of the giant. And there was again a battle in Gob with the Philistines, where Elhanan the son of Jaare-oregim, a Beth-lehemite, slew the

brother of Goliath the Gittite, the staff of whose spear was like a weaver's beam. And there was yet a battle in Gath, where was a man of great stature, that had on every hand six fingers, and on every foot six toes, four and twenty in number; and he also was born to the giant. And when he defied Israel, Jonathan the son of Shimeah the brother of David slew him."

— 2 SAMUEL 21:15-21

Almighty God, raise godly people to reign over every kingdom on earth, in the name of Jesus. Any witch or wizard in the position of authority in my community, city or nation, be dethroned, in the name of Jesus. Blood of Jesus, cry against my problems, the oppressors and deliver the oppressed, in the name of Jesus. Any part of me under satanic arrest in every evil altar, be delivered now, in the name of Jesus. Any evil program assigned to waste my life, be terminated, in the name of Jesus. Let the reign of any strong man be terminated in shame, in the name of Jesus. Any satanic roadblock on my way to the top, be violently removed, in the name of Jesus. Any spiritual warfare going on against my life, be terminated to my favor, in the name of Jesus. I put on the whole armor of God to stand against every enemy of my leadership in the battle field, in the name of Jesus. I command every soldier on the other side fighting against me to wax faint in defeat, in the name of Jesus.

Day 15

Expectations:

1. **Commanding heaven to raise soldiers that will represent you in times of trouble**
2. **The destruction of every satanic agent in the battle field of your life**
3. **The killing of every satanic stubborn soldier against your life and destiny**
4. **Commanding the power of your enemies to be reduced to nothing**

Almighty God, raise soldiers that will represent me in times of battle, spiritually and physically, in the name of Jesus. Every satanic giant in the battle field to kill me, your time is up, receive destructive defeats, in the name of Jesus. I command the weapons of darkness against me to become impotent, in the name of Jesus. Almighty God, send me helps from heaven to defeat my enemies, in the name of Jesus. Any satanic stubborn soldier that refuses to run away, die in the battle field, in the name of Jesus. Father Lord, send your arresting power to arrest every enemy in the garden of my life, in the name of Jesus. I command the strength of my enemies to be reduced to nothing, in the name of Jesus. Let the weight of my enemies be destroyed by the weight of the Lord in my life without resistance, in the name of Jesus. I command my enemies to repent or use their weapons against themselves in the name of Jesus. Let the light of my spiritual and physical strength be rekindled, in the name of Jesus. Father Lord, renew my strength and empower me to win every battle, spiritually and physically, in the name of Jesus. Let the powers of darkness empowered to quench my light and fire be frustrated, in the name of Jesus. Every bad person and strong enemy that's trying to fight against me, fall down and never rise again, in the name of Jesus. Let the slaying power of God slay every giant assigned to kill me, spiritually and physically, in the name of Jesus. By the power of divine supernatural investigation, I command the secrets of the devil against me to be discovered and destroyed, in the name of Jesus. Let the backbone of the devil and his agents in my life be broken to pieces, in the name of Jesus. Let the rising of God's spirit in my life bring down every satanic uprising in my life, in the name of Jesus. I withdraw every satanic knowledge and information about me, in the name of Jesus. Let my going out and coming in be withdrawn from the devil and his agents, in the name of Jesus.

"Them also king David dedicated unto the LORD, with the silver and the gold that he brought from all these nations; from Edom, and from Moab, and from the children of Ammon, and from the Philistines, and from Amalek."

— 1 CHRONICLES 18:11

"And David sent messengers unto the men of Jabesh-gilead, and said unto them, Blessed be ye of the LORD, that ye have shewed this kindness unto your Lord, even unto Saul, and have buried him. And now the LORD shew kindness and truth unto you: and I also will requite you this kindness, because ye have done this thing. Therefore, now let your hands be strengthened, and be ye valiant: for your master Saul is dead, and also the house of Judah have anointed me king over them."

— 2 SAMUEL 2:5-7

I dedicate myself to God without reservation, in the name of Jesus. Father Lord, I bring back everything you have ever blessed me with for rededication and cleansing, in the name of Jesus. Let the accepting power of God accept me and everything about me for forever, in the name of Jesus. Father Lord, increase my prayer life and the grace to always enquire from you before action, in the name of Jesus. Father Lord, increase your kindness before me, in the name of Jesus. Ancient of days, help me to motivate men and women that matter to help support and sponsor my mission here on earth, in the name of Jesus. Let kindness from God and man be multiplied in my life forever, in the name of Jesus.

Day 16

Expectations:

1. **Commanding every good thing that belongs to you but have been buried by the enemy to be exhumed.**
2. **Restraining the devil from operating in your life.**
3. **Commanding the destroying power of God to destroy every satanic structure against you**
4. **Commanding every evil thought and imagination against your life to be pulled down.**

Every good thing the enemy has buried against me, be exhumed by thunder, in the name of Jesus. I use the weapons of truth against every enemy in the battle field of my life, in the name of Jesus. By the power of God's restraining power, I restrain the devil and his agents from operating in my life, in the name of Jesus. Father Lord, by your mercy, I command your angels to guide me everywhere I go in life, in the name of Jesus. Let the destroying power of God destroy every satanic structure in my life, in the name of Jesus. Every blessing attached to my name, in the hands of the devil and his agents, I take you away, in the name of Jesus. Every evil thought and imagination against my life, I pull you down, in the name of Jesus. Almighty God, assist me in the battles of life, in the name of Jesus. Every demonic property in any part of my life, catch fire and burn to ashes, in the name of Jesus.

"Then came all the tribes of Israel to David unto Hebron, and spake, saying, Behold, we are thy bone and thy flesh. Also, in time past, when Saul was king over us, thou wast he that leddest out and broughtest in Israel: and the LORD said to thee, thou shalt feed my people Israel, and thou shalt be a captain over Israel. So all the elders of Israel came to the king to Hebron; and king David made a league with them in Hebron before the LORD: and they anointed David king over Israel. David was thirty years old when he began to reign, and he reigned forty years."

— 2 SAMUEL 5:1-4

Every enemy of my promotion, your time is up, be frustrated, in the name of Jesus. I command every evil personality that has vowed to deny me of my rights, benefits and entitlement to be frustrated, in the name of Jesus. Every evil voice speaking against the plans of God for my life, be silenced by the speaking blood of Jesus. Every evil gang up against my destiny, scatter in shame, in the name of Jesus. O Lord arise and take me to my place in life without struggle, in the name of Jesus. Any human blood and sacrifice crying against my prosperity and breakthrough, be silenced unto death, in the name of Jesus. Any witch or wizard, boasting to waste my life, fail woefully and be wasted, in the name of Jesus. Every evil fire burning the good things in my life, be quenched by the speaking blood of Jesus, in the name of Jesus.

Day 17

Expectations:

1. **The destruction of every demonic spirit blocking your path to progress**
2. **The destruction of every negative word opposing the word of God in your life**
3. **The destruction of every visible and invisible evil mark of hatred affecting you**

Every enemy of divine program in my life, fail woefully, in the name of Jesus. Every demonic spirit blocking my path of progress in life, I bind and cast you out, in the name of Jesus. Let the Lord Jesus control every aspect of my life, in the name of Jesus. Every negative word opposing the word of God for my life, be frustrated to nothing, in the name of Jesus. Every visible or invisible evil mark of hatred in any area of my life, be cleansed by the blood of Jesus. Let the blood sacrifice speaking against my destiny be frustrated, in the name of Jesus. Every organized satanic program against my life, be disorganized to death, in the name of Jesus.

> "For a day in thy courts Is better than a thousand. I had rather be a doorkeeper in the house of my God, than to dwell in the tents of wickedness. For the LORD God is a sun and shield: The LORD will give grace and glory: No good thing will he withhold from them that walk uprightly."
>
> — PSALMS 84:10, 11

> "Then said David, O LORD God of Israel, thy servant hath certainly heard that Saul seeketh to come to Keilah, to destroy the city for my sake. Will the men of Keilah deliver me up into his hand? will Saul come down, as thy servant hath

heard? O LORD God of Israel, I beseech thee, tell thy servant. And the LORD said, He will come down."

— SAMUEL 23:10-11

I command every part of my life; my heart, and my flesh to cry ceaselessly for the manifestation of the living God, in the name of Jesus. Anointing to live for God alone and praise Him without ceasing, possess me, in the name of Jesus. Let the strength and power to function be of the Lord, in the name of Jesus. Almighty God, take me from strength to strength every day of my life, in the name of Jesus. Let the mercy of God attract the hearing ears of God to hear my prayers with immediate answers, in the name of Jesus. Father Lord, keep me by your side every day and cause me never depart from your presence, in the name of Jesus. Deliver me from the tent of the wicked, from his court and keep me in your court forever, in the name of Jesus. Let the LORD my God be my sun, my shield with enough of his grace and glory upon me every day, in the name of Jesus. I command the good things among God's creation to rush into my life and minister to me, in the name of Jesus. Anointing to walk uprightly every day of my life forever and ever, fall upon me, in the name of Jesus. O Lord of host, bless me with every good thing and empower me to trust you under every situation, in the name of Jesus. Alpha and Omega, deliver me from every unfriendly friend, in the name of Jesus. Any secret and open mischief being practiced against me, fail woefully and back fire, in the name of Jesus. Every evil plot to take away my life, be frustrated, in the name of Jesus.

Day 18

Expectations:

1. **The destruction of every demonic attachment in your life.**
2. **Complete deliverance from the destruction of the devil and his agents.**
3. **Commanding the whole universe to minister to your needs.**
4. **Receiving God's inventing power**

Every demonic attachment in my life, catch fire and burn to ashes, in the name of Jesus. Wonderful knowledge of God for my life, begin to manifest, in the name of Jesus. Almighty God, bless me with your divine inventing power, in the name of Jesus.

"And it came to pass after this, that David enquired of the LORD, saying, Shall I go up into any of the cities of Judah? And the LORD said unto him, Go up. And David said, whither shall I go up? And he said, Unto Hebron."

— 2 SAMUEL 2:1

"Behold, the Lord GOD will come with strong hand, and his arm shall rule for him: behold, his reward is with him, and his work before him. He shall feed his flock like a shepherd: he shall gather the lambs with his arm, and carry them in his bosom, and shall gently lead those that are with young." "Who hath measured the waters in the hollow of his hand, and meted out heaven with the span, and comprehended the dust of the earth in a measure, and weighed the mountains in scales, and the hills in a balance? Who hath directed the Spirit of the LORD, or being his counsellor hath taught him? With whom took he counsel, and who instructed him, and taught him in the path of judgment, and taught him knowledge, and shewed to him the way of understanding? Behold, the nations are as a drop of a bucket, and are counted as the small dust of the balance: behold, he taketh up the isles as a very little thing."

— ISAIAH 40:12-15

Father Lord, give me detailed information about the evil plans of the wicked and save me from every danger, in the name of Jesus. By your mercy Oh Lord, deliver me and my household from the destruction of the devil and his agents, in the name of Jesus. Ancient of days, prepare me for a day of my promotion and ordination, in the name of Jesus. By the power that measured the waters in the hollow of God's hand, I command every creature to bow to God's will in my life, in the name of Jesus. Anointing of God's grace, his mercy that meted out heaven with the span, I command the whole universe to minister to my needs, in the name of Jesus. By the power that comprehended the dust of the earth and measured it without mistake, I command every good thing to arrest my life forever, in the name of Jesus. Almighty God, you weighed the mountains in scales and the hills in a balance, by the same power, put in me everything that will prosper my relationship with you, in the name of Jesus. Let the directing power of God's Spirit direct me to the place of God and keep me spotless without sin and its consequences, in the name of Jesus. Let the counsellorship of God rule and reign over my life forever, in the name of Jesus. By the power of God's teaching ability, I receive the ministry to teach with understanding, in the name of Jesus. By divine instruction and teaching, I walk into the path of judgment, in the name of Jesus. Let the knowledge and wisdom of God begin to manifest into my life without hindrance, in the name of Jesus.

Day 19

Expectations:

1. **The destruction of every yoke of misunderstanding upon your life.**
2. **Handing over your life completely to God for him to take control and be in charge.**
3. **The destruction of every power that wants to limit you and hinder you from achieving God's ordained greatness.**
4. **The destruction of every yoke of impossibility.**

Every yoke of misunderstanding upon my life, break to pieces, in the name of Jesus. Let the supplying strength of God begin to supply every good thing in my life until I am filled, in the name of Jesus. Let God be in charge of every area of my life, in the name of Jesus. I command all the works of the devil and his agents, sin and its consequences to melt before the presence of God with me, in the name of Jesus. Almighty God, help me to attain the height you have destined for me here on earth, in the name of Jesus. Every yoke of impossibility, assigned to hold me down to captive, break to pieces, in the name of Jesus. I command every evil spirit in my life to flee and never look back again, in the name of Jesus. Let the flying Spirit of God empower me to fly away from every satanic roadblock, in the name of Jesus. By the power in God's deliverance, I deliver myself wherever I need deliverance, in the name of Jesus.

> "Ah Lord GOD! behold, thou hast made the heaven and the earth by thy great power and stretched out arm, and there is nothing too hard for thee:"
>
> — JEREMIAH 32:17

> "and all the inhabitants of the earth are reputed as nothing: and he doeth according to his will in the army of heaven, and among the inhabitants of the earth: and none can stay his hand, or say unto him, What doest thou?"
>
> — DANIEL 4:35

Let my life stick to the power that made heaven and earth in greatness, forever without a break, in the name of Jesus. Let God's great power attract the greatness that will make me great among the creation, in the name of Jesus. Everything that used to be impossible in my life, your time is up, become possible by force, in the name of Jesus. I withdraw my fears, respect, honor, and every relationship with every enemy of God, in the name of Jesus. Father Lord, I surrender everything, all my life and activity here on earth forever, in the name of Jesus. Let the loving kindness of God, goodness and mercy flow into my life and settle forever, in the name of Jesus. Let the blessings of God enter into my bosom and minister to me forever, in the name of Jesus. Let the ending power of God end the activity of the devil, his agents, sin and its ministry in my life, in the name of Jesus. Let the lifting and promoting power of God, begin to manifest in my life forever, in the name of Jesus. Divine understanding, wherever you are, begin to occupy every space in my life, in the name of Jesus. Let the multiplying anointing of God start its work in every area of my life, in the name of Jesus.

Day 20

Expectations:

1. **Commanding every creature to bow before the spirit and image of God in you.**
2. **Commanding the everlastingness of God to bring you into everlasting prosperity**
3. **Breaking the arms of the devil, his agents, sin and its work off your life**
4. **The destruction of every demonic spirit attached to your life**
5. **Commanding the release of all your blessings that were locked up**

By the power in the dominating anointing of God, I command every creature to bow before the Spirit and image of God in me, in the name of Jesus. Let the everlastingness of God bring me to everlasting prosperity in every aspect of my life, in the name of Jesus. I command the inhabitants of the earth and all creation to surrender and submit before the Spirit and likeness of God in me, in the name of Jesus. I command the arms of the devil, his agents, sin and its work to be broken in my life, in the name of Jesus. Let the staying and establishing power of God, establish me according to his purpose, in the name of Jesus. Any evil force questioning the leadership of God in my life, close your mouth and perish, in the name of Jesus. All my blessings, locked up in satanic storeroom, I release you by force, in the name of Jesus. Any demonic spirit attached to my life, my bedroom and presence, I bind and cast you out, in the name of Jesus. Every spirit of hell fire in any area of my life, I bind and cast you out, in the name of Jesus. I reject every satanic food and drink given to me physically and spiritually, in the name of Jesus. I command my morning, day and night to be withdrawn from every satanic control, in the name of Jesus.

"But Jesus beheld them, and said unto them, with men this is impossible; but with God all things are possible."

— MATTHEW 19:26

Every blessing, riches, and everything among God's creation assigned to take me to hell fire, be frustrated to failure and total defeat, in the name of Jesus. Every demonic blockage against me in the door of heaven, be violently removed without a trace, in the name of Jesus. By the power invested in the blood of Jesus, I command everything in and outside me to be disengaged from Satan and sin forever and ever, in the name of Jesus. Let the speaking power in the blood of Jesus speak me out of every relationship with Satan and sin forever and ever, in the name of Jesus. Let the destroying power of God arise in anger and destroy without remaining the powers of impossibility in my life, in the name of Jesus. Let the anointing possibility of God make the manifestations of God's plan, his purpose possible in my life, in the name of Jesus. Every dark angel assigned to minister to me, be blinded and be crippled on your way to my life, in the name of Jesus.

Day 21

Expectations:

1. **The destruction of every yoke of second affliction against your life**

2. **The termination and frustration of every satanic judgment against you**

3. **Commanding the keeping power of God to keep you from sin and from the activities of the devil forever**

Every yoke of second time afflictions from the devil, his agents in my life, break to pieces, in the name of Jesus. Father Lord, by the power in your flushing ability, flush every satanic deposit, plantations in my life in and out, in the name of Jesus. Let that power that drove the devil, his loyal angels out from heaven manifest in my life and drive them again out of my life, in the name of Jesus. Every satanic judgment ever pronounced against me, be reverse by the reversing strength of God, in the name of Jesus. Every satanic estate, evil structures built inside or outside me, be uprooted, catch fire, burn to ashes and perish forever, in the name of Jesus. Let the keeping power of God keep me out of sin and the activities of the devil forever, in the name of Jesus. With the everlasting chain of God Almighty, I bind, cast out every demonic spirit out of my life and chain them, in the name of Jesus. Every darkness established by the devil, his agents and sin against me, be replaced with divine light, in the name of Jesus. Any strange fire programmed into my life to burn me, be quenched by the quenching power in the blood of Jesus, in the name of Jesus. Any evil spirit promoting Satan and sin in my life, I bind and cast you out, in the name of Jesus. Let the vengeance of God appear in every area of my life and take vengeance against every demonic activity in my life, past, present and future, in the name of Jesus. Every dream from satanic kingdom in my life, past, present and future, fail woefully in my life, in the name of Jesus. Every satanic plantation in my life in the dreams, die from your root, in the name of Jesus. I break and loose myself from filthy dreams, polluted and defiled dreams, in the name of Jesus.

Day 22

Expectations:

1. **Commanding the contaminating strength of the devil to be broken off your life.**
2. **The scattering of every evil brain thinking and planning against you.**
3. **Complete deliverance from every negative thought.**

Almighty God, empower me, help me to overcome and dominate the fallen angels, in the name of Jesus. Let the defiling, polluting, contaminating strength of the devil and his agents fail woefully in my life, in the name of Jesus. Any evil brain thinking against me, scatter with confusion, in the name of Jesus. Almighty God, deliver me from every negative thought, in the name of Jesus. Father Lord, take me away from every evil presence, in the name of Jesus. Let my dwelling place in life be adequately protected by the angel of God, in the name of Jesus. I command the uttermost part of the earth to rise to my defense, in the name of Jesus. Father Lord, fuel the tank of my life with your ability, in the name of Jesus. Let the leadership of God take over the leadership of my life, in the name of Jesus.

"And, behold, I am with thee, and will keep thee in all places whither thou goest, and will bring thee again into this land; for I will not leave thee, until I have done that which I have spoken to thee of. And Jacob awaked out of his sleep, and he said, Surely the LORD is in this place; and I knew it not."

— GENESIS 28:15,16

Every demonic inherited plague, that I have attracted to myself, loose your hold over my life, in the name of Jesus. Almighty God, give me a sign that will destroy every satanic sign in my life and family, forever, in the name of Jesus. Almighty God, begin to do great and marvelous things in my life without stopping, in the name of Jesus. Let the filling power of God fill me to overflowing with the best things of life, in the name of Jesus. Father Lord, send your wrath to the camp of my enemies until they repent or perish, in the name of Jesus. Let the worse judgement of God mingled with pain, suffering, hardship, famine and every bad thing among the creation combined without a minus to invade the camp of my unrepentant enemies, in the name of Jesus. I withdraw the services of God, victory and the manifestations of every positive attribute of God from my determined enemies until they repent, in the name of Jesus. Every mark of the devil and anti-Christ in my life, visible and invisible, known and unknown, be cleansed and cleared away permanently by the blood of Jesus. Almighty God, give me a permanent new song that will keep me far away from satanic manifestations forever, in the name of Jesus. Let the praising power, rejoicing power, happiness anointing invested in the Almighty loyal angels in heaven fall upon me here on earth, in the name of Jesus. By the end of today's night, I declare that all my problems shall perish without a trace, in the name of Jesus. Evil agreement against my destiny in the kingdom of darkness, fail woefully, in the name of Jesus.

Day 23

Expectations:

1. **The destruction of every demonic established darkness against you.**
2. **The destruction of anything in you and around you that is from the satanic kingdom.**
3. **Complete deliverance for every part of your life possessed by the devil.**

Every demonic established darkness in my life, receive destruction, in the name of Jesus. Let the multiplying power of God, multiply the best things of life into my life, in the name of Jesus. Anything in me from satanic kingdom, catch fire and burn to ashes, in the name of Jesus. I command the sorrows in my life to be converted to divine joy and happiness, in the name of Jesus. Any part of my life possessed by the devil, receive deliverance, in the name of Jesus. Let the covering strength of God by the blood of Jesus cover me from satanic manipulations, in the name of Jesus.

> "And as soon as we had heard these things, our hearts did melt, neither did there remain any more courage in any man, because of you: for the LORD your God, he is God in heaven above, and in earth beneath."
>
> — JOSHUA 2:11

> "Whither shall I go from thy spirit? Or whither shall I flee from thy presence? If I ascend up into heaven, thou art there: If I make my bed in hell, behold, thou art there. If I take the wings of the morning, and dwell in the uttermost parts of the sea; Even there shall thy hand lead me, and thy right hand shall hold me. If I say, Surely the darkness shall cover me; Even the night shall be light about me. Yea, the darkness hideth not from thee; But the night shineth as the day: The darkness

and the light are both alike to thee. For thou hast possessed my reins: Thou hast covered me in my mother's womb."

— PSALMS 139:7-12

Anointing to start and finish well without delay, begin to manifest in my life, in the name of Jesus. Any death designed to delay my movement to my place of rest, be frustrated, in the name of Jesus. I command every place the sole of my foot shall tread upon to become mine forever, in the name of Jesus. I command the wilderness, great rivers, every land occupied by wicked people among the creation, unto the great sea, in every coast to become mine forever, in the name of Jesus. Any evil personality prepared and equipped by the devil to stand against me anywhere in this life, fail and fall, in the name of Jesus. Let the presence of God, unconditionally refuse to leave me by all means, all the days of my life, in the name of Jesus. I command the spirits in charge of failures and defeat to run far away from me forever, in the name of Jesus. By the strength of God Almighty, I overcome every satanic reigning strength in every environment, in the name of Jesus.

Day 24

Expectations:

1. **Commanding the discouraging power of darkness to be discouraged**
2. **The destruction of every evil personality in any nation sitting on your inheritance**
3. **Commanding the strength of God to take over you and replace every satanic weakness projected against you**

I command the discouraging power of darkness to be discouraged and overcome before divine courage apportioned to my life, in the name of Jesus. Any evil personality in any nation sitting upon my inheritance, be unseated by heavenly force, in the name of Jesus. Let the dividing power of God divide my enemies against each other, in the name of Jesus. I command the devil by force to begin to fail and disappoint all his agent of all level without a stop, in the name of Jesus. Anointing to observe and to do all the commandments of God, fall upon every human race without discrimination, in the name of Jesus. I command every part of my life to depart from evil presence and demonic activity, in the name of Jesus. Let the word of God displace every opposing word in my life and fully take charge, in the name of Jesus. Almighty God, empower me to be prosperous and have good success in every area of my life, in the name of Jesus. Let the strength of the LORD replace every satanic planted weakness in my life, in the name of Jesus. Any demonic spy in my life, spiritually or physically, be crippled and be blinded, in the name of Jesus. Any evil wall built to prevent my divine motivated movements in my life, collapse from your foundation, in the name of Jesus. Let the searching power of the devil and monitoring anointing fail woefully before me, in the name of Jesus. I command every satanic embargo militating against my life to be lifted, in the name of Jesus. Let the taking away power of God take me away from evil captivity, in the name of Jesus. Every good door shut against my destiny, open by force and remain open, in the name of Jesus. I command the overtaking power of the devil and his agents to be crippled before me, in the name of Jesus. By the power of God's quickness, I overcome every evil personality ahead of me in every competition, past, present and future, in the name of Jesus. Father Lord, with your rain of quality in every good thing, overflow my life with divine motivated qualities, in the name of Jesus. Any demon with the ability to walk, crawl, fly or run, your time is up, I bring you to everlasting lameness, in the name of Jesus. I command every creature to rise against the enemy of my relationship with God and my place in heaven, in the name of Jesus. Let the pursuing power of God pursue out every problem in my life to its grave, in the name of Jesus. Every skilled man and woman in evil practices, avoid me like a plague, in the name of Jesus. I command the wealth and the prosperity of the wicked to be cleansed and be transferred to me, in the name of Jesus. I command the whole creation to move my problems far away from me, in the name of Jesus. Let the properties of the devil in my life be roasted by fire, in the mighty name of Jesus.

Day 25

Expectations:

1. **Commanding the cutting off of every evil head and hand raised against you.**

2. **Commanding the shocking earthquake of God to move into the camp of all unrepentant enemies of your life and destiny and waste them.**

3. **The complete destruction of the operational base of witches and wizards.**

I command every evil head and hand raised or will ever be raised against me to be cut off, in the name of Jesus. I command every creature to open their mouth and swallow my problems and refuse to vomit them back to me, in the name of Jesus. Let the shocking earthquake from God move into the camp of my unrepentant enemies and waste them, in the name of Jesus. The power that shut the third heaven against the devil, shut the devil, his agents, sin and live problems out of my life forever, in the name of Jesus. Almighty God, make me a great terrorist against the devil, demons, satanic agents, sin and the problems they carry, in the name of Jesus. Let the operational base of the witches and wizard against me catch fire and be overturned, in the name of Jesus. Let my problems' ear and strength to walk away from divine destructions be destroyed, in the name of Jesus. I command the waters in the bodies of my unrepentant enemies to be defiled with deaths, in the name of Jesus. Every evil pursuer of my life, receive confusion and walk into the red sea, in the name of Jesus. I command unknown and known problems to invade the foundation of my unrepentant enemies, in the name of Jesus. Any evil personality reigning as king or queen in my life, be dethroned, in the name of Jesus. Let the destroying weapons in the camp of my enemies be used in confusion against them, in the name of Jesus. I command the remaining problem in life to avoid me and my family members, in the name of Jesus. Anointing to prevail over evil circumstances, possess me, in the name of Jesus. I command any witchcraft womb that has swallowed my blessings to open and vomit them, in the name of Jesus. Any blessing that will move me away from my present level, begin to manifest, in the name of Jesus. Almighty God, lead me to a skill that will end suffering and hardship, in the name of Jesus. Anything in me, rebelling against the divine plan of God for my life, I bring you to divine obedience, in the name of Jesus.

Day 26

Expectations:

1. **The rejection of every name given to you by the devil and his agents.**

2. **The creation of a mountainous mountain that will separate you permanently from poverty, shame, lack, sickness and reproach.**

3. **The closing of every evil mouth opened to mock you.**

Every evil movement in any branch of satanic kingdom, be demobilized, in the name of Jesus.

> "He telleth the number of the stars; He calleth them all by their names." "He that planted the ear, shall he not hear? He that formed the eye, shall he not see? He that chastiseth the heathen, shall not he correct? He that teacheth man knowledge, shall not he know? The LORD knoweth the thoughts of man, that they are vanity."
>
> — PSALMS 147:4; 94:9-11

Thou God that counts and tell the number of the stars, count my problems in life present and future and destroy them, in the name of Jesus. Every name given to me by the devil, his agents and sin, I reject you and change to my God given name, in the name of Jesus. Let the greatness of God Almighty begin to manifest in my life unstopped, forever and ever, in the name of Jesus. Father Lord, increase my wisdom to infinity without distractions, in the name of Jesus. Father Lord, empower me with the fruits of your Spirit and lift me up above every height, in the name of Jesus. By the power in the blood of Jesus, I cast down the wicked ones in the list of God, in the name of Jesus. Let the singing, praising, abilities and capacity of God's holy angels possess me, in the name of Jesus. Almighty God, prepare me for your rain of blessings and command prosperity to rain upon me, in the name of Jesus. Father Lord, create a mountainous mountain between me and poverty, famine and all the work of the devil, sin and every evil, in the name of Jesus. Let the delight of God and his pleasure be taken away from every evil activity in my life, in the name of Jesus. I command the fear of God to flood my life and to do away with everything called demonic fear in my life forever, in the name of Jesus. Almighty God, once again and again without a stop, strengthen your bars of protection in the gates of my life against satanic activities, in the name of Jesus. I command everyone within the gates of my life, my family members everywhere to be blessed without measure, in the name of Jesus. You my prayers, carry the answers from God with peace and joy, in the name of Jesus. Let peace and the nine fruits of the Spirit compass the borders of my life with the finest thing here on earth, in the name of Jesus. Let the snow like wool, mixed with painful judgment enter into the foundations of my enemies and force them to repent or perish, in the name of Jesus. Any evil mouth opened to mock me, close in shame and in defeat without victory, in the name of Jesus. Every little effort I will put in life from now must prosper to please God, in the name of Jesus.

Day 27

Expectations:

1. **The termination of every satanic program against you and your family.**
2. **The destruction of every evil achievement in your life and family.**
3. **The frustration of all demonic efforts against you and your family.**

Let the eyes of the devil and his agents against my life be blinded, in the name of Jesus. By the power of God's terminating grace, I terminated every satanic program for my life forever, in the name of Jesus. Let all evil achievement and successes in my life be destroyed, in the name of Jesus. Books written by the devil and his agents against my life, catch fire and burn to ashes, in the name of Jesus. Let He that planted ears and eyes hear and see me through in times of troubles and prosperity without defilement, in the name of Jesus. Let the hearing ears of God and his seeing eyes minister deliverance into every area of my life, in the name of Jesus. Every heathen in my life, receive divine chastisement for correction and repentance, in the name of Jesus. I bring every satanic effort against me to vanity, in the name of Jesus. Any evil thought, evil imagination and desires against me, be discovered and be destroyed by God, in the name of Jesus. Let the knowledge of God in my life destroy every evil knowledge contending against God, in the name of Jesus. Let the chastisement of God bring me to correction and divine elevations, in the name of Jesus.

> "And he said unto them, Ye are they which justify yourselves before men; but God knoweth your hearts: for that which is highly esteemed among men is abomination in the sight of God."
>
> — LUKE 16:15

> "Neither is there any creature that is not manifest in his sight: but all things are naked and opened unto the eyes of him with whom we have to do."
>
> — HEBREWS 4:13

Father Lord, examine every aspect of my life and help me to understand myself for possible adjustment, in the name of Jesus. Let my life be justified by God's Spirit and empower me to accept your judgment for my life for a better life, in the name of Jesus. Blood of Jesus, justify me before God and qualify me to make heaven, in the name of Jesus. Father Lord, deliver me from wrong self-esteem assigned to destroy your plans for my life, in the name of Jesus. I break and loose myself from every yoke of abomination designed to waste my life, in the name of Jesus. Every demonic plan to take me out of divine presence, fail woefully, in the name of Jesus. Blood of Jesus, sanctify me and qualify me to stand in God's presence qualified to enter heaven by the special grace of God at last, in the name of Jesus. I command every creature to manifest before God and be empowered to do me good every day, in the name of Jesus. I bring every part of my life body, soul and spirit before God to be blessed without a curse, in the name of Jesus. Every hidden evil thing in my life, be exposed and be replaced with God's blessings, in the name of Jesus.

Day 28

Expectations:

1. **Commanding the deliverance power of God to manifest in every area of your life.**

2. **Bringing into manifestation all God's thought and plan for you.**

3. **The destruction of all the determined enemies of your life and destiny.**

Anointing to hold fast my faith and profession for Christ without any record of sin, I command you to come upon me, in the name of Jesus. Father Lord, let my life be precious before you by the power in the blood of your son, in the name of Jesus. Let your deliverance power manifest in every area of my life without a break, in the name of Jesus. Every divine thought and imagination for my life, begin to manifest, in the name of Jesus. Let my blessing be more than numbers from this year, in the name of Jesus. Almighty God, strengthen my relationship with you and keep me pure forever, in the name of Jesus. Every determined enemy of my life, your time is up, receive divine judgment, in the name of Jesus. Let the multiplying grace of God multiply the mercy of God in my life, in the name of Jesus.

> "The woman saith unto him, I know that Messias cometh, which is called Christ: when he is come, he will tell us all things. The woman then left her waterpot, and went her way into the city, and saith to the men, Come, see a man, which told me all things that ever I did: is not this the Christ? Then they went out of the city, and came unto him. and said unto the woman, now we believe, not because of thy saying: for we have heard him ourselves, and know that this is indeed the Christ, the Saviour of the world."
>
> — JOHN 4:25, 28-30, 42

Blood of Jesus, flow into my life and clean the water in the well of my life, in the name of Jesus. Father Lord, give me water to drink to quench every thirst in every area of my life, in the name of Jesus. Anointing for direct encounter with Christ without delay, fall upon my life, in the name of Jesus. Let the deep in the well of my life be filled with the living water of life from heaven, in the name of Jesus. Anything in my life ignorantly arguing with Christ, receive divine knowledge and surrender to the leadership of Christ, in the name of Jesus. Almighty God, deliver me from spiritual blindness and weakness, in the name of Jesus. Almighty God, empower me with prophetic anointing for spiritual perfection, in the name of Jesus. I command every part of my life to get deeply involved in worshipping God in Spirit and in truth, in the name of Jesus. Let the manifestation of Christ in my life be perfected with full knowledge of God without a minus, in the name of Jesus. Everything I need to know in life to complete my life in Christ, begin to manifest, in the name of Jesus. Almighty God, empower me to witness for Christ with the right manner of approach everywhere I go, in the name of Jesus. I command the whole creature to prosper my witness for Christ with the result of true repentances, in the name of Jesus. I command the believing power of God to manifest in my ministry and move people to believe in Christ with ease, in the name of Jesus.

Day 29

Expectations:

1. **The destruction of every evil sacrifice that has ever been offered against you.**
2. **The killing of every evil personality that married you spiritually.**

3. **The destruction of all determined problems and enemies after your life and destiny.**
4. **The destruction of every evil force that has vowed to waste you.**

Almighty God, empower me to show forth your power physically with signs and wonders following everywhere I go, in the name of Jesus. Almighty God, give me heavenly injection that will kill every sin and its consequences in my life, in the name of Jesus. Any evil sacrifice ever offered against my destiny, expire and leave me alone, in the name of Jesus. Any evil personality that has married me spiritually, I divorce you by force, in the name of Jesus.

"And God said unto Moses, I AM THAT I AM: and he said, thus shalt thou say unto the children of Israel, I AM hath sent me unto you."

— EXODUS 3:14

"And as a vesture shalt thou fold them up, and they shall be changed: But thou art the same, and thy years shall not fail."

— HEBREWS 1:12

"Before the mountains were brought forth, or ever thou hadst formed the earth and the world, Even from everlasting to everlasting, thou art God."

— PSALMS 90:2

Almighty God, by your power and name; I AM THAT I AM, destroy every determined problem and enemies with an oath to waste my life, in the name of Jesus. Let your presence in my life disengage every demonic presence in my life and family, in the name of Jesus. Let God be the same as He was in the life of Abraham, Isaac and Jacob, in the name of Jesus. I command every enemy ahead of me in any competition to be made my foot stool, in the name of Jesus. Let the ministering Spirit of God begin to minister to me as an heir of God's salvation, in the name of Jesus. By the power of the ministering Spirit of God, I receive the power to rise above my problems, in the name of Jesus. I command every evil action ever taken against me to receive their just reward, in the name of Jesus. Any man, woman or power with a vow to waste my destiny, be frustrated, in the name of Jesus. Any evil voice witnessing against me in the spirit or physical, be silence by the truth, in the name of Jesus. Let the perishing power among the creation combine their forces and to perish all my past, present and future problems in life, in the name of Jesus. Every grave yard here on earth, open your mouth and swallow my problems, in the name of Jesus. Let the transforming grace of God transform my life to the best ever, in the name of Jesus. I command the spirit of failure to capture my troubles and every negative thing in my life to fail woefully in my life, in the name of Jesus. Father Lord, cause me to sit quietly in peace and watch you fight my battles, in the name of Jesus. I refuse to give heed to the devil and his agents in any area of my life forever, in the name of Jesus. Let the power attached to the power in the word "escape" enter into every organ of my life to escape from every satanic attack, in the name of Jesus.

Day 30

Expectations:

1. **Commanding all the problems in your life to end.**
2. **The termination of every Pharaoh after your life and destiny.**
3. **The destruction of every demonic mobilization against you.**
4. **Standing firm against the pestilence that walk-in darkness and the destruction that wastes at noonday.**

Almighty God, by your mercy, bring me into your dwelling place in all generation, in the name of Jesus. Almighty God, manifest in my life and show every problem in my life that you are still God from everlasting to everlasting, in the name of Jesus. By the power that terminated the life of Pharaoh and the Egyptian army in the red sea, I terminate the lives of my problems, in the name of Jesus. I command my lost blessings of the yester years to be recovered today and tomorrow forever, in the name of Jesus. Let the increasing power of God increase my strength and renew my age, in the name of Jesus. Every activity of the snare of the fowler from the noisome pestilence of life, avoid my life forever, in the name of Jesus. I pluck out all the feather of the flying witches and wizards against me, in the name of Jesus. By the power in the multiplying grace of God, I command my enemy's problem to multiply without control, in the name of Jesus. Let the brains of my enemies receive confusion to forget me without action, in the name of Jesus. By the reversing anointing of God, I reverse every demon mobilized against me from any evil altar, in the name of Jesus. You the power of darkness that causes people to fall, I break your strength in my life, in the name of Jesus. Every demonic expectation against my life, be frustrated without success, in the name of Jesus. You the pestilence that walk-in darkness and the destructions that waste at noonday, avoid me and my family, in the name of Jesus. You the evil that falls upon people and plagues that draw near to people in my generation, avoid me from afar, in the name of Jesus. Wherever my name will be mentioned for evil, blood of Jesus, manifest and answer for me, in the name of Jesus. Any satanic taskmaster working hard to keep me in bondage, be frustrated, in the name of Jesus. Any wicked action ever taken against me by anyone living or dead, back fire, in the name of Jesus. I command the forces of darkness militating against me to be disgraced, in the name of Jesus. I command the weapons of household wickedness against my life to be rendered impotent, in the name of Jesus.

Day 31

Expectations:

1. **The termination of every witchcraft crusade against you**
2. **Commanding every troubler of your life to be troubled**
3. **Commanding an end to the voice of groaning in your life and family**
4. **Reconnecting your foundation to God**

Every witchcraft crusade staged against my life, be terminated by the crying blood of Jesus.

> "I said, O my God, take me not away in the midst of my days: Thy years are throughout all generations. Of old hast thou laid the foundation of the earth: And the heavens are the work of thy hands. They shall perish, but thou shalt endure: Yea, all of them shall wax old like a garment; As a vesture shalt thou change them, and they shall be changed: But thou art the same, and thy years shall have no end."
>
> — PSALMS 102:24-27

I command the moving strength of my prayers and cry to God to be increased and meet God for answers, in the name of Jesus. Every troubler of my life, be troubled unto death without mercy, in the name of Jesus. I command the death of my deaths to fight against each other until they die forever before me, in the name of Jesus. Almighty God, arise in your power and end the voice of groaning in my family, in the name of Jesus. Every yoke of shame, reproach, disgrace, defeat and failure in my life, break to pieces, in the name of Jesus. You my stubborn enemies, your time is up, whither like grass and die without resurrection, in the name of Jesus. Every demonic spirit of madness injected into people in order for them not to favor me, back fire, in the name of Jesus. Any demonic spirit attacking my strength, your time is up, I bind and cast you out, in the name of Jesus. Let the eaters of flesh and drinkers of blood assigned against me, eat their own flesh and drink their own blood, in the name of Jesus. Let the years of God which extend to every generation begin to manifest in my life for constant renewal, in the name of Jesus. By the power of God that laid the foundation of this world, I command my foundation to connect with God for strength, in the name of Jesus. Every creature that has refused to cooperate with God's program for my life, avoid me forever, in the name of Jesus. I command all my problems to wax old and die immediately now, in the name of Jesus. Let the life of God, his breath in me be renewed at all time without expiration, in the name of Jesus. I command all demons ever assigned against my life ever before I was born till now to relocate base back to their senders, in the name of Jesus. Let the establishing power of God arise and establish me and my children, in the name of Jesus. Any demonic show case in my life, your time is up, break to pieces and burn to ashes, in the name of Jesus. Any evil voice of witchcraft speaking against my life, be silenced by the speaking voice of Jesus, in the name of Jesus. Any garment of witchcraft in my life, visible or invisible, catch fire and be roasted, in the name of Jesus. Let the strength of the strongman of my place of birth be destroyed without remedy, in the name of Jesus. Every witchcraft animal in the garden of my life, die, in the name of Jesus.

Day 32

Expectations

1. **Complete deliverance from all the enemies that seem stronger than you.**

2. **Commanding every negative thing in your life to change.**

3. **The destruction of every enemy of the manifestation of divine truth in your life.**

4. **The killing of every demonic lion roaring against your life and destiny.**

Almighty God, deliver me from enemies that are stronger than me, in the name of Jesus.

> "For I am the LORD, I change not; therefore, ye sons of Jacob are not consumed."
>
> — MALACHI 3:6

> "For the law was given by Moses, but grace and truth came by Jesus Christ."
>
> — JOHN 1:17

> "The law of the LORD is perfect, converting the soul: The testimony of the LORD is sure, making wise the simple."
>
> — PSALMS 19:7

By the power in the unchangeable name of God, I command every negative thing in my life to change, in the name of Jesus. Let the powers in silver and gold bow before me and serve me better to serve God all the days of my life, in the name of

Jesus. Let every consuming power in the hands of the devil fail woefully before me, in the name of Jesus. Let the powers of darkness assigned against my life be reversed without delay, in the name of Jesus. O Lord arise and bring your anointing into my life to change every demonic plan against my life, in the name of Jesus. Every enemy of the manifestations of divine truth in my life, be disgraced out of my life, in the name of Jesus. Almighty God, arise and frustrate every satanic invented error in my life with the power of the truth in the word of God, in the name of Jesus. Let the perfection attached to your law begin to bring your conversion power into my life, in the name of Jesus. I command my body, soul and Spirit to receive the conversion power in the law of God, in the name of Jesus. Let testimonies from God increase in my life by fire, in the name of Jesus. Almighty God, give me your sure testimony that will promote my relationship with you, in the name of Jesus. Every fake lion roaring against my destiny, be destroyed by the Lion of the Tribe of Judah in my life, in the name of Jesus. Any evil movement assigned to stop my movement in life, be demobilized to failure, in the name of Jesus. I break every link with the devil, his agents, sin and its consequences, in the name of Jesus. Long- and short-time problems in my life, your time is up, die, in the name of Jesus. I break and loose myself from every inherited covenant, curses and nemesis, in the name of Jesus.

"But whoso looketh into the perfect law of liberty, and continueth therein, he being not a forgetful hearer, but a doer of the work, this man shall be blessed in his deed."

—   JAMES 1:25

"For I am the LORD: I will speak, and the word that I shall speak shall come to pass; it shall be no more prolonged: for in your days, O rebellious house, will I say the word, and will perform it, saith the Lord GOD."

— EZEKIEL 12:25

"God forbid: yea, let God be true, but every man a liar; as it is written, that thou mightest be justified in thy sayings, and mightest overcome when thou art judged."

— ROMANS 3:4

Any power assigned to steal the word of God from me, be frustrated, in the name of Jesus. Heavenly father, empower me to put your word to practice without diverting, in the name of Jesus. Let the anointing that is in the perfect law of liberty liberate my life from every bondage, in the name of Jesus. Father Lord, give me divine focus to look unto Jesus, the author and the finisher of my faith, without ceasing, in the name of Jesus. Anointing to walk with God continually without stopping, fall upon me, in the name of Jesus. Any satanic distraction against my walk with God, be frustrated, in the name of Jesus. Father Lord, help me to take the action that will favor the kingdom of God and displease the devil and his agents forever, in the name of Jesus. Let the word of God, spoken on my behalf, stand the test of time without shaking, in the name of Jesus. Every negative word ever spoken against me by anyone living or dead, expire, in the name of Jesus.

Day 33

Expectations:

1. **The destruction of every evil force prolonging the manifestation of God's word in your life**
2. **Complete deliverance upon any part of your life that is rebelling against the will of God**
3. **Complete deliverance from the effects and consequences of past sins**
4. **Commanding the marking ink of God to mark you for promotion**
5. **The destruction of every satanic witchcraft network against you.**

Any evil force prolonging the manifestation of God's word in my life, scatter in shame, in the name of Jesus. Any part of my life rebelling against the will of God for my life, receive deliverance, in the name of Jesus. Let the performing power in the word of God begin to manifest in my life, in the name of Jesus. I command all my suspended testimonies, miracles and promotions to be lifted, in the name of Jesus. Let the mobilizing power of God mobilize God's angels to take me to my promised land, in the name of Jesus. Father Lord, deliver me from evil spirits visitation from my past sins, in the name of Jesus. Let the marking ink of God mark me for promotion this season, in the name of Jesus. Every satanic witchcraft network against my life, be destroyed, in the name of Jesus.

"God is faithful, by whom ye were called unto the fellowship of his Son Jesus Christ our Lord."

— 1 CORINTHIANS 1:9

"That the LORD spake unto me, saying, thou art to pass over through Ar, the coast of Moab, this day: and when thou comest nigh over against the children of Ammon, distress them not, nor meddle with them: for I will not give thee of the land of the children of Ammon any possession; because I have given it unto the children of Lot for a possession."

— DEUTERONOMY 2:17-19

Every satanic weapon of mass destruction, avoid me and go back to your senders, in the name of Jesus. I command my enemies to repent or make heart breaking mistakes that will favor me in life, in the name of Jesus. Almighty God, upgrade my brain to rise above my competitors, in the name of Jesus. I command every destiny manipulator to fail woefully in my life, in the name of Jesus. Let the power that justifies every spoken word of God bring justice in every area of my life, in the name of Jesus.

"And Balaam said unto God, Balak the son of Zippor, king of Moab, hath sent unto me, saying, Behold, there is a people come out of Egypt, which covereth the face of the earth: come now, curse me them; peradventure I shall be able to overcome them, and drive them out."

— NUMBERS 22:10-11

"God is faithful, by whom ye were called unto the fellowship of his Son Jesus Christ our Lord."

— 1 CORINTHIANS 1:9

Any iniquity in my life attracting satanic curse against me, be destroyed by the saving power in the blood of Jesus, in the name of Jesus. Let the strength of every curse in my life be destroyed without fulfillment, in the name of Jesus. Every altar of darkness built to minister against me, catch fire and burn to ashes, in the name of Jesus. Any evil priest hired to attack me, receive confusion, in the name of Jesus. Any evil spirit ever raised against me in any evil altar, I bind and cast you out, in the name of Jesus. Blood of Jesus, speak me out of the captivity of every evil altar, in the name of Jesus. Any blood sacrifice crying against me in any evil altar, be silenced by the crying blood of Jesus, in the name of Jesus. Any evil eye monitoring against me from any evil altar, be blinded spiritually and physically, in the name of Jesus.

Day 34

Expectations:

1. The scattering of every evil gang up against your life.
2. The destruction of all the evil meeting places of your enemies.
3. The destruction of every lie going on against your life from witches and wizards.
4. Complete deliverance from the effect of every negative word ever spoken against you.

Every evil gang up against my life from any evil altar, scatter in shame, in the name of Jesus. Any human blood sacrifice, bullock and ram ever offered in any evil altar to attack my life, fail woefully and attack your sender, in the name of Jesus. Let the meeting places of my enemies collapse and swallow them, in the name of Jesus. Every lie going on against my life from witches and wizards, back fire, in the name of Jesus. Almighty God, deliver me from the spirit of perversion assigned to expose me to evil sacrifices and curses, in the name of Jesus. By the power of God's presence in my life, I break away from every negative word ever spoken against me, in the name of Jesus. Let the shout of a king, divine motivated leader be around me always, in the name of Jesus. By the counsel of the Almighty God, I destroy every satanic attack programmed against me from evil altars, in the name of Jesus. Any satanic packing store in my life, catch fire and burn to ashes, in the name of Jesus. Father Lord, fill my life with the best things of life and promote me above my competitors, in the name of Jesus. Ancient of days, deliver me from every lying word about to manifest against me, in the name of Jesus. Let the marching power of God march out every problem in my life and the powers behind them, in the name of Jesus. Every evil door opened for my destruction, I walk away from your place, in the name of Jesus. Father Lord, open the door of prosperity and walk me into it with ease, in the name of Jesus. Any power that is assigned to break my fellowship with God the father, son and the Holy Ghost, fail woefully, in the name of Jesus.

"Faithful is he that calleth you, who also will do it."

— 1 THESSALONIANS 5:24

> "that by two immutable things, in which it was impossible for God to lie, we might have a strong consolation, who have fled for refuge to lay hold upon the hope set before us:"

— HEBREWS 6:18

By the power of God's faithfulness, I destroy every work of the devil and his agents in my life, in the name of Jesus. Almighty God, increase and manifest your faithfulness in every area of my life, in the name of Jesus. Every enemy of the manifestations of the faithfulness of God in my life, be frustrated, in the name of Jesus. Every promise of God for my life, begin to manifest by the power in the faithfulness of God in my life, in the name of Jesus. Any evil personality standing against the fulfillment of God's work in my life, be frustrated, in the name of Jesus.

Day 35

Expectations:

1. **Commanding the resuscitation of every good thing that belongs to you that the devil buried.**
2. **The destruction of every lying spirit working against the manifestation of God's will in your life.**

3. **The destruction of every fake news arranged and released from satanic kingdoms against you, to destroy your reputation.**

4. **The destruction of every mountain from any demonic kingdom standing on your way to progress.**

Almighty God, show yourself strong in every part of my life, in the name of Jesus. Lord Jesus, stand by me and command every good thing that the devil and his agents killed and buried against me to rise, in the name of Jesus. Every part of my life lacking the presence of God, receive divine action without delay, in the name of Jesus. O Lord arise and release the answers to my prayers for the termination of my problems, in the name of Jesus. Let the immutability nature of God stand against every impossibility in my life until they bow, in the name of Jesus. Every lying spirit working against the manifestation of God's will for my life, I bind and cast you out, in the name of Jesus. Every fake news arranged and released from the satanic kingdom to destroy my reputation, be disregarded to my promotion, in the name of Jesus. Mountains from demonic kingdom standing on my way to progress, disappear before me, in the name of Jesus. Any evil program organized to demote my life, fail woefully, in the name of Jesus.

> "if we believe not, yet he abideth faithful: he cannot deny himself."
>
> — 2 TIMOTHY 2:13

By the power of God's abiding faithfulness, I command every long-term problem and impossibility to bow in my life, in the name of Jesus. Any mountainous problem in my life, your time is up, be frustrated to destruction, in the name of Jesus. Every evil power, denying me of my rights, benefits and entitlements, I bind and cast you out, in the name of Jesus. Every agent of the devil standing as God in my life, be frustrated from your place in my life, in the name of Jesus. Every enemy of the success of God's program for my life, your time is up, be exposed and be disgraced, in the name of Jesus. Almighty God, arise in your power and faithfulness and defend your word in my life, in the name of Jesus.

Day 36

Expectations:

1. **The destruction of every evil power that is attacking your relationship with God.**
2. **The dethronement of every evil throne militating against your life.**
3. **Complete deliverance from the yoke of negative reports.**

4. Commanding the release of all the answers to your prayers.

Any evil power attacking my relationship with God, fail woefully, in the name of Jesus. By the power of God's name in my life, I dethrone every evil throne militating against my life, in the name of Jesus. Every yoke of witchcraft and occultism in my life, break to pieces, in the name of Jesus. I receive the anointing of how did it happen in everything I do in life henceforth, in the name of Jesus. I break and loose myself from the yoke of negative reports, in the name of Jesus.

> "And the LORD gave unto Israel all the land which he sware to give unto their fathers; and they possessed it, and dwelt therein. And the LORD gave them rest round about, according to all that he sware unto their fathers: and there stood not a man of all their enemies before them; the LORD delivered all their enemies into their hand. There failed not ought of any good thing which the LORD had spoken unto the house of Israel; all came to pass."
>
> — JOSHUA 21:43-45

By the giving power in the nature of God, I receive every good thing I ever asked for in my prayers, in the name of Jesus. Let all my heart desire according to God's word be release to me without delay, in the name of Jesus. Father Lord, no matter the number of the enemies on my way, deliver me from their evil plans, in the name of Jesus. Any evil hand stealing from me, whither and lose your hold over my blessings, in the name of Jesus. I command every enemy that is occupying my place in life to be removed by heavenly force, in the name of Jesus. Any evil personality that has vowed to deny me of God's blessings, fail woefully, in the name of Jesus. Heavenly father, take me to my promised land and settle me there without a rival, in the name of Jesus. Almighty God, dispose my enemies of anything here on earth they are using to serve the devil, in the name of Jesus. I command the strength of my enemies in the promised land to be withdrawn, in the name of Jesus. Every promise that God made to Abraham, begin to manifest in my life, in the name of Jesus. Let the fear of God drive away any evil personality sitting in my place in life, in the name of Jesus. Every satanic giant in my promise land, be destroyed without mercy, in the name of Jesus. Every spiritual and physical backing of my enemies in the promised land, be withdrawn, in the name of Jesus. Blood of Jesus, cry against every evil occupancy in my land of promise, in the name of Jesus. Every evil altar in my promised land, be dismantled by thunder, in the name of Jesus.

Day 37

Expectations:

1. The destruction of every satanic structure in your land of promise.
2. The destruction of every evil sacrifice offered to bring evil spirits into your promise land.
3. The complete withdrawal of every invitation to your promise land, ever given to the devil, evil spirits and demonic agents.
4. The destruction of the spirits behind all evil and demonic witnesses against you.
5. Commanding all the enemies against your life to surrender and disengage from you

Every satanic structure in my land of promise, catch fire, and burn to ashes, in the name of Jesus. Every evil sacrifice ever offered to invite evil spirits in my promised land, expire, in the name of Jesus. Any invitation ever given to the devil, demonic spirits and all satanic agents in my promised land, I withdraw you now, in the name of Jesus. Let the property of the devil in my land of promise catch fire and burn to ashes, in the name of Jesus. Let the oath of God to bless me with every good thing be fulfilled, in the name of Jesus. Any strongman or woman that has vowed not to vacate my promised land, your time is up, leave now or perish, in the name of Jesus. Almighty God, command your peace to fall upon my life forever, in the name of Jesus. Let the presence of God Almighty occupy my promised land, in the name of Jesus. Anything my ancestors have handed over to the devil, I recover you double, in the name of Jesus. Any evil personality on assignment to take my place in life, be frustrated, in the name of Jesus. Every dream of defeat attacking me in my promised land, perish, in the name of Jesus.

Father Lord, deliver me from every organized enemy assigned to stand against my life, in the name of Jesus. Let the standing ground and supporters of my enemies collapse and disappear forever, in the name of Jesus. I command every enemy in my life to surrender and be disengaged, in the name of Jesus. By the unfailing power of God, I command all the promises of God to manifest in my life with joy, in the name of Jesus. Let the staying anointing of God, keep me in God's blessing forever and ever, in the name of Jesus. Almighty God, deliver me from every second-time affliction that has been assigned to take me to the grave yard, in the name of Jesus. Let the anointing of God upon me rise against every satanic plan against my life, in the name of Jesus. Let every mischief in the heart of my enemies against me back fire, in the name of Jesus. Any evil gang up against my financial life, scatter in failure, in the name of Jesus. Any evil tongue speaking against my life, I cut you off, in the name of Jesus. Every evil arrangement to destroy my efforts in life, fail woefully, in the name of Jesus. All evil witnesses against me spiritually and physically end your promotion and operation now, in the name of Jesus. I command every creature to release everything attached to my name in the hand of others, in the name of Jesus. Let the running away power, walking, moving and flying strength of God enter into all my blessings and inheritance in the hands of others and come to me with ease, in the mighty name of Jesus.

TEN

PRAYERS AND BLESSINGS FROM RESTITUTION

DECREES-1

(Luke 17:3-5, Luke 19:9-10, Acts 19:18, Psalms 24:3, Genesis 20:1-11, 17-18, 1 King 20:34, 2 Kings 8:1-6, Proverbs 6:30-31, Nehemiah 5:6-13, Ezekiel 33:14-16, Matthew 5:23, 24, Matthew 18:15-17; 23:23)

Day 1

Expectations:

1. Genuinely repenting from all sins and obtaining pardon and forgiveness from God.

2. Commanding all the consequences of your past sins to be wiped out

3. Commanding your complete deliverance from the spirit of malice, anger and bitterness.

4. The destruction of all the spirits assigned to weaken your decision in Christ.

5. The destruction of every chain of bondage pulling you back to sin.

Almighty God, give me victory over every offence that will come my way in my Christian journey, in the name of Jesus. Father Lord forgive me for every sin I have ever committed against you and everyone, in the name of Jesus. I repent genuinely from every problem I have caused that has brought people to sin or stumble in faith, in the name of Jesus. Let the consequences of my past sins be wiped out of my life by the blood of Jesus. Anointing to truly repent and confess my sins before God and man, come upon me, in the name of Jesus. Father Lord, empower me to acknowledge my sins, repent, restitute and forsake them forever, in the name of Jesus.

> Take heed to yourselves: If thy brother trespass against thee, rebuke him; and if he repent, forgive him. And if he trespass against thee seven times in a day, and seven times in a day turn again to thee, saying, I repent; thou shalt forgive him.
>
> 5 And the apostles said unto the Lord, Increase our faith.
>
> — LUKE 17:3-5

I pray for my trespassed brother to accept his mistakes, repent, confess and forsake his sins, in the name of Jesus. Father Lord, help me to receive people who will rebuke me when I trespass against you, in the name of Jesus. Let the power to repent when the Holy Ghost rebukes me, possess me in the name of Jesus. Let my repentance and confession to God and people I've offended attract God's forgiveness upon my life, in the name of Jesus. Father Lord, increase my faith and righteousness to forgive my offenders just like you forgave the world, in the name of Jesus. I bind and loose myself from the spirit of malice and unforgiving spirit, in the name of Jesus. Let the sins of repented believers be forgiven them, in the name of Jesu. Any power assigned to weaken my decision for Christ and against sin, be frustrated away from my life, in the name of Jesus. Every chain of bondage pulling me back to sin, your time is up, break to pieces and loose your power over my life, in the name of Jesus. I break and loose myself from the yoke of sin, especially ancestral sins, in the name of Jesus. Blood of Jesus, Holy Ghost fire, enter into my life and cleanse my blood from every sin, in the name of Jesus.

> This day is salvation come to this house, forsomuch as he also is a son of Abraham. For the Son of man is come to seek and to save that which was lost.
>
> — LUKE 19:9-10

Lord Jesus, enter into my life and pass through every organ of my body, in the name of Jesus. Almighty God, empower me spiritually and make me rich materially, in the name of Jesus. Any evil spirit attached to my riches and prosperity in life, I bind and cast you out, in the name of Jesus. I command everything in my body, soul and spirit to see Jesus, in the name of Jesus. Almighty

God, command everything in me to grow tall in size to see Jesus with ease, in the name of Jesus. Let my little stature grow spiritually in size and be empowered to see Jesus from every side, in the name of Jesus. I command the strength of sin and Satan in my life to be reduced to nothing and grow me spiritually in righteousness, in the name of Jesus. Lord Jesus, look up to my side in the midst of the multitude and see me with your power, in the name of Jesus. I command every part of my life to make haste joyfully to meet Jesus wherever He is, in the name of Jesus.

Day 2

Expectations:

1. **The destruction of every sin standing as a mountain between you and Christ**
2. **Receiving the grace and anointing to do your restitution**
3. **Commanding the salvation that comes through Christ to begin to manifest in your life**
4. **Commanding the blessings of Abraham to begin to manifest in your life**
5. **Complete deliverance from every form of vanity**

Any sin in my life, standing as a mountain between me and Jesus, disappear, in the name of Jesus. Anointing to restitute and give back all wrongly acquired wealth, fall upon me, in the name of Jesus. Everything I have denied the poor and the rich through false accusation, I return them back, in the name of Jesus. Let the salvation that comes through Jesus Christ begin to manifest in my life, in the name of Jesus. I command the spirit of pride in my life to be bound and cast out of my life forever, in the name of Jesus. Powers of darkness moving me to claim to be right when I am wrong; shift blames, complain and find fault in others, I bind and cast you out, in the name of Jesus. Let the forsaking power of God to forsake every sin and hate them, fall upon me, in the name of Jesus. By the power in the death and the blood shed of Jesus, I command the blessings of Abraham to manifest in my life, in the name of Jesus. Let the saving power in the blood of Jesus save me, in the name of Jesus.

And many that believed came, and confessed, and shewed their deeds.

— ACTS 19:18

Who shall ascend into the hill of the LORD? or who shall stand in his holy place?

— PSALMS 24:3

I break and loose myself from the captivity of vagabond spirit, in the name of Jesus. Let my repentance and salvation reject every evil deed and every property of the devil, in the name of Jesus. I set ablaze publicly all the material for idolatrous spirit and occultic materials in my possession, in the name of Jesus. Let the word of God grow and prevail over the words of the devil in my life style and ministry, in the name of Jesus. Father Lord, use me to establish your kingdom in my environment and all over the globe, in the name of Jesus. Anointing to ascend into the hill of the Lord and stand in his place forever, possess me, in the name of Jesus. Blood of Jesus, wash my hands and heart and make them clean without pollution, in the name of Jesus. I withdraw my body, soul and spirit and deliver them from every form of vanity, in the name of Jesus. Father Lord, help me to see reasons to remain pure and holy in the midst of sinners in every situation and circumstances, in the name of Jesus. Anointing to say sorry immediately when need be without delay, fall upon me, in the name of Jesus. Any evil spirit using me or anyone to promote or attract sin here on earth, I bind and cast you out, in the name of Jesus. Let my repentance be genuine and accepted by God, in the name of Jesus. I break and loose myself from every evil covenant and curse, in the name of Jesus. Every negative word ever spoken against me among the creation, expire, in the name of Jesus.

And Abraham journeyed from thence toward the south country, and dwelled between Kadesh and Shur, and sojourned in Gerar.

And Abraham said of Sarah his wife, she *is* my sister: and Abimelech king of Gerar sent, and took Sarah.

But God came to Abimelech in a dream by night, and said to him, Behold, thou *art but* a dead man, for the woman which thou hast taken; for she *is* a man's wife.

But Abimelech had not come near her: and he said, Lord, wilt thou slay also a righteous nation?

Said he not unto me, she *is* my sister? and she, even she herself said, He *is* my brother: in the integrity of my heart and innocence of my hands have I done this.

And God said unto him in a dream, Yea, I know that thou didst this in the integrity of thy heart; for I also withheld thee from sinning against me: therefore, suffered I thee not to touch her.

Now therefore restore the man *his* wife; for he *is* a prophet, and he shall pray for thee, and thou shalt live: and if thou restore *her* not, know thou that thou shalt surely die, thou, and all that *are* thine.

Therefore, Abimelech rose early in the morning, and called all his servants, and told all these things in their ears: and the men were sore afraid.

Then Abimelech called Abraham, and said unto him, what hast thou done unto us? and what have I offended thee, that thou hast brought on me and on my kingdom a great sin? thou hast done deeds unto me that ought not to be done.

And Abimelech said unto Abraham, what sawest thou, that thou hast done this thing?

And Abraham said, Because I thought, Surely the fear of God *is* not in this place; and they will slay me for my wife's sake.

And Abraham said unto God, O that Ishmael might live before thee!

— GENESIS 20:1-11, 17-18

Let my journey out of the Satanic kingdom be perfected and completed by the power in the blood of Jesus. Anything appealing to me from the world, your time is up, I reject you, in the name of Jesus. Every spirit of lie and fear in my life, I bind and cast you out, in the name of Jesus. I break and loose myself from the spirit that destroys in the day and night, in the name of Jesus.

Day 3

Expectations:

1. **Complete deliverance from the spirit behind lying.**
2. **Commanding your blessings that are still in the camp of the enemy to be restored to you.**
3. **The destruction of every satanic achievement in your life.**
4. **The destruction of the enemies of the manifestation of God's presence in your life.**
5. **Commanding the complete restoration of all that you ever lost.**

Let every good thing in the life of my captors be dead without life, in the name of Jesus. Every sin of lying determined to separate me from God and His blessings for me, be destroyed, in the name of Jesus. Almighty God, visit every sinner assigned to separate me from your comfort and judge them, in the name of Jesus. I command every one of my blessings in the camp of the wicked to be restored back to me, in the name of Jesus. Let the fear of God in me rise and intimidate the enemies of my destiny, in the name of Jesus. I command the strength of the remaining power of sin in my life to be broken to pieces, in the name of Jesus. Every satanic achievement in my life through sin and the consequences of sin, be destroyed by the speaking blood of Jesus. Every enemy of the manifestation of God's presence in my life, be destroyed, in the name of Jesus. Whatever plan the devil and his agents have over my life, I command them to fail, in the name of Jesus. Blood of Jesus, speak me out of the captivity of sin, sickness and disease, in the name of Jesus. Any part of my life completely captured by sin and its consequences, receive perfect deliverance, in the name of Jesus. You my reproductive organ, receive power to say no to every sin, in the name of Jesus. I command my body, soul and spirit to escape from the captivity of Satan, his agents and all sin, in the name of Jesus. I command every work of the devil and his agents to be terminated, in the name of Jesus. Let my prayers deliver the repentant wicked ones, witches and wizards, in the name of Jesus.

> And *Benhadad* said unto him, the cities, which my father took from thy father, I will restore; and thou shalt make streets for thee in Damascus, as my father made in Samaria. Then *said Ahab,* I will send thee away with this covenant. So he made a covenant with him, and sent him away.
>
> — 1 KING 20:34

Everything I need to restore to perfect my salvation, I refuse to keep them back, I restore them now, in the name of Jesus. Almighty God, create in my divine express way that will attract your blessings and keep the devil out of my life forever, in the name of Jesus. Let the entrance door of my life close against Satan and every evil, in the name of Jesus. By the power in God's restoring nature, I command every good thing handed over to the devil from the day of Adam and Eve to be restored back to me, in the name of Jesus. I bring back my life, body, soul and spirit to the covenant of God Almighty, in the name of Jesus.

> Then spake Elisha unto the woman, whose son he had restored to life, saying, Arise, and go thou and thine household, and sojourn wheresoever thou canst sojourn: for the LORD hath called for a famine; and it shall also come upon the land seven years.

And the woman arose, and did after the saying of the man of God: and she went with her household, and sojourned in the land of the Philistines seven years.

And it came to pass at the seven years' end, that the woman returned out of the land of the Philistines: and she went forth to cry unto the king for her house and for her land.

And the king talked with Gehazi the servant of the man of God, saying, tell me, I pray thee, all the great things that Elisha hath done.

And it came to pass, as he was telling the king how he had restored a dead body to life, that, behold, the woman, whose son he had restored to life, cried to the king for her house and for her land. And Gehazi said, my lord, O king, this *is* the woman, and this *is* her son, whom Elisha restored to life.

And when the king asked the woman, she told him. So, the king appointed unto her a certain officer, saying, restore all that *was* hers, and all the fruits of the field since the day that she left the land, even until now.

— 2 KINGS 8:1-6

Let the guiding power of the Almighty guide me into all truth without confusion, in the name of Jesus. Almighty God, empower me to know the truth and lead me to your perfect will by your power, in the name of Jesus. Almighty God, restore everything good that is dead in my life, in the name of Jesus. Let the Spirit of life from above minister into every part of my life, in the name of Jesus. Ancient of days, take me to the right places in life and prosper me with ease, in the name of Jesus. Every good thing I lost in the battle of life, I recover you double, in the name of Jesus.

Day 4

Expectations:

1. **Commanding your spiritual ears to open to divine counsel.**
2. **The destruction of the spirit of disobedience.**
3. **Total recovery of all that you lost due to disobedience**
4. **The uprooting of every evil altar in your place of abode.**
5. **The destruction of every satanic involvement in all the areas of your life.**
6. **Total and complete deliverance from every ditch and trouble.**

Father Lord, open my ears spiritually to hear your counsels, in the name of Jesus. I break and loose myself from the spirit of disobedience, in the name of Jesus. Anointing to obey God without resistance, fall upon me, in the name of Jesus. O Lord arise and take me to a journey you are fully in control and in charge of, in the name of Jesus. Every good thing the devil denied me because of my obedience to God's command, I recover you double, in the name of Jesus. Almighty God, deliver me from the general famine and dangers of life in my generation, in the name of Jesus. I command my living place to be conducive for divine habitations, in the name of Jesus. Any evil altar in my place of abode, be uprooted by thunder, in the name of Jesus. O Lord arise and prepare me for the journey of life ahead, in the name of Jesus. I refuse to embark on any journey that God is not in control of, in the name of Jesus. Father Lord, deliver me in times of famine, lack and poverty, in the name of Jesus. Let the hand of God lead me out of every present and future pandemic in this world, in the name of Jesus. Anointing to walk away from the place of danger at the right time, fall upon me, in the name of Jesus. Almighty God, prepare my future and bless my present with the fullness of your presence, in the name of Jesus. Every satanic involvement in every area of my life, be destroyed, in the name of Jesus. I command the devil, his agents, sin and lives problem to be very uncomfortable in my life, in the name of Jesus. Ancient of days, pull me out of every ditch and troubles of life, in the name of Jesus. Let my household be delivered from the past, present and future consequences of the ghost of our pasts, in the name of Jesus. By the power in God's provisional grace, I receive everything I need in times of famine, in the name of Jesus. I command the problems in my life to end by the ending power of the Almighty, in the name of Jesus. Every satanic nature planted in my life, be uprooted by the power in the blood of Jesus, in the name of Jesus. Father God, help me to do every restitution and empower me to stand against sin forever, in the name of Jesus. I break and loose myself from every sinful relationship no matter who is involved, in the name of Jesus. Every fire of sin and its property in my life, catch fire and burn to ashes, in the name of Jesus. Every enemy of the manifestation of God's word, his truth in my life, be frustrated, in the name of Jesus. Every messenger of sin in my life, I reject you and your message, in the name of Jesus.

> *Men* do not despise a thief, if he steals to satisfy his soul when he is hungry;
>
> But *if* he be found, he shall restore sevenfold; he shall give all the substance of his house.
>
> — PROVERBS 6:30-31

I command every part of my soul to receive the satisfying power of God, in the name of Jesus. Every creature, I command you to begin to minister to the needs of my soul without delay, in the name of Jesus.

Day 5

Expectations:

1. Commanding an end to every problem in your life and destiny.
2. The destruction of every problem that has vowed to waste you.
3. The destruction of every evil personality and authority sitting on your inheritance.
4. The destruction of the structure of the devil, and his agents in your life and family.
5. Commanding the powers that be in every community, city and nation to favor you

Every thirsty part of my soul, receive divine supply by the power in the speaking blood of Jesus. Let the hand of God that satisfies the soul satisfy my soul with the best things of life, in the name of Jesus. Every problem in my life, I command you to embrace your end without extension, in the name of Jesus. Father Lord, return me to my place of abundance without lack, in the name of Jesus. I command every problem in my life to come to an end while I am alive, in the name of Jesus. I refuse to die in the battle field without fulfilling my destiny and serving my generation according to God's will, in the name of Jesus. Any problem that vowed to end my life, you are a liar, end and die while I am alive, in the name of Jesus. Father Lord, let my, life be filled with testimonies of your goodness and take me to heaven by yourself and not by the powers of the devil or his agents, in the name of Jesus. Let my life be cleared from evil presence now, and in the times to come, in the name of Jesus. Any evil personality, satanic power that has vowed to write the last chapter of my life, fail woefully, in the name of Jesus. Let the whole creature rise and command the restoration of every good thing I have ever lost in the battles of life, in the name of Jesus. I command my heart desires to be honored by the whole creation, in the name of Jesus. I command the cries, voices in my prayers to attract divine attention and immediate response from among the creatures, in the name of Jesus. I command the powers that be in every community, city and nations to favor me without struggle, in the name of Jesus. Any evil personality, authorities and strong people of life sitting on my inheritance, spiritually or physically to be unseated, in the name of Jesus. Any place here on earth, among the living and the dead, known and unknown, begin to favor me and fight for me, in the name of Jesus. Let the testimonies of my good relationship with God reach to the end of the earth forever and ever, in the name of Jesus. Father Lord, anoint me with the power to make heaven, in the name of Jesus. Let the structures of the devil, his agents and sin in my life be roasted by fire, and burn to ashes, in the name of Jesus. Any evil personality, agents of the devil manipulating me to sin, be exposed and disgraced out of my life, in the name of Jesus. Every good thing that Satan has stolen away from me, I recover them back, in the name of Jesus. Any darkness in my life inhabiting Satan and sin, be replaced with divine light, in the name of Jesus. Let the shining light of God in my life, expose and expel Satan and his work in my life, in the name of Jesus.

And I was very angry when I heard their cry and these words.

Then I consulted with myself, and I rebuked the nobles, and the rulers, and said unto them, Ye exact usury, every one of his brother. And I set a great assembly against them.

And I said unto them, we after our ability have redeemed our brethren the Jews, which were sold unto the heathen; and will ye even sell your brethren? or shall they be sold unto us? Then held they their peace, and found nothing to answer.

Also, I said, it *is* not good that ye do: ought ye not to walk in the fear of our God because of the reproach of the heathen our enemies?

I likewise, *and* my brethren, and my servants, might exact of them money and corn: I pray you, let us leave off this usury.

Restore, I pray you, to them, even this day, their lands, their vineyards, their olive yards, and their houses, also the hundredth *part* of the money, and of the corn, the wine, and the oil, that ye exact of them.

Then said they, we will restore *them,* and will require nothing of them; so, will we do as thou sayest. Then I called the priests, and took an oath of them, that they should do according to this promise.

Also I shook my lap, and said, So God shake out every man from his house, and from his labour, that performeth not this promise, even thus be he shaken out, and emptied. And all the congregation said, Amen, and praised the LORD. And the people did according to this promise.

—   NEHEMIAH 5:6-13

Let the anger of God descend upon my captors and force them to release me, in the name of Jesus. Everything I or my ancestors mortgaged to receive deliverance, I recover you by the power in the blood of Jesus.

Day 6

Expectations:

1. **Commanding the blood of Jesus to flow into your foundation.**
2. **The destruction of every agent of the devil causing you pain.**
3. **The destruction of every evil personality, men and women in authority sitting on your right.**
4. **The destruction of every evil movement in any part of your life.**
5. **The breaking of every demonic attachment in your life, family and destiny**

I command the spirit of debt, borrowing and begging in my life to be bound and cast out of my life, in the name of Jesus. I release myself, my born and unborn children from the consequence of my past sins, in the name of Jesus. Blood of Jesus, flow into my foundation and wipe the tears of my born and unborn children, in the name of Jesus. Let the agents of the devil causing me pains be rebuked by the angels of the living God, in the name of Jesus. Any evil personality, men and women in authority sitting upon my rights, benefits or entitlement, release them by force, in the name of Jesus. Let the whole creature rise in judgment against every enemy of my joy, peace and happiness, in the name of Jesus. By the ability in the blood of Jesus, I command my redemption to manifest, in the name of Jesus. Almighty God, transfer into my life the wealth of the heathen, in the name of Jesus. Blood of Jesus, repurchase me from every satanic captivity, in the name of Jesus. I command every inflicted shame, disgrace and reproach in my life to be destroyed, in the name of Jesus. Every enemy of the manifestation of my financial prosperity, fail woefully, in the name of Jesus. Let the restoration power of God restore back to me everything that I ever lost in life, in the name of Jesus. I break and loose myself from the yoke of slavery and servant hood, in the name of Jesus. Almighty God, shake out of my life every demonic attachment, in the name of Jesus. Anointing to enjoy the fruits of my labor, fall upon me, in the name of Jesus. Almighty God, by your mercy, command your promises to start manifesting in my life every day, in the name of Jesus. I command the congregations of the wicked against my life to scatter, in the name of Jesus. Miracles from above that will enable me to start praising and worshipping God non-stop, manifest in my life, in the name of Jesus. Every pollution of the waters and the blood in my life, be cleansed by the cleansing blood of Jesus. Any evil movement in any part of my life, be demobilized to death, in the name of Jesus. Father Lord, give me your wisdom to approach every matter without committing sin, in the name of Jesus.

> Though these three men, Noah, Daniel, and Job, were in it, they should deliver *but* their own souls by their righteousness, saith the Lord GOD.
>
> If I cause noisome beasts to pass through the land, and they spoil it, so that it be desolate, that no man may pass through because of the beasts:
>
> Though these three men *were* in it, *as* I live, saith the Lord GOD, they shall deliver neither sons nor daughters; they only shall be delivered, but the land shall be desolate.
>
> — EZEKIEL 33:14-16

Any spirit of wickedness on assignment to resist the word of God, I bind and cast you out, in the name of Jesus. I break and loose myself, my ministry and destiny from the yoke of condemnation, in the name of Jesus. Any type of sin that has taken any part of my life to captive, be frustrated, in the name of Jesus. Heavenly father, empower me to minister to the wicked until they are restored back to you in righteousness, in the name of Jesus. Let the yoke of sin be broken down to pieces in the lives of the wicked ones in my ministry, in the name of Jesus. I break and loose myself from wrong reaction because of the sinful lifestyle of the wicked, in the name of Jesus.

Day 7

Expectations:

1. **Putting an end to every punishment, suffering and hardship affecting you.**

2. **Commanding the blood of Jesus to silence every voice crying against you.**

3. **Commanding the frustrating power of God to frustrate the devil and his works in your life.**

4. **Commanding the ancient of days to prosper your life and ministry.**

5. **The destruction of every evil plan to keep you away from God's blessings.**

6. **The destruction of every yoke of hypocrisy, pretense and deceit**

Father Lord, empower my ministry to turn the wicked ones away from their wickedness, in the name of Jesus. Every punishment, suffering and hardship in my life coming from my past sins and mistakes, be terminated by the speaking blood of Jesus. Let the crying blood of Jesus silence every evil voice crying against my destiny, in the name of Jesus. Let the frustrating power of God frustrate the devil and his works in my life, in the name of Jesus. Ancient of days, deliver me wherever I need deliverance and keep me holy forever, in the name of Jesus.

> Therefore, if thou bring thy gift to the altar, and there rememberest that thy brother hath ought against thee;
>
> Leave there thy gift before the altar, and go thy way; first be reconciled to thy brother, and then come and offer thy gift.
>
> — MATTHEW 5:23, 24

Ancient of days, empower me to prosper in the ministry of reconciliation through the power in the blood of Jesus. Anointing to follow peace with all men, possess me and make me a peace maker every day of my life, in the name of Jesus. Every enemy of Christ's type of peace in my life, be frustrated, in the name of Jesus. I command trouble making demons in my life to be bound and cast out, in the name of Jesus. Any evil spirit separating me from good people, your time is up, I bind and cast you out, in the name of Jesus. I command the garden of my life to be purged by the power in the blood of Jesus, in the mighty name of Jesus. Let the fire of God enter into every area of my life and consume the presence of the devil without mercy, in the name of Jesus. Every evil plan to keep me away from God's blessings, fail woefully, in the name of Jesus. Almighty God, anoint me to say no to every evil suggestion and appearances, in the name of Jesus.

> Moreover, if thy brother shall trespass against thee, go and tell him his fault between thee and him alone: if he shall hear thee, thou hast gained thy brother.
>
> But if he will not hear *thee, then* take with thee one or two more, that in the mouth of two or three witnesses every word may be established.
>
> And if he shall neglect to hear them, tell *it* unto the church: but if he neglects to hear the church, let him be unto thee as an heathen man and a publican.
>
> Woe unto you, scribes and Pharisees, hypocrites! for ye pay tithe of mint and anise and cummin, and have omitted the weightier *matters* of the law, judgment, mercy, and faith: these ought ye to have done, and not to leave the other undone.
>
> — MATTHEW 18:15-17; 23:23

Father Lord, empower me with boldness, the right manner of approach to tell people their faults, in the name of Jesus. By the power in the word of God, I command the spirit of misunderstanding, quarrels and disagreement to avoid me forever, in the name of Jesus. Father Lord, empower me with my lifestyle and my ministry to win many to Christ, in the name of Jesus. Anointing to win backsliders back to Christ, fall upon me, in the name of Jesus. Let the hearing ears of the people I minister to hear the gospel and turn away from their sins, in the name of Jesus. Father Lord, help me to do everything right without sin, in the name of Jesus. I break and loose myself from the yoke of hypocrisy and pretense, in the name of Jesus. I receive God's abundant grace to do everything I suppose to do according to God's word, in the name of Jesus. Let the resisting power of God empower me to resist Satan, sin and every agent of sin, in the name of Jesus. Any evil voice crying against me from the altars of sin, be silenced by the crying blood of Jesus, in the name of Jesus. Almighty God, deliver me from the fake miracle workers, in the name of Jesus.

ELEVEN

BELIEVERS CALL UNTO HOLINESS

DECREE-1

(Leviticus 20:7-8, John 17:17, 19, 21-23, 1 Corinthians 1:30, 1 Thessalonians 4:3-4, 7-8, 2 Thessalonians 2:13, 15, 17, 1 Peter 1: 2; Romans 6:19, 22, Romans 2:29, 1 Timothy 2:15, Hebrews 12:14, Luke 1:75, 1 Peter 1:15-16, Psalms 24:3-4; 73:1, Matthew 5:8, 48, Deuteronomy 30:6, Colossians 2:11, Genesis 17:1, 2 Corinthians 13:9, 1 John 4:17, 18)

Day 1

Expectations:

1. **The destruction of all the enemies of the manifestation of God's righteousness upon your life.**

2. **Receiving the anointing from above to experience of holiness.**

3. **The purification of your foundation by the nature of God.**

4. **Commanding the spirit of God to arrest every part of your life**

5. **The destruction of every messenger of sin in your life.**

6. **Commanding every part of your life to submit perfectly to the word of God.**

Strength, wisdom, knowledge and understanding to take action and to sanctify myself, manifest in my life, in the name of Jesus. Almighty God, turn everything about me to holiness, in the name of Jesus. By the power attached to the whole creation, I command every organ of my body to respond to the call of God for my sanctification, in the name of Jesus. Anointing of God to live holy, wherever you are, possess me, in the name of Jesus. Every enemy of the manifestation of God's righteousness in my life, be disgraced, in the name of Jesus. Let the power of God take me to God's sanctifying grace, body, soul and spirit, in the name of Jesus. Almighty God, soak me inside the blood of Jesus to witness the purging and sanctification of my soul into righteousness, in the name of Jesus. Anointing from above that will bring me to divine experience of holiness, fall upon me, in the name of Jesus. Heavenly father, drop your complete nature from above to purify my foundation, in the name of Jesus. Let the blessed Holy Trinity sanctify me and keep me out of sin forever, in the name of Jesus.

Sanctify yourselves therefore, and be ye holy: for I *am* the LORD your God.

And ye shall keep my statutes, and do them: I *am* the LORD which sanctify you.

— LEVITICUS 20:7-8

Almighty God, by your mercy, fill me with your nature without measure, in the name of Jesus. Let the sanctifying power of God arrest every area of my life and bring them to purity, in the name of Jesus. Anointing of self-sanctification, enter into my life with deep thirst and hunger for purity, in the name of Jesus. Spirit of the living God, arrest every part of my body, soul and spirit for inner purity, in the name of Jesus. Let the sanctifying power in the blood of Jesus penetrate into my life and nullify every contention of the devil against my sanctification, in the name of Jesus. Father Lord, keep me away from every sin and empower me to keep your statues and abide by them with joy, in the name of Jesus. By the power in the LORD that sanctifies, I receive the strength to be sanctified, in the name of Jesus. Let the power in the LORD my God penetrate into every organ of my life with sanctifying strength, in the name of Jesus. Let the cooperating grace of God command every part of my life to surrender to sanctification, in the name of Jesus.

Sanctify them through thy truth: thy word is truth.

Then said the chief priests of the Jews to Pilate, Write not, The King of the Jews; but that he said, I am King of the Jews.

Pilate answered, What I have written I have written.

Then the soldiers, when they had crucified Jesus, took his garments, and made four parts, to every soldier a part; and also *his* coat: now the coat was without seam, woven from the top throughout.

— JOHN 17:17, 19, 21-23

I command the backbone of sin and Satan to be broken to pieces in every area of my life, in the name of Jesus. Every messenger of sin in my life, your time is up, fail woefully without success, in the name of Jesus. Let the power in the word of God be consecrated and focus on my sanctification without withdrawal, in the name of Jesus. Father Lord, bring down from heaven the hour of my personal sanctification and sanctify me through your word, in the name of Jesus. I command every branch of my life to receive power over the flesh to live a holy life, in the name of Jesus. Let my eternity embrace holiness without any relationship with sin and every form of defilement, in the name of Jesus. By the power of the only true God, I command the sanctification of my life to become real, in the name of Jesus. Anointing from above, filled with purity, empower me to glorify God without compromise here on earth, in the name of Jesus. I receive the ability from the word of God to live without sin and to glorify God forever here on earth, in the name of Jesus. Let the name of Christ be manifested in my life before everyone here on earth, in the name of Jesus. Anointing to keep God's word in righteousness to my last moment here on earth, possess me, in the name of Jesus. Almighty God, increase my joy in living right without cooperating with Satan and sin, in the name of Jesus. I break and loose myself from the defiling activities of this world, in the name of Jesus. Father Lord, help me to handle the word of life without modification or change, in the name of Jesus. By the power in keeping anointing of God, I keep myself holy and undefiled by God's word, in the name of Jesus. I bring my life to perfect submission to God's word, God's name, the blood of Jesus and under the guidance of the Holy Spirit, in the name of Jesus. I break and loose myself from the control of the son of perdition forever and ever, in the name of Jesus. Let the word of God and every part of the scriptures be filled positively in every area of my life, in the name of Jesus. Let the joy of the Lord and his strength be fulfilled in every area of my life without struggle, in the name of Jesus. Let the joy of being hated by the world and loved by Jesus Christ flood my life, in the name of Jesus. Father Lord, while I am still in this world, keep me holy without defilement, in the name of Jesus. Anointing from above that keeps saints from sin and every evil in this world, fall upon me, in the name of Jesus. Powers from above that separates believers from the activities of this world while still in the world, arrest me and refuse to release me forever, in the name of Jesus. Anointing to operate in this world, doing what is right without compromise, fall upon me, in the name of Jesus. By the power of unity between the three God-heads, father Lord, unite me with all true believers all over the world without struggle, in the name of Jesus. I command every fake one in the body of Christ like Judas Iscariot to be easily identified and be carefully handled, in the name of Jesus. Spirit of joy from above, empower me to differentiate true believers from fake ones with wisdom to deal with each of them, in the name of Jesus. I receive the grace of God to discern and operate in the nine gifts of the Holy Ghost, in the name of Jesus. I command everything in me, outside me to be conscious of the presence of God with honor to Him, everywhere I find myself, in the name of Jesus.

But of him are ye in Christ Jesus, who of God is made unto us wisdom, and righteousness, and sanctification, and redemption:

— 1 CORINTHIANS 1:30

For this is the will of God, *even* your sanctification, that ye should abstain from fornication:

That every one of you should know how to possess his vessel in sanctification and honour;

For God hath not called us unto uncleanness, but unto holiness.

He therefore that despiseth, despiseth not man, but God, who hath also given unto us his holy Spirit.

— 1 THESSALONIANS 4:3-4, 7-8

Let the perfecting power that is in the word of God, in the name of Christ Jesus perfect me in holiness, in the name of Jesus. Almighty God, show your power, love and your nature through me in every situation, in the name of Jesus. By the power of Christ in me, father Lord perfect your wisdom, righteousness, sanctification and redemption, in the name of Jesus. By the grace of God in the redeeming power of God, I command every part of my life to be perfectly redeemed and sanctified, in the name of Jesus. Sanctification from above, you are God's perfect will for me, manifest in my life, in the name of Jesus.

Day 2

Expectations:

1. Receiving the anointing to abstain from fornication and all sexual perversion

2. The destruction of every organized power of sin against your life and destiny

3. Commanding the reigning power in the righteousness of Christ to reign and rule forever in your life and destiny

4. The destruction of every yoke of uncleanness in your life.

5. Putting an end to every infirmity in your life

Anointing to abstain from fornication, all sexual perversion and every other kind of sin, possess me, in the name of Jesus. I command every part of my life, body, soul and spirit to possess the vessel in sanctification and the anointing to honor God forever, in the name of Jesus. Every enemy of the manifestation of God's image, nature, his likeness and power in my life, fail woefully, in the name of Jesus.

> But we are bound to give thanks alway to God for you, brethren beloved of the Lord, because God hath from the beginning chosen you to salvation through sanctification of the Spirit and belief of the truth:
>
> Therefore, brethren, stand fast, and hold the traditions which ye have been taught, whether by word, or our epistle.
>
> Comfort your hearts, and stablish you in every good word and work.
>
> — 2 THESSALONIANS 2:13, 15, 17

Holy Spirit, arrest me and detain me forever to give thanks to you always, in the name of Jesus. Let the strength and the power of my salvation and sanctification from the beginning be preserved forever, in the name of Jesus. By the power in the truth of the word of God, I command my life to prosper in holiness, in the name of Jesus. Let the glory of God frustrate every demonic activity fighting against the truth and the nature of God in my life, in the name of Jesus. Almighty God, empower every area of my life to stand fast and hold the tradition, the foundational truth in the word of God, in the name of Jesus. Let the love of God and other fruits of the Holy Spirit abide in me without shaking, in the name of Jesus. Let the everlasting consolation, the goodness and hope in Christ prevail over every circumstance in my life forever, in the name of Jesus. By the ministering power in God's grace and mercy, I command every organized power of sin to be disorganized in my life, in the name of Jesus. Let the reigning power in righteousness of Christ reign and rule forever in my life, in the name of Jesus. Father Lord, comfort my heart and establish me in every good word and work, in the name of Jesus. Let the commanding power in God's truth and sanctification take me far away from failure and defeat, in the name of Jesus. Almighty God, command everything in me and outside me to answer the call of holiness, in the name of Jesus. Every yoke of uncleanness in my life, your time is up, break to pieces, in the name of Jesus. Let the responding power of God in holiness fill me to respond promptly to holiness, in the name of Jesus. Let the believing power of God help me to believe in God's word without doubting, in the name of Jesus. God forbid that I will despise God, I command my spirit and soul to act positively to the word of God without doubting, in the name of Jesus. Let the Holy Spirit by God's mercy overshadow my life and begin to manifest without hindrance, in the name of Jesus.

Elect according to the foreknowledge of God the Father, through sanctification of the Spirit, unto obedience and sprinkling of the blood of Jesus Christ: Grace unto you, and peace, be multiplied.

— 1 PETER 1:2;

I speak after the manner of men because of the infirmity of your flesh: for as ye have yielded your members servants to uncleanness and to iniquity unto iniquity; even so now yield your members servants to righteousness unto holiness.

But now being made free from sin, and become servants to God, ye have your fruit unto holiness, and the end everlasting life.

— ROMANS 6:19, 22

By the power in God's abundance of mercy, I receive the ministry of God's sanctifying grace, in the name of Jesus. By the power in the foreknowledge of God the father, through sanctification of the Spirit, bring me close to God for perfect sanctification, in the name of Jesus. Let the blood of Jesus be sprinkled into the foundation of my life to speak unto death every root of sin, in the name of Jesus. By the ministry of God's sanctification in my life, I command every part of my life to willingly submit to God's plan in obedience, in the name of Jesus. Almighty God, multiply your grace and peace in every area of my life, in the name of Jesus. Every infirmity in my flesh against the manifestation of God's nature in my life, be cut-off by the power in the blood of Jesus. Almighty God, deliver me from spiritual weakness and empower me with your lifestyle, in the name of Jesus. Every demonic arrest in any area of my life, be terminated, in the name of Jesus. O Lord, arise and deliver me from the power of the devil and every evil character, in the name of Jesus. Father Lord, help me to live like you without regret, in the name of Jesus. Every satanic property in any area of my life, catch fire and burn to ashes, in the name of Jesus. Every yoke of iniquity in my life, break to pieces, in the name of Jesus. I command every part of my life to refuse to yield but to break Satan and sin, in the name of Jesus. Everything from the kingdom of darkness pulling me down to sin, be destroyed by the destroying power of God, in the name of Jesus. Everything that needs to happen for my life to be sanctified, body, soul and spirit, begin to happen, in the name of Jesus. I command the spirit that is in charge of uncleanness in my life to be bound and cast out of my life, in the name of Jesus. Let the power that enabled Jesus Christ to live above Satan and sin here in this world arrest me and do likewise in my life, in the name of Jesus. I command every part of my life to rise above Satan and sin forever, in the name of Jesus. Any evil force assigned to bring me low to serve Satan and sin, scatter and fail woefully, in the name of Jesus. Any fire of sin burning in any area of my life, be quenched by the speaking blood of Jesus, in the name of Jesus. Almighty God, plant the fruit of holiness and righteousness in my life, in the name of Jesus.

> But he *is* a Jew, which is one inwardly; and circumcision *is that* of the heart, in the spirit, *and* not in the letter; whose praise *is* not of men, but of God.
>
> — ROMANS 2:29

> Notwithstanding she shall be saved in childbearing, if they continue in faith and charity and holiness with sobriety.
>
> — 1 TIMOTHY 2:15

I command my heart to submit to divine circumcision that will uproot sin out of my life forever, in the name of Jesus. Let the Spirit of God capture every part of my heart and sanctify it, in the name of Jesus. I command my body, soul and spirit to surrender to the sanctification of the Lord Jesus, in the name of Jesus. Let the praising power of God possess me with the gift of praise and worship, in holiness without sin, in the name of Jesus. Father Lord, sanctify and empower me to continue in faith, charity and in holiness to eternity, in the name of Jesus. Every property of the devil in my life, be roasted by the fire of the Holy Ghost, in the name of Jesus. Let the speaking ability in the blood of Jesus speak death unto every demonic existence in my life forever, in the name of Jesus. Lord Jesus, inflict in me the sanctifying ability to live holy without sin the rest of my life on earth, in the name of Jesus. Mountain moving faith in Christ Jesus, move everything in me to attract your type of sanctification, in the name of Jesus. Let the destroying power in the resurrection power destroy every strength of sin and Satan in my life, in the name of Jesus. I command the yoke of inherited iniquity in my life to be broken to pieces, in the name of Jesus. Let the rain of judgmental fire as it was in the days of Sodom fall upon every structure of Satan and sin in my life, in the name of Jesus. Blood of Jesus, cleanse every mark of Satan and sin in my life and destroy their works without a trace, in the name of Jesus. I command every part of my life to receive the willing ability to say no to Satan and sin forever, in the name of Jesus.

Day 3

Expectations:

1. The destruction of every evil deposit and witchcraft plantation in your life.

2. Commanding the strength of Satan and sin to be crippled out of your life, family and destiny.

3. The destruction of every chain of sin and sickness affecting you.

4. The termination of every evil influence in any area of your life.

5. The termination of every satanic revival affecting the body of Christ these last days.

6. The destruction of every demonic spirit of 'the pride of life' affecting you.

7. The breaking of the yoke of worldly enjoyment, pleasures and every evil gathering against your life.

Every evil deposit and witchcraft plantation in my life, be uprooted and be wiped away by divine power, in the name of Jesus. Let the forces of witchcraft be defiled and be disengaged from every area of my life, in the name of Jesus. Let the ability to live holy begin to manifest in my life without a break, in the name of Jesus. I command the strength of Satan and sin to be crippled in every area of my life, in the name of Jesus. Blood of Jesus, enter into the battlefield of my life, fight for me and give me victory, in the name of Jesus.

Follow peace with all *men*, and holiness, without which no man shall see the Lord:

— HEBREWS 12:14

In holiness and righteousness before him, all the days of our life.

— LUKE 1:75

Let the holiness that will empower me to see the LORD and to live with Him eternally possess me, in the name of Jesus. Any chain of sin, Satan and hell in my life, visibly or invisibly, break to pieces, in the name of Jesus. Father Lord, equip me with holiness and righteousness all the days of my life, forever and ever, in the name of Jesus. I command every area of my life to lay aside every weight and the sin which is holding me in captive now, in the name of Jesus. Anointing to run my Christian race with patience to overcome easily every sin, possess me, in the name of Jesus. I command every part of me to be disengaged from Satan and sin; and be focused on Jesus forever, in the name of Jesus. Let the grace to look unto Jesus and to follow peace with all men come upon me, in the name of Jesus. Father Lord, circumcise my heart and purge me of every sin and evil presence, in the name of Jesus. Let the presence of the Holy Spirit dominate every evil presence and expel them out of my life, in the name of Jesus. I terminate every evil influence in any area of my life and I command the whole creation to fight for my purity, in the name of Jesus. I command every part of my life, body, soul and spirit to inhabit holiness in truth and in Spirit, in the name of Jesus. Father Lord, make me a holy influence in the church of the living God, the pillar and the ground of the truth, in the name of Jesus. I separate myself from those who defile the church and pollute the holy altar, in the name of Jesus. Without controversy, empower me to promote godliness, holy conversation and the revival in the body of Christ globally, in the name of Jesus. Father Lord, empower me and use me to revive the body of Christ globally, in the name of Jesus.

But as he which hath called you is holy, so be ye holy in all manner of conversation;

Because it is written, be ye holy; for I am holy.

— 1 PETER 1:15-16

Let the call of God in my life come along with holiness and all the manner of joy and holy conversation, in the name of Jesus. By God's mercy, I receive the holy nature of God without a minus, in the name of Jesus. Anointing to work for God and walk with Him in holiness and righteousness, fall upon me, in the name of Jesus. Any satanic revival in the body of Christ in these last days, be terminated by my last days contribution, in the name of Jesus. I break and loose myself from every satanic revival going on in the body of Christ, in the name of Jesus. Almighty God, use me and my ministry to raise renewed men and women that will overturn satanic activities in the body of Christ worldwide, in the name of Jesus. Let my maturity in Christ influence others to imitate Christ in me and to rise to defend the truth, in the name of Jesus. Father Lord, through me, raise men and women that will carry the work of God in truth and holiness all over the world, in the name of Jesus. Let men who are truly saved, sanctified and zealous for God be raised through me, in the name of Jesus. Empower me to practice self-denial and equip me with supernatural power to dethrone the devil in every community, in the name of Jesus. Almighty God, cloth me with humility and make me wise as serpents, harmless as doves and simple as children, in the name of Jesus. I receive the anointing and grace to be compassionate as Jesus and be strong in faith, not staggering in the promises of God, in the name of Jesus.

> Who shall ascend into the hill of the LORD? or who shall stand in his holy place?
>
> He that hath clean hands, and a pure heart; who hath not lifted up his soul unto vanity, nor sworn deceitfully.
>
> Truly God *is* good to Israel, *even* to such as are of a clean heart.
>
> — PSALMS 24:3-4; 73:1

Father Lord, take me to your hill and empower me to stand with you in holiness without defilement, in the name of Jesus. Blood of Jesus, clean my hands and heart and make me pure forever, in the name of Jesus. Let my body, soul and spirit be humbled before God and be delivered from vanity and deceit, in the name of Jesus. By the power of God's cleansing anointing, I command my heart to be perfectly cleansed, in the name of Jesus. I command every part of my life to be crucified to the world and the world crucified to me forever, in the name of Jesus. Let the authority in my faith and prayer lock and unlock, bind and loose with ease against evil kingdoms, in the name of Jesus. Let the rivers of the living waters flow into every area of my life unhindered, in the name of Jesus. By the power of God, I command every part of my life to be energized by the Holy Spirit, in the name of Jesus. Father Lord, empower me supernaturally with sound principles, saintly purpose and scriptural preaching, in the name of Jesus.

> Blessed *are* the pure in heart: for they shall see God.
>
> Be ye therefore perfect, even as your Father which is in heaven is perfect.
>
> — MATTHEW 5:8, 48

Let the purification anointing of God purify my heart and empower me to see God and to live with Him till eternity, in the name of Jesus. Blood of Jesus, flow into my heart and make it perfect without sin, in the name of Jesus. Demonic spirit of the love of the world in my life, I bind and cast you out, in the name of Jesus. Demonic spirit of lust of the flesh of the things of this world, I bind and cast you out, in the name of Jesus. Demonic spirit of lust of the eyes possessing my eyes, I bind and cast you out, in the name of Jesus. Demonic spirit of the pride of life in this world, I bind and cast you out of my life, in the name of Jesus. Almighty God, separate me by your power and distinguish me from evil affections and defiled desires of the world, in the name of Jesus. Almighty God, deliver me from every demonic program in this world, in the name of Jesus. I break and loose myself from all manner of carnal feasts in this world, in the name of Jesus.

> And the LORD thy God will circumcise thine heart, and the heart of thy seed, to love the LORD thy God with all thine heart, and with all thy soul, that thou mayest live.
>
> — DEUTERONOMY 30:6

> In whom also ye are circumcised with the circumcision made without hands, in putting off the body of the sins of the flesh by the circumcision of Christ:
>
> — COLOSSIANS 2:11

Let the circumcising power of God circumcise my heart and make it holy forever, in the name of Jesus. By the circumcising power of God, I command my body, soul and spirit to be circumcised, in the name of Jesus. Every sin in my flesh, I put you away by the speaking blood of Jesus, in the name of Jesus. Anything here on this world pushing me away from pleasing God, I bind and cast you out, in the name of Jesus. Blood of Jesus, flow into my foundation and empower me to live for God only, in the name of Jesus. Every yoke of worldliness in any area of my life, break to pieces, in the name of Jesus. Every yoke of disobedience against the word of God in my life, break to pieces, in the name of Jesus. All the little foxes in my life bringing me to defilement, I command you to die, in the name of Jesus. Every unprofitable character working against the plans of God in my life, receive destruction, in the name of Jesus. Almighty God, deliver me and set me free from worldly dressing, in the name of Jesus.

> And when Abram was ninety years old and nine, the LORD appeared to Abram, and said unto him, I *am* the Almighty God; walk before me, and be thou perfect.
>
> — GENESIS 17:1

> For we are glad, when we are weak, and ye are strong: and this also we wish, *even* your perfection.
>
> — 2 CORINTHIANS 13:9

Let the Almightiness of God make me perfect without sin and every demonic influence, in the name of Jesus. Let the walking power of God walk me out of every sin and make me perfect, in the name of Jesus. Any evil arrow fired against my relationship with God, I fire you back, in the name of Jesus. Father Lord, bring me into perfection without sin forever and ever, in the name of Jesus. Almighty God, help me to dress modestly according to your word, in the name of Jesus. I break and loose myself from the influence of worldly cares and day dreaming motivated by the devil, in the name of Jesus. Father Lord, deliver me from worldly pursuits and demonic ambitions, in the name of Jesus.

> Herein is our love made perfect, that we may have boldness in the day of judgment: because as he is, so are we in this world.
>
> There is no fear in love; but perfect love casteth out fear: because fear hath torment. He that feareth is not made perfect in love.
>
> — 1 JOHN 4:17, 18

Let the perfect fear of God deliver me from every satanic fear, in the name of Jesus. Let the love of God for Christ in me bring me to divine perfection, in the name of Jesus. Father Lord, help me to be bold before you and before every evil kingdom, in holiness and perfection without sin, in the name of Jesus. Every demonic fear in any area of my life, I bind and cast you out, in the name of Jesus. Every satanic judgment against my life, be reversed by the speaking blood of

Jesus, in the name of Jesus. I command the yoke of worldly enjoyment, pleasures and every evil gathering to break to pieces in my life, in the name of Jesus. Almighty God, deliver me from worldly music and every marine-spirit motivated dancing, in the name of Jesus. Every spirit of alcohol and drunkenness in my life, I bind and cast you out, in the name of Jesus. Every enemy of true purity in any area of my life, be frustrated, in the name of Jesus. Almighty God, deliver me from every carnal relationship, in the name of Jesus. Let the righteousness of Christ begin to rule and reign in my life, in the name of Jesus.

TWELVE

EVIDENCE OF A SANCTIFIED LIFE

DECREE-1

(2 Corinthians 4:2, Hebrews 4:9; 12:14; 2:11, Matthew 5:6, 8, 48, Philippians 1:9-11; 2:5, 21; 1:27, Psalms 15:1-5; 24:3-4, Psalms 133:1-3, Luke 1:74-75, Titus 2:14, Revelation 19:5-9, Deuteronomy 30:6, Matthew 22:37, Ephesians 4:3, 1 Corinthians 1:10, John 8:36; 17:22-23, Romans 13:10, 1 Corinthians 13:5-6, 1 Peter 1:15, 16, 1 John 4:17-21)

Day 1

Expectations:

1. The frustration of every arrow of spiritual fainting fired against your life and destiny.

2. The destruction of the yoke of living a fake life, deceit and craftiness.

3. Commanding every part of your life to manifest divine truth.

4. The destruction of every demonic arrow fired against your strength.

5. The destruction of every force blocking the manifestation of God's promise upon your life.

6. Commanding the rest and peace apportioned in God's word to begin to manifest in your life and destiny.

I break and loose myself from the arrows of spiritual fainting demons fired against my ministerial strength, in the name of Jesus. Anointing to renounce the hidden things of dishonesty, assigned to destroy my services to God, fall upon me, in the name of Jesus. Every yoke of living a fake life, craftiness and deceit in my life, break to pieces, in the name of Jesus. I command every part of my life to manifest divine truth with pure conscience in the sight of God and man, in the name of Jesus.

> But have renounced the hidden things of dishonesty, not walking in craftiness, nor handling the word of God deceitfully; but by manifestation of the truth commending ourselves to every man's conscience in the sight of God.
>
> — 2 CORINTHIANS 4:2

> There remaineth therefore a rest to the people of God.

> Follow peace with all *men*, and holiness, without which no man shall see the Lord:
>
> For both he that sanctifieth and they who are sanctified *are* all of one: for which cause he is not ashamed to call them brethren,
>
> — HEBREWS 4:9; 12:14; 2:11

Power of God to keep my salvation, sanctification and my relationship with God, manifest in my life, in the name of Jesus. By the power of God's mercy, O Lord, I receive divine support to fulfill my ministry, in the name of Jesus. Every demonic arrow fired against my strength to cause me to faint, be frustrated, in the name of Jesus. I command my body, soul and spirit to renounce every force of dishonesty that has been assigned against my walk with God, in the name of Jesus. I break and loose myself from every demon promoting sin in my life, in the name of Jesus. Every enemy of the reign of God's word in my life, be frustrated, in the name of Jesus. I command the powers of darkness that twist, manipulate and misinterpret the word of God to avoid me and my ministry, in the name of Jesus. Almighty God, help me to live holy all the days of my life on earth, in the name of Jesus. I command the manifestations of the devil in my life and ministry to be terminated, in the name of Jesus. Every enemy of the reign of the doctrine of truth and holiness in my life and ministry, fail woefully, in the name of Jesus. Almighty God, expose me to the life of purity and the manifestation of the power of the gospel, in the name of Jesus. I break and loose myself from the captivity of the gods of this world and mind blindness, in the name of Jesus. Let the light of the glorious gospel of Christ displace every work of the devil and the dark part of my life, in the name of Jesus. Almighty God, release your fear into my life without measure, in the name of Jesus. Any evil force, blocking the manifestation of God's promises in my life and ministry, scatter and fail woefully, in the name of Jesus. Father Lord, empower my ministry, my teaching and preaching to be mixed in faith with God's word, in the name of Jesus. Let the rest and peace apportioned to God's word begin to manifest in my life and ministry, in the name of Jesus. Father Lord, command your plans and purpose to be manifested in every area of my life, in the name of Jesus. Let the wrath of God fall upon every evil force militating against the reign of God and his word in my life, in the name of Jesus. Almighty God, lay your hand upon my body, soul, spirit and bring them to your rest and peace, in the name of Jesus. Every yoke of unbelief and doubts to the word of God in my life, break to pieces, in the name of Jesus. Every satanic limitation to the manifestation of God's word in my life and ministry, break to pieces, in the name of Jesus. I command everything in me to be receptive and accessible to God's word without restrictions, in the name of Jesus. I command every plan of God and the purpose of Christ to begin to manifest in my life, in the name of Jesus. Let the ceasing power and hindering power of the devil and his agents fail woefully in my life, in the name of Jesus. Almighty God, help me to labor with your strength to enter into your own rest, in the name of Jesus. I reject every promise and deceitful blessing that comes from the devil, in the name of Jesus. Let the quickness, powerfulness and sharpness in the word of God penetrate into every area of my life and destroy the works of the devil, in the name of Jesus. Father Lord, send your piercing power, dividing asunder anointing in your word into my body, soul and spirit for my deliverance, in the name of Jesus. I command every joint in my life, every marrow in my body to receive the cleansing power in the word of God, in the name of Jesus. Blood of Jesus, penetrate into my blood, all area of my life and purify them, in the name of Jesus. Every hidden power of darkness in any area of my life, be discerned, be located and be destroyed, in the name of Jesus. Let the evil intent and thoughts of my heart be discerned and destroyed by the word of God, in the name of Jesus. Almighty God, by your word, I stripe the works of the devil naked for destruction, in the name of Jesus. I command every part of my life, body, soul and spirit to die with Christ and resurrect with Him, in the name of Jesus. Father

Lord, help me to live the life of Christ, here on earth, in the name of Jesus. I break and loose myself from the yoke of every demonic control, in the name of Jesus. Almighty God, give me the grace to go through everything I must go through here on earth to make heaven at last, in the name of Jesus. Almighty God, gather me together and help me never to deny Christ forever and ever, in the name of Jesus.

> Blessed *are* they which do hunger and thirst after righteousness: for they shall be filled.
>
> Blessed *are* the pure in heart: for they shall see God.
>
> Be ye therefore perfect, even as your Father which is in heaven is perfect.
>
> — MATTHEW 5:6, 8, 48

(Anointing and boldness in Christ to open my mouth and teach God's word, fall upon me, in the name of Jesus. Father Lord, help me to be poor in Spirit and to always want more of you, in the name of Jesus. Heavenly father, let me never have enough of you in every area of my life with increasing desire to make heaven, in the name of Jesus. Let the mourning Spirit of God overshadow me with divine comfort in every area of my life, in the name of Jesus. Father Lord, fill me with your fruit of meekness without measure and enable me to inherit this earth, in the name of Jesus. Heavenly father, fill me with divine hunger and thirst after your kind of righteousness, in the name of Jesus. Let divine type of mercifulness begin to manifest in every area of my life, in the name of Jesus. By your grace, O Lord, empower every part of my life to obtain your mercy without measure, in the name of Jesus. Almighty God, send your purification power into my heart and foundation to penetrate into every part of me and sanctify me, in the name of Jesus. Father Lord, help me to spend the rest of my life here on earth, making peace without troubles, in the name of Jesus. Grace of God to be a peacemaker and anointing to see God and live with Him forever, fall upon me, in the name of Jesus.

Day 2

Expectations:

1. Receiving the joy and happiness that comes from God

2. Commanding the light of God to shine into every dark area of your life and destiny.

3. Commanding the removal of every demonic roadblock on your way to prosperity, success, righteous living and heaven.

4. The reversal of every evil judgment passed against you.

5. The expelling of every demonic spirit in any part of your body.

6. The destruction of every demonic bond and agreement against you

Father Lord, deliver me from every persecution, especially the ones that come with unrighteousness, in the name of Jesus. Anointing to do great and mighty things for God's kingdom and the grace to make heaven, fall upon me, in the name of Jesus. Every mockery, insult, persecution, injustice or evil against me, because of Christ's sake, bring me to heavenly joy and peace, in the name of Jesus. Let the rejoicing power of God from above overshadow my life in every situation, in the name of Jesus. Father Lord, release your happiness to gladden my life in every situation and reward me in heaven, in the name of Jesus. I command every part of my life to be turned into salt in this bitter world, in the name of Jesus. The salt of God in me will not lose its savor, but will sweeten the world in the midst troubles, in the name of Jesus. Almighty God, use me to bring hope to a hopeless world, in the name of Jesus. I command every part of my life to be good, in the name of Jesus. By the special grace and mercy of God, I command every part of my life to be a light of the world, in the name of Jesus. Every darkness in any area of my life, receive the light of God, in the name of Jesus. Almighty God, help my life, ministry and your image in me to bring revival, in the name of Jesus.

Anything here in this world, among the creation, hiding divine investment and power in my life, give up the ghost, in the name of Jesus. I command the whole creature to rise in power and announce all about God in me without restriction, in the name of Jesus. You the light of God in me, your time is up, begin to shine and spread all over the world, in the name of Jesus. I command every eye on earth to open and see the light of God in me, in the name of Jesus. You the light of God in me, burst out and spread to the whole creation, in the name of Jesus. Every stubborn darkness anywhere in the whole universe, receive the light of Christ and vanish, in the name of Jesus. I command all my activity here on earth to be good without bad, for divine glory to manifest, in the name of Jesus. By the forces invested in God's word in me, I command God's promises to be fulfilled positively through me, in the name of Jesus. Almighty God, help me never to have issue with your word, no matter how small, in the name of Jesus. Let the manifestation of God's word in my life and ministry save sinful souls and bring them to heaven, in the name of Jesus. Father Lord, prosper my teaching ministry and spread them all over the universe, in the name of Jesus. Every enemy of the positive manifestation of God's commandment in my life, fail woefully, in the name of Jesus. Almighty God, help me to be called great in your heavenly kingdom and not the least, in the name of Jesus. You the righteousness of God in me, rise and exceed the righteousness of the scribes and the Pharisees, in the name of Jesus. Every demonic roadblock on my way to heaven, be removed by heavenly forces, by God's mercy, in the name of Jesus. Almighty God, deliver me from the danger of hell and judgment, in the mighty name of Jesus. Every spirit of anger and unforgiving spirit assigned to take me to hell fire, I bind and cast you out, in the name of Jesus. Almighty God, bridle my tongue and close it up against evil speaking, in the name of Jesus. I break and lose my tongue from demonic arrest of evil utterances forever, in the name of Jesus. Every demonic arrest to my tongue and heart, receive deliverance by fire, in the name of Jesus.

Every agent of tongue and heart pollution, contamination and defilement, be frustrated out of my life, in the name of Jesus. Anointing to forgive from my heart and to settle every issue with my offenders, fall upon me, in the name of Jesus. I break and loose myself from malice, grudges and everything that harbors sin in the heart, in the name of Jesus. Let my memory, body, soul and spirit discharge everything that is designed to block my entry into heaven, in the name of Jesus. Father Lord by your mercy, cause my services here on earth to be accepted before you, in the name of Jesus. Every agreement, even with my adversaries that will qualify me for heaven, begin to take place, in the name of Jesus. Any demonic spirit in my eyes, ears and tongue, I bind and cast you out, in the name of Jesus. Father Lord, deliver me from police case, court case, hospital case and poverty case, in the name of Jesus. Any evil judgment passed against me, be reversed by the power in the speaking blood of Jesus, in the name of Jesus. Almighty God, provide for me and help me to pay all my debts, in the name of Jesus. Any spiritual or physical prison locking me behind the bars, open and release me, in the name of Jesus. Almighty God, deliver me from every kind of sexual perversion and unclean relationship, in the name of Jesus. Blood of Jesus, flow into my eyes, ears, hands, legs and tongues; deliver me from every pollution, defilement and contamination, in the name of Jesus. Every heart and organ pollution in my life, be delivered by the speaking blood of Jesus, in the name of Jesus. Any organ of my body, captured to take me to hell fire, be delivered or cut off, in the name of Jesus. Almighty God, take me far away from unprofitable marriage, evil relationships and every form of evil soul-tie, in the name of Jesus. Let the perishing power of the devil and his agents with a vow to take me to hell fire perish and die forever in my life, in the name of Jesus. Father Lord, deliver me from every marital problem, hostility, disagreement, separation and divorce, in the name of Jesus. I break and loose myself from every careless visitation, unclean conversation, evil plot and the spirit of lying, in the name of Jesus. Let my yes be my yes and my no be my no without sin, in the name of Jesus. Every spirit of unforgiveness, vengeance and retaliation, I bind and cast you out, in the name of Jesus. Father Lord, control and guide me to have the right manner of approach in every situation, in the name of Jesus. I break and loose myself from every trouble, fighting and quarrelling without peace, in the name of Jesus. Father Lord, impart your true love in me and the nine fruits of your Spirit, with perfect holiness, in the name of Jesus. I command the spirit of hatred and rejection in me and in others to be cast out from my affairs, in the name of Jesus. Father Lord, teach me to love my enemies without harm and sin, in the name of Jesus. I receive divine wisdom, knowledge and understanding on how to approach all manner of things, without sin, in the name of Jesus.

Day 3

Expectations:

1. Receiving the perfect nature of God and the ability to moderate things
2. Commanding the discharging nature of God to discharge every sin out of your life and destiny
3. Victory over temptation and persecution attempting to make you displease God
4. The destruction of every evil force contending against your relationship with God
5. Commanding the terribleness of God to descend on every problem and demonic challenges affecting your life
6. Complete deliverance from every satanic captivity against your life

Almighty God, show me how to handle difficult and impossible situations in the midst of my loved ones and enemies without doing wrong, in the name of Jesus. Father Lord, impart your character in me to relate with the just and the unjust, without sin, in the name of Jesus. I receive the perfect nature of God and the ability to moderate things without offending God and man, in the name of Jesus Matthew 5:1-48). (I command my body, soul and spirit to lay aside every weight and sin that is ministering against my life and ministry, in the name of Jesus. Let the discharging strength of God Almighty arise in my life to discharge every iota of sin in my life, in the name of Jesus. I receive power to run my Christian race with patience, without compromise, in the name of Jesus. By the power in God's looking ability, I queue up to look unto Jesus, the author and finisher of my faith, forever, in the name of Jesus. Let the joy that awaits me at the end of my life and ministry here on earth motivate me to live holy every day of my life here on earth, in the name of Jesus. Anointing to endure the cross, despise the shame attached to the gospel, the cross, fall upon me, in the name of Jesus. Every temptation and persecution on my way to please God, I receive victory over you, in the name of Jesus. Every arrow of weakness, fainting spirit and compromise fired against my life, I reject you, in the name of Jesus. Father Lord, help me to resist Satan and sin, even with the last drop of my blood, in the name of Jesus. Let the chastising of the Lord in my life make me a better Christian and bring me closer to God, in the name of Jesus. Anointing to continually lift up my hands towards God, and my knees without weakness, fall upon me, in the name of Jesus. Let the blood of Jesus make my life straight, without sin, to my last breath on earth, in the name of Jesus. Almighty God, blind and cripple any evil force militating against my sanctification, in the name of Jesus. I command every part of my life to follow peace with all men, in the name of Jesus. Let the compromising force from every satanic kingdom bow before me, in the name of Jesus. Anointing of God's mercy and grace to see God and live with Him forever, fall upon my life, in the name of Jesus. I command every area of my life to be married to God's grace and mercy; I refuse to be separated from God, in the name of Jesus. Any evil force, contending against my relationship with Christ and my birthright, scatter and fail woefully, in the name of Jesus. Almighty God, by your mercy, remove far away from me your rejecting power and accept my body, soul and spirit forever, in the name of Jesus. Let the destroying power in God's strength to destroy Satan, sin and its consequences in my life, in the name of Jesus. Every sound of Satan, sin and every evil trumpet in my life, be silenced by the voice of the speaking blood of Jesus, in the name of Jesus. Let the terribleness of God's anger descend upon the power of Satan, sin and every problem in my life; destroy them, in the name of Jesus. Almighty God, at my last moment here on earth, take me to the heavenly Jerusalem, to an innumerable company of angels, to the general assembly; to the church of the first born in heaven, in the name of Jesus. Let the creative power of God create God's holiness in me and keep me holy forever, in the name of Jesus. Lord Jesus, by your mercy, reconcile me back to God the father, God the Holy Ghost with everlasting covenant, in the name of Jesus. Let the blood of Jesus be sprinkled in every area of my life to cleanse me and make me pure, in the name of Jesus. Blood of Jesus, minister holiness in me forever, in the name of Jesus. Almighty God, repurchase me back with the speaking and pleadings of the voice of Jesus Christ, in the name of Jesus. I silence every blood speaking sin and all its consequences in my life, by the speaking blood of Jesus, in the name of Jesus. Let the blood that shook the earth speak into my foundation to rescue me from every satanic captivity, spiritually and physically, in the name of Jesus. Let the shaking power that shook the heaven and the earth, shake me out of every sin and land me to the domain of holiness without sin, forever, in the name of Jesus. Almighty God, by the invested power in the blood of Jesus, arise for my sake and deliver me where I need deliverance, in the name of Jesus. Every remaining problem in my life, be destroyed by the destroying power in the blood of Jesus, in the name of Jesus. Father Lord, take me away from every satanic kingdom and bring me to your kingdom, in the name of Jesus. Let my services to God here on earth be made pure and acceptable with reverence and godly fear, in the name of Jesus. By the power in God's consuming fire, I command Satan, sin and every evil structure in my life to be consumed by fire, in the name of Jesus-Hebrews 12:1-29). Almighty God, plant your image and likeness in every area of my life and destroy the image and work of the devil, in the name of Jesus. Let Christ be seen in me from every side, without the manifestation of the devil, in the name of Jesus. Every satanic embargo placed upon the manifestation of God's true nature in me, be lifted, in the name of Jesus. Every satanic dark room in any part of my life, receive divine shining light forever, in the name of Jesus. Almighty God, sanctify my body, soul, spirit; purge my conscience, in the name of Jesus. Father Lord, command your light to shine out of darkness everywhere I go, in the name of Jesus.

And this I pray, that your love may abound yet more and more in knowledge and *in* all judgment;

That ye may approve things that are excellent; that ye may be sincere and without offence till the day of Christ;

Being filled with the fruits of righteousness, which are by Jesus Christ, unto the glory and praise of God.

Let this mind be in you, which was also in Christ Jesus

For all seek their own, not the things which are Jesus Christ's.

Only let your conversation be as it becometh the gospel of Christ: that whether I come and see you, or else be absent, I may hear of your affairs, that ye stand fast in one spirit, with one mind striving together for the faith of the gospel;

— PHILIPPIANS 1:9-11; 2:5, 21; 1:27

Let the love of God in my life abound and connect to every area of my life, in the name of Jesus. In my knowledge and judgment in everything I do in life, let the love of God be honored, in the name of Jesus. Father Lord, by your love in my life, help me to discern things that are wrong, right or excellent before taking any decision and action, in the name of Jesus. By the power of God's love in me, let my actions be freed from every offense, in the name of Jesus. Almighty God, keep me in your love and purity till the day of Christ, in the name of Jesus. Almighty God, prepare everything in me to be filled with the fruits of righteousness, in the name of Jesus. Let my life be prepared and well-filled with God's nature unto the glory and praise of God, to the day of Christ, in the name of Jesus. Everything that will take place in my life from now, Oh Lord, use them to promote the gospel of Christ, in the name of Jesus.

Day 4

Expectations:

1. The frustration and uprooting of every satanic deposition in your life.
2. The destruction of everything in you promoting the deeds of strife and vainglory.
3. The destruction of every power conflicting and contending with the reign of Christ in your life.
4. The destruction of every arrow of spiritual weakness fired against you.
5. The destruction of every satanic establishment against your life and destiny.
6. Commanding every good thing from God to begin to manifest in your life.

Father Lord, deliver me from preaching Christ in envy, jealousy and strife, in the name of Jesus. Oh Lord, bring my mind to see things the way Jesus Christ would, in the name of Jesus. Every satanic deposition in me, be frustrated and be uprooted, in the name of Jesus. Anything in me, promoting the deeds of strife or vainglory, your time is up, be destroyed, in the name of Jesus. Father Lord, give me the exact mind that is in Christ Jesus and uproot every negativity in me, in the name of Jesus. Any power conflicting the rule and reign of Christ in me, I bind and cast you out, in the name of Jesus. I command everything in and outside me to seek to promote and honor Christ on earth, in the name of Jesus. I break and loose myself, especially my tongue from unprofitable conversations, in the name of Jesus. Henceforth, let my conversations be like that of Christ without defilement, in the name of Jesus. Any evil personality attached to my life to bring me to defiled conversations, I break away from you, in the name of Jesus. Let every information about me far and near be without blemish, spot or wrinkle, in the name of Jesus. I command every part of my body, soul and spirit to receive the light of the gospel of Christ, in the name of Jesus. Let the knowledge of Christ, his wisdom and understanding be released along with the power of holiness, in the name of Jesus. Every enemy of the manifestation of God's glory in my life, your time is up, be destroyed, in the name of Jesus. Almighty God, command your light in me to shine-out to the entire globe; let it outshine every darkness and restriction, in the name of Jesus. Every arrow of spiritual weakness fired against my life from every side, go back to your sender, in the name of Jesus.

> LORD, who shall abide in thy tabernacle? who shall dwell in thy holy hill?
>
> *He that* putteth not out his money to usury, nor taketh reward against the innocent. He that doeth these *things* shall never be moved.
>
> Who shall ascend into the hill of the LORD? or who shall stand in his holy place?
>
> He that hath clean hands, and a pure heart; who hath not lifted up his soul unto vanity, nor sworn deceitfully.
>
> — PSALMS 15:1-5; 24:3-4

(O Lord my God, the owners of heaven and earth, and its fullness thereof, meet me wherever I have been abandoned and supply my needs, in the name of Jesus. I command everything on earth to cooperate with the plans of God for my life and minister to me, in the name of Jesus. Let the blood of Jesus connect me to the saving and sanctifying experience from God, in the name of Jesus. I command all the blessings in the rivers, sea, ocean and everything in the waters to find their way into my life, in the name of Jesus. Every demonic establishment against my destiny, scatter and perish before me, in the name of Jesus. Anointing from God's grace and mercy, prepare me and bring me to God without sin, in the name of Jesus. Let the ascending power of God bring me to the hill of the Lord without iniquity, in the name of Jesus. Father Lord, make me holy, settle me and establish me in the holy place of God, in the name of Jesus. Blood of Jesus, wash my hands, purify my heart and make them clean, in the name of Jesus. By the power of God's lifting ability, father Lord, take me far away from vanity, evil oath and deceit, in the name of Jesus. Almighty God, sanctify me and bring me to receive your blessings, in the name of Jesus. Every good thing from the Lord, wherever you are, begin to manifest in my life with divine arrest, in the name of Jesus. Blood of Jesus, speak me into God's righteousness and his salvation, in the name of Jesus. Almighty God, use me to raise a generation of people that will seek your face and find you, in the name of Jesus. I command every stubborn ancient head, gate and door to be lifted for the King of glory to come into my life, in the name of Jesus. Any satanic block to the manifestation of my salvation and sanctification, be removed, in the name of Jesus. I command everlasting doors, evil threats of impossibilities to give way and disappear from me, in the name of Jesus. Almighty God, come into my life and take over without a rival, in the name of Jesus. Let the King of glory, the LORD Jesus Christ, take full control of everything concerning me, in the name of Jesus. Father Lord, by your strong and mighty name, the mighty Lord in battle, arise and fight for me, in the name of Jesus. Let the forces of God's soldiers force every evil authority on my way, the everlasting doors closed by the dark kingdom to open for me now, in the name of Jesus. Almighty God, show your almightiness in my life, sanctify me and empower me with all your gift, in the name of Jesus. Let the coming in of God's power into my life bring everything that will perfect my relationship with Christ forever, in the name of Jesus Psalms 24:1-10). (By God's abiding strength, I receive the mercy to abide in the word of God forever, in the name of Jesus. I break and loose myself from every demonic influence and corruption, in the name of Jesus. Anointing to honor God, fear Him and to maintain my integrity forever, fall upon me, in the name of Jesus. Let the dwelling ability and strength from God bring me to heaven at last and keep me forever, in the name of Jesus. Every divine instrument of God's sanctifying power, manifest in my life and sanctify me, in the name of Jesus. Father Lord, help me to walk uprightly from today till my last breath on earth, in the name of Jesus. Ancient of days, put your righteousness in me and empower me to speak the truth, in the name of Jesus. Blood of Jesus, flow into my tongue and discharge every work of the devil, in the name of Jesus. I break away and set myself free from the evil powers that promote evil, shame, reproach and disgrace, in the name of Jesus. Every evil force and defiler, my life is not your candidate, in the name of Jesus. Let the unchanging nature of God in doing good, completely arrest me and keep me holy forever, in the name of Jesus. I command the stopping power of the devil and his agents to bow before me and avoid me forever, in the name of Jesus. Almighty God, move me to use all the blessing you have given me rightly, in the name of Jesus. I command everything about me to refuse to give attention or service to the devil and his unrepentant agents, in the name of Jesus. Almighty God, use me to do good and to show justice to the innocent, in the name of Jesus. Any evil force, commissioned to move me out of divine coverage, divine security, fail woefully, in the name of Jesus-Psalms 15:1-5). Troubles, distress, persecution assigned to put me to fear, confusion and despair, fail woefully, in the name of Jesus. Anointing to bear in my body the dying of the Lord Jesus without giving up in living holy, possess me, in the name of Jesus. Let the destroying power in the name of God Almighty destroy every property of the devil in my life, in the name of Jesus.

Behold, how good and how pleasant *it is* for brethren to dwell together in unity!

It is like the precious ointment upon the head, that ran down upon the beard, *even* Aaron's beard: that went down to the skirts of his garments;

As the dew of Hermon, *and as the dew* that descended upon the mountains of Zion: for there the LORD commanded the blessing, *even* life for evermore.

— PSALMS 133:1-3

Day 5

Expectations:

1. Commanding the unity of the blessed trinity to manifest between you and other believers.
2. Complete deliverance from every demonic relationship affecting your life and destiny.
3. The frustration of every problem designed to separate you from God.
4. The destruction of every evil mark in your life, family and destiny.
5. Commanding an end to every form of famine affecting you (spiritual and physical famine).
6. Commanding God's deliverance to liberate and touch every part of your life.

Father Lord, bless me and bring me in your unity with your Son, Holy Spirit and my destiny helpers all over the world, in the name of Jesus. Let the unity of the blessed Holy Trinity manifest between me and believers all over the world, in the name of Jesus. If I am where I don't suppose to be, father Lord, take me to where I supposed to be, in the name of Jesus. By divine commandment from above, let the blessings of God begin to manifest in my life from every side, in the name of Jesus. Any evil mark in my life, visible or invisible, be cleansed by the crying blood of Jesus, in the name of Jesus. Almighty God, deliver me from every demonic relationship, in the name of Jesus. Every yoke of death to the life of God in my life, be destroyed and receive destruction, in the name of Jesus. Let the life of Christ begin to manifest in my mortal body against the plans of the devil and his agents, in the name of Jesus.

That he would grant unto us, that we being delivered out of the hand of our enemies might serve him without fear,

In holiness and righteousness before him, all the days of our life.

— LUKE 1:74-75

In the midst of corruption, defilement and pollution, father Lord, sanctify me and keep me holy, in the name of Jesus. I receive the divine strength to serve God with all my heart, without sin, forever and ever, in the name of Jesus. Divine grace to worship God, keep his commandments and statues, fall upon me, in the name of Jesus. Any problem in my life designed to separate me from God, be frustrated, in the name of Jesus. Father Lord, empower me to live holy and obey you in every situation I find myself, in the name of Jesus. I command every long-time problem in my life that is attacking my relationship with God to expire and die, in the name of Jesus. Prayer answering God, manifest in my situation and answer every prayer I have ever prayed, in the name of Jesus. Almighty God, send your angel to visit me with answers to my prayers and guide me into your path, in the name of Jesus. Any satanic roadblock on my way to victory and establishment be dismantled, in the name of Jesus. Almighty God, empower me to conceive everything good with power to deliver them to my generation, in the name of Jesus. Every spiritual and physical famine of God's righteousness in my life, be frustrated, in the name of Jesus. Father Lord, put your hand upon me and transfer your righteousness in me, in the name of Jesus. Every satanic opposition standing against the manifestation of divine purity in my life, be removed, in the name of Jesus. I command my body, soul and spirit to thirst, hunger and be saturated with divine purity, in the name of Jesus. Almighty God, visit me and transfer your nature into my life without measure, in the name of Jesus. I command every area of my life to be flooded with all manner of divine nature, in the name of Jesus. I command the doors leading to every organ of my body, soul and spirit to open and swallow divine purity, in the name of Jesus. Any part of my life lacking divine image and likeness, be filled with holiness, in the name of Jesus. Let my deliverance from above affect every part of my life without measure, in the name of Jesus. I break and loose myself from the presence of the devil and his contaminating agents, in the name of Jesus. I break and loose myself from the captivity of my enemies, Satan and sin, in the name of Jesus. Every fear from the kingdom of darkness, ministering against me, your time is up, disappear, in the name of Jesus. Almighty God, fill me with your fear, love and power without end, in the name of Jesus. Let my services to God Almighty be filled with God's fear, holiness and righteousness of Christ all the days of my life, in the name of Jesus. Every demonic plantation of sin in any area of my life, your time is up, be uprooted, in the name of Jesus. I break and loose myself from every demonic plantation in my body, soul and spirit in my dreams, in the name of Jesus. Any witchcraft animal living with me in the same house, manifest and die, in the name of Jesus.

That they may teach the young women to be sober, to love their husbands, to love their children,

— TITUS 2:14

And a voice came out of the throne, saying, praise our God, all ye his servants, and ye that fear him, both small and great.

And I heard as it were the voice of a great multitude, and as the voice of many waters, and as the voice of mighty thundering's, saying, Alleluia: for the Lord God omnipotent reigned.

Let us be glad and rejoice, and give honour to him: for the marriage of the Lamb is come, and his wife hath made herself ready.

And to her was granted that she should be arrayed in fine linen, clean and white: for the fine linen is the righteousness of saints.

And he saith unto me, Write, Blessed *are* they which are called unto the marriage supper of the Lamb. And he saith unto me, these are the true sayings of God.

— REVELATION 19:5-9

Let the aborting and miscarrying strength of God abort every root of sin in my life, in the name of Jesus. Let the saving and the redeeming power in the blood of Jesus penetrate into my foundation and sanctify me, in the name of Jesus. I command the strength of every iniquity assigned against my life to be broken by the speaking blood of Jesus, in the name of Jesus. Let the mobilizing power of God, mobilize every creature to rise against the devil, his agents, and every problem in my life, in the name of Jesus. Almighty God, fill me with your Spirit and bring me to a divine motivated purity, in the name of Jesus. Almighty God, bring me to experience a sanctification that will make me special and zealous of good work every day, in the name of Jesus. Fire of God, enter into my life and sanctify my spirit from sin, in the name of Jesus. Every evil presence around me, be destroyed by God's presence in me, in the name of Jesus. Every voice and presence of Satan, sin and trouble in my life, be silenced by the voice of Jesus. Every pillar of sin, mounted against my life, be uprooted, in the name of Jesus. Every satanic program, organized against my purity, be frustrated unto death, in the name of Jesus. Every enemy of the manifestation of God's glory in my life, be frustrated, in the name of Jesus. Almighty God, empower me to live a life of holiness to honor your name, every day and forever, in the name of Jesus. I command the power of Satan and sin in my life to be frustrated, in the name of Jesus. Let the judgment of the devil and his agents against my life be reversed, in the name of Jesus. Any evil personality promoting sin in my life, be exposed and disgraced, in the name of Jesus. Almighty God, deliver me from every enemy of my qualification to partake in the marriage supper of the Lamb, in the name of Jesus. Anointing to praise God in heaven after the rapture of the saints; to remain forever with God, fall upon me, in the name of Jesus. Any evil personality attached to my life to promote a sinful character in me, I break away from you, in the name of Jesus. Any evil presence in my life, influencing me to act against God's plan for my life, disappear forever, in the name of Jesus. I command the backbone of sin and Satan to be broken to pieces in my life, in the name of Jesus.

> And the LORD thy God will circumcise thine heart, and the heart of thy seed, to love the LORD thy God with all thine heart, and with all thy soul, that thou mayest live.
>
> — DEUTERONOMY 30:6

> Jesus said unto him, thou shalt love the Lord thy God with all thy heart, and with all thy soul, and with all thy mind.
>
> — MATTHEW 22:37

Father Lord, turn away my captivity and deliver me perfectly from the powers of Satan and sin, in the name of Jesus. Let the gathering power of God gather all my stolen and scattered blessing all over the world, spiritually and physically, in the name of Jesus.

Day 6

Expectations:

1. The circumcision of your heart.

2. Complete liberation from every form of captivity against your life.

3. Complete deliverance and liberation from greed, pride, anger, immorality, jealousy and covetousness.

4. Deliverance from every yoke of 'the love of money', financial misappropriation and unfaithfulness.

5. Complete deliverance from every counterfeit of the devil and his agents, designed to separate you from Christ.

6. The destruction of every satanic gang up against your purity and the manifestation of divine nature.

Ancient of days, circumcise my heart and cleanse me totally with cleansing power in the blood of Jesus, in the name of Jesus. I command my body, soul and spirit to receive the sword of God's circumcision ministry, in the name of Jesus. Almighty God, help me to love you, your word with all my heart, body, mind and spirit, in the name of Jesus. Almighty God, increase my hatred against Satan, sin and every evil presence, in the name of Jesus. Let the power that raised Jesus from the grave take me away from every captivity of Satan and sin, in the name of Jesus. Let the presentation power of God present me body, soul and spirit for sanctification, in the name of Jesus. By the power in the sanctifying anointing in the blood of Jesus, I command every part of my life to be sanctified, in the name of Jesus.

Endeavoring to keep the unity of the Spirit in the bond of peace.

Now I beseech you, brethren, by the name of our Lord Jesus Christ, that ye all speak the same thing, and *that* there be no divisions among you; but *that* ye be perfectly joined together in the same mind and in the same judgment.

— 1 CORINTHIANS 1:10

Father Lord, I willingly surrender and dedicate my body, soul and spirit, use me for your glory, in the name of Jesus. Anointing to walk worthy of the vocation wherewith you have called me to your glory, fall upon me, in the name of Jesus. Let everything in me by your grace, endeavor to keep the unity of the Spirit, in the bond of peace without compromise, in the name of Jesus. Father Lord, deliver me from living a hypocritical life and practicing religion without the righteousness of Christ, in the name of Jesus. Almighty God, deliver me from manifesting your gifts without the grace of living a holy life, in the name of Jesus. I break and loose myself from greed, pride, anger, immorality, jealousy and covetousness, in the name of Jesus. Every yoke of the love of money, financial misappropriation and unfaithfulness to my family in my life, break to pieces, in the name of Jesus. Almighty God, deliver me from the counterfeit of the devil and his agents, designed to separate me from Christ, in the name of Jesus. I disengage myself from operating with power without holiness and the fruits of the Spirit of God, in the name of Jesus. I command all things, every creature to frustrate the works of the devil and his agents in every area of my life, in the name of Jesus. Almighty God, allocate every good thing you have created to my life in abundance, in the name of Jesus. Every demonic voice militating against the rule and reign of God's voice in my life, be silenced by the speaking blood of Jesus. Let the multiplying power of God multiply his nature into my life without measure, in the name of Jesus. Galatians 1:10; John 5:41; 10:10 … I receive divine motivated power without fear to please God at all cost, in every situation, in the name of Jesus. I withdraw myself from serving the devil, his agents and the things of the world and I dedicate my services to God, in the name of Jesus. Let my promotion, prosperity, and breakthrough come from God and not from the corrupting influence of the world, in the name of Jesus. Every good thing that must come to me shall be purified and approve by God, in the name of Jesus. Almighty God, bring me into your kingdom through your son, Jesus Christ, in the name of Jesus. I break and loose myself from the devil and his agents in this world and in the spiritual realm, in the name of Jesus. Every good thing the devil has stolen from me, let the restoration power of God restore them back, in the name of Jesus. Lord Jesus, intervene in my life and give your kind of life in abundance, in the name of Jesus. Ancient of days, restore my lost spiritual life and energize me to pray aright, in the name of Jesus. Father Lord, by your mercy, bring your kingdom right inside my heart, body, soul and spirit, in the name of Jesus. Almighty God, fill every part of my life with the spirit of forgiveness and purity, in the name of Jesus. Empower me Lord to use everything, all my blessings, to please you without reserve, in the name of Jesus. Every satanic gang up against my purity and the manifestation of divine nature, scatter and fail woefully, in the name of Jesus. By the power of God's renewal grace, I receive divine newness in every part of my life, in the name of Jesus. Every demonic affliction, poverty and lack in my life assigned to defile me, fail woefully, in the name of Jesus.

If the Son therefore shall make you free, ye shall be free indeed.

And the glory which thou gavest me I have given them; that they may be one, even as we are one:

I in them, and thou in me, that they may be made perfect in one; and that the world may know that thou hast sent me, and hast loved them, as thou hast loved me.

— JOHN 8:36; 17:22-23

I command my deliverance to manifest only through Christ by God's mercy, in the name of Jesus. Let the spirit of unity, oneness from above manifest before me and among all true believers, in the name of Jesus. I command my entire life, in and out to be taken over by Christ for purity and preservation to eternity, in the name of Jesus. Every enemy of the manifestation of the perfect lifestyle of Christ in my life, be frustrated, in the name of Jesus. Father Lord, fill my morning, afternoon, night and every moment of my life with your presence, in the name of Jesus. Let the arresting power of the devil and his agents to sin, fail woefully in my life, in the name of Jesus. Every stone of Satan and sin raised against me, drop by divine intervention, in the name of Jesus. Almighty God, deliver me from sin and sanctify me in and out, in the name of Jesus. Every good-looking thing, prepared by the devil to entice me to sin, I reject you and the devil, in the name of Jesus. Let the accusing strength of the devil and his polluting power fail woefully in my life, in the name of Jesus. Almighty God, help me to recover my true identity and likeness without struggle, in the name of Jesus. Let the blessing of God in his grace and mercy flow into my life without hindrance, in the name of Jesus. Every enemy of the manifestation of God's lifestyle in my life, be frustrated, in the name of Jesus.

Love worketh no ill to his neighbor: therefore, love *is* the fulfilling of the law.

— ROMANS 13:10

Doth not behave itself unseemly, seeketh not her own, is not easily provoked, thinketh no evil;

Rejoiceth not in iniquity, but rejoiceth in the truth;

— 1 CORINTHIANS 13:5-6

Every anti-love of God in my life, be frustrated without survival, in the name of Jesus. Father Lord, deposit in me your type of love without measure, in the mighty name of Jesus. Let the enduring power and anointing to suffer-long in God's charity, begin to manifest in my life, in the name of Jesus. Let the charity to overcome envy, pride, jealousy, malice and all the lifestyle of the devil begin to occupy every part of my life, in the name of Jesus. I break and loose myself from every manifestation that lacks the fruits of the spirit, in the name of Jesus. Father Lord, release into my life your abundant, sufficient, sustaining and strengthening grace to keep your type of holiness in me forever, in the name of Jesus. Almighty God, sanctify me inwardly and outwardly and keep me holy all the days of my life, in the name of Jesus.

Day 7

Expectations:

1. Commanding God's holiness to touch every area of your life
2. The destruction of every satanic defiling agent assigned against your life and destiny
3. Commanding every evil to fade away from your life forever
4. The frustration of every attempt to separate you from God.
5. The scattering of every demonic developing force assigned to develop evil in your life.
6. The destruction of everything working against the manifestation of God's perfect love and fear in your life.

Let the nature of God in and outside me receive the company of eternal weight and abiding grace forever, in the name of Jesus.

> But as he which hath called you is holy, so be ye holy in all manner of conversation;
>
> Because it is written, be ye holy; for I am holy.
>
> — 1 PETER 1:15, 16

Let my calling and services to God embrace God's holiness without delay, in the name of Jesus. Father Lord, empower me to resemble you in everything, especially in holiness, in the name of Jesus. I command my holiness from God to touch every area of my life, even in all manner of conversation, in the name of

Jesus. Father Lord, enter into my life with all your qualities and likeness without measure, in the name of Jesus. I break and loose myself from every satanic defiling agent that has been assigned to defile my life and separate me from God, in the name of Jesus. By the power of God's abiding presence in my life, I command evil to fade away from my life forever, in the name of Jesus. Almighty God, invade my life and capture me completely with your kind of nature, in the name of Jesus. Let the depriving power of God deny the devil and his agents access into my life, forever, in the name of Jesus. By the power of God's miscarrying anointing, I command every work of the devil and his agent to be miscarried out of my life, in the name of Jesus. Let the presence of Satan and sin be completely abolished from my life, forever, in the name of Jesus.

Herein is our love made perfect, that we may have boldness in the day of judgment: because as he is, so are we in this world.

There is no fear in love; but perfect love casteth out fear: because fear hath torment. He that feareth is not made perfect in love.

We love him, because he first loved us.

If a man say, I love God, and hateth his brother, he is a liar: for he that loveth not his brother whom he hath seen, how can he love God whom he hath not seen?

And this commandment have we from him, that he who loveth God love his brother also.

— 1 JOHN 4:17-21

Let the love of God in me be transformed exactly like the love of Christ to the world, in the name of Jesus. Father Lord, arise in your power and perfect your love in my life, in the name of Jesus. By the power of God's love in my life, I receive the grace to be as bold as God before every creature, in the name of Jesus. Every demonic inflicted fear in my life, be displaced with the perfect fear of God, in the name of Jesus. Anything anywhere, working against the manifestation of God's perfect love and fear in my life, receive death, in the name of Jesus. Let my love for God exceed the love I have for any creature, including myself, in the name of Jesus. Let the love of God in me hate what God hates and love what God loves, in the name of Jesus. Lord Jesus, help me by your mercy to love exactly the way you love without discrimination, in the name of Jesus. Almighty God, by the power in your word, two-edged sword, cut me off from Satan, sin and every evil, forever, in the name of Jesus. Blood of Jesus, speak me out of every evil presence and satanic demonstration, in the name of Jesus. Every sinful inheritance in my life, be uprooted, in the name of Jesus. Almighty God, deliver me from Satan, sin and use me as your instrument to deliver others, in the name of Jesus. Any evil mouth speaking sin into my life, close and speak no more, in the name of Jesus. Let the demonic developing force assigned to develop evil in my life scatter and perish, in the name of Jesus.

THIRTHEEN

EVIDENCE OF A SANCTIFIED LIFE -2

DECREE-1

(2 Corinthians 4:2, Hebrews 4:9; 12:14; 2:11, Matthew 5:6, 8, 48, Philippians 1:9-11; 2:5, 21; 1:27)

Day 1

Expectations:

1. Deliverance from every arrow fired against you by spiritual fainting demons
2. Deliverance from every hidden thing of dishonesty assigned to destroy your service to God
3. The destruction of every demonic arrow fired against your strength
4. The destruction of every yoke of unbelief and doubt

I break and loose myself from the arrows of spiritual fainting demons fired against my ministerial strength, in the name of Jesus. Anointing to renounce the hidden things of dishonesty, assigned to destroy my services to God, fall upon me, in the name of Jesus. Every yoke of living a fake life, craftiness and deceit in my life, break to pieces, in the name of Jesus. I command every part of my life to manifest divine truth with pure conscience in the sight of God and man, in the name of Jesus.

> But have renounced the hidden things of dishonesty, not walking in craftiness, nor handling the word of God deceitfully; but by *manifestation* of the truth commending ourselves to every man's conscience in the sight of God.
>
> — 2 CORINTHIANS 4:2

> There remaineth therefore a rest to the people of God.
>
> Follow peace with all *men*, and holiness, without which no man shall see the Lord:
>
> For both he that sanctifieth and they who are sanctified *are* all of one: for which cause he is not ashamed to call them brethren,
>
> — HEBREWS 4:9; 12:14; 2:11

Power of God to keep my salvation, sanctification and my relationship with God, manifest in my life, in the name of Jesus. By the power of God's mercy, O Lord, I receive divine support to fulfil my ministry, in the name of Jesus. Every demonic arrow fired against my strength to cause me to faint, be frustrated, in the name of Jesus. I command my body, soul and spirit to renounce every force of dishonesty that has been assigned against my walk with God, in the name of Jesus. I break and loose myself from every demon promoting sin in my life, in the name of Jesus. Every enemy of the reign of God's word in my life, be frustrated, in the name of Jesus. I command the powers of darkness that twist, manipulate and misinterpret the word of God to avoid me and my ministry, in the name of

Jesus. Almighty God, help me to live holy all the days of my life on earth, in the name of Jesus. I command the manifestations of the devil in my life and ministry to be terminated, in the name of Jesus. Every enemy of the reign of the doctrine of truth and holiness in my life and ministry, fail woefully, in the name of Jesus. Almighty God, expose me to the life of purity and the manifestation of the power of the gospel, in the name of Jesus. I break and loose myself from the captivity of the gods of this world and mind blindness, in the name of Jesus. Let the light of the glorious gospel of Christ displace every work of the devil and the dark part of my life, in the name of Jesus. Almighty God, release your fear into my life without measure, in the name of Jesus. Any evil force, blocking the manifestation of God's promises in my life and ministry, scatter and fail woefully, in the name of Jesus. Father Lord, empower my ministry, my teaching and preaching to be mixed in faith with God's word, in the name of Jesus. Let the rest and peace apportioned to God's word begin to manifest in my life and ministry, in the name of Jesus. Father Lord, command your plans and purpose to be manifested in every area of my life, in the name of Jesus. Let the wrath of God fall upon every evil force militating against the reign of God and his word in my life, in the name of Jesus. Almighty God, lay your hand upon my body, soul, spirit and bring them to your rest and peace, in the name of Jesus. Every yoke of unbelief and doubts to the word of God in my life, break to pieces, in the name of Jesus. Every satanic limitation to the manifestation of God's word in my life and ministry, break to pieces, in the name of Jesus. I command everything in me to be receptive and accessible to God's word without restrictions, in the name of Jesus. I command every plan of God and the purpose of Christ to begin to manifest in my life, in the name of Jesus. Let the ceasing power and hindering power of the devil and his agents fail woefully in my life, in the name of Jesus. Almighty God, help me to labor with your strength to enter into your own rest, in the name of Jesus. I reject every promise and deceitful blessing that comes from the devil, in the name of Jesus. Let the quickness, powerfulness and sharpness in the word of God penetrate into every area of my life and destroy the works of the devil, in the name of Jesus. Father Lord, send your piercing power, dividing asunder anointing in your word into my body, soul and spirit for my deliverance, in the name of Jesus. I command every joint in my life, every marrow in my body to receive the cleansing power in the word of God, in the name of Jesus. Blood of Jesus, penetrate into my blood, all area of my life and purify them, in the name of Jesus. Every hidden power of darkness in any area of my life, be discerned, be located and be destroyed, in the name of Jesus. Let the evil intent and thoughts of my heart be discerned and destroyed by the word of God, in the name of Jesus. Almighty God, by your word, I stripe the works of the devil naked for destruction, in the name of Jesus. I command every part of my life, body, soul and spirit to die with Christ and resurrect with Him, in the name of Jesus. Father Lord, help me to live the life of Christ, here on earth, in the name of Jesus. I break and loose myself from the yoke of every demonic control, in the name of Jesus. Almighty God, give me the grace to go through everything I must go through here on earth to make heaven at last, in the name of Jesus. Almighty God, gather me together and help me never to deny Christ forever and ever, in the name of Jesus.

Blessed *are* they which do hunger and thirst after righteousness: for they shall be filled.

Blessed *are* the pure in heart: for they shall see God.

Be ye therefore perfect, even as your Father which is in heaven is perfect.

— MATTHEW 5:6, 8, 48

(Anointing and boldness in Christ to open my mouth and teach God's word, fall upon me, in the name of Jesus. Father Lord, help me to be poor in Spirit and to always want more of you, in the name of Jesus. Heavenly father, let me never have enough of you in every area of my life with increasing desire to make heaven, in the name of Jesus. Let the mourning Spirit of God overshadow me with divine comfort in every area of my life, in the name of Jesus. Father Lord, fill me with your fruit of meekness without measure and enable me to inherit this earth, in the name of Jesus. Heavenly father, fill me with divine hunger and thirst after your kind of righteousness, in the name of Jesus. Let divine type of mercifulness begin to manifest in every area of my life, in the name of Jesus. By your grace, O Lord, empower every part of my life to obtain your mercy without measure, in the name of Jesus. Almighty God, send your purification power into my heart and foundation to penetrate into every part of me and sanctify me, in the name of Jesus. Father Lord, help me to spend the rest of my life here on earth, making peace without troubles, in the name of Jesus. Grace of God to be a peacemaker and anointing to see God and live with Him forever, fall upon me, in the name of Jesus. Father Lord, deliver me from every persecution, especially the ones that come with unrighteousness, in the name of Jesus. Anointing to do great and mighty things for God's kingdom and the grace to make heaven, fall upon me, in the name of Jesus.

Day 2

Expectations:

1. **Commanding divine joy and happiness to be your portion**
2. **The destruction of every form of darkness in any area of your life**
3. **The destruction of every enemy of the positive manifestation of God's commandment in your life**
4. **Releasing your tongue from every form of demonic arrest**

Every mockery, insult, persecution, injustice or evil against me, because of Christ's sake, bring me to heavenly joy and peace, in the name of Jesus. Let the rejoicing power of God from above overshadow my life in every situation, in the name of Jesus. Father Lord, release your happiness to gladden my life in every situation and reward me in heaven, in the name of Jesus. I command every part of my life to be turned into salt in this bitter world, in the name of Jesus. The salt of God in me will not lose its savor, but will sweeten the world in the midst troubles, in the name of Jesus. Almighty God, use me to bring hope to a hopeless world, in the name of Jesus. I command every part of my life to be good, in the name of Jesus. By the special grace and mercy of God, I command every part of my life to be a light of the world, in the name of Jesus. Every darkness in any area of my life, receive the light of God, in the name of Jesus. Almighty God, help my life, ministry and your image in me to bring revival, in the name of Jesus. Anything here in this world, among the creation, hiding divine investment and power in my life, give up the ghost, in the name of Jesus. I command the whole creature to rise in power and announce all about God in me without restriction, in the name of Jesus. You the light of God in me, your time is up, begin to shine and spread all over the world, in the name of Jesus. I command every eye on earth to open and see the light of God in me, in the name of Jesus. You the light of God in me, burst out and spread to the whole creation, in the name of Jesus. Every stubborn darkness anywhere in the whole universe, receive the light of Christ and vanish, in the name of Jesus. I command all my activity here on earth to be good without bad, for divine glory to manifest, in the name of Jesus. By the forces invested in God's word in me, I command God's promises to be fulfilled positively through me, in the name of Jesus. Almighty God, help me never to have issue with your word, no matter how small, in the name of Jesus. Let the manifestation of God's word in my life and ministry save sinful souls and bring them to heaven, in the name of Jesus. Father Lord, prosper my teaching ministry and spread them all over the universe, in the name of Jesus. Every enemy of the positive manifestation of God's commandment in my life, fail woefully, in the name of Jesus. Almighty God, help me to be called great in your heavenly kingdom and not the least, in the name of Jesus. You the righteousness of God in me, rise and exceed the righteousness of the scribes and the Pharisees, in the name of Jesus. Every demonic roadblock on my way to heaven, be removed by heavenly forces, by God's mercy, in the name of Jesus. Almighty God, deliver me from the danger of hell and judgment, in the mighty name of Jesus. Every spirit of anger and unforgiving spirit assigned to take me to hell fire, I bind and cast you out, in the name of Jesus. Almighty God, bridle my tongue and close it up against evil speaking, in the name of Jesus. I break and lose my tongue from demonic arrest of evil utterances forever, in the name of Jesus. Every demonic arrest to my tongue and heart, receive deliverance by fire, in the name of Jesus. Every agent of tongue and heart pollution, contamination and defilement, be frustrated out of my life, in the name of Jesus. Anointing to forgive from my heart and to settle every issue with my offenders, fall upon me, in the name of Jesus. I break and loose myself from malice, grudges and everything that harbors sin in the heart, in the name of Jesus. Let my memory, body, soul and spirit discharge everything that is designed to block my entry into heaven, in the name of Jesus.

Father Lord by your mercy, cause my services here on earth to be accepted before you, in the name of Jesus. Every agreement, even with my adversaries that will qualify me for heaven, begin to take place, in the name of Jesus. Any demonic spirit in my eyes, ears and tongue, I bind and cast you out, in the name of Jesus. Father Lord, deliver me from police case, court case, hospital case and poverty case, in the name of Jesus. Any evil judgment passed against me, be reversed by the power in the speaking blood of Jesus, in the name of Jesus. Almighty God, provide for me and help me to pay all my debts, in the name of Jesus. Any spiritual or physical prison locking me behind the bars, open and release me, in the name of Jesus. Almighty God, deliver me from every kind of sexual perversion and unclean relationship, in the name of Jesus. Blood of Jesus, flow into my eyes, ears, hands, legs and tongues; deliver me from every pollution, defilement and contamination, in the name of Jesus. Every heart and organ pollution in my life, be delivered by the speaking blood of Jesus, in the name of Jesus. Any organ of my body, captured to take me to hell fire, be delivered or cut off, in the name of Jesus. Almighty God, take me far away from unprofitable marriage, evil relationships and every form of evil soul-tie, in the name of Jesus. Let the perishing power of the devil and his agents with a vow to take me to hell fire perish and die forever in my life, in the name of Jesus. Father Lord, deliver me from every marital problem, hostility, disagreement, separation and divorce, in the name of Jesus. I break and loose myself from every careless visitation, unclean conversation, evil plot and the spirit of lying, in the name of Jesus. Let my yes be my yes and my no be my no without sin, in the name of Jesus. Every spirit of unforgiveness, vengeance and retaliation, I bind and cast you out, in the name of Jesus. Father Lord, control and guide me to have the right manner of approach in every situation, in the name of Jesus. I break and loose myself from every trouble, fighting and quarrelling without peace, in the name of Jesus. Father Lord, impart your true love in me and the nine fruits of your Spirit, with perfect holiness, in the name of Jesus. I command the spirit of hatred and rejection in me and in others to be cast out from my affairs, in the name of Jesus. Father Lord, teach me to love my enemies without harm and sin, in the name of Jesus. I receive divine wisdom, knowledge and understanding on how to approach all manner of things, without sin, in the name of Jesus. Almighty God, show me how to handle difficult and impossible situations in the midst of my loved ones and enemies without doing wrong, in the name of Jesus. Father Lord, impart your character in me to relate with the just and the unjust, without sin, in the name of Jesus. I receive the perfect nature of God and the ability to moderate things without offending God and man, in the name of Jesus Matthew 5:1-48).

Day 3

Expectations:

1. **Commanding your body and soul to lay aside every weight and sin**
2. **Receiving the grace and power to run your Christian race patiently without compromise**
3. **Victory over every temptation and persecution on your way to pleasing God**
4. **Commanding the compromising force from every satanic kingdom to bow before you**

I command my body, soul and spirit to lay aside every weight and sin that is ministering against my life and ministry, in the name of Jesus. Let the discharging strength of God Almighty arise in my life to discharge every iota of sin in my life, in the name of Jesus. I receive power to run my Christian race with patience, without compromise, in the name of Jesus. By the power in God's looking ability, I queue up to look unto Jesus, the author and finisher of my faith, forever, in the name of Jesus. Let the joy that awaits me at the end of my life and ministry here on earth motivate me to live holy every day of my life here on earth, in the name of Jesus. Anointing to endure the cross, despise the shame attached to the gospel, the cross, fall upon me, in the name of Jesus. Every temptation and persecution on my way to please God, I receive victory over you, in the name of Jesus. Every arrow of weakness, fainting spirit and compromise fired against my life, I reject you, in the name of Jesus. Father Lord, help me to resist Satan and sin, even with the last drop of my blood, in the name of Jesus. Let the chastising of the Lord in my life make me a better Christian and bring me closer to God, in the name of Jesus. Anointing to continually lift up my hands towards God, and my knees without weakness, fall upon me, in the name of Jesus. Let the blood of Jesus make my life straight, without sin, to my last breath on earth, in the name of Jesus. Almighty God, blind and cripple any evil force militating against my sanctification, in the name of Jesus. I command every part of my life to follow peace with all men, in the name of Jesus. Let the compromising force from every satanic kingdom bow before me, in the name of Jesus. Anointing of God's mercy and grace to see God and live with Him forever, fall upon my life, in the name of Jesus. I command every area of my life to be married to God's grace and mercy; I refuse to be separated from God, in the name of Jesus. Any evil force, contending against my relationship with Christ and my birthright, scatter and fail woefully, in the name of Jesus. Almighty God, by your mercy, remove far away from me your rejecting power and accept my body, soul and spirit forever, in the name of Jesus. Let the destroying power in God's strength to destroy Satan, sin and its consequences in my life, in the name of Jesus. Every sound of Satan, sin and every evil trumpet in my life, be silenced by the voice of the speaking blood of Jesus, in the name of Jesus. Let the terribleness of God's anger descend upon the power of Satan, sin and every problem in my life; destroy them, in the name of Jesus. Almighty God, at my last moment here on earth, take me to the heavenly Jerusalem, to an innumerable company of angels, to the general assembly; to the church of the first born in heaven, in the name of Jesus. Let the creative power of God create God's holiness in me and keep me holy forever, in the name of Jesus. Lord Jesus, by your mercy, reconcile me back to God the father, God the Holy Ghost with everlasting covenant, in the name of Jesus. Let the blood of Jesus be sprinkled in every area of my life to cleanse me and make me pure, in the name of Jesus. Blood of Jesus, minister holiness in me forever, in the name of Jesus. Almighty God, repurchase me back with the speaking and pleadings of the voice of Jesus Christ, in the name of Jesus. I silence every blood speaking sin and all its consequences in my life, by the speaking blood of Jesus, in the name of Jesus. Let the blood that shook the earth speak into my foundation to rescue me from every satanic captivity, spiritually and physically, in the name of Jesus. Let the shaking power that shook the heaven and the earth, shake me out of every sin and land me to the domain of holiness without sin, forever, in the name of Jesus. Almighty God, by the invested power in the blood of Jesus, arise for my sake and deliver me where I need deliverance, in the name of Jesus. Every remaining problem in my life, be destroyed by the destroying power in the blood of Jesus, in the name of Jesus. Father Lord, take me away from every satanic kingdom and bring me to your kingdom, in the name of Jesus. Let my services to God here on earth be made pure and acceptable with reverence and godly fear, in the name of Jesus. By the power in God's consuming fire, I command Satan, sin and every evil structure in my life to be consumed by fire, in the name of Jesus-Hebrews 12:1-29). Almighty God, plant your image and likeness in every area of my life and destroy the image and work of the devil, in the name of Jesus. Let Christ be seen in me from every side, without the manifestation of the devil, in the name of Jesus. Every satanic embargo placed upon the manifestation of God's true nature in me, be lifted, in the name of Jesus. Every satanic dark room in any part of my life, receive divine shining light forever, in the name of Jesus. Almighty God, sanctify my body, soul, spirit; purge my conscience, in the name of Jesus. Father Lord, command your light to shine out of darkness everywhere I go, in the name of Jesus.

And this I pray, that your love may abound yet more and more in knowledge and *in* all judgment;

That ye may approve things that are excellent; that ye may be sincere and without offence till the day of Christ;

Being filled with the fruits of righteousness, which are by Jesus Christ, unto the glory and praise of God.

Let this mind be in you, which was also in Christ Jesus:

> For all seek their own, not the things which are Jesus Christ's.
>
> Only let your conversation be as it becometh the gospel of Christ: that whether I come and see you, or else be absent, I may hear of your affairs, that ye stand fast in one spirit, with one mind striving together for the faith of the gospel;
>
> — PHILIPPIANS 1:9-11; 2:5, 21; 1:27

Let the love of God in my life abound and connect to every area of my life, in the name of Jesus. In my knowledge and judgment in everything I do in life, let the love of God be honored, in the name of Jesus. Father Lord, by your love in my life, help me to discern things that are wrong, right or excellent before taking any decision and action, in the name of Jesus. By the power of God's love in me, let my actions be freed from every offense, in the name of Jesus. Almighty God, keep me in your love and purity till the day of Christ, in the name of Jesus. Almighty God, prepare everything in me to be filled with the fruits of righteousness, in the name of Jesus. Let my life be prepared and well-filled with God's nature unto the glory and praise of God, to the day of Christ, in the name of Jesus. Everything that will take place in my life from now, Oh Lord, use them to promote the gospel of Christ, in the name of Jesus. Father Lord, deliver me from preaching Christ in envy, jealousy and strife, in the name of Jesus. Oh Lord, bring my mind to see things the way Jesus Christ would, in the name of Jesus. Every satanic deposition in me, be frustrated and be uprooted, in the name of Jesus. Anything in me, promoting the deeds of strife or vainglory, your time is up, be destroyed, in the name of Jesus. Father Lord, give me the exact mind that is in Christ Jesus and uproot every negativity in me, in the name of Jesus. Any power conflicting the rule and reign of Christ in me, I bind and cast you out, in the name of Jesus.

Day 4

Expectations:

1. **Commanding everything in and outside you to seek to promote and honor Christ**

2. **The destruction of every evil personality attached to your life to bring you to defiled conversations**

3. **Commanding every part of your body, soul and spirit to receive the light of the gospel**

4. **Commanding all information about you far and near to be without blemish, spot and wrinkle**

I command everything in and outside me to seek to promote and honor Christ on earth, in the name of Jesus. I break and loose myself, especially my tongue from unprofitable conversations, in the name of Jesus. Henceforth, let my conversations be like that of Christ without defilement, in the name of Jesus. Any evil personality attached to my life to bring me to defiled conversations, I break away from you, in the name of Jesus. Let every information about me far and near be without blemish, spot or wrinkle, in the name of Jesus. I command every part of my body, soul and spirit to receive the light of the gospel of Christ, in the name of Jesus. Let the knowledge of Christ, his wisdom and understanding be released along with the power of holiness, in the name of Jesus. Every enemy of the manifestation of God's glory in my life, your time is up, be destroyed, in the name of Jesus. Almighty God, command your light in me to shine-out to the entire globe; let it outshine every darkness and restriction, in the name of Jesus. Every arrow of spiritual weakness fired against my life from every side, go back to your sender, in the name of Jesus.

(O Lord my God, the owners of heaven and earth, and its fullness thereof, meet me wherever I have been abandoned and supply my needs, in the name of Jesus. I command everything on earth to cooperate with the plans of God for my life and minister to me, in the name of Jesus. Let the blood of Jesus connect me to the saving and sanctifying experience from God, in the name of Jesus. I command all the blessings in the rivers, sea, ocean and everything in the waters to find their way into my life, in the name of Jesus. Every demonic establishment against my destiny, scatter and perish before me, in the name of Jesus. Anointing from God's grace and mercy, prepare me and bring me to God without sin, in the name of Jesus. Let the ascending power of God bring me to the hill of the Lord without iniquity, in the name of Jesus. Father Lord, make me holy, settle me and establish me in the holy place of God, in the name of Jesus. Blood of Jesus, wash my hands, purify my heart and make them clean, in the name of Jesus. By the power of God's lifting ability, father Lord, take me far away from vanity, evil oath and deceit, in the name of Jesus. Almighty God, sanctify me and bring me to receive your blessings, in the name of Jesus. Every good thing from the Lord, wherever you are, begin to manifest in my life with divine arrest, in the name of Jesus. Blood of Jesus, speak me into God's righteousness and his salvation, in the name of Jesus. Almighty God, use me to raise a generation of people that will seek your face and find you, in the name of Jesus. I command every stubborn ancient head, gate and door to be lifted for the King of glory to come into my life, in the name of Jesus. Any satanic block to the manifestation of my salvation and sanctification, be removed, in the name of Jesus. I command everlasting doors, evil threats of impossibilities to give way and disappear from me, in the name of Jesus. Almighty God, come into my life and take over without a rival, in the name of Jesus. Let the King of glory, the LORD Jesus Christ, take full control of everything concerning me, in the name of Jesus. Father Lord, by your strong and mighty name, the mighty Lord in battle, arise and fight for me, in the name of Jesus. Let the forces of God's soldiers force every evil authority on my way, the everlasting doors closed by the dark kingdom to open for me now, in the name of Jesus. Almighty God, show your almightiness in my life, sanctify me and empower me with all your gift, in the name of Jesus. Let the coming in of God's power into my life bring everything that will perfect my relationship with Christ forever, in the name of Jesus Psalms 24:1-10). (By God's abiding strength, I receive the mercy to abide in the word of God forever, in the name of Jesus. I break and loose myself from every demonic influence and corruption, in the name of Jesus. Anointing to honor God, fear Him and to maintain my integrity forever, fall upon me, in the name of Jesus. Let the dwelling ability and strength from God bring me to heaven at last and keep me forever, in the name of Jesus. Every divine instrument of God's sanctifying power, manifest in my life and sanctify me, in the name of Jesus. Father Lord, help me to walk uprightly from today till my last breath on earth, in the name of Jesus. Ancient of days, put your righteousness in me and empower me to speak the truth, in the name of Jesus. Blood of Jesus, flow into my tongue and discharge every work of the devil, in the name of Jesus. I break away and set myself free from the evil powers that promote evil, shame, reproach and disgrace, in the name of Jesus. Every evil force and defiler, my life is not your candidate, in the name of Jesus. Let the unchanging nature of God in doing good, completely arrest me and keep me holy forever, in the name of Jesus. I command the stopping power of the devil and his agents to bow before me and avoid me forever, in the name of Jesus. Almighty God, move me to use all the blessing you have given me rightly, in the name of Jesus. I command everything about me to refuse to give attention or service to the devil and his unrepentant agents, in the name of Jesus. Almighty God, use me to do good and to show justice to the innocent, in the name of Jesus. Any evil force, commissioned to move me out of divine coverage, divine security, fail woefully, in the name of Jesus-Psalms 15:1-5). Troubles, distress, persecution assigned to put me to fear, confusion and despair, fail woefully, in the name of Jesus. Anointing to bear in my body the dying of the Lord Jesus without giving up in living holy, possess me, in the name of Jesus. Let the destroying power in the name of God Almighty destroy every property of the devil in my life, in the name of Jesus. Father Lord, bless me and bring me in your unity with your Son, Holy Spirit and my destiny helpers all over the world, in the name of Jesus. Let the unity of the blessed Holy Trinity manifest between me and believers all over the world, in the name of Jesus. If I am where I don't suppose to be, father Lord, take me to where I supposed to be, in the name of Jesus. By divine commandment from above, let the blessings of God begin to manifest in my life from every side, in the name of Jesus. Any evil mark in my life, visible or invisible, be cleansed by the crying blood of Jesus, in the name of Jesus. Almighty God, deliver me from every demonic relationship, in the name of Jesus. Every yoke of death to the life of God in my life, be destroyed and receive destruction, in the name of Jesus. Let the life of Christ begin to manifest in my mortal body against the plans of the devil and his agents, in the name of Jesus. In the midst of corruption, defilement and pollution, father Lord, sanctify me and keep me holy, in the name of Jesus. I receive the divine strength to serve God with all my heart, without sin, forever and ever, in the name of Jesus. Divine grace to worship God, keep his commandments and statues, fall upon me, in the name of Jesus. Any problem in my life designed to separate me from God, be frustrated, in the name of Jesus. Father Lord, empower me to live holy and obey you in every situation I find myself, in the name of Jesus. I command every long-time problem in my life that is attacking my relationship with God to expire and die, in the name of Jesus. Prayer answering God, manifest in my situation and answer every prayer I have ever prayed, in the name of Jesus. Almighty God, send your angel to visit me with answers to my prayers and guide me into your path, in the name of Jesus. Any satanic roadblock on my way to victory and establishment, be dismantled, in the name of Jesus.

Day 5

Expectations:

1. Receiving the power to conceive good things
2. The destruction of every satanic opposition standing against the manifestation of divine purity in your life
3. Receiving the nature of Christ
4. Complete deliverance from every form of captivity

Almighty God, empower me to conceive everything good with power to deliver them to my generation, in the name of Jesus. Every spiritual and physical famine of God's righteousness in my life, be frustrated, in the name of Jesus. Father Lord, put your hand upon me and transfer your righteousness in me, in the name of Jesus. Every satanic opposition standing against the manifestation of divine purity in my life, be removed, in the name of Jesus. I command my body, soul and spirit to thirst, hunger and be saturated with divine purity, in the name of Jesus. Almighty God, visit me and transfer your nature into my life without measure, in the name of Jesus. I command every area of my life to be flooded with all manner of divine nature, in the name of Jesus. I command the doors leading to every organ of my body, soul and spirit to open and swallow divine purity, in the name of Jesus. Any part of my life lacking divine image and likeness, be filled with holiness, in the name of Jesus. Let my deliverance from above affect every part of my life without measure, in the name of Jesus. I break and loose myself from the presence of the devil and his contaminating agents, in the name of Jesus. I break and loose myself from the captivity of my enemies, Satan and sin, in the name of Jesus. Every fear from the kingdom of darkness, ministering against me, your time is up, disappear, in the name of Jesus. Almighty God, fill me with your fear, love and power without end, in the name of Jesus. Let my services to God Almighty be filled with God's fear, holiness and righteousness of Christ all the days of my life, in the name of Jesus. Every demonic plantation of sin in any area of my life, your time is up, be uprooted, in the name of Jesus. I break and loose myself from every demonic plantation in my body, soul and spirit in my dreams, in the name of Jesus. Any witchcraft animal living with me in the same house, manifest and die, in the name of Jesus. Let the aborting and miscarrying strength of God abort every root of sin in my life, in the name of Jesus. Let the saving and the redeeming power in the blood of Jesus penetrate into my foundation and sanctify me, in the name of Jesus. I command the strength of every iniquity assigned against my life to be broken by the speaking blood of Jesus, in the name of Jesus. Let the mobilizing power of God, mobilize every creature to rise against the devil, his agents, and every problem in my life, in the name of Jesus. Almighty God, fill me with your Spirit and bring me to a divine motivated purity, in the name of Jesus. Almighty God, bring me to experience a sanctification that will make me special and zealous of good work every day, in the name of Jesus. Fire of God, enter into my life and sanctify my spirit from sin, in the name of Jesus. Every evil presence around me, be destroyed by God's presence in me, in the name of Jesus. Every voice and presence of Satan, sin and trouble in my life, be silenced by the voice of Jesus. Every pillar of sin, mounted against my life, be uprooted, in the name of Jesus. Every satanic program, organized against my purity, be frustrated unto death, in the name of Jesus. Every enemy of the manifestation of God's glory in my life, be frustrated, in the name of Jesus. Almighty God, empower me to live a life of holiness to honor your name, every day and forever, in the name of Jesus. I command the power of Satan and sin in my life to be frustrated, in the name of Jesus. Let the judgment of the devil and his agents against my life be reversed, in the name of Jesus. Any evil personality promoting sin in my life, be exposed and disgraced, in the name of

Jesus. Almighty God, deliver me from every enemy of my qualification to partake in the marriage supper of the Lamb, in the name of Jesus. Anointing to praise God in heaven after the rapture of the saints; to remain forever with God, fall upon me, in the name of Jesus. Any evil personality attached to my life to promote a sinful character in me, I break away from you, in the name of Jesus. Any evil presence in my life, influencing me to act against God's plan for my life, disappear forever, in the name of Jesus. I command the backbone of sin and Satan to be broken to pieces in my life, in the name of Jesus. Father Lord, turn away my captivity and deliver me perfectly from the powers of Satan and sin, in the name of Jesus. Let the gathering power of God gather all my stolen and scattered blessing all over the world, spiritually and physically, in the name of Jesus. Ancient of days, circumcise my heart and cleanse me totally with cleansing power in the blood of Jesus, in the name of Jesus. I command my body, soul and spirit to receive the sword of God's circumcision ministry, in the name of Jesus. Almighty God, help me to love you, your word with all my heart, body, mind and spirit, in the name of Jesus. Almighty God, increase my hatred against Satan, sin and every evil presence, in the name of Jesus. Let the power that raised Jesus from the grave take me away from every captivity of Satan and sin, in the name of Jesus. Let the presentation power of God present me body, soul and spirit for sanctification, in the name of Jesus. By the power in the sanctifying anointing in the blood of Jesus, I command every part of my life to be sanctified, in the name of Jesus. Father Lord, I willingly surrender and dedicate my body, soul and spirit, use me for your glory, in the name of Jesus. Anointing to walk worthy of the vocation wherewith you have called me to your glory, fall upon me, in the name of Jesus. Let everything in me by your grace, endeavor to keep the unity of the Spirit, in the bond of peace without compromise, in the name of Jesus. Father Lord, deliver me from living a hypocritical life and practicing religion without the righteousness of Christ, in the name of Jesus. Almighty God, deliver me from manifesting your gifts without the grace of living a holy life, in the name of Jesus. I break and loose myself from greed, pride, anger, immorality, jealousy and covetousness, in the name of Jesus. Every yoke of the love of money, financial misappropriation and unfaithfulness to my family in my life, break to pieces, in the name of Jesus. Almighty God, deliver me from the counterfeit of the devil and his agents, designed to separate me from Christ, in the name of Jesus. I disengage myself from operating with power without holiness and the fruits of the Spirit of God, in the name of Jesus. I command all things, every creature to frustrate the works of the devil and his agents in every area of my life, in the name of Jesus. Almighty God, allocate every good thing you have created to my life in abundance, in the name of Jesus. Every demonic voice militating against the rule and reign of God's voice in my life, be silenced by the speaking blood of Jesus. Let the multiplying power of God multiply his nature into my life without measure, in the name of Jesus. I receive divine motivated power without fear to please God at all cost, in every situation, in the name of Jesus. I withdraw myself from serving the devil, his agents and the things of the world and I dedicate my services to God, in the name of Jesus. Let my promotion, prosperity, and breakthrough come from God and not from the corrupting influence of the world, in the name of Jesus. Every good thing that must come to me shall be purified and approve by God, in the name of Jesus. Almighty God, bring me into your kingdom through your son, Jesus Christ, in the name of Jesus. I break and loose myself from the devil and his agents in this world and in the spiritual realm, in the name of Jesus. Every good thing the devil has stolen from me, let the restoration power of God restore them back, in the name of Jesus. Lord Jesus, intervene in my life and give your kind of life in abundance, in the name of Jesus. Ancient of days, restore my lost spiritual life and energize me to pray aright, in the name of Jesus. Father Lord, by your mercy, bring your kingdom right inside my heart, body, soul and spirit, in the name of Jesus. Almighty God, fill every part of my life with the spirit of forgiveness and purity, in the name of Jesus. Empower me Lord to use everything, all my blessings, to please you without reserve, in the name of Jesus. Every satanic gang up against my purity and the manifestation of divine nature, scatter and fail woefully, in the name of Jesus. By the power of God's renewal grace, I receive divine newness in every part of my life, in the name of Jesus. Every demonic affliction, poverty and lack in my life assigned to defile me, fail woefully, in the name of Jesus. John 8:36; 17:22-23 ... I command my deliverance to manifest only through Christ by God's mercy, in the name of Jesus. Let the spirit of unity, oneness from above manifest before me and among all true believers, in the name of Jesus. I command my entire life, in and out to be taken over by Christ for purity and preservation to eternity, in the name of Jesus. Every enemy of the manifestation of the perfect lifestyle of Christ in my life, be frustrated, in the name of Jesus. Father Lord, fill my morning, afternoon, night and every moment of my life with your presence, in the name of Jesus. Let the arresting power of the devil and his agents to sin, fail woefully in my life, in the name of Jesus. Every stone of Satan and sin raised against me, drop by divine intervention, in the name of Jesus. Almighty God, deliver me from sin and sanctify me in and out, in the name of Jesus. Every good-looking thing, prepared by the devil to entice me to sin, I reject you and the devil, in the name of Jesus. Let the accusing strength of the devil and his polluting power fail woefully in my life, in the name of Jesus. Almighty God, help me to recover my true identity and likeness without struggle, in the name of Jesus. Let the blessing of God in his grace and mercy flow into my life without hindrance, in the name of Jesus. Every enemy of the manifestation of God's lifestyle in my life, be frustrated, in the name of Jesus. Romans 13:10; 1; Corinthians 13:5-6 ... Every anti-love of God in my life, be frustrated without survival, in the name of Jesus. Father Lord, deposit in me your type of love without measure, in the mighty name of Jesus. Let the enduring power and anointing to suffer-long in God's charity, begin to manifest in my life, in the name of Jesus. Let the charity to overcome envy, pride, jealousy, malice and all the lifestyle of the devil begin to occupy every part of my life, in the name of Jesus. I break and loose myself from every manifestation that lacks the fruits of the spirit, in the name of Jesus. Father Lord, release into my life your abundant, sufficient, sustaining and strengthening grace to keep your type of holiness in me forever, in the name of Jesus. Almighty God, sanctify me inwardly and outwardly and keep me holy all the days of my life, in the name of Jesus. Let the nature of God in and outside me receive the company of eternal weight and abiding grace forever, in the name of Jesus. 1 Peter 1:15, 16 ... Let my calling and services to God embrace God's holiness without delay, in the name of Jesus. Father Lord, empower me to resemble you in everything, especially in holiness, in the name of Jesus. I command my holiness from God to touch every area of my life, even in all manner of conversation, in the name of Jesus. Father Lord, enter into my life with all your qualities and likeness without measure, in the name of Jesus. I break and loose myself from every satanic defiling agent that has been assigned to defile my life and separate me from God, in the name of Jesus. By the power of God's abiding presence in my life, I command evil to fade away from my life forever, in the name of Jesus. Almighty God, invade my life and capture me completely with your kind of nature, in the name of Jesus. Let the depriving power of God deny the devil and his agents access into my life, forever, in the name of Jesus. By the power of God's miscarrying anointing, I command every work of the devil and his agent to be miscarried out of my life, in the name of Jesus. Let the presence of Satan and sin be completely abolished from my life, forever, in the name of Jesus. 1 John 4:17-21 ... Let the love of God in me be transformed exactly like the love of Christ to the world, in the name of Jesus. Father Lord, arise in your power and perfect your love in my life, in the name of Jesus. By the power of God's love in my life, I receive the grace to be as bold as God before every creature, in the name of Jesus.

Every demonic inflicted fear in my life, be displaced with the perfect fear of God, in the name of Jesus. Anything anywhere, working against the manifestation of God's perfect love and fear in my life, receive death, in the name of Jesus. Let my love for God exceed the love I have for any creature, including myself, in the name of Jesus. Let the love of God in me hate what God hates and love what God loves, in the name of Jesus. Lord Jesus, help me by your mercy to love exactly the way you love without discrimination, in the name of Jesus. Almighty God, by the power in your word, two-edged sword, cut me off from Satan, sin and every evil, forever, in the name of Jesus. Blood of Jesus, speak me out of every evil presence and satanic demonstration, in the name of Jesus. Every sinful inheritance in my life, be uprooted, in the name of Jesus. Almighty God, deliver me from Satan, sin and use me as your instrument to deliver others, in the name of Jesus. Any evil mouth speaking sin into my life, close and speak no more, in the name of Jesus. Let the demonic developing force assigned to develop evil in my life scatter and perish, in the name of Jesus.

FOURTEEN

CHARACTERS OF UNSANCTIFIED LIFE

DECREE-1

(Romans 6:6, Ephesians 4:22, 18, Colossians 3:9, 5-6, 1 Corinthians 2:14; 6:9, 10, 1 Thessalonians 4:3-4, 7, Matthew 5:8, 48; Hebrews 12:14, 1 Thessalonians 5:24-25, Psalms 51:7-10, Psalms 118:27, Songs 2:15, Matthew 5:6, 2 Corinthians 13:5, Jeremiah 6:16; 1:12; 32:17, Luke 1:74, 75, Ezekiel 36:25-27)

Day 1

Expectations:

1. The destruction of every demonic character in your life.
2. Complete deliverance from the grip and captivity of sin and sinful appetite.
3. The termination of the continuing power of sin and Satan.
4. The destruction of every sinful structure and establishment in your life and destiny.
5. The cleansing of all filthiness in your life.
6. The frustration of every evil force from the witchcraft world targeted at making you live a sinful life.

Every demonic character in my life, be aborted and be destroyed, in the name of Jesus. Every inherited sin in any area of my life, your time is up, be uprooted, in the name of Jesus. Every sin I have ever committed, wherever you are now, die with your consequences, in the name of Jesus. I break and loose myself from the reign of any sin, in the mighty name of Jesus. Let the continuing power of Satan and sin in my life be terminated, in the name of Jesus. Every yoke of unforgiving spirit in my life, break to pieces, in the name of Jesus. Any sinful structure and evil establishment in my life, catch fire, burn to ashes and be uprooted, in the name of Jesus. Father Lord, deliver me from every manipulator that has been assigned to manipulate me into sin, in the name of Jesus. I break and loose myself from every bewitchment and every spell that has been cast upon me to sin, in the name of Jesus. Every property of the devil, sin and its consequence in my life, catch fire, burn to ashes, in the name of Jesus. Any evil force from the witchcraft world against my living righteous, scatter in defeat, in the name of Jesus. By the uprooting power of God, I command the body of sin in my life to be uprooted, in the name of Jesus. Sin living inside me, I bind and cast you out, in the name of Jesus. Every filthiness in my life, your time is up, be cleansed by the blood of Jesus, in the name of Jesus.

> Knowing this, that our old man is crucified with *him*, that the body of sin might be destroyed, that henceforth we should not serve sin.
>
> — ROMANS 6:6

> That ye put off concerning the former conversation the old man, which is corrupt according to the deceitful lusts;
>
> Having the understanding darkened, being alienated from the life of God through the ignorance that is in them, because of the blindness of their heart:
>
> — EPHESIANS 4:22, 18

I command every part of my life, body, soul and spirit to put off evil conversation, in the name of Jesus. Any agent of corruption, pollution and defilement in my life, be exposed and be disgraced, in the name of Jesus. I break and loose myself from every lust and deceit, in the name of Jesus. Any evil sacrifice ever offered to bring me to sin, expire by the sacrifice of the blood of Jesus, in the name of Jesus. Any evil hand planting in the garden of my life, wither and dry up, in the name of Jesus. Anything in me, harboring the devil and sin in my life, receive immediate deliverance, in the name of Jesus. Any evil voice calling me to sin, be silenced by the speaking blood of Jesus, in the name of Jesus. I command the backbone of Satan and sin to be broken in my life, in the name of Jesus. Any witchcraft animal promoting sin in my life, die, in the name of Jesus. Blood of

Jesus, flow into my foundation, quench the fire of sin and uproot them from their roots, in the name of Jesus. I terminate the ministry of Satan and sin in every area of my life, in the name of Jesus. I command the strength of Satan and sin in my life to be destroyed by the speaking blood of Jesus, in the name of Jesus. Let the capacity and ability invested in the blood of Jesus cripple the powers of Satan and sin in every part of my life, in the name of Jesus.

Lie not one to another, seeing that ye have put off the old man with his deeds;

Mortify therefore your members which are upon the earth; fornication, uncleanness, inordinate affection, evil concupiscence, and covetousness, which is idolatry:

For which things' sake the wrath of God cometh on the children of disobedience:

— COLOSSIANS 3:9, 5-6

I bind and cast out every lying spirit militating against my life, in the name of Jesus. Let the yoke of falsehood, pretense and evil deeds be put away from my life forever, in the name of Jesus. Father Lord, empower me to put on the new man, new life that is in Christ Jesus forever, in the name of Jesus. Almighty God, renew my knowledge and wisdom in Christ and deliver me from spiritual ignorance, in the name of Jesus. I receive divine grace to see the things above where Christ is sitting on the right hand of God, in the name of Jesus. I command every area of my life to follow Christ and move with Him without a stop, in the name of Jesus. Let Jesus Christ be my life and let every enemy of this fail woefully before me, in the name of Jesus. Almighty God, mortify every part of my body and protect them from every sin and Satan, in the name of Jesus. I break and loose myself from every yoke of sin, especially the sin of idolatry, in the name of Jesus. You the old man in my life, you are crucified with Christ, long age, be frustrated in my life, in the name of Jesus. I command the body of sin in my life to be destroyed, in the name of Jesus. Any part of my life, serving Satan and sin, receive deliverance, in the name of Jesus. Every yoke of carnality, mind defiler in any part of my life, break to pieces, in the name of Jesus. Any evil character that has dominated my life, be destroyed, in the name of Jesus. I break and loose myself from downward and inward enemy, in the name of Jesus. Every enemy of my eternal life with God corrupting my nature, be frustrated, in the name of Jesus. Father Lord, stretch your hand of mercy and take me far away from the captivity of Satan and sin, in the name of Jesus. Any evil personality equipped to keep me in sinful character, be frustrated, in the name of Jesus. Almighty God, deliver me from every negative influence, in the name of Jesus. Blood of Jesus, help me to say no to every sin without delay, in the name of Jesus. Every organized darkness in any area of my life, your time is up, be disorganized, in the name of Jesus. Any evil river flowing into my life from my pasts, dry up, in the name of Jesus. Father Lord, arise in your power and deliver me wherever I need deliverance, in the name of Jesus. Let the destroying power of God destroy every demonic plantation in my life, in the name of Jesus. Almighty God, enlighten my understanding and deliver me from every darkness in my body, soul and spirit, in the name of Jesus. Father Lord, bring me back to spiritual knowledge and wisdom, in the name of Jesus. I command the works of the devil in my life to be terminated, in the name of Jesus. Every enemy of the illumination of God's light in my life, be frustrated, in the name of Jesus. Father Lord, deliver me from spiritual and physical ignorance, in the name of Jesus. Almighty God, restore into me the life of Christ, in the name of Jesus.

But the natural man receiveth not the things of the Spirit of God: for they are foolishness unto him: neither can he know *them,* because they are spiritually discerned.

Know ye not that the unrighteous shall not inherit the kingdom of God? Be not deceived: neither fornicators, nor idolaters, nor adulterers, nor effeminate, nor abusers of themselves with mankind,

Nor thieves, nor covetous, nor drunkards, nor revilers, nor extortioners, shall inherit the kingdom of God.

— 1 CORINTHIANS 2:14; 6:9, 10

Father Lord, help me, guide me to rightly discern the things of the spirit and follow it to the end, in the name of Jesus. Every yoke of unrighteousness upon my life, break to pieces, in the name of Jesus. Every enemy of my entering heaven and inheriting my inheritance, fail woefully, in the name of Jesus. Almighty God, empower me with enough of your grace to receive the things of the Spirit, in the name of Jesus. I command the entering point of the devil and sin into my life to be closed against them forever, in the name of Jesus. Almighty God, open the doors of my life and chase Satan and sin out of my life, in the name of Jesus.

Day 2

Expectations:

1. **Banning and blocking the devil and sin from returning into your life.**
2. **Deliverance from every form of spiritual blindness.**
3. **The dismantling of every form of unclean feeling assigned to dominate your heart.**
4. **The destruction of every evil mark in your life.**
5. **The destruction of every satanic arrow of sin fired against you.**

6.   The destruction of every worldly character in your life.

Let the returning back of Satan, demonic spirits and sin into my life be banned and forbidden forever, in the name of Jesus. Anointing to look foolish before God and to sheepishly obey the word of God without questioning, fall upon me, in the name of Jesus. Blood of Jesus, speak me out of the wrath of God forever and empower me to stay away from Satan and sin, in the name of Jesus. Father Lord, help me to live a life of obedience to your word without a break forever, in the name of Jesus. I break and loose myself from spiritual and physical blindness, in the name of Jesus. Father Lord, send your light into my heart and keep me far away out of sin assigned against me, in the name of Jesus. Every unclean feeling assigned to dominate my heart, body and mind, be destroyed, in the name of Jesus. Every enemy of the manifestations of God's holiness in my life, fail woefully, in the name of Jesus. Father Lord, deliver me from every demonic soul-tie designed to take me away from God's mercy, in the name of Jesus. Any evil sinful partner attached to my life, be frustrated, in the name of Jesus. Every satanic arrow of sin fired into my life, go back to your sender, in the name of Jesus. Almighty God, arise in your anger and rescue me from every satanic arrest, spiritually and physically, in the name of Jesus. Everything in my life fighting against the rule and the reign of God's nature, fail woefully, in the name of Jesus. Any evil mark in my life, spiritually or physically, be erased by the speaking blood of Jesus, in the name of Jesus. Blood of Jesus, penetrate into my heart of hearts and purify me whole without sin, in the name of Jesus. Every enemy of God's full control of my life, your time is up, fail woefully, in the name of Jesus. I completely forbid evil thought, evil desires, feelings of any sin from any access to my heart, in the name of Jesus. Father Lord, deliver me from sin within and sin without forever, in the name of Jesus. Let the cleansing power in the speaking blood of

Jesus forever occupy my body, soul and spirit without leaving, in the name of Jesus. Any evil force moving with sin into my life, be crippled, in the mighty name of Jesus. Ancient of days, plant in me your likeness and empower to live holy without sin, in the name of Jesus. Any worldly character in my life, be destroyed, in the name of Jesus. Every tree of sin planted in my life, seen or unseen, be uprooted, in the name of Jesus. Father Lord, take me far away from the presence of Satan and sin forever, in the name of Jesus. Anything that must happen for my life to be completely out of sin, begin to happen, in the name of Jesus. I command the powers of sin put together to be crippled out of my life without delay in and out of my life, in the name of Jesus.

For this is the will of God, *even* your sanctification, that ye should abstain from fornication:

That every one of you should know how to possess his vessel in sanctification and honour;

For God hath not called us unto uncleanness, but unto holiness.

— 1 THESSALONIANS 4:3-4, 7

Almighty God, help me to know how to walk with you and empower me to please you without a break all the days of my life, in the name of Jesus. By the power attached to God's will to sanctify me, I receive divine touch for my sanctification now, in the name of Jesus. Almighty God, by the power attached to your promise to sanctify, I receive my sanctification, in the name of Jesus. Let the sanctifying power in the blood of Jesus penetrate deep into my life, in the name of Jesus.

Father Lord, help me to abstain from every unclean character, in the name of Jesus. I receive divine grace and knowledge to possess my vessel in sanctification, in the name of Jesus. Almighty God, help me to respond positively without delay to your call for my sanctification, in the name of Jesus. I break and loose myself from every evil voice calling me into uncleanness, in the name of Jesus. I refuse to ignore, despise or reject the call of God for my sanctification, in the name of Jesus. Spirit of the living God, appear in my life and sanctify me, body, soul and spirit, in the name of Jesus. Every shame, reproach and disgrace that accompanied Satan and sin into my life, receive total destructions, in the name of Jesus. Every yoke of pride and the love of money in my life, break to pieces, in the mighty name of Jesus. Almighty God, deliver me from the pull of demonic ambition and the pursuit of wealth in a wrong way, in the name of Jesus. I break and loose myself from every demonic movement to the presence of Satan and sin, in the name of Jesus. Any evil force bringing me under the captivity of sin, fail woefully and scatter, in the name of Jesus. Any evil project going on in my life, known or unknown to me, be terminated, in the name of Jesus. Almighty God, take me out of sin and move me far away from every demonic camp, in the name of Jesus. I break and loose myself from every sinful and unprofitable relationship, in the name of Jesus.

Blessed *are* the pure in heart: for they shall see God.

Be ye therefore perfect, even as your Father which is in heaven is perfect.

Follow peace with all *men*, and holiness, without which no man shall see the Lord:

— MATTHEW 5:8, 48; HEBREWS 12:14

Anointing and blessings attached to divine purity, begin to manifest in my life, in the name of Jesus. I command my heart to submit and surrender to divine purity and perfect cleansing, in the name of Jesus. Let the perfecting power in the word of God and in the blood of Jesus begin to perfect my life from sin and all form of defilement, in the name of Jesus. My father, which is in heaven, perfect your work in my heart and sanctify me, body, soul and spirit without sin, in the name of Jesus. I receive abundance grace to follow peace with all men and the ability to be a peacemaker, in the name of Jesus. I refuse to join the multitudes to do evil against my soul, in the name of Jesus. Any sin that woke up with me this morning, you will not go to bed with me tonight, in the name of Jesus. Any serpent and scorpion in the garden of my life, your time is up, die, in the name of Jesus. Blood of Jesus, appear in the battle field of my life and destroy the works of the devil in my life, in the name of Jesus. Every throne of Satan and sin in my life, be dethroned, in the name of Jesus. Any evil seed planted in my life, be uprooted, in the name of Jesus. Father Lord, empower me to receive the fulfilment of the promise of sanctification, in the name of Jesus. I receive divine abundant grace to abstain from all the appearance of evil and the enemies of sanctification, in the name of Jesus. Let the flowing blood of Jesus flow into my foundation and speak me out of every sin, sickness and diseases, in the name of Jesus. Every anti-sanctification doctrine in my life, be destroyed, in the name of Jesus.

Faithful *is* he that calleth you, who also will do *it*.

Brethren, pray for us.

— 1 THESSALONIANS 5:24-25

Almighty God, arise in your power, sanctify me to show the world your faithfulness in my life, in my life, in the name of Jesus. Every enemy of God's manifestations in my life, fail woefully, in the mighty name of Jesus. Father Lord, confirm your love and care in my life physically through the washing power in the precious blood of Jesus. Let the prayers of Jesus for the sanctification of believers manifest fully in every area of my life, in the name of Jesus. Any part of God's promises yet to manifest in my life positively, your time is up, begin to manifest, in the name of Jesus. Almighty God, help me to be holy, to remain holy in every situation without considering sin as an option, in the name of Jesus. Almighty God, keep me holy without sin in the day of the Lord's coming, in the name of Jesus. Every chain of Satan and sin in my life, visible or invisible, break to pieces, in the name of Jesus. Almighty God, help me to escape from every sinful trap, in the name of Jesus.

> Purge me with hyssop, and I shall be clean: wash me, and I shall be whiter than snow.
>
> Create in me a clean heart, O God; and renew a right spirit within me.
>
> — PSALMS 51:7-10

By the power in God's mercy, let the loving kindness of God destroy every transgression in my life and sanctify me, in the name of Jesus. By the power of God's cleansing anointing in the blood of Jesus, I command my body, soul and spirit to be washed and made pure, in the name of Jesus. I command the presence of every type of sin to disappear forever from my life, in the name of Jesus. Every sin I have ever inherited or committed, wherever you are, be destroyed by the speaking power in the blood of Jesus. Every shape of iniquity and manner of sin in my life, be uprooted, in the name of Jesus. Every yoke of evil desire in my life, your time is up, be destroyed by the anointing of God, in the name of Jesus. Let the purging power in the word of God purge me of every sin and satanic presence, in the name of Jesus. Let the joy of my salvation, sanctification and relationship with God be multiplied in my life, in the name of Jesus. Let the hiding strength in God hide me far away from Satan and sin forever, in the name of Jesus. Let the creating power of the Almighty God create a clean heart in me, in the name of Jesus. Almighty God, empower me to live holy and renew your Spirit within me, in the name of Jesus. Let the overtaking powers of darkness in my life be crippled and demobilized, in the name of Jesus. Any part of my destiny under demonic captivity, receive total deliverance, in the name of Jesus. Let the yoke of every inherited sinful lifestyle in my life break to pieces, in the name of Jesus.

Day 3

Expectations:

1. **The destruction of all the enemies of the rule and reign of God's presence.**

2. **The termination of all the programs of the devil and his agents against you.**

3. **Complete deliverance from every satanic link and relationship.**

4. **The destruction of every evil force keeping you in sin.**

5. **Deliverance from every evil power that has been keeping you in bondage.**

6. **The destruction of every evil force standing between you and the fulfillment of God's plan for your life.**

Almighty God, flash your divine touch light in my life and leave it to shine steadily, in the name of Jesus.

> God *is* the LORD, which hath shewed us light: bind the sacrifice with cords, *even* unto the horns of the altar.
>
> — PSALMS 118:27

> Take us the foxes, the little foxes, that spoil the vines: for our vines *have* tender grapes.
>
> — SONGS 2:15

Let my coming, staying, going and actions in life from today bring honor to God, in the name of Jesus. Father Lord, open my eyes to see the light you are showing me everywhere I go, in the name of Jesus. Father Lord, move in action, help me to take away the foxes, the little foxes that spoils vines in my life, in the name of Jesus. Every enemy of the rule and reign of God's presence and nature in my life, I cut you off, in the name of Jesus. Any satanic engagement in my destiny, be disengaged by the speaking blood of Jesus. I terminate every program of the devil and his agents in my life, in the name of Jesus. Father Lord, deliver me from every satanic link and relationship, in the name of Jesus. Father Lord, deliver me from every evil activity designed to deny me of the rapture, in the name of Jesus. I break and loose myself from any evil soul-tie with any creature, in the name of Jesus.

> Blessed *are* they which do hunger and thirst after righteousness: for they shall be filled.

> — MATTHEW 5:6

> Examine yourselves, whether ye be in the faith; prove your own selves. Know ye not your own selves, how that Jesus Christ is in you, except ye be reprobates?

> — 2 CORINTHIANS 13:5

Almighty God, fill my soul with hunger and thirst for your righteousness, in the mighty name of Jesus. Ancient of days, deliver me from the famine and poverty of your word and the fruits of the Holy Spirit, in the name of Jesus. Anointing to obtain divine mercy for the sanctification of my body, soul and Spirit, fall upon me, in the name of Jesus. Every satanic inflicted and inherited sin in any area of my life, be purged by the speaking blood of Jesus, in the name of Jesus. Almighty God, establish your word in my life and fulfill all your promises, in the name of Jesus. Let the word of God, the power in the speaking blood of Jesus, spare no sin in my life, in the name of Jesus. By the power of the resurrection, I command everything that is good in my life to get better, in the name of Jesus. Anointing to rightly examine myself at all times, fall upon me, in the name of Jesus. Father Lord, help me always to give the right judgment of myself without compromise, in the name of Jesus. I receive the grace to deal with every sinful character in my life and to get rid of them, in the name of Jesus. Father Lord, by your keeping power, keep me in Christ forever, in the name of Jesus. I receive the grace to tell myself the truth about myself, in the name of Jesus. Let the amending anointing in the word of God empower me to repent and amend my ways, in the name of Jesus. By the power of God's discovering truth, I receive the grace to discover the truth and to keep it at all cost, in the name of Jesus. I break and loose myself from the spirit of error, foolishness and reprobate behavior, in the name of Jesus. Every invisible and visible mark of Satan and sin in my life, be cleansed by the cleansing power in the blood of Jesus, in the name of Jesus. Father Lord, take me away from every evil presence, in the name of Jesus. Any promotion, breakthrough or prosperity, designed to take me away from Christ, I reject you, in the name of Jesus. Let the promises of sanctification begin to manifest in my life, in the name of Jesus. Lord Jesus, take me away to safety and minister holiness into my life, in the name of Jesus. By the power in the word of God, I command sanctification to manifest in my life, in the name of Jesus.

Thus saith the LORD, stand ye in the ways, and see, and ask for the old paths, where *is* the good way, and walk therein, and ye shall find rest for your souls. But they said, we will not walk *therein*

Then said the LORD unto me, thou hast well seen: for I will hasten my word to perform it.

Ah Lord GOD! behold, thou hast made the heaven and the earth by thy great power and stretched out arm, *and* there is nothing too hard for thee:

— JEREMIAH 6:16; 1:12; 32:17

Father Lord, fish me out and deliver me from every sin and keep me from every evil presence, in the name of Jesus. Let the hunters from above locate me and take me away from the destructive powers of sin, in the name of Jesus. Any evil force, keeping me in sin and captivity, loose your hold over my life, in the name of Jesus. Almighty God, deliver me from the hills, holes, rocks and mountains of sin, in the name of Jesus. Let the power in God's performance to his promises begin to manifest and deliver me from every sin, in the name of Jesus. Any evil force militating against the fulfillment of God's promises in my life, scatter and fail woefully, in the name of Jesus. Let the promises of God manifest in my life with all positivity, in the name of Jesus. Let the word of God replace every negative word in my life forever, in the name of Jesus. By the power that made heaven and earth, I receive the immediate fulfillment of God's promises in every area of my life, in the name of Jesus. Let the great power of God's word and his stretched-out arm take me away from the works of the devil, in the name of Jesus. I command every yoke of impossibility in my life to break to pieces, in the name of Jesus. Every fire of sin burning in any part of my life, be quenched by the Holy Ghost fire and the blood of Jesus. Let the sudden destruction from God fall upon the works of the devil in my life and consume them, in the name of Jesus. Let the frustrating power of God from above frustrate Satan and sin in my life, in the name of Jesus.

That he would grant unto us, that we being delivered out of the hand of our enemies might serve him without fear,

In holiness and righteousness before him, all the days of our life.

— LUKE 1:74, 75

Anointing to serve God with boldness and sound mind, possess me, in the name of Jesus. By the power of God's purity and divine righteousness, I receive the strength to serve God forever without sin, in the name of Jesus. Almighty God, cause your granting power from above to appear in my life for my perfect deliverance, in the name of Jesus. Any evil power keeping me in bondage, your time is up, release me by force from above, in the name of Jesus. Every enemy of the manifestation of God's promises in my life, be exposed and disgraced, in the name of Jesus. Any evil power standing between me and the fulfillment of God's plans for my life, fail woefully, in the name of Jesus. I command every area of my life to begin to travail and abort every pregnancy of iniquity in my life unto death, in the name of Jesus. Any evil plantation of sin in my life, be uprooted, in the name of Jesus. By the power in the resurrection and anointing of God, I receive life against every sinful character in my life, in the name of Jesus. I break and loose myself from every demonic appetite, in the name of Jesus. Almighty God, increase my hunger and thirst for righteousness, in the name of Jesus.

Then will I sprinkle clean water upon you, and ye shall be clean: from all your filthiness, and from all your idols, will I cleanse you.

And I will put my spirit within you, and cause you to walk in my statutes, and ye shall keep my judgments, and do *them*.

— EZEKIEL 36:25-27

Every property of the devil, be removed by the hand of God, in the name of Jesus. Any evil investment within me, catch fire and burn to ashes, in the name of Jesus. Almighty God, give me your heart of flesh and perfect your promises of sanctification in my life, in the name of Jesus. Let the promises of God's sprinkle clean waters from above and begin to manifest in my life, in the name of Jesus.

By the power in God's cleanness, I cleanse my body, soul and spirit, in the name of Jesus. Every demonic created and invested filthiness in my life, receive divine cleansing, in the name of Jesus. Every idolatrous property in my life, your time is up, receive divine purging, in the name of Jesus. By the power in the promises of God's word, I receive a new heart, void of sin, in the name of Jesus. Let the promise of God to give His children new hearts and new Spirits manifest in my life, in the name of Jesus. I put on the breastplate of righteousness against the forces of sin and Satan into my life, in the name of Jesus. Let the ending power of God's anointing end the activities of sin and Satan in my life forever, in the name of Jesus. I bind myself under the continual power of God's righteousness, in the name of Jesus. I bring myself under the perfect control of God's righteousness, in the name of Jesus. Let the salvation of my soul and the sanctification of my body, soul and spirit be permanent, in the name of Jesus. Let the promises of God manifest in every area of my life positively, in the name of Jesus. Let the forces of God from heaven force every part of my body, soul and spirit out of the presence of the devil, in the name of Jesus. Anointing to walk in God's statues and keep his commandments, fall upon me, in the name of Jesus. I command every evil force, sitting upon my blessings, to be removed by heavenly force, in the name of Jesus. I break and loose myself from every satanic program, in the name of Jesus. Almighty God, show yourself God in every area of my life without a minus, in the name of Jesus. Let the saving power of God enter into my life and save me from every trouble, in the name of Jesus. I break and loose myself from the yokes of every evil, in the name of Jesus. Father Lord, cleanse me from every uncleanness and perfect your word in my life, in the name of Jesus. Let the increasing power of God increase his presence in my life forever, in the name of Jesus. I break and loose myself from every lack and famine connected to the devil and sin, in the name of Jesus. I break and loose myself from every demonic leadership, in the name of Jesus. Almighty God, settle me and establish me in my place of life and, fulfil your promises without remaining, in the name of Jesus. Any evil force multiplying evil into my life, I bind and cast you out, in the name of Jesus. Any evil tree bearing the seed of sin and its consequence in my life, be uprooted, in the name of Jesus. Every messenger of shame and reproach in my life, I reject you and your message, in the name of Jesus. Father Lord, arise in your mercy and walk me out of the wrong ways of life, in the name of Jesus. Father Lord, bring me into your perfect will, plan and purpose, in the name of Jesus.

FIFTEEN

THE AUTHORITY OF BELIEVERS

DECREE-1

(Luke 11:21, 22, Luke 10:17-19, 1 Samuel 17:48-50, Colossians 1:17, 18, 2 Chronicles 16:9)

Day 1

Expectations:

1. Total freedom from all demonic spirits and sicknesses.
2. Deliverance from evil spirit and all lunatic demons.
3. The destruction of every evil hand planting evil in your life, family and destiny.
4. The destruction of the backbone of your problems.
5. The termination of all the activities of the devil and his agents against your life.

Almighty God, empower me to remain under your care and under the authority that comes from Christ, in the name of Jesus. By the authority I receive from Christ to cast out demons, I bind and cast out every demonic spirit behind all manner of sickness and disease in my life, in the name of Jesus. Any part of my life possessed with evil spirits and lunatic demons, receive full deliverance now, in the name of Jesus. Any evil hand planting evil into my life, wither and dry up, in the name of Jesus. I command every part of my body, soul and spirit to receive divine promotion without delay, in the name of Jesus. Every enemy of the manifestation of God's peace in my life, fail woefully, in the name of Jesus. I command the backbone of my problems to die forever, in the name of Jesus. Every disease in my body, soul and spirit, die, in the name of Jesus. Any serpent in the garden of my life challenging my authority, I bind and cast you out, in the name of Jesus. Every arrow of deceit from the satanic kingdom fired against my destiny, I fire you back, in the name of Jesus. Almighty God, empower me to resist the devil and say no to all his words, in the name of Jesus. Father Lord, help me to truly acknowledge my sins, repent, confess and forsake them, in the name of Jesus. I break and loose myself from the evil desires of forbidden fruits, in the name of Jesus. Almighty God, deliver me from shifting blames and excusing myself for my faults, in the name of Jesus. Every curse placed upon me because of my past sins, O Lord, by your mercies, remove them from me, in the name of Jesus. Any tree of sin glowing in my life, be uprooted by the hand of God, in the name of Jesus. I take authority over the activities of the devil in my life and I terminate them, in the name of Jesus (Genesis 3:1-24).

When a strong man armed keepeth his palace, his goods are in peace:

But when a stronger than he shall come upon him, and overcome him, he taketh from him all his armour wherein he trusted, and divideth his spoils.

— LUKE 11:21, 22

Any strong man in charge of my case file, your time is up, release it now, in the name of Jesus. By the power and authority given to me by Jesus Christ, I disarm the strong man assigned against me, in the name of Jesus. Any evil personality in the palace of my destiny, I bind and cast you out, in the name of Jesus. Every darkness in any area of my life, be replaced by the light of God, in the name of Jesus. O Lord arise and take me away from the captivity of the strong man, in the name of Jesus. Every serpent of darkness in the territory of my life, I cut you to pieces, in the name of Jesus. Any satanic structure in any area of my life, catch fire and burn to ashes, in the name of Jesus. I command every organ of my life to be free from every satanic presence, in the name of Jesus. Every good thing assigned to minister to my life here on earth or in the camp of the devil, be released, in the name of Jesus. I take back every good thing my ancestors, from the days of Adam, have handed over to the devil, in the name of Jesus. Any evil movement among the creation against my life, be crippled, in the name of Jesus. Any strange fire burning in any area of my life, be quenched by the speaking blood of Jesus, in the name of Jesus. Let the capturing power in the blood of Jesus lose its power over my life forever, in the name of Jesus. I command every evil spirit to fly-out and leave my presence, forever, in the name of Jesus. Let the crippling power of God cripple every evil action going on against my life among the creatures, in the name of Jesus. Every satanic limitation placed before me by the devil and his agents, disappear, in the name of Jesus. Every enemy of my joy, happiness and peace of mind, your time is up, die, in the name of Jesus. Every messenger of failure and defeat in my life, wherever you are, show up and die with your message, in the name of Jesus. I set on fire the camp of the strong man and I command every evil property to burn to ashes, in the name of Jesus. Let the multiplying power of God multiply every good thing in my life to the glory of God, in the name of Jesus. I command every organ of my body, soul and spirit to submit to Jesus Christ, forever, in the name of Jesus. Lord Jesus, arise, rule and reign forever and ever in my life, in the name of Jesus. I command the devil, his agents; sin and its consequences to be frustrated forever in every area of my life, in the name of Jesus. Let the overcoming anointing in Jesus Christ overcome the devil, his agents and all evil in my life, in the name of Jesus. Almighty God, prosper me beyond human imagination and use me to share your blessings rightly among others, in the name of Jesus. I command my life to be a channel of blessing to others all over the world without an end, in the name of Jesus. Any evil force militating against divine purpose, plan and goals in my life, be frustrated, in the name of Jesus. O Lord arise and bless me beyond others all over the world, in the name of Jesus. Any demonic spirit attached to my life or on God's blessing in my life, I bind and cast you out, in the name of Jesus. Every unclean spirit of leprosy, blindness, curses, poverty and demonic fear in my life, come out now, in the name of Jesus. Any evil spirit, plague, impotence and death, tormenting my destiny, your time is up, I bind and cast you out, in the name of Jesus. I take authority against evil forces attacking me from the waters, grave yard and heavenlies, in the name of Jesus.

Day 2

Expectations:

1. **Total deliverance from every form of witchcraft manipulation.**
2. **The calming of every storm raging against your destiny.**
3. **The complete restoration of everything that the enemy stole from you.**
4. **The destruction of every yoke of idolatry and evil sacrifice affecting you and your destiny.**
5. **The destruction of every curse placed on you due to stubbornness and sinful lifestyle.**
6. **The destruction of all the spirits behind evil lifestyles**

Lord, deliver my brain, hands, head and feet from witchcraft manipulations, in the name of Jesus. Every great storm raging against my destiny, be calmed by force, in the name of Jesus. Every weeping part of my life, be comforted, in the name of Jesus. Let the deliverance messengers from heaven begin to minister deliverance into my life, in the name of Jesus. Every good thing the enemy has stolen from my life, I command them to be restored, in the name of Jesus. I stretched forth my hand for divine touch and full deliverance with all manner of blessings, in the name of Jesus. I break and loose myself from every yoke of idolatry and evil sacrifices, in the name of Jesus. Father Lord, deliver me from the spirit of religion without Christ, in the name of Jesus. Let my faith in Christ frustrate every work of the devil in my life, in the name of Jesus. Any evil action ever taken against me in any evil altar, be frustrated unto failure, in the name of Jesus. Let the sacrifice of the blood of Jesus frustrate every evil sacrifice ever offered against my destiny, in the name of Jesus. Every anger and action of the devil and his agents against my life, back fire, in the name of Jesus. Every evil sacrifice going on against my life and relationship with God, expire and lose your power over my life, in the name of Jesus. Any agent of the devil with a vow to kill me or destroy works of my hands, here on earth, fail woefully, in the name of Jesus. Any demonic spirit of complaining, finding fault without repentance, I bind and cast you out, in the name of Jesus. Every curse placed upon my life because of my stubbornness and sinful lifestyle, father Lord, remove them by your mercy, in the name of Jesus. I break and loose myself from the spirit of fugitive and vagabond, in the name of Jesus. Spirit of murder, assigned to kill every good thing in my life, and my relationship with Christ, I bind and cast you out, in the name of Jesus. I take authority and I destroy every satanic program going on against my life, in the name of Jesus (Genesis 4:2-16).

> And the seventy returned again with joy, saying, Lord, even the devils are subject unto us through thy name.
>
> And he said unto them, I beheld Satan as lightning fall from heaven.
>
> Behold, I give unto you power to tread on serpents and scorpions, and over all the power of the enemy: and nothing shall by any means hurt you.
>
> — LUKE 10:17-19

I use my power and authority over all devils, sicknesses and diseases to destroy every demonic operation in my life, in the name of Jesus. I command every incurable sickness and disease in my life to be cured by force, in the name of Jesus. Every demonic infection in my body, soul and spirit, die from your roots, in the name of Jesus. Almighty God, arise and help me to use my authority rightly with eternity in view, in the name of Jesus. Let the healing power in the stripes of Jesus begin to manifest in my life, family and ministry, in the name of Jesus. Any evil kingdom, fighting against the manifestations of the authority of Christ in my life, be dethroned, in the name of Jesus. Let my encounters with evil spirits in the battle field end by casting them out without struggle, in the name of Jesus. I command every demonic spirit to be subjected to my command through the name of Jesus, in the name of Jesus. I command the devil and every demonic spirit engaged in evil action here on earth to be destroyed through my ministry, in the name of Jesus. Let the falling of demonic kingdoms be noticeable in my ministry everywhere, in the name of Jesus. With the power given to me by Jesus Christ, I tread upon serpents and scorpions all the days of my life without harm, in the name of Jesus. I command the powers of my enemies to be wasted by the divine authority given to me, in the name of Jesus. I command every pain causing power on earth and among creations to avoid me and refuse to hurt me, in the name of Jesus. I command every demonic arrested area of my life to rise, take up your bed and walk, in the name of Jesus. I command every container of my marriage that has been dried and emptied of wine to be refilled with waters that will be turned to wine, in the name of Jesus. By the mercies of God Almighty, I command every part of my life to be connected to Christ, in the name of Jesus. Almighty God, deliver me from the spirit of the last days, Sodom and Gomorrah, in the name of Jesus. Every enemy of my settlement and establishment on earth, be exposed and be disgraced, in the name of Jesus. I break and loose myself from every demonic influence and wrong decisions, in the name of Jesus. Every arrow of failure and destruction, fired against my marriage, I fire you back, in the name of Jesus. O Lord arise and deliver me from the lifestyle of Sodom and Gomorrah, in the name of Jesus. Every spirit of wickedness against me and God, I bind and cast you out of my presence, in the name of Jesus. Father Lord, deliver me from the plans of the devil and his agents, in the name of Jesus. I break and loose myself from the yoke of wrong marriage, in the name of Jesus. Blood of Jesus, deliver my mind and thoughts from the habitations of the devil, in the name of Jesus.

You the waters that destroyed the whole world in the days of Noah, flow into the camp of my unrepentant enemies and destroy them, in the name of Jesus (Genesis 6:1-24). Let my imaginations and desires be cleansed by the speaking blood of Jesus, in the name of Jesus. Let the yearn to continue in sin be terminated in my life, by the Almighty God, in the name of Jesus. Let the powers of God that destroyed the whole world in the past arise for my sake and destroy every work of the devil and his agents, in the name of Jesus.

Day 3

Expectations:

1. The destruction of every evil group building Babylon around you.
2. The destruction of all the enemies of your life, family and destiny
3. The destruction of every evil gang up against you.
4. Commanding God's plan for your life to manifest.
5. The termination of every reproach, shame and disgrace in your life.

Any evil group building Babylon within me and within nations, receive destructive confusion, in the name of Jesus. I command the languages of my enemies to be confounded, in the name of Jesus. I withdraw the understanding and the wisdom of my enemies, in the name of Jesus. I take authority against every evil gang up against me and God, in the name of Jesus. Any evil plan against God and his plans for my life, fail woefully, in the name of Jesus. O Lord arise and deliver me from every satanic arrow, in the name of Jesus. Let the scattering power of God spare me and scatter my unrepentant enemies, in the name of Jesus. I break every evil unity designed to fight God in me, in the name of Jesus. I command every evil unrepentant enemy's program going on against my destiny to be terminated, in the name of Jesus. Every satanic structure, built against me, spiritually or physically, catch fire and burn to ashes, in the name of Jesus. Father Lord, single me out from general punishment and judgments that come from you, in the name of Jesus (Genesis 11:1-0).

> And it came to pass, when the Philistine arose, and came and drew nigh to meet David, that David hasted, and ran toward the army to meet the Philistine.

And David put his hand in his bag, and took thence a stone, and slang *it,* and smote the Philistine in his forehead, that the stone sunk into his forehead; and he fell upon his face to the earth.

So David prevailed over the Philistine with a sling and with a stone, and smote the Philistine, and slew him; but *there was* no sword in the hand of David.

—   1 SAMUEL 17:48-50

Any battle and warfare going on against me among the creations, end to my favor, in the name of Jesus. Every evil gathering, organized against me, my family and God's people on earth, scatter and fail woefully, in the name of Jesus. Let the standing ground of all my enemies collapse and swallow them, in the name of Jesus. Any evil drawing near and closer to my place, be crippled and blinded, in the name of Jesus. Any evil mouth opened against my life, close forever, in the name of Jesus. I terminate every reproach, shame and disgrace in my life, by the speaking blood of Jesus, in the name of Jesus. Let the prevailing power of God empower me to prevail over my enemies in the battle field, in the name of Jesus. Father Lord, empower me to slay every Goliath in the battle field of my life, in the name of Jesus. Let the sword of my enemies enter into their hearts and slay them, in the name of Jesus. I receive victory to liberate me and all my loved ones, in the name of Jesus. Every hungry and thirsty part of my life, open your mouths and be filled up with the best of life, in the name of Jesus. Let the washing and cleansing power in the blood of Jesus wash and clean me, inside out, in the name of Jesus. Let the forces of heaven that raised Lazarus from the grave enter into every area of my life and give me life in abundance, in the name of Jesus. Almighty God, increase my faith to exercise authority over the powers of the devil, in the name of Jesus. I stand against every enemy of my destiny and God's plan, in the name of Jesus. I command every satanic embargo placed upon my life to be lifted, in the name of Jesus. Every satanic military force, assigned against me, scatter and fail woefully, in the name of Jesus. Father Lord, separate me from anything that has vowed to separate me from you, in the name of Jesus (Genesis 12:10-16). Anointing of God's grace to hear and respond to the will of God for my life, possess me, in the name of Jesus. Father Lord, empower me to walk out from the camp of the devil to your own camp, in the name of Jesus. Any evil force delaying my prompt obedience to divine call, scatter and leave me alone, in the name of Jesus. Almighty God, help me never to return to Egypt, no matter the situation where you keep me, in the name of Jesus. Every enemy of my permanent settlement and establishment in God's will, fail woefully, in the name of Jesus. Almighty God, empower me to stay put in your will, place and purpose forever, in the name of Jesus. Father Lord, increase your grace to help me stay with you, no matter the situation, in the name of Jesus. Every demonic fear assigned to take me away from God's will, I bind and cast you out, in the name of Jesus.

And he is before all things, and by him all things consist.

And he is the head of the body, the church: who is the beginning, the firstborn from the dead; that in all *things* he might have the pre-eminence.

— COLOSSIANS 1:17, 18

For the eyes of the LORD run to and fro throughout the whole earth, to shew himself strong in the behalf of *them* whose heart *is* perfect toward him. Herein thou hast done foolishly: therefore, from henceforth thou shalt have wars.

— 2 CHRONICLES 16:9

I command all creation to join me in the battle field against all my enemies, in the name of Jesus. Any visible or invisible forces of darkness assigned to destroy me and my people, turn around and destroy yourselves, in the name of Jesus. I command every throne of darkness, principality or power against me to be dethroned, in the name of Jesus. Father Lord, by your presence, I manifest to destroy every evil appearance among the creation, in the name of Jesus. Almighty God, command your fighting spirit to possess me to defeat every demonic force, in the name of Jesus. Any evil head that will ever be raised against me in the battle field of life, I cut you off, in the name of Jesus. Let the beginning and the end of my problems be terminated in shame without survival, in the name of Jesus. Every good thing that is dead in my life and ministry, receive abundant life, in the name of Jesus. Father Lord, blessed Holy Spirit, take full pre-eminence over my life forever and ever, in the name of Jesus. Let the eyes of God Almighty possess my eyes to see clearly spiritually and physically, in the name of Jesus. Let the hide out of the devil and his agents be exposed and destroyed in my life, in the name of Jesus. Any evil force, marching towards me with destructive weapons, be destroyed on your way without delay, in the name of Jesus. By the power of God's searching eyes, I command every evil eye monitoring my life to be blinded, in the name of Jesus. Father Lord, discover and destroy every evil habitation of the devil against me, in the name of Jesus. Father Lord, look at the whole earth and discover my problems and waste them before they manifest, in the name of Jesus. Father Lord, arise in your strength and destroy the strength of the devil and his agents against me, in the name of Jesus. I command every evil arrow that has been assigned against my heart to go back to its sender, in the name of Jesus. Almighty God, send the blood of your son, Jesus, to enter into my heart and other organs of my body and sanctify them, in the name of Jesus. Almighty God, deliver me from every sin and replace my foolishness with your pure wisdom, in the name of Jesus. Every warfare going on against me in the spirit ream and in the physical ream, end to my favor, in the name of Jesus. Every Pharaoh that is standing in my inheritance, be destroyed, in the name of Jesus. Almighty God, deliver me from any fear assigned to put me into trouble, in the name of Jesus. Father Lord, by your power, I bring plague upon every living and non-living thing in the house of my enemies with barrenness, in the name of Jesus. I command the activities of my unrepentant enemies to be destroyed without fruits, in the name of Jesus. Every yoke of loneliness upon my life, break to pieces, in the name of Jesus. I command the handworks of my enemies to be destroyed without survival, in the name of Jesus (Genesis12:14-17). Father Lord, prepare me for the manifestation of your promises and fill me with the fruits and the gifts of your Spirit, in the name of Jesus. I command every evil voice speaking inside me to hold their peace and come out by force, in the name of Jesus. Every power behind my problems, your time is up, I rebuke you, in the name of Jesus. I command every creature supporting my enemies to withdraw their support immediately, in the name of Jesus. Any strange fire burning in any area of my life, be quenched by the flowing blood of Jesus, in the name of Jesus. Every organized darkness militating against me, be disorganized, in the name of Jesus.

SIXTEEN

UNKNOWN PRAYERS AND JESUS' SPIRITUAL WARFARE

DECREE-1

(Matthew 4:1-11, Matthew 15:33-39, Matthew 27:62-66, Matthew 28:2-4, Acts 26:9-15, Acts 9:13-19, Philippians 3:7, 8)

Day 1

Expectations:

1. Receiving God's anointing to live above sin
2. Deliverance from every custom and tradition conflicting with your desire to serve God.
3. The destruction of every power attempting to drive Christ out of your life.
4. The destruction of every satanic weapon aimed at destroying you.
5. The breaking of every idolatrous nature affecting church leaders.

Father Lord, empower me and lead me by your Spirit in everything I do in life without sin and compromise, in the name of Jesus. Anointing to live above sin in everything, especially in hard times, fall upon me, in the name of Jesus. I receive power to continue with God, even in times of prosperity and abundance, in the name of Jesus. Almighty God, deliver me from any tradition and custom conflicting with my decision to serve you with my whole heart, in the name of Jesus. I break and loose myself from every life of luxury (Matthew 8:19, 20) preventing me from following Christ, in the name of Jesus. Every demonic motivated goal in my life, affecting my relationship with Christ, I reject you, in the name of Jesus. I break and loose myself from every demonic demand (Matthew 8:21) from the dead, in the name of Jesus. Any evil force assigned to drive Christ out of any coast, from any department in my life (Matthew 8:34), scatter, in the name of Jesus. Any demon residing in me with any problem to mock Jesus (Matthew 9:18, 19, 23-26), I bind and cast you out, in the name of Jesus. Any satanic weapon with the Herod of my time (Matthew 14:1-13) to cut any part of my life or head, back fire, in the name of Jesus.

Then was Jesus led up of the Spirit into the wilderness to be tempted of the devil.

And when he had fasted forty days and forty nights, he was afterward an hungred.

And when the tempter came to him, he said, if thou be the Son of God, command that these stones be made bread.

But he answered and said, it is written, Man shall not live by bread alone, but by every word that proceedeth out of the mouth of God.

Then the devil taketh him up into the holy city, and setteth him on a pinnacle of the temple,

And saith unto him, if thou be the Son of God, cast thyself down: for it is written, He shall give his angels charge concerning thee: and in *their* hands they shall bear thee up, lest at any time thou dash thy foot against a stone.

Jesus said unto him, it is written again, thou shalt not tempt the Lord thy God.

Again, the devil taketh him up into an exceeding high mountain, and sheweth him all the kingdoms of the world, and the glory of them;

And saith unto him, all these things will I give thee, if thou wilt fall down and worship me.

Then saith Jesus unto him, get thee hence, Satan: for it is written, thou shalt worship the Lord thy God, and him only shalt thou serve.

Then the devil leaveth him, and, behold, angels came and ministered unto him.

— MATTHEW 4:1-11

Every temptation before me, father Lord, give me victory and divine support, in the name of Jesus. Any evil force contending against my faith in the battle field of life, scatter and fail woefully, in the name of Jesus. Almighty God, prepare me and keep me righteous without sin before, during and after fasting, in the name of Jesus. Hunger for physical food, sin and sexual perversion after fasting, I bring you under my control, in the name of Jesus. Any tempter and temptress in and outside the church assigned to pull me down with sexual perversion be disgraced, in the name of Jesus. Any demon possessed prophet or prophetess assigned to pollute the church through false prophesy, fail woefully, in the name of Jesus. Let the corrupting powers of darkness in every city of the world, be frustrated, in the name of Jesus. Every negative influence and worldliness, pulling me out of my faith in Christ, I reject you, in the name of Jesus. I break and loose myself from every worldly activity going on in the church, in the name of Jesus. Any worldly kingdom brought into the church to destroy souls, be frustrated out of the ministry, in the name of Jesus. Every yoke of idolatry in the lives of the church leadership and members, break to pieces in the ministry, in the name of Jesus. Father Lord, deliver me from occultism and idolatrous worship in the body of Christ, in the name of Jesus. Anointing to serve only one true God everywhere I go in life, fall upon me, in the mighty name of Jesus. Father Lord, protect me from every satanic attack hindering me from standing for the truth, in the name of Jesus. I command the devil and his agents assigned to pull me down to be frustrated in defeat, in the name of Jesus. I command the devil and his agents working against me to be disengaged without success, in the name of Jesus. Almighty God, command your angels to come to my rescue and minister to me without break, in the name of Jesus. Almighty God, deliver me from the spirit of slumber (Matthew 26:37-46) in the times of battle, in the name of Jesus. Any spirit against Christ in my life, assigned to use me to betray Christ (Matthew 26:47-50), I bind and cast you out, in the name of Jesus. Almighty God, help me to stand for the truth without bearing false witness (Matthew 26:57), in the name of Jesus. I refuse to follow the multitude to do any evil against Christ (Matthew 26:51-75), in the name of Jesus. Almighty God, empower me to stand for justice and to render righteous judgment under any pressure (Matthew 27:11), in the name of Jesus. I refuse to join others to fight Jesus (Matthew 27:27-31, 34-37), in the name of Jesus. Father Lord, deliver me from conspiracy against Christ, in the name of Jesus. Almighty God, help me to get to my cross and empower me to stand by the right hand of Christ (Matthew 27:38-44) to plead for mercy, in the name of Jesus.

Day 2

Expectations:

1. **The frustration of everything in you and around you insulting Christ**
2. **Deliverance from every form of corruption and bribery**
3. **Deliverance from every form of satanic arrest aimed at moving you against Christ**
4. **Commanding the blood of Jesus to speak you out of every danger**

Anything in me, outside me, insulting Christ (Matthew 27:39-40), be frustrated, in the name of Jesus. I withdraw every organ of my life from accepting to give Jesus vinegar to drink (Matthew 27:48-50), in the name of Jesus. Almighty God, deliver me from corruption and the spirit of bribery (Matthew 28:11-15) against Christ, in the name of Jesus. Mark 14:36-40, 42 ... Almighty God, deliver me from the spirit of self-confidence and overestimation of myself, in the name of Jesus. I break and loose myself from every satanic arrest assigned to move me against Christ, in the name of Jesus. Father Lord, lead me to my Gethsemane and empower me to pray for the preparation of the battles ahead, in the name of Jesus. I refuse to sit, lie or stay in silent when I supposed to pray, in the name of Jesus. I command every organ of my body, soul and spirit to be fervent in prayer, in the name of Jesus. Every arrow of weakness fired against my prayer life, go back to your sender, in the name of Jesus. Any spirit of heaviness attacking my prayer life, I bind and cast you out, in the name of Jesus. Father Lord, command your perfect will to start manifesting in my life, in the name of Jesus. Let the redemption power in the speaking blood of Jesus speak me out of every danger, in the name of Jesus. Lord Jesus, you are my burden bearer, take away every burden in my life, in the name of Jesus. Almighty God, command your will to manifest in my life, in the name of Jesus. Every spirit of slumber, heaviness in my life, I bind and cast you out, in three names of Jesus. Father Lord, fill me with the Holy Spirit and empower me to receive deliverance, in the name of Jesus. Almighty God, deliver me from sleeping on duty, in the mighty name of Jesus. Let the sending power of God send me out of every satanic altar, in the name of Jesus. I break and loose myself from the spirit of failure and defeat, in the mighty name of Jesus. I receive enough grace to help me to fast, pray and watch at all times against satanic diversion, in the name of Jesus. Almighty God, prepare me to have victory concerning every temptation assigned to destroy my life, in the name of Jesus. Every unfriendly friend assigned to betray me, your time is up, be frustrated, in the name of Jesus. Almighty God, anoint me with spiritual alabaster box of ointment of spikenard, very precious to sustain my purity, in the name of Jesus. I command my head to carry divine anointing that will scare away every demonic presence, in the name of Jesus. I refuse to spare anything that will bring me closer to Christ and prepare me for heaven, in the name of Jesus. Father Lord, deliver me from the spirit of Judas Iscariot and every betrayal demon, in the name of Jesus. Any conspiracy against my relationship with Christ, your time is up, scatter, in the name of Jesus. I break and loose myself from the spirit of covetousness and the love of money, in the name of Jesus. Any evil gang-up against Christ in me, fail woefully and scatter, in the name of Jesus. Almighty God, deliver me from every satanic plan and evil designed against my destiny, in the name of Jesus. I break and loose myself from the spirit of bribery and corruption, in the name of Jesus. Any part of my life, bound in spiritual or physical prison (Mark 6:17-28), I command you to be released by fire, in the name of Jesus. Every demonic accusation against me by the devil and his agents, fail woefully, in the name of Jesus. O Lord arise and deliver me from every satanic motivated conspiracy, in the name of Jesus. Any satanic tradition or custom (Mark 7:1-5, 20-23) designed to bring me to bondage, be frustrated, in the name of Jesus. Any agent of defilement, pollution and contamination against my life, be exposed and be disgraced, in the name of Jesus. Let the beheading power of the devil and his agents avoid my head, in the name of Jesus. Almighty God, deliver me from all manner of temptation in this generation (Mark 8:11-13), in the name of Jesus. Every enemy of my stand with God in righteousness, your time is up, be frustrated, in the name of Jesus.

Day 3

Expectations:

1. **The destruction of every spirit responsible for confusion and fighting for position in the body of Christ.**
2. **Receiving the ability to make the right choice in marriage.**
3. **The breaking of 'the yoke of impossibility' affecting any area of your life.**
4. **Complete deliverance from every form of depression, envy, indignation and carnality.**

Every spirit of confusion, in fighting for position in the body of Christ (Mark 9:33-37), I am not your candidate, in the name of Jesus. Any evil spirit questioning my authority and looking for fault to discredit me (Marl 10:2-12), be disappointed, in the name of Jesus. Father Lord, empower me to do your will in my marriage without any mistake, in the name of Jesus. Any evil spirit monitoring my life to lead me into making wrong choices in life, I bind and cast you out, in the name of Jesus. Father Lord, empower me to train younger ones in ministry with true conversion and holiness (Mark 10:13-16), in the name of Jesus. Let my lifestyle bring little children to Jesus and empower them to serve Christ forever, in the name of Jesus. Father Lord, bless me with riches, great wealth (Mark 10-17) and empower me to use it to serve you, in the name of Jesus. Father Lord, deliver me from the love of money and anything standing between me and you, in the name of Jesus. Let the gifts and talents in me, plus my time and strength be dedicated to serve God without any reservation, in the name of Jesus. Everything here on earth, standing between me and God as an idol, receive destruction, in the name of Jesus. Blood of Jesus, speak me out of idolatry and occultism, in the name of Jesus. Every spirit of hypocrisy in me, your time is up,

I bind and cast you out, in the name of Jesus. Every yoke of impossibility in any area of my life, break to pieces, in the name of Jesus. You the spirit of position seeking demon in my life (Mark 10:35-40), I bind and cast you out, in the name of Jesus. Father Lord, deliver me from carnal desires and unprofitable ambitions, in the name of Jesus. Almighty God, deliver me from depression, envy, indignation and carnality (Mark 10:41-45), in the name of Jesus. I command the spirit of merchandise, buying and selling in the temple to be cast out from the body of Christ, in the name of Jesus. Every enemy of purity, decency, right way of doing things in the church (Mark 11:15-17), be frustrated, in the name of Jesus. I receive divine strength and leading to stop every carnality going on in the church, in the name of Jesus. Every satanic activity going on against divine activity in the ministry, be terminated, in the name of Jesus. Father Lord, anoint me to overthrow every satanic establishment in my ministry, in the name of Jesus. Any evil personality, organizing the establishment of false doctrines in my ministry, be frustrated, in the name of Jesus. Almighty God, use me to destroy and terminate any evil that I have brought into the ministry by myself, in the name of Jesus. I burn every satanic table I have allowed into the ministry, in the name of Jesus. Any business going on in the ministry against the Lord's business, be terminated by force, in the name of Jesus. I terminate every lifestyle that is promoting the devil and his works in the ministry, in the name of Jesus. Blood of Jesus, speak me out of everything that promotes the devil and his agents, in the name of Jesus. Father Lord, deliver me from stealing in the ministry and from every wrong doing, in the name of Jesus. Any evil gang up against the will of God (Mark 11:18-19) in my ministry, scatter, in the name of Jesus. Almighty God, deliver me from every congregational conspiracy against the truth, in the name of Jesus. Any evil group (Mark 11:27-33), questioning my authority in Christ, your time is up, scatter, in the name of Jesus. Almighty God, arise and deliver me from every satanic plan to frustrate me, in the name of Jesus. Father Lord, empower me with your wisdom to overcome every satanic wisdom militating against my services to your name, in the name of Jesus. I receive divine knowledge and understanding to over match the schemes of the devil and his agents against me, in the name of Jesus. Let the tempting power of the devil and his agents be disgraced by your Spirit, in the name of Jesus.

Day 4

Expectations:

1. The closing of all satanic entrance doors into your life.
2. The destruction of every agent of darkness sent to use your words against you.
3. The conquering of every satanic agent against your faith.
4. The destruction of every organized darkness trying to deceive you into falsehood.
5. Total deliverance from the spirit of religion

Almighty God, possess my brain and tongues to release words that will disgrace the devil and his agents in the battlefield of my life, in the name of Jesus. I close every satanic entrance door into my life and I block them from every route of escape, in the name of Jesus. Almighty God, give me divine motivated questions to cripple the wisdom of the devil and his agents before me, in the name of Jesus. Every agent of the devil that has been (Mark 12:13-17) sent to use my words against me, receive pain and fall in defeat, in the name of Jesus. I confront and conquer every satanic agent in the battle field against my faith and mission in life, in the name of Jesus. I command the enemies of God to make heart wrenching mistakes that will promote me against their evil, in the name of Jesus. Father Lord, by your wisdom in me, disgrace and disappoint every satanic agent that has been assigned against me (Mark 12:18-27), in the name of Jesus. Every position seeker in the ministry of Christ (Mark 12:33-40), be disgraced, in the name of Jesus. Every organized darkness deceiving people with falsehood, your time is up, scatter, in the name of Jesus. Let the reward of damnation be released against every unrepentant agent dominating the plans of God, in the name of Jesus. I command every messenger of the devil with false doctrine in the ministry to be exposed and disgraced, in the name of Jesus. I break and loose myself and every member of this ministry from the spirit of religion without Christ, in the name of Jesus. Every yoke of pride upon my life because of my academic achievement, break to pieces, in the name of Jesus. I refuse to disobey God and his commandments, my social level, position and financial statues shall not stop me from being humble to God, in the name of Jesus. Father Lord, fill me with your Spirit and your fruits to humble myself, in the name of Jesus. Almighty God, deliver me from the crafty ones (Mark 14:1-2) in the ministry, in the name of Jesus. Every arrow of death fired against me in the ministry, I fire you back, in the name of Jesus. I bring the devil and his agents into a perfect failure in my life, in the name of Jesus. Father Lord, begin to reward all unrepentant agents of the devil raised against me, in the name of Jesus. I bring into captivity every evil thought and imagination against me to be obedient to Christ (Mark 14:3-9), in the name of Jesus. Any satanic exaltation against Christ in my life, I pull you down, in the name of Jesus. Every demonic embargo placed against me, be lifted, in the name of Jesus. Almighty God, bless every sponsor, supporter and servant of yours in this ministry, in the name of Jesus. Father Lord, raise men and women that will help me to complete my mission on earth, perfectly, to your own glory, in the name of Jesus. Father Lord, arise in your mercy and prepare me to fulfill my purpose on earth; empower me to make heaven, in the name of Jesus. Almighty God, give me victory in every temptation on my way to the end of my mission here on earth, in the name of Jesus. Every satanic indignation against the supporters of this mission, be frustrated, in the name of Jesus. Father Lord, encourage every true worshipper and helper in this ministry, in the name of Jesus. Every Judas in the ministry and in the midst of the workers in this ministry (Mark 14:10, 11, 45-48), be exposed, in the name of Jesus. Every agent of darkness hiding, in the midst of believers, be exposed and be disgraced, in the name of

Jesus. Let the betraying power of Judas take me to fulfill my purpose on earth, in the name of Jesus. Every evil plan to destroy the will of God for my life, fail woefully, in the name of Jesus. Let the kissing power of the devil in the life of every enemy in my life be disappointed, in the name of Jesus. Almighty God, give me victory over every unfriendly friend working against me, in the name of Jesus. Any evil personality that has been given the assignment to destroy me, your time is up, be frustrated, in the name of Jesus. I command all the deceived elders, workers, ministers in the ministry to repent or perish, in the name of Jesus.

Day 5

Expectations:

1. The destruction of every satanic stripe, sickness, disease and second affliction prepared against you.
2. Receiving the power to follow Christ
3. The destruction of every evil force that wants you to forsake Christ
4. The destruction of every satanic agent attacking your faith in Christ
5. The destruction of every arrow of confusion fired against you.

Every evil plan to dethrone Jesus Christ in my life and ministry, fail woefully, in the name of Jesus. Every satanic stripe, sickness, diseases and all second time affliction, prepared against my life, fail woefully (1 Peter 2:24; Mark 14:46, 53, 55, 56, 48, 49, 62), in the name of Jesus. I refuse to be sleep when I'm supposed pray; father Lord deliver me from fighting carnally (Mark 14:47), in the name of Jesus. Blood of Jesus, speak me out of denying Christ for any reason, in the name of Jesus. Father Lord, empower me to follow Christ to the cross; drop my cross at the calvary, in the name of Jesus. Any evil force that wants me to forsake Christ (Mark 14:50-52), you are a liar, fail woefully, in the name of Jesus. I refuse to join the disciples and the multitudes (Mark 14:54, 62-72) that denied Christ in the day of battle, in the name of Jesus. Almighty God, anoint me with your strength to follow Christ to the end, under any situation, in the name of Jesus. Every evil leader or agent of the devil, bounding Christ in my life (Mark 15:1-35), fail woefully, in the name of Jesus. Any evil council or demonic accuser spreading lies against my faith, be frustrated, in the name of Jesus. Almighty God, empower me to fight to the end no matter the battles against my faith, in the name of Jesus. Every Pilate in the judgment seat against my life (Mark 15:2, 45, 7, 10), receive silence in your cross examinations to me, in the name of Jesus. Let the scourging power of the devil and threat of death, even to crucifixion, be silenced by my determination to please God, in the name of Jesus. I command every satanic agent that is attacking my faith in Christ to fail woefully, in the name of Jesus. Almighty God, help me to pull through to the end under every trial and temptation, in the name of Jesus. Every satanic military personnel, urging me to deny Christ (Mark 15:16-28, 36), be frustrated, in the name of Jesus. I withdraw all my efforts to live in the flesh and focus my strength to live or die with Christ, in the name of Jesus. I command all mockers of my life because of my relationship with Christ to be disappointed, in the name of Jesus. Any evil nail in my body, soul and spirit, spiritually or physically (Mark 15:29), be removed by the crying blood of Jesus, in the name of Jesus. I command all that will follow through to the cross in this battle of life, including the thieves that were at the right hand of Christ to make it to Paradise, in the name of Jesus. Every property of the devil, weapon of darkness and evil words waging against me, be removed by the crying blood of Jesus. Every stumbling block on my way to calvary to drop my burdens, be violently removed, in the name of Jesus. Anointing to push through, despise the insults from armed robbers, all sinners (Mark 15:27, 32), fall upon me, in the name of Jesus. Almighty God, increase your faith in me, grant me more mercies to make heaven at all cost in the midst of every warfare, in the mighty name of Jesus. Every satanic promise and arrow of confusion fired against me to disobey God, I reject you forever, in the name of Jesus. Every tempter and temptress assigned to overthrow my faith in Christ, fail woefully, in the name of Jesus. Any evil spirit challenging my faith and faithfulness in God, I bind and cast you out, in the name of Jesus. I reject every demonic demand against my life, in the mighty name of Jesus. Blood of Jesus, go before me and speak me out of every evil, in the name of Jesus.

And his disciples say unto him, whence should we have so much bread in the wilderness, as to fill so great a multitude?

And Jesus saith unto them, how many loaves have ye? And they said, Seven, and a few little fishes.

And he commanded the multitude to sit down on the ground.

And he took the seven loaves and the fishes, and gave thanks, and brake *them,* and gave to his disciples, and the disciples to the multitude.

And they did all eat, and were filled: and they took up of the broken *meat* that was left seven baskets full.

And they that did eat were four thousand men, beside women and children.

And he sent away the multitude, and took ship, and came into the coasts of Magdala.

— MATTHEW 15:33-39

Let the compassionate power of God flow into my life without measure, in the name of Jesus. Blood of Jesus, speak me out of every problem, in the name of Jesus. I break and loose myself from physical and spiritual fainting spirit, in the name of Jesus. By the power in Christs' multiplying anointing, I command every good thing in my life to multiply, in the name of Jesus. Almighty God, feed me spiritually and physically with the little in me, in the name of Jesus.

Day 6

Expectations:

1. **Divine empowerment so that you can feed God's people**
2. **Divine supply to meet every need in your life**
3. **Deliverance from every danger and satanic rough road**
4. **Commanding the presence of God to bring you into divine strength, comfort, rest and hope forever**

Almighty God, empower me to be able to feed the followers of Christ through me with good diet, spiritually and physically, in the name of Jesus. I abort every food poison that has been swallowed by any follower of Christ, in the name of Jesus. Every spiritual and physical lack in my life, receive divine provision, in the name of Jesus. Let the renewal power in the word of God, renew every good thing in my life, in the name of Jesus. Father Lord, guide me to every truth and instruct me in righteousness, in the name of Jesus. Father Lord, give me courage in times of danger without fear, in the name of Jesus. Almighty God by your miraculous provision, provide everything I need, in the name of Jesus. Father Lord, put your quality and strength into everything in my life, in the name of Jesus. Almighty God, accompany me to every battle and fight for me, in the name of Jesus. Father Lord, walk into my life and take over, walk the devil and his problems out of my life, in the name of Jesus. Father Lord, lead me out of every danger and satanic rough road, in the name of Jesus. Almighty God, lead me and guide me to walk in faith, always, in the name of Jesus. Father Lord, empower me to be delivered from the valleys and perils of this world, in the name of Jesus. Oh Lord, hold me and strengthen me to stand firm in your word, without falling, in the name of Jesus. Let the promises of God be fulfilled to the glory of his name in mt life, in the name of Jesus. Let the name EMMANUEL, God be with me, be perfectly fulfilled in my life, in the name of Jesus. I frustrate every satanic danger and peril, known and unknown, in the name of Jesus. Father Lord, empower me to recognize your voice and empower me to obey your commands, in the name of Jesus. Let the protection and the provision in obeying God's word begin to manifest in my life, in the name of Jesus. Let the assurance of help in the word of God begin to manifest in every area of my life, in the name of Jesus. Let the sufficient power of God provide protection, security and preservation in every area of my life, in the name of Jesus. Let the presence of God bring me into divine strength, comfort, rest and hope forever, in the name of Jesus. Father Lord, let your promise of complete supply of every one of my needs manifest in my life from every side, in the name of Jesus. Let the goodness of God, his mercy, loving-kindness and grace be multiplied into my life, in the name of Jesus. Father Lord, help me to break every evil covenant in my life and help me to uphold my covenant with you, in the name of Jesus. Let heaven, which is my goal be preserved for me without negotiation forever, in the name of Jesus. Father Lord, cause your blessings in my life to run over with joy and goodness that cannot fade away, in the name of Jesus. I break and loose myself from the prison yard of the Herod of my time and place, in the name of Jesus. Every judgment passed against me from every evil personality (Luke 3:19, 20), be reversed, in the name of Jesus. I break and loose myself from every evil spirit influencing me to reject divine counsels (Luke 7:29, 30), in the name of Jesus. Almighty God, deliver me from every demonic spirit fighting against the presence of Jesus Christ (Luke 8:37) in my life, in the name of Jesus. Father Lord, help me to remain in the position and place apportioned for me in your kingdom without seeking for a place for myself (Luke 9:46-48), in the name of Jesus. Father Lord, empower me to collaborate and work in unity (Luke 49-50) with other believers without envy and jealousy, in the name of Jesus. Anointing to discern true believers and accept them for the progress of evangelism (Luke 9:51-56), possess me, in the name of Jesus. Father Lord, fill me with the spirit of forgiveness, help me to forgive my offenders the way Jesus forgave his persecutors in the bible, in the name of Jesus. Any spirit in me moving me to wish others evil (Luke 9:51-56), I bind and cast you out, in the name of Jesus. Every spirit of hatred, envy, jealousy and rejection against others (9:51-56), your time is up; I bind you and cast you out, in the name of Jesus.

Day 7

Expectations:

1. **The frustration of every evil spirit fighting to overthrow Christ in your life.**
2. **The destruction of every demonic power by the power of God's word.**
3. **The uprooting and removal of every satanic deposit in your life.**
4. **The termination of every marine spirit activity going on against your life and destiny.**

Father Lord, fill me with the spirit of Christ to love and care like He cares for us, in the name of Jesus. Any evil spirit fighting to overthrow Christ in my life, be frustrated, in the name of Jesus. Let the destroying power in the word of God destroy every demonic character in my life, in the name of Jesus. Almighty God, empower me to give Jesus every support He needs to take over everything going on in my life, in the name of Jesus. I command every organ in my body to abort every satanic deposit in me, in the name of Jesus. Every spiritual battle going on in the spirit and physical against my destiny, end to my favor, in the name of Jesus. Let the killing anointing in the word of God kill every evil presence in every part of my life, in the name of Jesus. Any marine spirit activity going on against my destiny, be terminated, in the name of Jesus. Let the tempting power of the devil and his agents (Luke 10:25-37) fail woefully in my life, in the name of Jesus. Almighty God, deliver me from every tempter and temptress that has been assigned against my faith in Christ, in the name of Jesus. Almighty God, by your grace and mercy, let me be among the people that will hear the sound of the trumpet, in the name of Jesus. I break and loose myself from every spirit of hypocrisy, in the name of Jesus. Every enemy of the reign and manifestation of truth in my life, fail woefully, in the name of Jesus. Almighty God, empower me to keep a balance in obeying the law and obeying the word of God without sinning against your kingdom, in the name of Jesus. Oh lord my God, give me wisdom to strike a balance between my service to mankind with my service to you (Luke 10:38-42), in the name of Jesus. Every influential brother, sister or friend, pulling me away from serving God, fail woefully, in the name of Jesus. Almighty God, deliver me from every opposite sex that the devil has assigned to divert my life from God's divine plans for my life, in the name of Jesus. Almighty God, help me to make the right choices and the right decisions with eternity in view, in the name of Jesus. Father Lord, help me to always take the right path in my relationship with Christ, without compromise, in the name of Jesus. Every demonic motivated accusation against my life and my work for God (Luke 11:14, 15, 17, 26), be frustrated, in the name of Jesus. Anointing to cast out the spirit of Beelzebub and Satan from their victims, possess me, in the name of Jesus. Father Lord, empower me to seek Jesus and find Him (Luke 11:16, 17) before seeking for his signs, in the name of Jesus. Any evil spirit moving me to provoke Jesus or tempt Him for any reason (Luke 11:53, 54), I bind and cast you out, in the name of Jesus. I break and loose myself from every demonic arrest by evil spirits (Luke 12:16-21) assigned to waste my life, in the name of Jesus. I command every demonic spirit influencing me to plan my life without God to be frustrated (Luke12:16-21) out of my life, in the name of Jesus. Father Lord, help me to withdraw all my trust in money, material things or every other thing here on earth, in the name of Jesus. Almighty God, prepare me to fulfil my destiny before you call me for eternity, in the name of Jesus. Anything here on earth, depriving me or delaying my perfect service to God, receive total destruction, in the name of Jesus. Father Lord, empower me to serve you and my generation in holiness (Acts 13:36) according to your will, in the name of Jesus. Any evil force manipulating my life to divert me from God's divine purpose, scatter in defeat, in the name of Jesus. I break and loose myself from everything in this world that is contending with God and his will for myself, in the name of Jesus. Let my trust in God rule and reign in every part of my life without a rival, in the name of Jesus. Anything or person, among the creatures, that wants to take the place of God in my life, be frustrated out of my life, forever, in the name of Jesus. Every Jezebel, Delilah, wife of Potiphar or demonic filled person in my life, be exposed and be disgraced, in the name of Jesus. Almighty God, deliver my soul from anything that will cause it to sin on its last day on earth.

Day 8

Expectations:

1. **The perfecting of your holiness and your relationship with God**
2. **Deliverance from false accusers and hypocritical rulers in the body of Christ**
3. **Deliverance from every conspiracy and evil arrow fired against you**
4. **The destruction and removal of every demonic roadblock mounted against you**
5. **The destruction of every demonic plantation in people's hearts, hindering them from yielding completely to God and being saved.**

Father Lord, perfect my holiness and relationship with you from now on, especially in my last moment here on earth, in the name of Jesus. Father Lord, increase my fighting spirit against Satan and sin every day of my life, in the name of Jesus. Let my hatred against Satan and sin be multiplied, in the name of Jesus. Almighty God, deliver me from false accusers, and hypocritical rulers in the body of Christ (Luke 13:14-17), in the name of Jesus. Every enemy of the sound teaching of the word of God in my ministry, be exposed and be disgraced, in the name of Jesus. Almighty God, increase my boldness in spreading the truth without compromising it, in the name of Jesus. I break and loose myself from every conspiracy and evil arrow that the enemy has fired against my ministry, in the name of Jesus. Let the power of Christ dethrone every agent of the devil that is exalting themselves above Christ, in the name of Jesus. Every organized evil elder, blocking the move of God in the body of Christ, be disorganized, in the name of Jesus. I command all the evil ones sitting in the place of Christ in my ministry to be unseated and replaced by God Himself, in the name of Jesus. Every enemy of divine motivated change and revival in my life, your time is up, be exposed and disgraced, in the name of Jesus. Almighty God, move people from everywhere on earth to respond to divine invitation (Luke 14:15-24), in the name of Jesus. Every demonic roadblock mounted on the way to block me from Christ, the truth and the life, be dismantled, in the name of Jesus. I command every demonic plantation in human hearts against their true repentance and their salvation to die, in the name of Jesus. Every darkness in human understanding against God's plan for my life (Ephesians 4:18; 1 Corinthians 2:14), receive destruction, in the name of Jesus. Every seed of deceit and wickedness planted in my heart (Jeremiah 17:9), be uprooted, in the name of Jesus. Every satanic defilement in my mind and conscience (Titus 1:15), receive divine cleansing by the power of the speaking blood of Jesus, in the name of Jesus. Any evil force that has arrested my will and enslaved it (Romans 7:14-18), your time is up, release it by force, in the name of Jesus. Almighty God, deliver me from the spirit of waste and prodigality (Luke 15:11-24), in the name of Jesus. Almighty God, empower me with your knowledge to know who I am (Romans 8:17, 32), in the name of Jesus. Anointing to start operating as God's heirs and sons (John 1:12), possess me, in the name of Jesus. Every spirit of ignorance and slavery in any area of my life (2 Corinthians 5:20), I bind and cast you out, in the name of Jesus. Anointing to rule like a king (Revelation 1:5, 6), fall upon me now, in the name of Jesus. I command the Eagle of my destiny to fly out from the ground and fly into the skies (Isaiah 40:31), in the name of Jesus. I refuse to operate like the elder brother of the prodigal son, suffering and complaining in the midst of plenty, in the name of Jesus. Father Lord, deliver me from every form of self-righteousness (Luke 18:9-14), in the name of Jesus. Father Lord, fill me with the fruits of the spirit and humility, in the name of Jesus. Almighty God, command my promotion and prosperity to come from you, in the name of Jesus. Almighty God, empower me to bring little children to Christ (Luke 18:15-17), in the name of Jesus. Anointing to introduce little children, youths and everyone to Christ, fall upon me, in the name of Jesus. Let the rebuking power of Christ rebuke every character in me that is discouraging sinners from receiving Jesus Christ, in the name of Jesus. I command my lifestyle to draw others to Christ before I preach the gospel, in the name of Jesus. Father Lord, help me to love Jesus Christ above my life and everything that is of the world (Luke 18:18-27), in the name of Jesus. I receive the grace to share my wealth rightly with the poor and the needy according to divine direction, in the name of Jesus.

Day 9

Expectations:

1. **Deliverance from the activities of every flattering and mocking spirit**
2. **The destruction of every yoke of laziness affecting you.**
3. **The dethroning of every evil spirit reigning as king and queen in your life.**
4. **The scattering of every evil spirit fighting hard to convert the house of prayer to den of thieves.**

I break and loose myself from every flattering and mocking spirit, in the mighty name of Jesus. Let the forgiving power in the blood of Jesus minister heavily into my life and forgive my sins, in the name of Jesus. By the power of God's qualifying power, father Lord, qualify me to make heaven, in the name of Jesus. Any wealth attached to my life and assigned to drag me to hell fire, I distribute you to the poor, in the name of Jesus. Any riches empowered to separate me from Jesus

Christ, I reject you, in the name of Jesus. Every yoke of laziness upon my life (Luke 19:20-27), your time is up, break to pieces, in the name of Jesus. Father Lord, deliver me from the spirit of covetousness, complaining and fault finding, in the name of Jesus. Every demonic spirit fighting against the rule and the reign of Christ in my life (Luke 19:37-40), I bind and cast you out, in the name of Jesus. Any evil spirit reigning as a king or queen in my life, be dethroned by force, in the name of Jesus. Let the Kingship of Christ in my life reign forever and ever in my life, in the name of Jesus. Any evil voice, speaking against Christ in my life, be silenced by the speaking blood of Jesus, in the name of Jesus. I command the stones of the earth to fight against the enemies of the reign of Christ in my life, in the name of Jesus. Let the voice of every creature silence every negative voice speaking against the manifestation of Christ in my life, in the name of Jesus. Every demonic spirit of selling and buying in the temple of God in my life (Luke 19:45-48), I bind and cast you out, in the name of Jesus. Almighty God, deliver me from joining people that convert your house to a place of buying and selling, in the name of Jesus. Any evil group fighting hard to convert the house of prayer to a den of theft, scatter, in the name of Jesus. Father Lord, convert every church that has backslidden in prayer, in our lands, to houses of prayer by your power, in the name of Jesus. Every evil gang up against true believers in the house of God, scatter and fail woefully, in the name of Jesus. Let every spy of the devil that has been sent to monitor me spiritually and physically be blinded and crippled, in the name of Jesus. Almighty God, give me the wisdom to overcome every evil agent that has been assigned to terminate my ministry, in the name of Jesus. Any evil conspiracy, against the divine purpose and plan of God for my life, fail woefully, in the name of Jesus. Anointing and wisdom to approach every matter without sin, fall upon me, in the name of Jesus. I break and loose myself from the arrest of false doctrines (Luke 20:27-38; Colossians 2:8; 2 Timothy 1:5-18), in the name of Jesus. Almighty God, deliver me from every demon that has been assigned to destroy my marriage, in the name of Jesus. Father Lord, deliver me from any marriage that will take me to hell fire, in the name of Jesus. I break and loose myself from every yoke of marital failure, in the name of Jesus. Father Lord, command your power of resurrection to quicken every good thing the devil has killed in my life, in the name of Jesus. I break and loose myself from the spirit of pride, evil desire and wickedness (Luke 20:45-47), in the name of Jesus. Let the wickedness of every unrepentant enemy be judged without delay, in the name of Jesus. Let the devourers of the widows, the poor and righteous ones, and the needy repent or perish, in the name of Jesus. You killers of Jesus, on assignment to kill me (Luke 22:1-6), your time is up, repent or perish, in the name of Jesus. Any witch or wizard, firing arrows of spiritual or physical blindness against me, repent or receive your arrows back, in the name of Jesus. Any evil personality attacking me with stripes, be frustrated (1 Peter 2:24), in the name of Jesus. Every sickness and disease in my life, receive healing by the stripes of Jesus, in the name of Jesus. Father Lord, deliver me from every shame, reproach, disgrace, defeat, failure and death (Luke 22:1-6, 47, 52, 55, 63-71; 23:1-6, 10), in the name of Jesus. Almighty God, deliver me from quarreling, gossiping and position seeking in the house of God (22:24-30), in the name of Jesus.

Day 10

Expectations:

1. **Deliverance from the spirit of slumber and spiritual weakness.**
2. **Deliverance from every yoke of the devil and demonic manipulation.**
3. **Victory over the devil and his agents.**
4. **Complete deliverance from every form of satanic arrest.**

Father Lord, humble me and impart the spirit of children, in the name of Jesus. Almighty God, teach me how to put on your whole armor to avoid fighting carnally with physical swords (Luke 22:31-38, 49-51, 54-62), in the name of Jesus. Any evil force, confusion or fear designed to cause me to deny Christ for any reason, scatter and fail, in the name of Jesus. I command the Peter in me to stand strong and refuse to deny Christ under any pressure, in the name of Jesus. Father Lord, deliver me from the spirit of slumber and spiritual weakness (Luke 22:43-46), in the name of Jesus. Almighty God, empower me to be fervent in prayer, especially in a time of battle, in the name of Jesus. I refuse to follow the multitudes to fight against Christ and His mission on earth (Luke 23:1-39), in the name of Jesus. Any demonic spirit seeking for a seat in my life to judge Christ, I bind and cast you out, in the name of Jesus. I refuse to compromise and yield to pressure from any group against Jesus Christ (Luke 23:3-7, 13-25), in the name of Jesus. Any spirit of Herod, asking in mockery for miracles in my ministry with insulting words (Luke 23:8-12, 15, 34), be silenced, in the name of Jesus. Almighty God, deliver me from the last rebellion and every evil force that has been assigned to use me in my last moment here on earth (Luke 23:32, 39, 34), in the name of Jesus. Father Lord, in my last day, hours, minutes and moment here on earth, forgive me all my sins and remember me when I come into your kingdom (Luke

23:40-43), in the name of Jesus. I break and loose myself from every satanic ensign and convert them to signs and wonders, in the name of Jesus. I break and loose myself from the yoke of the devil and his manipulations, in the name of Jesus. Almighty God, put your word in my mouth against the word of the devil, in the name of Jesus. Let the written word of God prevail over the spoken, written and unwritten word of the devil in my life, in the name of Jesus. I confront and conquer the devil and his agents; I receive victory over them in the battle field of my life, in the name of Jesus.

> Now the next day, that followed the day of the preparation, the chief priests and Pharisees came together unto Pilate,
>
> Saying, Sir, we remember that that deceiver said, while he was yet alive, after three days I will rise again.
>
> Command therefore that the sepulchre be made sure until the third day, lest his disciples come by night, and steal him away, and say unto the people, He is risen from the dead: so the last error shall be worse than the first.
>
> Pilate said unto them, Ye have a watch: go your way, make *it* as sure as ye can.
>
> So they went, and made the sepulchre sure, sealing the stone, and setting a watch.
>
> — MATTHEW 27:62-66

Any satanic arrest of my destiny in the grave yard, your time is up, be released by heavenly force, in the name of Jesus. Every satanic command to keep my destiny under an evil watch, fail woefully, in the name of Jesus. Any evil soldier, monitoring my destiny in their altar, be blinded and be crippled, in the name of Jesus. Every stone of hindrance keeping me in bondage, be rolled away by force, in the name of Jesus. Almighty God, take me away from where I am, to where you want me to be, in the name of Jesus. Every organized darkness, spiritually and physically assigned to hinder me from rising to the global level, be disorganized, in the name of Jesus. Almighty God, by your mercy, deliver me from the despising power of the devil and his agents (John 1:45-47), in the name of Jesus. Every inherited set back and limitation in my life, your time is up, be terminated, in the name of Jesus. I recover every good thing that the devil has denied to my ancestors, in the name of Jesus. I break and loose myself from every inherited bondage and yoke, in the name of Jesus. Father Lord, empower me to take back every good thing my ancestors handed over to the devil, in the name of Jesus. Every problem in my life as a result of sin, wherever you are, die without mercy, in the name of Jesus. Blood of Jesus, speak me out from the powers of sin and its consequences, in the name of Jesus. Every organized darkness militating against my destiny, your time is up, be disorganized, in the name of Jesus. Every enemy of my relationship with God, I cut you off, in the name of Jesus. Every satanic attack against my life and destiny, be frustrated and terminated, in the name of Jesus. I command the backbone of the devil and sin in my life to break to pieces, in the name of Jesus. Every enemy of the manifestation of God's divine nature in my life, be disappointed, in the name of Jesus. Father Lord, take me away from every demonic presence, in the name of Jesus. I command every continuous sin in my lineage to receive perfect failure, in the name of Jesus.

Day 11

Expectations:

1. **Complete deliverance from everything that is not of God in your life**
2. **Divine empowerment to be able to drive out every agent of defilement and pollution.**
3. **Recovering every place your ancestors gave to the devil and his agents**
4. **Deliverance from every yoke of immorality and adultery.**

Almighty God, perfect your will in every part of my life and make me holy in and out, in the name of Jesus. Father Lord, manifest yourself in every area of my life, in the name of Jesus. Ancient of days, deliver me where I need deliverance, in the mighty name of Jesus. Wherever the enemy will call my life for evil, blood of Jesus, answer for me, in the name of Jesus. Almighty God by your power, make me a wonder in the midst of defeat and failure, in the name of Jesus. I break and loose myself from every defiling power and evil pollution, in the name of Jesus. Father Lord, empower me to drive away every agent of defilement and pollution in the house of God (John 2:12-16), in the name of Jesus. I receive the grace to take spiritual and physical actions against the devil and his agents in the house of God, in the name of Jesus. Every office created for the devil and his agents in the house of God, I close it down, in the name of Jesus. Father Lord, empower me to refuse the devil and his agents a place in my life and family, in the name of Jesus. I take away every place my ancestors have given to the devil and his agents in my life and ministry, in the name of Jesus. I break and loose myself from the ministry of satanic agents (John 2:12-16; Ephesians 4:27; Revelation 2:12-17), in the name of Jesus. Almighty God, deliver me from every satanic doctrine, tradition and every evil establishment (John 5:8-18, 5), in the name of Jesus. Every yoke of religion without Christ in my life (Colossians 2:8), break to pieces, in the name of Jesus. Anointing to maintain my holiness and walk like God, fall upon me, in the name of Jesus. I break and loose myself from every spirit of Judas and conspiracy (John 6:44-71), in the name of Jesus. Almighty God, deliver me from every unfriendly friend and wicked kiss, in the name of Jesus. Any evil spirit in me assigned to accuse Christ through me (John 7:10-13, 20, 21), I bind and cast you out, in the name of Jesus. Every spirit of murmuring and gossiping, against Christ in my life, I bind and cast you out, in the name of Jesus. Every satanic arresting demon assigned against me (John 7:32, 41-53), be frustrated, in the name of Jesus. Anointing to seek Jesus and find Him (John 7:34), fall upon me, in the name of Jesus. Every yoke of immorality and adultery in my life (John 8:1-11), break to pieces, in the name of Jesus. Almighty God, deliver me from every lust of the flesh, in the name of Jesus. Father Lord, empower me to repent truly with the power to go and sin no more, in the name of Jesus. Father Lord, deliver me from the power of the law and replace it with your grace (John 8:3-10; Matthew 7), in the name of Jesus. I command every satanic stone that is hitting on me because of my sins to become powerless, in the name of Jesus. I rebuke every religious sinful man or woman (John 8:13, 48, 59) that is stoning my destiny to be frustrated, in the name of Jesus. Father Lord, empower me to do your work without restrictions (John 9:13-41), in the name of Jesus. Every enemy of God's deliverance, miracles, signs and wonders in my life, fail woefully, in the name of Jesus. Any wicked spirit promoting evil doctrines to stop the work of God, miracles, signs and wonders, be disgraced, in the name of Jesus. Almighty God, deliver me from the fear of men and fill me with your fear (John 9:18-23), in the name of Jesus. I break and loose myself from every lying spirit and every spirit of religion without Christ, in the name of Jesus. Almighty God, empower me to testify of your goodness and help me to stand for the truth (John 9:28-41), in the name of Jesus. I refuse to join the multitudes to do evil or speak ill against Christ

(John 10:19, 20, 31, 33, 39), in the name of Jesus. Father Lord, by your power, let the work I do in your name bear me witness (John 10:25), in the name of Jesus. Almighty God, deliver me from the conspiracy of evil leaders and religious fanatics (John 11:45-57), in the name of Jesus. Anointing to raise the dead and escape satanic murderers (John 11:47, 48; 10:25), fall upon me, in the name of Jesus. Father Lord, deliver me from every murderer of good things and every enemy of your work (John 12:10, 11, 18, 19), in the name of Jesus.

Day 12

Expectations:

1. **The removal of any man or woman trying to block the move of God in your life.**
2. **The scattering of those assigned by the devil to kill young and vibrant ministers.**
3. **The frustration of all the opposers of God's work.**
4. **Complete deliverance from every satanic verdict, judgment and punishment against you.**

I break and loose myself from the murderous demon- possessed religious elders, in the name of Jesus. Father Lord, deliver me from every evil possessed men, assigned to kill revival in ministries, in the name of Jesus. Every enemy of truth, signs and wonders in the body of Christ, fail woefully, in the name of Jesus. Any man or woman, blocking the move of God anywhere in my life, be disgraced to death, in the name of Jesus. Almighty God, raise men and women that will move your work forward in every city, in the name of Jesus. Killers of young vibrant ministers, fail woefully, in the name of Jesus. Any man or woman standing against the end time revival, be exposed and disgraced, in the name of Jesus. I command the opposers of God's work to be frustrated out of the pulpits and leadership positions (John 12:3-8; 18:2), in the name of Jesus. Any agent of the devil occupying the chief seats in the house of God (John 12:42-44), be dethroned, in the name of Jesus. I break and loose myself from every evil relationship with the devil and his agents (John 13:2, 18, 26, 27, 30), in the name of Jesus. Almighty God, deliver me from the love of money and every spirit of Judas (Luke 10:17, 18), in the name of Jesus. I break and loose myself from the arrest of the denying power of the devil (John 13:36-38), in the name of Jesus. Almighty God, deliver me from the spirit of betrayal and wickedness (John 18:1-5), in the name of Jesus. I break and loose myself from the spirit of rejection, hatred, lies and every manner of insult (John 18:1-8, 12-14, 19-24, 28-40), in the name of Jesus. I command the returning spirit of Satan and his agents to avoid me (Isaiah 53:3-9; 1 Peter 2:24) forever, in the name of Jesus. Almighty God, help me to put on your whole armor to fight my battles and shield me from the enemy (John 18:10, 15; Ephesians 6:10-18), in the name of Jesus. Almighty God, deliver me from giving or receiving evil counsel against Christ (John 18:14; 2 Samuel 15:31; 16:15-23; 17:1-6; 23), in the name of Jesus. Any evil personality assigned to judge Christ in my life (John 18:29-40; 19:1, 4-16, 19-22), your time is up, be frustrated, in the name of Jesus. Almighty God, deliver me from police case, court case, hospital case and prison case, in the name of Jesus. Any evil personality sitting in the judgment seat against me to condemn me, be frustrated, in the name of Jesus. Every spiritual or physical judgment delivered against me, be reversed to my favor, in the name of Jesus. Father Lord, deliver me from every satanic verdict and punishment in my life, physically and spiritually, in the name of

Jesus. I refuse to go through suffering the second time, in Jesus name; Jesus Christ has paid the price for my sake. Blood of Jesus, speak me out of second time afflictions, in the name of Jesus. Any satanic crown of thorn the devil has planted for or already upon my head (John 19:2-5, 22-24, 34), catch fire, burn to ashes, in the name of Jesus. I command every pain, sickness, diseases and the stripes (John 19:2-5, 22-24, 34) going on against me to cease, in the name of Jesus. Every demonic soldier mobilized against me to torment me, I terminate your assignment, in the name of Jesus. Almighty God, connect me to my destiny helpers everywhere I go (John 19:38), in the name of Jesus. You my Joseph of Arimathea, wherever you are, locate me and help me, in the name of Jesus. I command all my secret disciples to manifest in my time trouble, in the name of Jesus. Almighty God, show me where to cast my net and at the same time, serve you with my profession (John 21:2-3, 14-20; Luke 5:1-11), in the name of Jesus. Anointing to catch men for Christ through my profession, fall upon me, in the name of Jesus. Every agent of the devil serving Satan in the church and assigned to pull me down, fail woefully, be exposed and disgraced, in the name of Jesus. Any evil personality sitting on the highest seat in the church assigned to overthrow my faith in Christ, be publicly frustrated, in the name of Jesus. Any promotion presented to me to destroy my relationship with Christ, I reject you without consideration, in the name of Jesus.

Day 13

Expectations:

1. Deliverance from every bondage and deceit of the devil and his agents
2. The removal of every stone put in place by the devil and his agents against you and against God's work
3. The destruction of every enemy against the reign of Christ
4. The destruction of every demonic established darkness against you

I break and loose myself from the bondage and deceit of the devil and his agents, in the name of Jesus.

> And, behold, there was a great earthquake: for the angel of the Lord descended from heaven, and came and rolled back the stone from the door, and sat upon it.
>
> His countenance was like lightning, and his raiment white as snow:
>
> And for fear of him the keepers did shake, and became as dead *men*.
>
> — MATTHEW 28:2-4

I bring earth quakes upon the businesses, positions, wealth and health of the wicked, in the name of Jesus. Angels from heaven, arise and roll away every stone the devil and his agents have put in place against the move of Christ, in the name of Jesus. Every demonic stone put in place by the powers that are in my family, place of work, community or city, be removed, in the name of Jesus. Every stone of darkness blocking the door of the rise, and reign of Christ in my life, on earth, be removed, in the name of Jesus. Let the removing power of God Almighty enter into every space among the creations and roll away every evil stone, in the name of Jesus. Let the stone of impossibility placed against the reign of Christ be rolled away, in the name of Jesus. Every local or global stone against the reign of Christ, be rolled away, in the name of Jesus. I command the earth, the sea, the air and every creature to quake against every enemy of the rising of Christ in every soul on earth, in the name of Jesus. Any evil power or stone of hindrance, holding the rise of Christianity among the creations, be rolled away, in the name of Jesus. Any evil stone, standing against my life, your time is up, be rolled away, in the name of Jesus. I command every satanic blockage to the rising of my destiny, glory and the works of my hands to disappear, in the name of Jesus. Angels from God, take away by force every enemy on my way to divine purpose, in the name of Jesus. Let the countenance of the angel of God in the battle field of my life be like lightening, in the name of Jesus. Every satanic established darkness in my life and community, be displaced with divine lightening, in the name of Jesus. I command all my buried virtue and everything that belongs to me to be exhumed by thunder, in the name of Jesus. Every organized darkness blocking the entrance doors of my life, be disorganized unto total destruction, in the name of Jesus. I command weakness and infirmity from above and below to visit the camp of my unrepentant enemies, in the name of Jesus. Let the operational base of the devil and his agents against my life and neighborhood, everywhere, catch fire and burn to ashes, in the name of Jesus. I command the functional power and the strength of my unrepentant enemies to cease and die, in the name of Jesus. Let the fear of God Almighty fall upon every satanic gate keeper of my life and shake them out of their position, in the name of Jesus. I command every creature standing against my rising out of bondage to become as good as dead, in the name of Jesus. Every enemy of the full manifestation of Christ in my life, your time is up, repent or perish, in the name of Jesus. Any demonic geniuses twisting the word of God to destroy me and break my good relationship with God, fail woefully, in the name of Jesus. Every demonic demand to cause me to tempt God, I reject you forever, in the name of Jesus. Almighty God, deliver me from lust and covetousness of anything of the world, in the name of Jesus. I command the hindering power of the devil and his agents to avoid me forever, in the name of Jesus.

I verily thought with myself, that I ought to do many things contrary to the name of Jesus of Nazareth.

Which thing I also did in Jerusalem: and many of the saints did I shut up in prison, having received authority from the chief priests; and when they were put to death, I gave my voice against *them*.

And I punished them oft in every synagogue, and compelled *them* to blaspheme; and being exceedingly mad against them, I persecuted *them* even unto strange cities.

Whereupon as I went to Damascus with authority and commission from the chief priests,

At midday, O king, I saw in the way a light from heaven, above the brightness of the sun, shining round about me and them which journeyed with me.

And when we were all fallen to the earth, I heard a voice speaking unto me, and saying in the Hebrew tongue, Saul, Saul, why persecutest thou me? *it is* hard for thee to kick against the pricks.

And I said, Who art thou, Lord? And he said, I am Jesus whom thou persecutest.

— ACTS 26:9-15

Any man, woman or power under oath to waste my life to stop the move of Christ in me, repent or perish, in the name of Jesus. Anything in me fighting the move of God and the reign of Christ, die, in the name of Jesus. Every enemy of Christ, inside or outside me, your time is up, die, in the name of Jesus. Almighty God, forgive me of all my wrong deeds against Christ and deliver me, in the name of Jesus. I break and loose myself from every inherited religion without the righteousness of Christ, in the name of Jesus. Let the dismantling power of God dismantle me completely from every ignorance, in the name of Jesus. Let the forfeiting power of God empower me to forfeit anything standing between me and Christ, in the name of Jesus. Father Lord, deliver me from every crying blood, crying against me because of my past sins, in the name of Jesus. Almighty God, deliver me from every satanic prison yard, spiritually and physically, in the name of Jesus. I disengage myself from every authority, relationship and the benefit of Satan, in the name of Jesus. Any evil voice crying against the manifestation of Christ in my life, be silenced by the crying blood of Jesus. Let the compelling power of Christ compel me to reject and hate the devil, forever, in the name of Jesus. Let the abandoning power of God empower me to abandon the devil and his assignments and every connection with him, in the name of Jesus. Any evil mouth opened against me and my mission for Christ, close and be silenced forever by the speaking blood of Jesus, in the name of Jesus. Any strange fire, burning inside me from the satanic kingdom, be quenched by the blood of Jesus. Every demonic anger against me for rejecting Satan and his kingdom, be converted to blessings in heaven, in the name of Jesus. Almighty God, send your light on my way and turn me against the devil, his works and sin forever, in the name of Jesus. Let the brightness of God's light in me destroy every satanic established darkness everywhere I go, in the name of Jesus. I command the sun and every creature to fight for me until the last darkness in my life is displaced forever, in the name of Jesus. Every place in my life, and among the creatures, that has been given to the devil and his agents, be taken away by force, in the name of Jesus. I command every enemy of the shining light of God in my life and ministry to perish forever, in the name of Jesus. I end every evil journey that will ever be embarked against me; end in disaster and complete failure, in the name of Jesus. Let every power behind my problems collapse and rise no more, in the name of Jesus. Every satanic voice against my destiny, be silenced by the speaking voice in the blood of Jesus, in the name of Jesus. Almighty God, send the rescuing power in the blood of Jesus to rescue me from every satanic captivity, in the name of Jesus. Any satanic pricking power, working against me, be frustrated unto death, in the name of Jesus. Every satanic achievement in my life, body, soul and spirit, receive total destruction, in the name of Jesus. Father Lord, empower me to recognize the voice of Christ and obey Him to the end, in the name of Jesus. I silence every negative voice, trying to move me against Christ, in the name of Jesus.

Day 14

Expectations:

1. **Deliverance from every evil personality disguising as a believer**
2. **Commanding everything in you to bow to the will of God**
3. **Commanding your evil past to bow before the presence of God**
4. **The crippling of all evil personalities armed with letters from rulers and authorities to do evil against believers**

Father Lord, help me to identify what is right and what is wrong; the gift of God and the gift of the devil, in the name of Jesus.

Then Ananias answered, Lord, I have heard by many of this man, how much evil he hath done to thy saints at Jerusalem:

And here he hath authority from the chief priests to bind all that call on thy name.

But the Lord said unto him, go thy way: for he is a chosen vessel unto me, to bear my name before the Gentiles, and kings, and the children of Israel:

For I will shew him how great things he must suffer for my name's sake.

And Ananias went his way, and entered into the house; and putting his hands on him said, Brother Saul, the Lord, *even* Jesus, that appeared unto thee in the way as thou camest, hath sent me, that thou mightest receive thy sight, and be filled with the Holy Ghost.

And immediately there fell from his eyes as it had been scales: and he received sight forthwith, and arose, and was baptized.

And when he had received meat, he was strengthened. Then was Saul certain days with the disciples which were at Damascus.

— ACTS 9:13-19

Father Lord, open my spiritual eyes to discern the truly repented people and empower me to associate with them, in the name of Jesus. I discover and break away from every evil personality disguising as a true believer in the midst of Christians, in the name of Jesus. Father Lord, use me to disciple every repentant wicked and evil men to true repentance, in the name of Jesus. I receive the manifestation of God's gift to know the truth and follow it to the end, in the name of Jesus. I break and loose myself from every self-knowledge that conflicts with the knowledge of God, in the name of Jesus. Let everything in me bow to God's will and purpose without disagreement, in the name of Jesus. Every worldly and defiled information assigned to displace God's divine information in my brain, be discarded, in the name of Jesus. I command my evil pasts to bow before the presence of God in obedience, in the name of Jesus. Let the repenting power of God destroy every demonic assignment, in the name of Jesus. By the power in God's presence, I destroy every demonic authority over my life, in the name of Jesus. By the power in divine movement, I command every demonic movement to surrender, in the name of Jesus. By the power in God's authority, I disengage and bring to nothing every demonic authority, in the name of Jesus. Every demonic movement against God, be terminated by the move of God in me, in the name of Jesus. Anointing to pray all manner of prayer to cripple every satanic movement, fall upon me, in the name of Jesus. Father Lord, whatever I must do to bring my enemies to true repentance, help me to achieve it, in the name of Jesus. Any evil personality with letters of authority to do evil against Christianity, be blinded and crippled on your way, in the name of Jesus. Let the ending power of God end every demonic assignment against believers everywhere, in the name of Jesus. Every occultic personality and satanic agent in my family, office, community, city or nation, assigned to stand on my way, be blinded and crippled, in the name of Jesus. Any witch or wizard authorized by the power in the church and from the world government against me, be crippled, in the name of Jesus. I command every problem that will influence sinners in my family, office, community, city or nation to repent to manifest, in the name of Jesus. Let the killing power of God arise and kill every determined Pharaoh pursuing me to the red sea, in the name of Jesus. Every satanic vow with any determined and unrepentant agent to waste my life, back fire, in the name of Jesus. Every weapon that Satan and his agents have prepared to bind me with, turn around and bind yourselves, in the name of Jesus. Every enemy of my service to God, repent or become blind, in the name of Jesus. Every enemy of the manifestation of the name of Christ in my life and family, repent or perish, in the name of Jesus. I command every chosen vessel of God in the camp of the devil to change to the camp of Christ, in the name of Jesus. Father Lord, release your power of conversion to convert all chosen vessels that are under satanic arrest, in the name of Jesus. I withdraw every protection, satanic benefit and power from every satanic agent on their way to destroy me, in the name of Jesus. Let all the truly repented blindfolded and crippled satanic agents on assignment to destroy receive their freedom, in the name of Jesus. Almighty God, bring true repentance to the lives of our persecutors kicking against the pricks, in the name of Jesus. Almighty God, empower me to reject the devil and his gifts, no matter how good they look, in the name of Jesus. Every demonic demand to separate me from true worship, I reject you with my body, soul and spirit, in the name of Jesus. Every enemy of my worship to God and sanctification, be frustrated, in the name of Jesus.

But what things were gain to me, those I counted loss for Christ.

> Yea doubtless, and I count all things *but* loss for the excellency of the knowledge of Christ Jesus my Lord: for whom I have

> — PHILIPPIANS 3:7, 8

Blood of Jesus, flow into the foundation of my life and separate me completely from the immoral lifestyle of dogs, in the name of Jesus. Any spirit of dog, living inside me or influencing me, I bind and cast you out, in the name of Jesus. Father Lord, empower me to live holy and separate me from every manner of sexual perversion, in the name of Jesus. I break and loose myself from the company of evil workers and concision, in the name of Jesus. Almighty God, circumcise my body, soul and spirit and energize me to worship you in Spirit and in truth, in the name of Jesus. Anything that gives wealth by disobedience and gain outside Christ, I reject you, in the name of Jesus. I break and loose myself from having confidence in the flesh without eternity in view, in the mighty name of Jesus. I reject everything on earth that is profitable but is standing between me and God, in the name of Jesus. Almighty God, lead me to your perfection, excellence, knowledge and in your wisdom, in the name of Jesus. I refuse to pursue anything here on earth no matter how profitable that will separate me from Christ, in the name of Jesus. Almighty God, empower me to pursue everything that will help me improve my relationship with Christ on earth, in the name of Jesus. Anything that will make me a better Christian and take me to heaven on the last day, begin to manifest in my life, in the name of Jesus. Almighty God, help me to pay any price that will lead me to perfection and obedience to God's word, in the name of Jesus. I refuse to dodge or run away from every battle that has been designed to perfect God's divine plan for my life, in the name of Jesus. Father Lord, take me to the way of truth and life that comes from following Christ, in the name of Jesus. Every demonic threat against me because of my decision to live for Christ without compromise, fail woefully, in the name of Jesus. I command my body, soul and Spirit to abort every fear and satanic intimidation against my life, in the name of Jesus. Anointing to take decision to do good and live holy without compromise, fall upon me, in the name of Jesus. Any satanic oppression going on against me because of my decision to honor God and work for Him, be terminated, in the name of Jesus. Any evil force attacking my faith in Christ, scatter and fail woefully, in the name of Jesus. Father Lord, help me to confront and conquer every demonic army assigned to fight me on my way to please God, in the name of Jesus. Any position, prosperity, respect, offer and gain, designed to keep me away from God's will, I dump you, in the name of Jesus. Anointing to be to suffer happily, and do anything that will help me to in order to obey Christ, possess me, in the name of Jesus. Any evil spirit ministering to me, your time is up, I bind and cast you out, in the name of Jesus. Heavenly father, take me from wilderness experience, promote me, settle and establish me in your will, in the name of Jesus. Let the plan of the devil be aborted and destroyed forever before me, in the name of Jesus. Satan, get thee behind me and be forever frustrated in my life by the power in the word of God, in the name of Jesus. Anointing to worship the only true God and serve Him in truth and in Spirit all the days of my life, possess me, in the name of Jesus. Father Lord, assign your angels to start ministering to me from today and forever, in the name of Jesus.

SEVENTEEN

THE POWER OF RESURRECTION

DECREE-1

(Matthew 16:21,20:17-19, Matthew 17:22, 23, Matthew 20:17-19, Mark 10:32-34, Luke 9:20-22; 18:31-34, Matthew 22:29-33   , Luke 14:13, 14, John 5:24-29, Matthew 28:1-7, Matthew 28:8-13, Matthew 28:14-17, Mark 16:11, Acts 23:8, 2 Timothy 2:15-18, 1 Corinthians 15:12-23, Luke 24:36-43, Luke 24:4, 5, 23, John 11:1-3, Revelation 20:4, 5, 11-15)

Day 1

Expectations:

1. **Receiving the anointing to fulfill destiny and serve your generation according to God's will**

2. **The destruction of every demonic power projecting sin into your life**

3. **Commanding the spirit of God to enter into you and quicken every part of your life**

4. **Complete deliverance from every form of suffering, pain, lack and shame**

Almighty God, prepare me to live for you in this earth without sin, in the mighty name of Jesus. Anointing to fulfill destiny, serve my generation according to God's will, possess me, in the name of Jesus. Every sin that has vowed to die with me here on earth, fail woefully and die now, in the name of Jesus. Father Lord, replace my self-righteousness with Christ's righteousness, in the name of Jesus. Every life of sin assigned to write the last chapter of my life here on earth, be frustrated out of my life, in the name of Jesus. I break away from the life of sin and any relationship with the devil and his agents, in the name of Jesus.

> From that time forth began Jesus to shew unto his disciples, how that he must go unto Jerusalem, and suffer many things of the elders and chief priests and scribes, and be killed, and be raised again the third day.
>
> And Jesus going up to Jerusalem took the twelve disciples apart in the way, and said unto them,
>
> Behold, we go up to Jerusalem; and the Son of man shall be betrayed unto the chief priests and unto the scribes, and they shall condemn him to death,
>
> And shall deliver him to the Gentiles to mock, and to scourge, and to crucify *him:* and the third day he shall rise again.
>
> — MATTHEW 16:21, 20:17-19

Almighty God, enter into every part of my life with your Spirit and quicken every part of my body, soul and spirit that is weak or dead, in the name of Jesus. I receive victory over every trial in any area of my life, in the name of Jesus. Any evil personality standing on my way to Calvary, be frustrated, in the name of Jesus. Any agent of corruption in any area of my life, be frustrated, in the name of Jesus. Every demonic killing power in my life, your time is up, fail woefully, in the name of Jesus. By the power of the resurrection, I command every part of my life to be touched by the resurrection power, in the name of Jesus. Let the renewal power in the resurrection renew every area of my life, body, soul and spirit, in the name of Jesus.

> And while they abode in Galilee, Jesus said unto them, The Son of man shall be betrayed into the hands of men:
>
> And they shall kill him, and the third day he shall be raised again. And they were exceeding sorry.
>
> — MATTHEW 17:22, 23

I break and loose myself from the betrayal power of the devil and his agents, in the name of Jesus. Almighty God, deliver me from the hand of men and keep me holy every day of my life, in the name of Jesus. Father Lord, replace every dead part of my life with the resurrection power and quicken me to live again, in the name of Jesus. By the raising ability in the resurrection of God, I connect myself to divine liberation, in the name of Jesus. Father Lord, help me to end my journey here on earth without the involvement compromising my faith in Christ, in the name of Jesus. Father Lord, deliver me from any suffering here on earth with your full support, in the name of Jesus.

And Jesus going up to Jerusalem took the twelve disciples apart in the way, and said unto them,

Behold, we go up to Jerusalem; and the Son of man shall be betrayed unto the chief priests and unto the scribes, and they shall condemn him to death,

And shall deliver him to the Gentiles to mock, and to scourge, and to crucify *him:* and the third day he shall rise again.

— MATTHEW 20:17-19

Almighty God, lead me to every necessary journey ahead of me in this life, in the name of Jesus. Let my relationship with God be perfected and empowered to attract divine purity, in the name of Jesus. Almighty God, increase my prayer life and deliver me from the spirit of slumber in the day of battle, in the name of Jesus. Any conspiracy going on against me spiritually and physically, end to my favor, in the name of Jesus. Every yoke of condemnation upon my life, visible and invisible, break to pieces, in the name of Jesus. Any battle targeted against my life from the church and from the world, be frustrated, in the name of Jesus. Father Lord, be with me to pass every trial and temptation in life without sin, in the name of Jesus. Anything among the creation, designed to hinder me at the moment of the death or resurrection of the saints, be destroyed, in the name of Jesus. I break and loose myself from every negative influence assigned to separate me from God and his righteousness, in the name of Jesus. I break and loose myself from the spirit of religion without Christ, in the name of Jesus. Father Lord, give me enough grace to pass through any suffering, trial and hardship here on earth without sin, in the name of Jesus. I break and loose myself from any relationship or business that will corrupt my life, in the name of Jesus. Any death prepared to kill me with unconfessed and unforgiven sin, fail woefully, in the name of Jesus. Every enemy of my resurrection to life with Christ, be frustrated, in the name of Jesus. Mark 8:31 ... I refuse to ignore every battle I must fight to keep my relationship with God, in the name of Jesus. Almighty God, help me to remain pure in heart under any situation I find myself, in the name of Jesus.

Father Lord, deliver me from the spirit of hatred and rejection because of my relationship with Christ, in the name of Jesus. Any evil force assigned to keep me in sin till my day of death or at the moment of rapture, scatter in defeat and fail woefully, in the name of Jesus.

> And they were in the way going up to Jerusalem; and Jesus went before them: and they were amazed; and as they followed, they were afraid. And he took again the twelve, and began to tell them what things should happen unto him,
>
> *Saying,* Behold, we go up to Jerusalem; and the Son of man shall be delivered unto the chief priests, and unto the scribes; and they shall condemn him to death, and shall deliver him to the Gentiles:
>
> And they shall mock him, and shall scourge him, and shall spit upon him, and shall kill him: and the third day he shall rise again.
>
> — MARK 10:32-34

I terminate any journey initiated by the devil and his agents in my life to take me away from Christ, in the name of Jesus. Father Lord, empower me to start and finish my journey with Christ without sin, in the mighty name of Jesus. Let the surprising power of God surprise me with the miracle of resurrection in everything I do, here on earth, in the name of Jesus. Every yoke of fear in my life from satanic kingdom, break to pieces, in the name of Jesus. Almighty God, furnish me with every divine information that will prepare me for victory in the battle of my life, in the name of Jesus. Everything the devil put on my way to frustrate my journey to heaven, catch fire and burn to ashes, in the name of Jesus. Almighty God, prepare me to discover and disgrace my unfriendly friends, in the name of Jesus. Every demonic attack against my faith in Christ, your time is up, be frustrated, in the name of Jesus. Every demonic judgment against my relationship with Christ, be reversed without delay, in the name of Jesus. Any arrow of death fired against my destiny, I fire you back, in the name of Jesus.

Father Lord, take away everything from me assigned to keep me in this world or in the grave in the day of rapture, in the name of Jesus. Almighty God, keep me in your will here on earth at all times without sin by your special grace, in the name of Jesus. I break the backbone of Satan, sin and all the work of the devil in every area of my life, in the name of Jesus.

> He said unto them, but whom say ye that I am? Peter answering said, The Christ of God.
>
> And he straitly charged them, and commanded *them* to tell no man that thing;
>
> Saying, The Son of man must suffer many things, and be rejected of the elders and chief priests and scribes, and be slain, and be raised the third day.
>
> Then he took *unto him* the twelve, and said unto them, Behold, we go up to Jerusalem, and all things that are written by the prophets concerning the Son of man shall be accomplished.
>
> For he shall be delivered unto the Gentiles, and shall be mocked, and spitefully entreated, and spitted on:
>
> And they shall scourge *him,* and put him to death: and the third day he shall rise again.
>
> And they understood none of these things: and this saying was hid from them, neither knew they the things which were spoken.
>
> — LUKE 9:20-22; 18:31-34

Any satanic soldier, waiting for me anywhere on earth, spiritually or physically, scatter in defeat, in the name of Jesus. Almighty God, separate me from the multitude and empower me to pray fervently for the battles ahead of me, in the name of Jesus. Father Lord, empower me with your Spirit to know Christ and to relate with Him without a break, in the name of Jesus. Almighty God, by your Spirit, change the name the enemy has given me to the name you want me to bear, in the name of Jesus. I disown by the power of the Holy Ghost, every demonic conversion in any area of my life, in the name of Jesus. Every good thing I have lost in the kingdom of darkness, I recover your double, in the mighty name of Jesus. I dethrone every evil force reigning over my life and I command them to bow down to Christ, in the name of Jesus. Anything the devil and his agents have put in place against my life in the spirit and physical, scatter, in the name of Jesus. Father Lord, empower me to keep your commandments, without a struggle, all the days of my life, in the name of Jesus. Spirit of obedience to the word of God, possess me and take me to my last stay here on earth without sin, in the name of Jesus. Every suffering I must go through on earth to avoid resurrection unto death, Father Lord, give me the grace to go through them without sin, in the name of Jesus. Every enemy of my living right and for God on earth, be frustrated, in the name of Jesus. Every satanic lifestyle in my life, be destroyed by the speaking blood of Jesus, in the name of Jesus. Almighty God, destroy everything assigned to separate me from Christ, in the name of Jesus.

> Jesus answered and said unto them, Ye do err, not knowing the scriptures, nor the power of God.
>
> For in the resurrection they neither marry, nor are given in marriage, but are as the angels of God in heaven.
>
> But as touching the resurrection of the dead, have ye not read that which was spoken unto you by God, saying,
>
> I am the God of Abraham, and the God of Isaac, and the God of Jacob? God is not the God of the dead, but of the living.
>
> And when the multitude heard *this,* they were astonished at his doctrine.
>
> — MATTHEW 22:29-33

Every demonic power militating against my life, be destroyed by the power of God, in the name of Jesus. I break and loose myself from the spirit of error and sinful character, in the mighty name of Jesus. Almighty God, equip me with your full knowledge and wisdom and empower me to obey your commandments without looking back, in the name of Jesus. I break and loose myself from every witchcraft manipulation and bewitchment, in the name of Jesus. Every evil movement against my relationship with Christ, be demobilized, in the name of Jesus. Let the intimidating power of God destroy every satanic opposition in my life, in the name of Jesus. Almighty God, empower me to understand you better and help me to put your word into practice, in the name of Jesus. I command everything in this world that is interfering with my time of resurrection or the rapture of the saints to be destroyed, in the name of Jesus. Let the ministering of the angels of God begin to prepare me for the resurrection day and my last stay here on earth without sin, in the name of Jesus. Every property of death in any area of my life, be destroyed by the power of the resurrection, in the name of Jesus. By the power of the living anointing of God, I command life from above to enter into every department of my life, in the name of Jesus. Almighty God, surprise me with miracles that come from the power of the resurrection, in the name of Jesus. Anointing to deny myself anything that will bring me to sin and bondage, possess me, in the name of Jesus. Father Lord, empower me to be faithful to your word, even unto death, in the name of Jesus. I reject in totality any gain, joy or happiness that will bring me under the servitude of the devil, in the name of Jesus. Every enemy of my soul, assigned to yoke me with the devil and his lifestyle, be frustrated out of my life forever, in the name of Jesus.

But when thou makest a feast, call the poor, the maimed, the lame, the blind:

And thou shalt be blessed; for they cannot recompense thee: for thou shalt be recompensed at the resurrection of the just.

— LUKE 14:13, 14

Almighty God, bring me to heavenly dining table for heavenly dinner before my last moment here on earth, in the name of Jesus. Every enemy of my dinner and supper with the blessed Holy Trinity and the holy angels in my last moments here on earth, perish, in the name of Jesus. Almighty God, use my lifestyle to bring many to Christ and eternity with you, in the name of Jesus. Anointing to make it to heaven on the day of rapture, possess me forever, in the name of Jesus. Father Lord, empower me to fulfill my ministry to everyone (the poor, maimed, lame, blind and the greatest) in the name of Jesus. I receive blessings from God without defilement, contamination or pollutions from the devil and his agents, in the name of Jesus. Father Lord, prepare me and empower me never to miss my rewards in heaven for any reason, in the name of Jesus. Every enemy of my resurrection, now and in the last day, be frustrated, in the name of Jesus. Almighty God, sanctify me and keep me just to my last moment here on earth, in the name of Jesus. Anointing to remain pure without defilement to partake in the resurrection of the just, possess me, in the name of Jesus. Blood of Jesus, flow into my foundation and abort every satanic investment, in the name of Jesus. Anything in this world, among the creation anywhere designed to exchange my soul, I reject you forever, in the name of Jesus. Heavenly father, give me enough preparation and keep me holy in the day of the rapture, dead or alive, in the name of Jesus.

Verily, verily, I say unto you, He that heareth my word, and believeth on him that sent me, hath everlasting life, and shall not come into condemnation; but is passed from death unto life.

Verily, verily, I say unto you, the hour is coming, and now is, when the dead shall hear the voice of the Son of God: and they that hear shall live.

For as the Father hath life in himself; so hath he given to the Son to have life in himself;

And hath given him authority to execute judgment also, because he is the Son of man.

> Marvel not at this: for the hour is coming, in the which all that are in the graves shall hear his voice,
>
> And shall come forth; they that have done good, unto the resurrection of life; and they that have done evil, unto the resurrection of damnation.

— JOHN 5:24-29

Father Lord, empower me to honor you, your only begotten son Jesus Christ and the blessed Holy Spirit all the days of my life, in the name of Jesus. I receive the Holy Ghost power to be sanctified and the ability to hear God's word and put them to practice, in the name of Jesus. Father Lord, impart in me your grace to connect with your everlasting life, forever, by your grace, in the name of Jesus. Every condemnation that Satan and sin has brought into my life, be destroyed by the speaking blood of Jesus, in the name of Jesus. Any evil force, bringing me into condemnation, your time is up, scatter, in the name of Jesus. Blessed Holy Spirit, pass me from death to life everlasting by your grace and mercy, in the name of Jesus. Father Lord, bless the rest hours of my stay on earth with your dominating presence, filled with purity, in the name of Jesus. I command every part of my, body, soul and spirit to hear the voice of resurrection without a fail, in the name of Jesus. Every negative voice speaking against the voice of the resurrection in my life, be silence by the holiness in the blood of Jesus. Blood of Jesus, enter into every creature and deliver every part of me under satanic arrest, in the name of Jesus. Every good thing, dead in my life now, hear the voice of the resurrection and live again without death, in the name of Jesus. I command the backbone of Satan and sin to be broken forever in my life, in the name of Jesus. Let the voice of Christ take over every aspect of my life and silence unto death every evil voice speaking against me, in the name of Jesus. By the power in God's word, I receive the grace to live for Christ, in the name of Jesus. I break and loose myself from any evil demonic interest in my life, in the mighty name of Jesus. I break and loose myself from every satanic activity and I join myself with God forever, in the name of Jesus. Anointing to have an everlasting life with God, fall upon me and stay forever, in the name of Jesus. Let the crossing power of the Holy Ghost cross me over to heaven in the day of rapture by the special grace of God, in the name of Jesus. I break and loose myself from every demonic association with Satan, sin and death, in the name of Jesus. Father Lord, destroy in me every satanic property, in the name of Jesus. Almighty God, impart your kind of life in me and clear me from every evil attachment, in the name of Jesus. Let the life of Christ enter into me to live and reign over me without a rival, in the name of Jesus. Let the authority given to Jesus Christ to execute judgment fall upon me and judge every work of the devil in my life, in the name of Jesus. I command Satan and sin to be judged and removed forever from my life, in the name of Jesus. Father Lord, send your light into my life to replace every darkness in every area of my life, in the name of Jesus. Father Lord, put me in the right condition to hear your voice everywhere I go and even from the grave, in the name of Jesus. Let the coming forth of God Almighty come with every enemy of Satan and sin for their destruction, in the name of Jesus. Anointing to do good as required by God in his sight without sin, manifest in my life, in the name of Jesus. I receive the grace and the mercy of God to partake in the resurrection of life unto life everlasting, in the name of Jesus.

Day 2

Expectations:

1. **The destruction of every strength of the devil aimed at condemning your soul and taking you to hell.**
2. **Commanding every part of you to be thirsty for God's righteousness.**
3. **The destruction of every enemy trying to stop you from making heaven.**
4. **The uprooting of every mountain standing against you.**

Every strength of the devil to condemn my soul and take me to hell fire, be broken to pieces without life and strength before me forever and ever, in the name of Jesus. Let the arresting, deceiving and condemning power of the devil and his agents fail woefully in every area of my life, in the name of Jesus. Any man, woman or power with a vow to deny me my rights, benefits and entitlement here on earth, be frustrated, in the name of Jesus. I command every part of my body, soul and spirit to be thirsty for God's righteousness every day of my life here on earth, in the name of Jesus. Oh Lord, help me to be poor in spirit and the yearn to always be like Christ till my last breath, here on earth, in the name of Jesus.

In the end of the sabbath, as it began to dawn toward the first *day* of the week, came Mary Magdalene and the other Mary to see the sepulchre.

And, behold, there was a great earthquake: for the angel of the Lord descended from heaven, and came and rolled back the stone from the door, and sat upon it.

His countenance was like lightning, and his raiment white as snow:

And for fear of him the keepers did shake, and became as dead *men*.

And the angel answered and said unto the women, Fear not ye: for I know that ye seek Jesus, which was crucified.

> He is not here: for he is risen, as he said. Come, see the place where the Lord lay.
>
> And go quickly, and tell his disciples that he is risen from the dead; and, behold, he goeth before you into Galilee; there shall ye see him: lo, I have told you.
>
> — MATTHEW 28:1-7

Almighty God, send your ending power to end the activities of the devil, his agents and sin over my life forever, in the name of Jesus. By the power in God's supernatural ability, I destroy every enemy of my making heaven and I forbid them forever in my life, in the name of Jesus. I command every part of my life, body, soul and spirit to receive a great quake that will bring my life into an everlasting life with Christ, in the name of Jesus. Let the surrounding power of God Almighty surround my body, soul and spirit against the activities of Satan and sin, in the name of Jesus. Almighty God, send your angel to remove everything that will oppose sanctification and holiness in my life, in the name of Jesus. I command my physical and spiritual presence here on earth to put fear into the heart of every satanic agent around, in the name of Jesus. Let the strength that rolled back the stone from the door of the grave of Christ roll away every shame, disgrace and reproach in my life, in the name of Jesus. I command all my physical and spiritual enemies to bow and leave the battle field or perish without help, in the name of Jesus. Any mountain standing before me and God's righteousness be removed without negotiation, in the name of Jesus. By the power of divine presence in my life, I command evil presence in my life to die, in the name of Jesus. Let the countenance of God's divine angel in my life destroy every physical or spiritual darkness in my life, in the name of Jesus. Every inch of satanic presence and darkness in my life, disappear and be replaced by the shining light from above, in the name of Jesus.

And they departed quickly from the sepulchre with fear and great joy; and did run to bring his disciples word.

And as they went to tell his disciples, behold, Jesus met them, saying, All hail. And they came and held him by the feet, and worshipped him.

Then said Jesus unto them, be not afraid: go tell my brethren that they go into Galilee, and there shall they see me.

Now when they were going, behold, some of the watch came into the city, and shewed unto the chief priests all the things that were done.

And when they were assembled with the elders, and had taken counsel, they gave large money unto the soldiers,

Saying, say ye, His disciples came by night, and stole him *away* while we slept.

— MATTHEW 28:8-13

Any satanic gate man or woman keeping watch over my life and destiny, be overwhelmed by God's fear, in the name of Jesus. Let the collapsing power in the word of God bring down every demon standing agent against my life, in the name of Jesus. Oh Lod, sanctify my heart and make it to abhor every kind of sin, in the name of Jesus. I command satanic and everlasting destruction upon the camp of every enemy of my life, in the name of Jesus. Any arrow of fear fired against me from any satanic kingdom, I fire you back, in the name of Jesus. Almighty God, arise by your mercy and take me wherever Jesus is without delay, in the name of Jesus. Father Lord, empower me to tell others about the ministry of your resurrection, in the name of Jesus. Almighty God, arrange a meeting that will unite me with Christ forever and keep me with Him forever, in the name of Jesus. I receive divine assignment that will keep me busy and pure all the days of my life here on earth, in the name of Jesus. Father Lord, send the resurrection power that raised Jesus Christ to minister into every department of my life, in the name of Jesus. Wherever the devil and his agents have taken me to, for spiritual or physical burial, let the resurrection power of God remove me, in the name of Jesus. Heavenly father, fill me with your joy and godly fear every day of my life with Christ's presence, in the name of Jesus.

> And if this come to the governor's ears, we will persuade him, and secure you.
>
> So they took the money, and did as they were taught: and this saying is commonly reported among the Jews until this day.
>
> Then the eleven disciples went away into Galilee, into a mountain where Jesus had appointed them.
>
> And when they saw him, they worshipped him: but some doubted.
>
> — MATTHEW 28:14-17

Almighty God, bring me to hold your feet to worship you forever without a break, in the name of Jesus. Every fearful situation in my life, be terminated by divine appearance and everlasting presence, in the name of Jesus. Let the telling of God's goodness in the word of God begin to manifest in my life, in the name of Jesus. Father Lord, deliver me from every bribery and kickback designed to shut my mouth against the truth, in the name of Jesus. Almighty God, deliver me from the spirit of the love of money and covetousness, in the name of Jesus. I break and loose myself from the spirit of lying and falsehood, in the mighty name of Jesus. Every yoke of a lying spirit and bearing false witness in my life, break to pieces, in the name of Jesus. Ancient of days, deliver me from every blessing and satisfaction that will come from the devil or through sin, in the name of Jesus. Father Lord, impart me with the character of Christ and his righteousness, every day of my life, in the name of Jesus. Anything that will lead me to inherit heaven after fulfilling my destiny here on earth, begin to manifest, in the name of Jesus.

> And they, when they had heard that he was alive, and had been seen of her, believed not.
>
> — MARK 16:11

Any satanic arrest to my believe to God's word and the promises of his resurrection, be frustrated, in the name of Jesus. Lord Jesus, appear to me in many forms with perfect understanding, in the name of Jesus. Anointing to walk with Jesus without sin, begin to manifest in every area of my life, in the mighty name of Jesus. Father Lord, teach me the right way and manner to share my faith in Christ with others with your special wisdom, in the name of Jesus. Almighty God, impart your convincing and converting anointing into my ministry, in the name of Jesus. Lord Jesus appearing to my hearers anytime I minister to them with your convincing and converting power, in the name of Jesus. Every enemy of the manifestation of truth and God's glory in my life, your time is up, fail woefully, in the name of Jesus. Father Lord, increase my hunger and thirst for righteousness every day of my life, in the name of Jesus. Let the filling power of God fill me with divine character, without measure, in the name of Jesus. Father Lord, empower me to be merciful according to your plan without sin, in the name of Jesus. Almighty God, deliver me from evil persuasion against the truth, in the mighty name of Jesus. I break and loose myself from the teachers of lies, false doctrines and negative reports, in the name of Jesus. Father Lord, help me stand on the side of truth, not with the devil and his agents, in the name of Jesus. Every established lie against the truth in my life, be over-throned by heavenly force, in the name of Jesus. Father Lord, empower me to be found at the right place all the time, filled with your presence, in the name of Jesus. I break and loose myself from every inherited appointment with the devil and any evil group, in the name of Jesus. I break and loose myself from doubting spirit against the word of God and the power of resurrection, in the name of Jesus (Luke 24:1-46) Any evil force keeping me in the grave, your time is up, I bind and cast you out, in the mighty name of Jesus. Every stone of hindrance, keeping me out of divine plan, be rolled away by the power of resurrection, in the name of Jesus. Any evil force covering my glory, scatter and fail woefully, in the name of Jesus. Almighty God, take me far away from every demonic altar that is holding me down, in the name of Jesus. I command every part of my body, soul and spirit to disappear from every satanic arrest and prison yard, in the name of Jesus. Every property of grave and death in any part of my life, visible and invisible, catch fire and burn to ashes, in the name of Jesus. I command every part of my life to leave the company of the dead and join the company of the living, in the name of Jesus. Father Lord, command your power of resurrection to minister to every part of my life, in the name of Jesus. By the mercies of God, I pray for the physical manifestation of God's promises in every area of my life, in the name of Jesus. Blood of Jesus, speak the manifestation of the resurrection power into my life forever, in the name of Jesus. Any area of my life in the hand and under the control of the devil and sinful men, be delivered, in the name of Jesus. I break and loose myself from the crucifying power of the devil and his agents, in the name of Jesus. Father Lord, reactivate my brain, mental storehouse to always remember your word, in the name of Jesus. Every negative influence pulling me away from Christ and his righteousness, I break away from you, in the name of Jesus. Let every purity from Christ that will empower me to see God and live with Him to eternity begin to manifest in my life, in the name of Jesus. Blood of Jesus, flow into my heart and sanctify me in and out, in the name of Jesus. Every enemy of the peace that comes from God in my life, your time is up, be exposed and disgraced, in the name of Jesus.

> For the Sadducees say that there is no resurrection, neither angel, nor spirit: but the Pharisees confess both.
>
> — ACTS 23:8

Father Lord, manifest your power of resurrection in every area of my life to put the devil and his agents to shame, in the name of Jesus. I break and loose myself from every false doctrine and tradition, in the mighty name of Jesus. Every negative confession against Christ and the doctrine of resurrection, be put to shame, in the name of Jesus. Any evil authority questioning the ability of God's word in my life, I put you to shame, in the name of Jesus. Any instrument of infirmity, weakness, sickness, disease and death in any area of my life, receive the resurrection power, in the name of Jesus. Any evil authority, spiritual or physical laying wait against me, scatter and perish, in the name of Jesus.

> Study to shew thyself approved unto God, a workman that needeth not to be ashamed, rightly dividing the word of truth.
>
> But shun profane *and* vain babblings: for they will increase unto more ungodliness.
>
> And their word will eat as doth a canker: of whom is Hymenaeus and Philetus;
>
> Who concerning the truth have erred, saying that the resurrection is past already; and overthrow the faith of some.
>
> — 2 TIMOTHY 2:15-18

Every organized darkness striving against my relationship with God, scatter and be disorganized forever, in the name of Jesus. Let the confronting power of God confront and conquer every satanic militant against my destiny, in the name of Jesus. Any satanic power subverting my hearers anywhere in the world, your time is up, be destroyed, in the name of Jesus. Father Lord, multiply my study and understanding grace to your word and empower me to obey you, in the name of Jesus. Anointing to divide the word of the truth rightly and practically obey them, fall upon me, in the name of Jesus. Father Lord, empower me to shun every profane and vain babbling against the doctrine of resurrection, in the name of Jesus. Every yoke of sin and every yoke of being around ungodly people, be frustrated, in the name of Jesus. Let the mouth and eating teeth of the devil and his agents against the word of God be broken to pieces, in the name of Jesus. Father Lord, deliver me from every satanic canker worm and every enemy of the truth, in the name of Jesus. Let the earring power of the devil against the power of resurrection be overthrown in my life, in the name of Jesus. Almighty God, strengthen my faith in Christ and invade my life with the power of resurrection, in the name of Jesus. Almighty God, by the power in the blood of Jesus, I restore the full image of God into my life, in the name of Jesus. Every demonic righteousness in my life, be uprooted by the hand of God, in the name of Jesus. I command the whole creature to come under my dominion, in the name of Jesus. Let the blessing of God from the day of creation begin to manifest in my life, in the name of Jesus.

Now if Christ be preached that he rose from the dead, how say some among you that there is no resurrection of the dead?

But if there be no resurrection of the dead, then is Christ not risen:

And if Christ be not risen, then *is* our preaching vain, and your faith *is* also vain.

Yea, and we are found false witnesses of God; because we have testified of God that he raised up Christ: whom he raised not up, if so be that the dead rise not.

For if the dead rise not, then is not Christ raised:

And if Christ be not raised, your faith *is* vain; ye are yet in your sins.

Then they also which are fallen asleep in Christ are perished.

If in this life only we have hope in Christ, we are of all men most miserable.

But now is Christ risen from the dead, *and* become the first fruits of them that slept.

For since by man *came* death, by man *came* also the resurrection of the dead.

— 1 CORINTHIANS 15:12-23

Let the power that raised Christ from the dead enter into my body, soul and spirit, and quicken my mortal body, in the name of Jesus. Every enemy of the doctrine of resurrection in my life, fail woefully, in the name of Jesus. By the mercy of our God Almighty, let the resurrection power begin to manifest in my life, in the name of Jesus. Lord Jesus, enter into my life and bring your plans for my life to be fulfilled, in the name of Jesus. Every satanic embargo against the manifestation of Christ's resurrection for my life, be lifted, in the name of Jesus. I command every part of my life to arise and attract the power of resurrection, in the name of Jesus. Let my faith in Christ begin to bring every divine benefit into manifestation without delay, in the name of Jesus. Every plan of the devil and his agents to make the death and resurrection of Christ ineffective in my life, fail woefully, in the name of Jesus. Every strength of Satan and sin in any area of my life, be broken to pieces, in the name of Jesus. Let the forgiving power of God forgive me and empower me to forgive others, in the name of Jesus. Let the purpose of the doctrine of resurrection be fulfilled in every area of my life positively, in the name of Jesus. Let the perishing power from God terminate every work of the devil and his agents in my life, in the name of Jesus. Let the hope of life after death with God eternally be rekindled in every area of my life, in the name of Jesus. Father Lord, deliver me from living a life of misery on earth and after death, in the name of Jesus. I disassociate myself from Satan, sin and every enemy of my eternity with Christ in heaven, in the name of Jesus. Every satanic program, organized to remove my name from the book of life, fail woefully, in the name of Jesus. Every evil movement among the creation against my destiny and the manifestation of God's power, be terminated, in the name of Jesus. Almighty God, take me far away from the consequences of the Sin of Adam and Eve, in the name of Jesus. Blood of Jesus, speak me into the divine program that will perfect my relationship with you, in the name of Jesus. Let the life of Christ be completely imparted into my life without measure, in the name of Jesus. Father Lord, prepare me adequately for the resurrection unto life with Christ forever, in the mighty name of Jesus. Every good thing that has been attached to my name by God from creation, begin to manifest before me, in the name of Jesus. Everything among the creation blocking my way to heaven, you time is up, be dismantled, in the name of Jesus. I command every part of my life to be fruitful and multiply according to divine decree from the beginning, in the name of Jesus. Let my blessings rise and shine beyond every boundary without a stop, in the name of Jesus. Let the dominating power of the devil against me be crushed to nothing, in the name of Jesus.

Day 3

Expectations:

1. **The frustration of everything coming against your life and destiny.**

2. **The destruction of every satanic embargo placed against your breakthrough.**

3. **Commanding every part of your life to attract God's holiness.**

4. **Deliverance from every satanic trap of sin and corruption.**

I command every living and non-living thing against my life to be frustrated, in the name of Jesus. Every satanic embargo placed against my breakthrough, be lifted, in the name of Jesus. Romans 3:3, 4; 2 Peter 1:1-4; 3:3 … Let the believing power of God displace every unbelief that has been injected into my life by the devil and his agents, in the name of Jesus. Every spirit of unbelief and fear in my life, your time is up, avoid me forever, in the mighty name of Jesus. By the power in God's truth, I command every spirit of telling lies to abandon my life forever, in the name of Jesus. Blood of Jesus, inject your anointing into my life and justify me with heavenly assurance, in the name of Jesus. Almighty God, by your mercies, justify me whenever I am judged, in life and in death, in the name of Jesus. Let the overcoming spirit of God empower me to overcome Satan, his agents and every sin, in the name of Jesus. Almighty God, directly ordain me as your servant, and make me an apostle of Jesus Christ without sin forever, in the name of Jesus. Father Lord, enlist my name among those that have obtained a precious faith in Christ with the power to live without sin, in the name of Jesus. Let the righteousness of Jesus Christ be imparted into my life and keep me holy in the day of the resurrection of the righteous, in the name of Jesus. Almighty God, multiply me with your grace, peace and mercy to enable me partake in the resurrection of the righteous, in the name of Jesus. By the power of God's knowledge, I destroy every satanic knowledge conflicting with the knowledge of

God in my life, in the name of Jesus. Let the anointing in God's divine power begin to supply into every part of my life and keep me holy, in the name of Jesus. I begin to receive without a stop the presence of God in every area of my life, in the name of Jesus. I command everything that will help me to stay holy and make heaven to begin to manifest, in my life, in the name of Jesus. Everything that pertains to the life of Christ, begin to manifest in every part of my life without a break, in the name of Jesus. I command every part of my life to attract every level of God's holiness, in the mighty name of Jesus. Almighty God, increase your knowledge into my life without measure and empower me to please you forever, in the name of Jesus. Let me be called to glory at the right timing of God with the fullness of God's virtue and divine purity, in the name of Jesus. Let the exceeding grace and God's precious promises begin to manifest in every area of my life, in the name of Jesus. Father Lord, by your special grace and mercy, empower me to inherit your divine nature, in the name of Jesus. Almighty God, empower me to escape every satanic trap of sin and corruption, in the name of Jesus. Heavenly father, by your mercy, stir up your pure mind to penetrate into my mind and purify me, in the name of Jesus. Anointing to be mindful to please God in every situation without sin, fall upon me, in the name of Jesus. Father Lord, help me to overcome scoffers, walking after their own lust, in the name of Jesus. I command every tree planted for my life by God, here on earth, to begin to yield fruits for me, in the name of Jesus. Any evil movement in the waters, heaven and earth against my life, be demobilized, in the name of Jesus. Every serpent in the garden of my life and destiny, your time is up, die, in the name of Jesus. Every negative word ever spoken against me by anyone living or dead, expire and lose your hold over my life, in the name of Jesus. I withdraw every invitation given to the devil and his agents over my life, in the name of Jesus. Father Lord, empower me with enough grace to obey your word at all cost, in the name of Jesus. Every messenger of death and hell in my life, I reject you and your message, in the name of Jesus.

And as they thus spake, Jesus himself stood in the midst of them, and saith unto them, Peace *be* unto you.

But they were terrified and affrighted, and supposed that they had seen a spirit.

And he said unto them, why are ye troubled? and why do thoughts arise in your hearts?

Behold my hands and my feet, that it is I myself: handle me, and see; for a spirit hath not flesh and bones, as ye see me have.

And when he had thus spoken, he shewed them *his* hands and *his* feet.

And while they yet believed not for joy, and wondered, he said unto them, Have ye here any meat?

And they gave him a piece of a broiled fish, and of an honeycomb.

And he took *it,* and did eat before them.

—   LUKE 24:36-43

Lord Jesus, appear to me in every situation and perfect my life with your purification grace, in the name of Jesus. Let the peace of Christ penetrate into my life and terrify every demonic crisis going on against me, in the name of Jesus. Every part of my life troubled by the devil and his agents, receive divine protection, in the name of Jesus. Let my thought, imagination and desire receive divine cleansing by the power in the speaking blood of Jesus. Every enemy of God's righteousness in my life, your time is up, be exposed and be disgraced, in the name of Jesus. Let the challenging power of God destroy every demonic settlement in my life, in the name of Jesus. Let the physical presence of the Lord Jesus manifest in the battle field of my life and set me free, in the name of Jesus. Almighty God, command the joy of the hope of your resurrection to take over my life, in the name of Jesus. Anointing to dine with Jesus all the days of my life, possess my body, soul and spirit, in the name of Jesus. Almighty God, empower me with the eating habit of Jesus and bless my body, soul and spirit, in the name of Jesus. Almighty God, deliver me from every satanic investment in my eyes and tongue, in the name of Jesus. Any evil voice among the creation calling me for evil, be silenced by the blood of Jesus, in the name of Jesus. I close my eyes and walk away from every gain of sin and every invitation to disobey God, in the name of Jesus. Father Lord, help me to see through your eyes and not through the eyes of the devil, in the name of Jesus. Let my understanding be connected to divine understanding by the power of God, in the name of Jesus. Father Lord, by your deliverance power, deliver me from carnal desires, in the mighty name of Jesus. Any part of my eyes that has been opened by the devil, be closed and be opened by God forever, in the name of Jesus. Let the voice of God in my life speak louder and silence every satanic voice in my life, in the name of Jesus. Any evil personality that has determined to kill me, use your weapon and kill yourself, in the name of Jesus. By the cleansing power in the speaking blood of Jesus, I cleanse any evil mark in my life, visible and invisible. Father Lord, deliver me from every satanic limitation that has been assigned to block my destiny, in the name of Jesus.

> And it came to pass, as they were much perplexed thereabout, behold, two men stood by them in shining garments:
>
> And as they were afraid, and bowed down *their* faces to the earth, they said unto them, why seek ye the living among the dead?
>
> And when they found not his body, they came, saying, that they had also seen a vision of angels, which said that he was alive.
>
> — LUKE 24:4, 5, 23

Almighty God, take me away from fear, the land of the dead to the land of the living, in the name of Jesus. Let the ministering angels of the Lord protect and give me full support here on earth and time of resurrection, in the name of Jesus.

Any evil mouth speaking against my life, close forever, in the mighty name of Jesus. Any evil and inherited garment of poverty, wickedness and the works of the devil in my life, catch fire and burn to ashes, in the name of Jesus. Every evil activity going on against my life, spiritually and physically, be terminated, in the name of Jesus. Every evil conspiracy and satanic gang up against my life, be exposed and disgraced, in the name of Jesus.

> Now a certain *man* was sick, *named* Lazarus, of Bethany, the town of Mary and her sister Martha.
>
> (It was *that* Mary which anointed the Lord with ointment, and wiped his feet with her hair, whose brother Lazarus was sick.)
>
> Therefore, his sisters sent unto him, saying, Lord, behold, he whom thou lovest is sick.
>
> — JOHN 11:1-3

Any sickness and disease that has been assigned to eat me up and take me to the grave, be disgraced by the resurrection power, in the name of Jesus. Lord Jesus, visit me and come to my rescue; confront and conquer every arrow of death that has been assigned to kill me and take me to the grave, in the name of Jesus. Anointing to keep good relationships like Mary and Martha, and prepare for every battle ahead of me, fall upon me, in the name of Jesus. Almighty God, increase my prayer life and prepare my prayers to be holy, without defilement, before the Lord Jesus, in the name of Jesus. I receive the special grace of God to guide and keep the love of Christ in my life till the day of battle, in the name of Jesus. Every yoke of slavery, suffering and hardship in my life, break to pieces, in the name of Jesus. Owners of evil load in my life, wherever you are, appear and carry your load, in the name of Jesus. Any evil noise raised against me anywhere among the creation, be terminated by the voice of Christ, in the name of Jesus.

Every dream of failure and defeat in my life, be reversed, in the name of Jesus (John 24-31). Every enemy of God's type of prosperity in my life and environment, fail woefully, in the name of Jesus. Let the returning power of God return me to his perfect plan from creation, in the name of Jesus. Every satanic weapon raised against up against my destiny on earth and among the creation, back fire, in the name of Jesus. Any battle going on against my life, your time is up, end to my favor, in the name of Jesus. Any strange fire, burning in any part of my life, be quenched by the blood of Jesus (1 Corinthians 15:35-54). Almighty God, deliver me from foolish thinking and unprofitable imaginations against the power of resurrection, in the name of Jesus. I command every part of my life that is getting weak and ready to die to receive the quickening power of God, in the name of Jesus. Almighty God, sow your seed of life in me and empower it to receive the power of resurrection, in the name of Jesus. Anointing to be raised in incorruption, without sin and death, forever, fall upon me, in the name of Jesus. Father Lord, raise everything in me to be glorious and powerful, in the name of Jesus. By the power in God's resurrection, I receive divine deliverance to quicken my spiritual body, in the name of Jesus. Let my spiritual body take full control over my physical body without resistance, in the name of Jesus. By the power in God's quickening spirit, I command every enemy of the life of Christ in me to bow, in the name of Jesus. You my body, soul and spirit, begin to respond to the quickening power of God, in the name of Jesus. Every reign of carnality (corruption, dishonor, weakness and every other sinful lifestyle) in my life, be dethroned by the power in the name of Jesus. I command my life to begin to respond to heavenly things against all earthly carnal demands, in the name of Jesus. Let the image of heaven in me from the Lord Jesus displace every worldly thing that is fighting against my spirit, in the name of Jesus. Any pollution, defilement and corruption in my blood, be cleansed by the speaking blood of Jesus. Let the Spirit of Christ in me frustrate every carnal desire that is fighting against my life, in the name of Jesus. Let the changing ability in the resurrection power of God transform everything in me to the glory of God, in the name of Jesus. I command the spirit of death, sin and Satan to bow before the appearance of the resurrection power in my life, in the name of Jesus. I paralyze every spirit of death that has been assigned to hold me down on the day of rapture, in the name of Jesus. Father Lord, destroy every corruptible thing in my life now and forever, in the mighty name of Jesus. Let the corruptible creatures and mortals in my life bow and surrender to incorruption and immortality, in the name of Jesus. Almighty God, arise and cause every death in my life to be swallowed up in victory without resistance, in the name of Jesus. I break and loose my body, soul and spirit from the sting of death, sin, and the powers of the grave, in the name of Jesus. Every victory and benefit attached to the death of Jesus our Lord, begin to manifest fully in my life, in the name of Jesus. Let the fire of God, burn every strange fire burning in every area of my life to ashes, in the name of Jesus. Everything the devil and his agents have concluded against my life, I command them to fail, in the name of Jesus. Father Lord, empower me to live for you alone without sin, in the mighty name of Jesus. Any demonic contribution in my life, receive destruction without break, in the name of Jesus. Almighty God, begin to plant in the garden of my life, in the name of Jesus. Any evil sacrifice ever offered against my life, expire by the sacrifice of Jesus, in the name of Jesus. O Lord arise and deliver me wherever I need deliverance, in the mighty name of Jesus. Any evil structure in any part of my life, catch fire and burn to ashes, in the name of Jesus. Father Lord, transfer me spiritually from my biological parent to your adopted child, in the name of Jesus. Almighty God, miraculously transform me to be like you in character and nature, in the name of Jesus. Let the purifying power in the blameless blood of Jesus sanctify me and keep me holy forever, in the name of Jesus. Let the powers that commit sin lose their grip over my life forever and ever, in the name of Jesus. Every yoke of transgression upon my life, your time is up, break to pieces, in the name of Jesus. Let the manifesting power of Christ show up in every area of my life and kill sin and death in my life, in the name of Jesus. Almighty God, detach me from the powers of sin, Satan and death forever, in the name of Jesus. I break every relationship, designed to deny me of my time of resurrection, in the name of Jesus. Almighty God, empower me to abide in you, in Christ and your word forever, in the name of Jesus. I command everything in me to be married to Jesus Christ; to divorce everything that will fight against Christ in my life, in the name of Jesus. Any evil assembly anywhere on earth against my life, your time is up, scatter in shame, in the name of Jesus. Any satanic tabernacle built to plan against God and his plans for my life, scatter, in the name of Jesus. Let the terminating power of God terminate every satanic initiation anywhere against my destiny, in the name of Jesus.

And I saw thrones, and they sat upon them, and judgment was given unto them: and *I saw* the souls of them that were beheaded for the witness of Jesus, and for the word of God, and which had not worshipped the beast, neither his image, neither had received *his* mark upon their foreheads, or in their hands; and they lived and reigned with Christ a thousand years.

But the rest of the dead lived not again until the thousand years were finished. This *is* the first resurrection.

And I saw a great white throne, and him that sat on it, from whose face the earth and the heaven fled away; and there was found no place for them.

And I saw the dead, small and great, stand before God; and the books were opened: and another book was opened, which is *the book* of life: and the dead were judged out of those things which were written in the books, according to their works.

And the sea gave up the dead which were in it; and death and hell delivered up the dead which were in them: and they were judged every man according to their works.

And death and hell were cast into the lake of fire. This is the second death.

And whosoever was not found written in the book of life was cast into the lake of fire.

— REVELATION 20:4, 5, 11-15

Almighty God, command your super angel to start ministering to me and prepare me for the day of the rapture of the saints, in the name of Jesus. Let God's angel ignore my cry, pain or anything that supports sin and separate me from Satan and sin, forever, in the name of Jesus. Angels of the living God, assigned to my life, lay your hand on the dragon, the old serpent, and take him far away from me, in the name of Jesus. Let the destroying power of God destroy every enemy of the life of Christ in me, in the name of Jesus. I command the works of the dragon, the old serpent, in my life to receive divine and total destruction, in the name of Jesus. Let the bounding power of God's angel arrest and bind the dragon, the old serpent, out of my life, forever, in the name of Jesus. Almighty God, separate me from Satan and hell fire, the bottomless pit, in the name of Jesus. Father Lord, shut the devil and his works out of my life forever, in the mighty name of Jesus. I command every power of deceit that is attached to the devil to fail woefully in every part of my life, in the name of Jesus. Every evil throne militating against my life, your time is up, be dethroned, in the name of Jesus. I terminate every evil reign in my body, soul and spirit, in the name of Jesus. Almighty God, by your mercy and the power attached to your promises, judge every enemy in my life, in the name of Jesus. Let the power in the word of God sustain me in truth and righteousness till my last breath here on earth, in the name of Jesus. God forbid that I will be among the people that will suffer the great tribulation, in the name of Jesus. Almighty God, by your mercy, help me never to have anything to do with the mark of the beast, 666, in the name of Jesus. Every demand to worship the devil openly or secretly, I reject you vehemently, in the name of Jesus. Let the swallowing power of God cause my enemies to be swallowed without resistance, in the name of Jesus. Heavenly father, take me from where I am now to where you want me to be, in the name of Jesus. Wherever they will call my name for evil, blood of Jesus, arise and answer for me, in the name of Jesus. Let the mouth of the earth, open and swallow all my problems, in the name of Jesus. By the power of the bulldozing anointing of God, I command my problems to be bulldozed out of this earth, in the name of Jesus. Father Lord, with your combined grace and mercy, help me to take part in the first resurrection, in the name of Jesus. I break and loose myself from the strength of the powers of the second death, in the name of Jesus. Almighty God, by your mercy, recruit me into the army of the Lord, into the camp of the saints, in the name of Jesus. Let me be brought into the armies of the Lord Jesus and to be forever separated from the devil and his agents, in the name of Jesus. Father Lord, use the blood of your son Jesus Christ to separate me from the devil and his agents, in the name of Jesus. I break and loose myself from the beasts of this earth, false prophets and every enemy of Christ, in the name of Jesus. Lord Jesus, by your mercy, remove my name from the book of death and write it in the book of life, in the name of Jesus. Let the evil powers that remove people's names from the book of life and write them in the books of death, avoid my name forever, in the name of Jesus. By the power in the ink of Jesus and his ever-speaking blood, let my name be written presently in the book of life, in the name of Jesus.

EIGHTEEN

FACTS OF RESURRECTION AND HEAVEN

DECREE-1

(Hebrews 11:17, 18, Job 19:25-27, Psalm 49:15, Daniel 12:2 , Isaiah 25:8, Isaiah 26:19, John 5:25, 28, 29 , John 11:23-25, Acts 24:15)

Day 1

Expectations:

1. The killing of everything that must die for your original nature to manifest.

2. Commanding every wall of Jericho standing against you to collapse.

3. The destruction of all the enemies that are against the manifestation of your testimonies.

4. The destruction of all the enemies that are against the manifestation of God's glory in your life.

Anything in my life that must die for my true life, originally from God, to manifest and resurrect, die, in the name of Jesus. Almighty God, receive my offering by faith and link me up with your promises and your only begotten son, the Lord Jesus, in the name of Jesus. Let my seed survive every satanic attack and be prepared for the day of resurrection, in the name of Jesus. Every wall of Jericho standing before me, spiritually or physically, collapse from your foundation, in the name of Jesus. Every enemy of the manifestation of my testimonies, receive death, in the name of Jesus. Let the compassing power of the devil against my destiny be frustrated, in the mighty name of Jesus. Every witchcraft animal, assigned to attack me, go back to your sender and attack them, in the name of Jesus. Every enemy of the manifestation of God's glory in my life, be exposed and be disgraced, in the name of Jesus.

> "By faith Abraham, when he was tried, offered up Isaac: and he that had received the promises offered up his only begotten son, of whom it was said, that in Isaac shall thy seed be called:"
>
> —   HEBREWS 11:17, 18

Any offering that will invoke the resurrection power of Christ in my life, be released by faith, in the name of Jesus. I refuse to withhold anything in me that will please God and bring me closer to heaven, in the name of Jesus. Let the receiving power of God receive my offerings, in the name of Jesus. Ancient of days, deliver me from being rejected in heaven, in the name of Jesus. Every instrument of the devil, made to hinder me from being raptured, be destroyed by God's grace and mercies, in the name of Jesus. Father Lord, by your resurrection power, quicken every part of my life to obey you without delay, in the name of Jesus. By the strength of the pleading blood of Jesus, I receive the strength to live above Satan and sin forever, in the name of Jesus. Let the power that took away the body of Jesus from the grave take me away from this world or from the grave in the day of rapture, in the name of Jesus. Every spiritual and physical force, keeping me away from the plan of God, be destroyed, in the name of Jesus. Let the power of God to raise every creature, come upon me and empower me to partake in the first resurrection, in the name of Jesus. Let the ability of God to raise the dead begin to show up in every area of my life against the ministry of death in my life, in the name of Jesus. I command every anti blessing spirit in my life to be paralyzed, in the mighty name of Jesus. Let the coming of God's power into my life come with all manner of blessing, in the name of Jesus. I command my last stay here on earth to be filled with divine strength without any contribution from the kingdom of darkness, in the name of Jesus. Anointing to worship God non-stop, fall upon me, in the name of Jesus. Let my mouth continue to mention God in truth and in spirit, even to my last breath here on earth, in the name of Jesus. Let the powers that pushed the devil and all his evil angels from heaven, begin to push away every property of the devil in my life, in the name of Jesus. Let the refusing power of God empower me to refuse and reject every form of sin in my life, in the name of Jesus.

"For I know that my redeemer liveth, and that he shall stand at the latter day upon the earth: And though after my skin worms destroy this body, yet in my flesh shall I see God: Whom I shall see for myself, and mine eyes shall behold, and not another; Though my reins be consumed within me."

— JOB 19:25-27

Any iron or stony grave, holding me spiritually and physically, be destroyed by the power of resurrection, in the name of Jesus. Let the power in the rock of ages, the Lord Jesus take me far away from every organized darkness, in the name of Jesus. By the power in the living redeemer, I command every part of my life to start living for God, in the name of Jesus. Let the standing power of God single me out from the strength of the devil, his agents and the grave in the day of resurrection, in the name of Jesus. Father Lord, perfect your original plan for my life, in the name of Jesus. Let my life become too uncomfortable for the devil and his evil schemes, in the name of Jesus. Almighty God, empower me to live for you in full righteousness, from now till I take my last breath on earth, in the name of Jesus. I command the powers of darkness that destroys the body and soul to fail woefully before me, even in the grave, in the name of Jesus. Let the gathering power of resurrection, gather me together and take me away from the world or from the grave, in the day of resurrection, in the name of Jesus. Let the divine power of God, from above, deliver me from every enemy of the manifestation of God's righteousness in me, in the name of Jesus. Blood of Jesus, purify me and keep me far away from sin and Satan; give me the grace to see you, in the name of Jesus. Father Lord, empower me to stand against every Pharaoh of my time, in the name of Jesus. Let the mobilizing power of God move me far away from every satanic doctrine, in the name of Jesus. By the power in God's disorganizing strength, I disorganize every organized darkness attacking my life, in the name of Jesus. Let the fighting spirit of God possess me to fight and defeat every strength of Satan and sin in my life, in the name of Jesus. O Lord arise and deliver me from every demonic captivity that has been assigned to delay my movements in life, in the name of Jesus.

Day 2

Expectations:

1. **The scattering of every evil force mobilized by your enemies against you**
2. **Commanding every part of your life to receive divine visitation**
3. **Complete freedom from every form of captivity**
4. **The destruction of every satanic structure built against you**

I scatter every evil force that has been mobilized by my enemies against my life, in the mighty name of Jesus. Every part of my life, lacking the fullness of divine presence and supply, receive divine visitation, in the name of Jesus.

> "But God will redeem my soul from the power of the grave: For he shall receive me. Selah."
>
> — PSALM 49:15

> "And many of them that sleep in the dust of the earth shall awake, some to everlasting life, and some to shame and everlasting contempt."
>
> — DANIEL 12:2

Almighty God, empower me to honor you, without sin, in every area of my life, in the name of Jesus. By the strength of God's purity, father Lord, sanctify my body, soul and spirit and keep me holy forever, in the name of Jesus. Let the redeeming strength in the precious blood of Jesus redeem me from the strength of Satan and sin, in the name of Jesus. I break and loose myself from every demonic captivity, in the name of Jesus. You the powers of the grave, Satan and sin, your time is up; avoid me forever, in the name of Jesus. Father Lord, by your receiving ability, through your grace and mercy, receive me in the air at the moment of rapture and resurrection, in the name of Jesus. Almighty God, by your deliverance power, deliver me from every captivity of the sin and grave, in the name of Jesus. I bind and cast out every demonic sleep or slumber that the devil and his agents have planned against me to cause me to miss the rapture, in the name of Jesus. Let the awaking power of God awake me and keep me awake to be raptured in the first resurrection, in the name of Jesus. Father Lord, empower me to destroy every satanic structure built to prevent me from rapturing with the saints, in the name of Jesus. By thy mercy O Lord, awake me to everlasting life in the day of the rapture of the saints, in the name of Jesus. I break and loose myself completely from every grip of Satan and sin, in the name of Jesus. Father Lord, deliver me from the type of resurrection that brings people to everlasting contempt, in the name of Jesus. Let the wisdom of God arrest me and detain me forever, without a release, in the mighty name of Jesus. Father Lord, by the strength of your wisdom, bring me to your knowledge, power and everlasting light, in the name of Jesus. Let the shining light of God, destroy the powers of Satan, sin and its consequences, in the name of Jesus. Let the wisdom of God upon me and shine as bright as the firmaments, in the name of Jesus. Almighty God, perfect my lifestyle and use my ministry to turn many to your righteousness, in the name of Jesus. Every property of the devil in any area of my life and destiny, catch fire and burn to ashes, in the name of Jesus. I receive the grace of God to reject every treasure of darkness designed to corrupt my life, in the name of Jesus. I break myself loosed from the bondage and the yoke of the devil, in the name of Jesus. Almighty God, deliver me from your wrath and empower me to confront and conquer the devil and his agents, in the name of

Jesus. By the power in God's subduing strength, I subdue every evil kingdom blocking my way to my promised land, in the name of Jesus.

"He will swallow up death in victory; and the Lord GOD will wipe away tears from off all faces; and the rebuke of his people shall he take away from off all the earth: for the LORD hath spoken it."

— ISAIAH 25:8

By the power of God that swallowed death in victory through the resurrection power, I command every part of my face to receive divine touch and wipe away my tears, in the name of Jesus. I destroy every weakness and death in my life, in the name of Jesus. Almighty God, by your power, take away every shame or failure far away from me, in this world and in the world to come, in the name of Jesus. By the power in the name of Jesus, I command every word that God has spoken for my sake to begin to manifest, without a hindrance. Let the strength that the angels use in praising God, fall upon me and praise Him in everything, in the name of Jesus. Let the exalting power of God exalt Christ in my life and dethrone Satan, sin and every power of death, in the name of Jesus. Let the wonders of God cripple Satan, sin and death, in my life, in the name of Jesus. Any evil counsel against my relationship with God and his purity in my life, be destroyed and put to shame, in the name of Jesus. I bring all the wisdom of the devil and his agents against my life into foolishness before the wisdom of God in me, in the name of Jesus. Every satanic structure anywhere against me, be roasted by fire, in the name of Jesus. Every messenger of defilement assigned against my life, be exposed and disgraced, in the name of Jesus. Any satanic billboard mounted against me anywhere, spiritually or physically, be dismantled, in the name of a Jesus. Every enemy of God's truth working against my relationship with God, receive destruction, in the name of Jesus. Blood of Jesus, speak me out of every condemnation and justify me before God by your mercy, in the name of Jesus. Let the pleading power in the blood of Jesus plead for me and deliver me from sin, forever, in the name of Jesus. By the defending power in the word of God, blood of Jesus, arise and defend me before God in the day of judgment, in the name of Jesus. Every strange thing happening among the creations, against my life, be terminated by the terminating power in the speaking blood of Jesus, in the name of Jesus. Any evil building, Babylon the great, that is against my faith in Christ, be pulled down, in the name of Jesus. Father Lord, join me with the saints that will praise you forever, in the kingdom of heaven, in the name of Jesus. I command every satanic memory that is stored in my brain and every satanic agent to forget me and be filled with confusion to my favor, in the name of Jesus. I release the terrifying power of God into the camp of my enemies; I scatter and abandon their evil program against me and the kingdom of God, in the name of Jesus.

Day 3

Expectations:

1. **The destruction of every satanic storm raised against you**
2. **Commanding every demonic wall constructed against God and his children to collapse**
3. **Commanding every satanic poison and demon in your body, soul and spirit to dry up**
4. **Commanding every area of your life to be delivered from sin**

Father Lord, help me to bless the poor and needy in distress and bring them to true salvation, in the name of Jesus. Every satanic storm, raised against me and the kingdom of God anywhere, I cause you to be calm, in the name of Jesus. Every demonic wall, constructed against God and his children, collapse by thunder, in the name of Jesus. Any visible and invisible mark of the devil against me in the day of the rapture, be cleansed by the blood of Jesus. I command every evil noise raised against my relationship with God and my entry into heaven to be put off by the voice of the blood of Jesus. Let the drying power in the word of God dry up every satanic poison and demon in my body, soul and spirit, in the name of Jesus. Every enemy of my joy, peace, rest and happiness, fail woefully, in the name of Jesus. Almighty God, fill me with your wine and help me to remain committed to you, forever, in the name of Jesus.

"Thy dead men shall live, together with my dead body shall they arise. Awake and sing, ye that dwell in dust: for thy dew is as the dew of herbs, and the earth shall cast out the dead."

I command every area of my life to be delivered from sin, by the power in the blood of Jesus, in the name of Jesus. I command every creature to release me to serve God from now to my last breath here on earth, in the name of Jesus. By the power in God's gathering strength, I command my body, soul and spirit to be gathered together at the moment of the first resurrection, in the name of Jesus. Father Lord, by the power in your grace and mercy, help me to take part in the first resurrection, in the name of Jesus. Let the power of the devil and his agents rise in support for me to make heaven on the last day, in the name of Jesus. Father Lord, put your song in my mouth and empower me to start singing to the glory of your name, in the name of Jesus. Let the disappointing power of God disappoint the power of sin in my life, in the name of Jesus. By the trusting ability in the word of God, I receive power to trust God in holiness, even to my last breath on earth, in the name of Jesus. Any evil spirit, mobilized against me from any evil kingdom, I bind and cast you out, in the mighty name of Jesus. Any strange fire burning in my foundation, be quenched by the speaking blood of Jesus, in the name of Jesus. Every shame, disgrace, reproach, failure and disgrace in my life, your time is up, be terminated, in the name of Jesus. Any evil chain of bondage tying me down, break to pieces, in the mighty name of Jesus. Every enemy of the manifestation of God's righteousness in my environment, be destroyed unto death, in the name of Jesus. Almighty God, empower me to obtain a new and undefiled promise that is not common, in the name of Jesus. Any evil mouth opened against me in the land of the living and the dead, close forever, in the name of Jesus.

"Verily, verily, I say unto you, the hour is coming, and now is, when the dead shall hear the voice of the Son of God: and they that hear shall live." "Marvel not at this: for the hour is coming, in the which all that are in the graves shall hear his voice, and shall come forth; they that have done good, unto the resurrection of life; and they that have done evil, unto the resurrection of damnation."

— JOHN 5:25, 28, 29

I command my ear to hear the voice of God and respond from now to the day of the rapture, in the name of Jesus. Almighty God, open my spiritual eyes to see you, my spiritual ears to hear you and obey you, in the name of Jesus. Almighty God, give me enough of your grace to serve you under any situation, in the name of Jesus. Let the living Christ take over my life to live for me without satanic contribution from today and forever, in the name of Jesus. Let the life of Christ in me rule and reign over sin and its consequences, in the name of Jesus. I receive divine authority to execute judgment against the devil and his activities here on earth, in the name of Jesus. I command my mouth to open and judge the devil, sin and every evil action, in the name of Jesus. Father Lord, help me to start doing good like Jesus Christ henceforth forever and ever, in the name of Jesus. Almighty God, wed me forever with the power of the first resurrection of the saints, in the name of Jesus. I command every part of my life to start doing good without a stop till the moment of the first resurrection of the saints, in the name of Jesus. By the power of God's forsaking anointing, I forsake the devil and all his works forever, in the name of Jesus. Every visible and invisible enemy of my destiny, be frustrated and be disappointed, in the name of Jesus. Blood of Jesus, flow into every part of my life and speak me out of satanic captivity, in the name of Jesus. Let the quenching power in the speaking blood of Jesus quench every strange fire burning anywhere against me, in the name of Jesus. Every satanic lion and serpent of darkness in the garden of my life, your time is up, die, in the name of

Jesus. Every demonic sword raised against my life, turn around and kill your owner, in the name of Jesus. Almighty God, increase my strength to fight until the last enemy in the battle field of my life is defeated, in the name of Jesus. I command the strength of my enemies to suddenly disappear and perish forever, in the name of Jesus. Let the powers behind the fighting strength of my enemies withdraw their power without notice, in the name of Jesus. Let the torturing power of God torture unto death every evil spirit assigned to torment my life, in the name of Jesus. Anointing to reject every gift from the devil and his agents that has been designed to blind my eyes, fall upon me, in the name of Jesus. Every enemy of my getting involved in the first resurrection to live with Christ forever, perish, in the name of Jesus. Anointing to obtain a better resurrection, fall upon me, in the mighty name of Jesus.

> "Jesus saith unto her, thy brother shall rise again. Martha saith unto him, I know that he shall rise again in the resurrection at the last day. Jesus said unto her, I am the resurrection, and the life: he that believeth in me, though he were dead, yet shall he live:"
>
> — JOHN 11:23-25

> "and have hope toward God, which they themselves also allow, that there shall be a resurrection of the dead, both of the just and unjust."
>
> — ACTS 24:15

You my life, listen to me very well; you shall rise in the first resurrection of the saints by God's special grace and mercy, in the name of Jesus. Even now, I command every good thing in my life that is weak or dead to receive the power of resurrection, in the name of Jesus. Jesus in me is the resurrection and life, therefore; let my life begin to show the glory of Christ and be without sin forever, in the name of Jesus. You my life, body, soul and spirit, I declare that you will remain pure till the day of the first resurrection, in the name of Jesus. I command the defiling power of the devil to avoid me for ever and ever, in the mighty name of Jesus. Father Lord, by the power in your blood, forbid me from taking part in the resurrection of the unjust, in the name of Jesus. Any evil movement in the spirit realm against my life, you are finished, perish, in the name of Jesus. By the power of God that destroyed the first born in Egypt, I receive the grace of God to destroy Satan and sin in my life, in the name of Jesus. I command my red sea to divide and destroy every satanic destruction, planned against me, in the name of Jesus. Any evil flow into my life from my ancestors and sinful past, dry up, in the name of Jesus. Any evil power sponsoring problems into my life, your time is up, die without delay, in the name of Jesus. I command the red sea of my environment to come together and swallow every stubborn enemy with vows to waste my life, in the name of Jesus.

NINETEEN

RESURRECTION TO HELL OR HEAVEN

DECREE-1

(Acts 9:4, 5, 11-12, Acts 9:18, 20, Philippians 3:7, 10, 11, Romans 8:11, 26, 27, 1 Corinthians 3:16; 6:19, 20, Matthew 12:28, Mark 16:17, 18)

Day 1

Expectations:

1. Commanding every enemy of your faith in Christ to be frustrated.
2. Deliverance from every force assigned to make you continue in your evil ways.
3. Commanding every enemy of the call of God upon your life to be frustrated.

Any threat to my relationship with Christ, father Lord, frustrate them and keep me alive, in the name of Jesus. Every enemy of my faith in Christ, your time is up, be frustrated, in the name of Jesus.

"And he fell to the earth, and heard a voice saying unto him, Saul, Saul, why persecutest thou me? And he said, Who art thou, Lord? And the Lord said, I am Jesus whom thou persecutest: it is hard for thee to kick against the pricks." "And the Lord said unto him, Arise, and go into the street which is called Straight, and enquire in the house of Judas for one called Saul, of Tarsus: for, behold, he prayed, and hath seen in a vision a man named Ananias coming in, and putting his hand on him, that he might receive his sight."

— ACTS 9:4, 5, 11-12

Father Lord, empower me to recognize your word and obey you without hesitation, in the name of Jesus. I refuse to continue in my evil ways for any reason, in the name of Jesus. Almighty God, empower me with your strength to leave where I am now to where you want me to be, in the name of Jesus. Every enemy of God's call to my life, be frustrated, in the name of Jesus. Father Lord, help me to obey you without negotiation, in the name of Jesus. Almighty God, connect me to the right people in life from today, in the name of Jesus. Let my life from today be guided by God without any error, in the name of Jesus. Father Lord, feed me with the food of champions from heaven, in the name of Jesus. Strength and energy to work with God without sin, wherever you are, flood my life, in the name of Jesus. Power to say no to Satan and say yes to God's will for my life, come upon me, in the name of Jesus. Father Lord, command my destiny helpers to look for me and find me by your guidance, in the name of Jesus. Let the mightiness of God come upon me and subdue every evil settlement in my life, in the name of Jesus. Almighty God, release your strength of salvation, purity and prayer upon me without weakness, in the name of Jesus. I command my prayer life to overcome every spirit of prayerlessness working against me, in the name of Jesus. Almighty God, give my destiny helpers vision to support me and help me to any extent, in the name of Jesus. Let God's revelational power open the eyes of people all over the world to see clearly how to support my God's given vision, in the name of Jesus. Father Lord, give men and women all over the world vision concerning me, in the name of Jesus. Every demonic vision against my life, be terminated to death, in the name of Jesus. I refuse to corporate with the devil and his evil plans for my life, in the name of Jesus. Father Lord, take me far away from every demonic assignment, in the name of Jesus. Every demonic focus against my life, be distracted and destroyed, in the name of Jesus. Blood of Jesus, silence every evil voice speaking against my destiny forever and ever, in the name of Jesus. Every enemy of the manifestation of the voice of Christ in my life, be silenced unto death, in the name of Jesus. Wherever they will ever call my name for evil, blood of Jesus, respond on my behalf, in the name of Jesus. Any strange movement against my destiny, spiritually and physically, be terminated, in the name of Jesus. Father Lord, arise and move me away from every danger, in the name of Jesus. Every fake blessing designed to destroy my life, I reject you forever, in the name of Jesus. I break and loose myself from every satanic bondage designed to waste my efforts in life, in the name of Jesus. Any mountain standing between me and God, disappear, in the name of Jesus. Every military movement from satanic army assigned to waste my life, be wasted, in the name of Jesus. Every evil gathering against my life, scatter without success, in the name of Jesus. Any war going on against me in the spirit, be terminated, in the mighty name of Jesus. Any evil mouth talking against my life anywhere, close forever in shame, in the name of Jesus. Almighty God, help me to hear your word and empower me to obey without hesitation, in the name of Jesus. Almighty God, link me up to the power of the resurrection, in the mighty name of Jesus. Every satanic decision to waste my destiny, be frustrated by the resurrection power, in the name of Jesus. Any evil organization, spiritually and physically assigned to block my way to God, scatter by the wind of the Holy Ghost, in the name of Jesus. Blood of Jesus, perfect your purpose in my life and speak me out of every demonic arrest, in the name of Jesus. Any evil assignment to cripple my relationship with God, fail woefully, in the name of Jesus. Father Lord, fail my failures and destroy my defeats in life, in the name of Jesus. Every yoke of bondage in my life, your time is up, break to pieces, in the name of Jesus. Any evil journey embarked to frustrate the plans of God for my life, be terminated with failures, in the name of Jesus. I command the failures and the defeats of my enemies to be multiplied, in the name of Jesus.

Day 2

Expectations:

1. **Commanding the backbone of every evil personality militating against you to be broken.**
2. **Commanding every satanic investment in your life to catch fire.**
3. **Complete deliverance from every satanic program prepared against your life and destiny.**

Let the backbone of every evil personality militating against my life be broken to pieces, in the name of Jesus.

> "And immediately there fell from his eyes as it had been scales: and he received sight forthwith, and arose, and was baptized. And straightway he preached Christ in the synagogues, that he is the Son of God."
>
> — ACTS 9:18, 20

Any satanic investment in my life, catch fire and burn to ashes, in the mighty name of Jesus. I break and loose myself from every satanic program designed to keep me in bondage forever, in the name of Jesus. Let the scales of the devil in my life be destroyed by the power of God, in the mighty name of Jesus. I command every satanic motivated darkness in any area of my life to disappear, in the name of Jesus. Any evil structure built against me anywhere, catch fire and burn to ashes, in the name of Jesus. Let the anointing of God bring deliverance into every part of my life, in the name of Jesus. Heavenly father, empower me to preach Christ everywhere without fear or favor, in the name of Jesus. Every enemy of the reign of Christ in my body, soul and spirit, be frustrated, in the name of Jesus. Almighty God, command your angels to surround me for protection without satanic oppression, in the name of Jesus. Let the earth open and swallow my problems and to vomit every good thing buried against my life, in the name of Jesus. Any evil voice speaking against my life from among the creation, be closed by the speaking blood of Jesus, in the name of Jesus. Almighty God, help me to withdraw from every negative thing going on in the world, in the name of Jesus. Any evil desire against me from every satanic kingdom, be frustrated, in the name of Jesus. O Lord arise and perfect your plan and purpose of creating me, in the name of Jesus. Heavenly father, arise and take me to my place in life, in the name of Jesus. Father Lord, frustrate every negative thought against my destiny, in the mighty name of Jesus. Let the overthrowing power of God overthrow every enemy of my destiny, in the name of Jesus.

"But what things were gain to me, those I counted loss for Christ. that I may know him, and the power of his resurrection, and the fellowship of his sufferings, being made conformable unto his death; if by any means I might attain unto the resurrection of the dead."

— PHILIPPIANS 3:7, 10, 11

Father Lord, arise in your power and expose me to the full knowledge and power of resurrection, in the name of Jesus. Every satanic blockage against the manifestation of the power of his resurrection in any area of my life, be removed, in the name of Jesus. Almighty God, bring me to the power of Christ's resurrection and the fellowship of his sufferings, in the name of Jesus. I command every part of my life, body, soul and spirit to be made conformable unto the death of Jesus, in the name of Jesus. Father Lord, by the power of your mightiness, help me to attain into your first resurrection power, in the name of Jesus. Let the pushing anointing of God help me to attain to God's perfection by the power in the blood of Jesus. I receive God's grace to push forward every day to reach the goal set for me by God, in the name of Jesus. Anointing to forget everything I suppose to forget and to remember what I suppose to remember, fall upon me, in the name of Jesus. Any strange fire from the satanic kingdom, burning in any area of my life, be quenched by the blood of Jesus, in the name of Jesus. I put behind me everything I need to put behind, forgetting them forever without struggle to please God at all cost, in the name of Jesus. Father Lord, empower me to press forward to reach divine height without struggle, in the name of Jesus. Ancient of days, move me into action to press towards the mark for the prize of the high calling of God in Christ Jesus. Father Lord, continue to perfect every area of my life until I get perfect to your expectation, in the name of Jesus. Let the revelational power of God overshadow me to get every knowledge that will bring me into God's divine will, in the name of Jesus. Anointing to walk by the rule of Christ, living like Him, fall upon me, in the name of Jesus. Father Lord, disengage me from Satan, his agents and every sin assigned to attack my fellowship with Christ, in the name of Jesus. I break and loose myself from every enemy of the cross that has been assigned to frustrate my walk with Christ, in the name of Jesus. Let my last days here on earth avoid sin, the second resurrection and destruction in hell fire, in the name of Jesus. I refuse to labor for my flesh alone but for the things concerning the kingdom of God, in the name of Jesus. Any evil wind blowing my faith in Christ, avoid me forever, in the mighty name of Jesus

Christ. Any yoke of earthly things holding me down in bondage, break to pieces, in the name of Jesus. Father Lord, help me to withdraw my conversations from every unprofitable thing, in the name of Jesus. Almighty God, let my conversation be dominated by the things of heaven without carnality, in the name of Jesus. Every enemy of the rule and the reign of Christ in my life, your time is up; be destroyed, in the name of Jesus.

Day 3

Expectations:

1. **Receiving the power to subdue sin**
2. **Commanding the righteousness of God to fill your life and take over you**
3. **Complete deliverance from all religious spirits**
4. **Commanding the carefulness of Christ to possess you.**

Almighty God, change my vile body and fashion it like the glorious body of Christ without sin, in the name of Jesus. Let my body, soul and spirit be empowered to subdue sin, in the name of Jesus. Almighty God, deliver me from dogs, evil workers and concision, in the mighty name of Jesus. I receive power to worship God in the spirit and rejoice in Christ Jesus without having confidence in the flesh, in the name of Jesus. Almighty God, by the power in the blood of Jesus, circumcise my heart, in the name of Jesus. Father Lord, make me a true Christian with a conscience purged by the precious blood of Jesus. Let the righteousness of Christ fill my life and take over me without any sin, in the name of Jesus. Any religious spirit in me, zeal without Christ, your time is up; I bind and cast you out, in the name of Jesus. Almighty God, sanctify me and make me blameless without any stain of sin, in the mighty name of Jesus. Any gain, profit, position and prosperity without Christ in my life, I reject you forever, in the name of Jesus. Every suffering I must go through to fulfil my destiny and serve my generation according to God's will, father Lord, help me to do so without sin, in the name of Jesus. Every yoke of sin in any area of my life, break to pieces, in the mighty name of Jesus. Anything in my life, fighting against the manifestation of God's righteousness in my life, I cut you off, in the name of Jesus. Let my faith in Jesus overcome every demonic operation in my life, in the name of Jesus. Blood of Jesus, flow into every part of my life and deliver me from every satanic work, in the name of Jesus. Every enemy of my complete knowledge of Christ, your time is up, be destroyed, in the mighty name of Jesus. Father Lord, increase my hope, joy and peace whenever I remember your intention to resurrect me to your heaven, in the name of Jesus. Anointing to moderate everything I do here on earth, bearing in mind about the first resurrection, fall upon me, in the name of Jesus. Let the carefulness of Christ possess me with the grace to remain holy to my last breath here on earth, in the name of Jesus. Almighty God, take over my prayer life and everything I do here on earth, in the name of Jesus. Oh Lord, let your peace excel in every area of my life and keep my heart and mind without sin, in the name of Jesus. Almighty God, help me to stand forever for things that are true, honest, just, pure and lovely, in the name of Jesus. I disassociate myself from every evil report, shameful act, reproach and evil manifestation, in the name of Jesus. Anointing to succeed in every situation, possess me, in the name of Jesus. Almighty God, empower me to be able to do all things with the strength of Christ without defilement, in the name of Jesus. Almighty God, by your mercy, supply all things I need now and that I will ever need, according to your riches in glory by Christ Jesus. Let my prayers, good thoughts and desires be empowered with ease to attract divine attention, in the name of Jesus. Almighty God, bless me and encourage me; comfort me and supply all my needs, in the name of Jesus. Every demonic fighting spirit militating against my life, receive shameful defeat, in the name of Jesus. Any witchcraft animal assigned to bewitch me, die, in the name of Jesus. Backbone of my problems, break to pieces, in the mighty name of Jesus. Any strange fire, burning in any part of my life, be quenched by the blood of Jesus, in the mighty name of Jesus.

"But if the Spirit of him that raised up Jesus from the dead dwell in you, he that raised up Christ from the dead shall also quicken your mortal bodies by his Spirit that dwelleth in you. Likewise, the Spirit also helped our infirmities: for we know not what we should pray for as we ought: but the Spirit itself maketh intercession for us with groanings which cannot be uttered. And he that searcheth the hearts knoweth what is the mind of the Spirit, because he maketh intercession for the saints according to the will of God."

— ROMANS 8:11, 26, 27

Father Lord, move into my life with your Spirit that raised Jesus from the dead, in the name of Jesus. I command every part of my life, body, soul and spirit to be quickened by the resurrection power, in the name of Jesus. Let my mortal body receive the power of resurrection by the Spirit of God that lives in me, in the name of Jesus. Father Lord, move me by your Spirit from every infirmity and weakness in prayer, in the name of Jesus. Holy Spirit, take over my life and help me to pray right, according to your will, in the name of Jesus. Father Lord, help me to pray without satanic obstruction, in the mighty name of Jesus. Let the intercession power of the Holy Spirit begin to rule and reign over my life, in the name of Jesus. By the searching power of the Holy Ghost, I destroy every anti-prayer demon militating against my life, in the name of Jesus. Every enemy of the ministry of the Holy Ghost in my life, your time is up, be disgraced, in the name of Jesus. Father Lord, purge my body, soul and spirit from every evil domination, in the name of Jesus. Holy Spirit of God, take your place in my life, ministry and make intercession for my life according to your will, in the name of Jesus. Almighty God, move me far from every condemnation, in the name of Jesus. Any evil force, pulling me away from Christ and his righteousness, scatter and be disgraced, in the name of Jesus. I command every part of my life to cease forever from walking after the flesh; begin to walk after the Spirit, in the name of Jesus.

Day 4

Expectations:

1. **Complete deliverance from every demonic law, custom and tradition holding you down.**
2. **Commanding every satanic injected weakness to die out of your life.**
3. **Receiving the power of God to walk in the spirit.**
4. **Total deliverance from every form of sin, corruption, pollution and carnality.**

Any demonic law, custom and tradition holding me down in bondage, be destroyed, in the name of Jesus. Father Lord, command your freedom to enter into my life and set me free from the law of sin and death, in the name of Jesus. Every satanic weakness injected into my life by the law of sin and death, be replaced with divine strength, in the name of Jesus. Father Lord, by your power that condemned sin through the depth of Christ, command every sin in my life to be condemned, in the name of Jesus. Father Lord, by your mercy and strength, stop me from walking in the flesh and empower me to walk after the Spirit. I break and loose every part of my mind from carnality, in the name of Jesus. Father Lord, help me to be spiritually minded and fill my mind with the peace of Christ, in the name of Jesus. Every carnality in me, fighting against the reign of Christ, receive destruction, in the name of Jesus. Almighty God, empower every aspect of my life to be subjected to the law of God, in the name of Jesus. You my spirit, begin to please God, in the name of Jesus. I command the everything about me to become dead to sin without negotiation, in the name of Jesus. Father Lord, help me to pay my debt to all men by living a holy life and preaching through my lifestyle, in the name of Jesus. Father Lord, deliver from sin and spiritual death, in the name of Jesus. Almighty God, help me to mortify the deeds of my body through your Spirit and live for Christ forever, in the name of Jesus. Lord Jesus, take over the leadership of my life and empower me with the resurrection anointing, in the name of Jesus. Every spirit of bondage in my life, break to pieces and be disengaged from my life forever, in the name of Jesus. I command every satanic fear in my life to die and be replaced with divine boldness, in the name of Jesus. Let the voice of the crying blood of Jesus enter into my life and cry Abba-Father in my life, in the name of Jesus. Spirit of the living God, begin to bear witness within my Spirit and confirm my sonship without condemnation, in the name of Jesus. Almighty God, command me to be your child and heir, in the name of Jesus. Anointing from God's grace and mercy, empower me to start glorifying God without a break all the days of my life here on earth, in the name of Jesus. Every yoke of vanity in my life, your time is up, break to pieces, in the name of Jesus. Almighty God, deliver me from every bondage of corruption, in the name of Jesus. I command every creature to accompany me and support me to fulfil divine destiny, in the name of Jesus. Almighty God, help me to manifest before every creature and command them to rise against every demonic hindrance, in the name of Jesus. By the power in God's liberating anointing, I liberate every part of my life from corruption without defilement, in the name of Jesus. Let the travailing and the groaning power of the whole creation in pain move everything to fight for me, in the name of Jesus. Almighty God, motivate your Spirit in me to groan in prayers for my sake until victory is achieved in every area of my life, in the name of Jesus. Every enemy of God's will for my life, be frustrated by the groaning power of God, in the name of Jesus. Let the whole creation open their mouths and groan against the devil and his work in my life, family and ministry, in the name of Jesus. Almighty God, make everything in me to be fully prepared for my final adaptation in the day of the first resurrection, in the name of Jesus. Let the redeeming power of God redeem me from every corruption, in the name of Jesus. Almighty God, fill my life with the nine fruits and nine gifts of the Holy Spirit, in the name of Jesus. Almighty God, fill my body, soul and spirit with your love, in the name of Jesus. I command all things to start working together for good in my life, in the name of Jesus. Almighty God, increase your presence in my life without measure, in the name of Jesus. Almighty God, empower me with your Spirit to lead me to your divine ordained destination, in the name of Jesus. Let the justification power of God fall upon me and justify me by the crying blood of Jesus. Father Lord, empower me to always walk with you and do your will to my last breath here on earth, in the name of Jesus. Every benefit and reward from the death of Jesus here on earth, begin to manifest in every area of my life, in the name of Jesus. Let the giving strength of God, the father, who gave us Jesus to die for our sins, give me every blessing, in the name of Jesus. Any satanic attack against my faith in Christ, be frustrated, in the name of Jesus. Blood of Jesus, flow into the foundation of my life and destroy every demonic plantation, in the name of Jesus.

Day 5

Expectations:

1. **Commanding every evil eye monitoring you to be blinded.**
2. **The scattering of every demonic force mobilized against you.**
3. **Complete deliverance from the influence of every spirit responsible for bad character.**
4. **The destruction of every spirit assigned to defile you.**
5. **Deliverance from every satanic captivity assigned to waste you**

Any evil eye, monitoring my life from any evil kingdom, be blinded, in the name of Jesus. I command every demonic force mobilized against my destiny to scatter and fail, in the name of Jesus.

> "Know ye not that ye are the temple of God, and that the Spirit of God dwelleth in you?" What? know ye not that your body is the temple of the Holy Ghost which is in you, which ye have of God, and ye are not your own? For ye are bought with a price: therefore, glorify God in your body, and in your spirit, which are God's."
>
> — 1 CORINTHIANS 3:16; 6:19, 20

Blood of Jesus, flow into my foundation and cleanse my life and make it holy for your habitation, in the name of Jesus. Every spirit of bad character in my life, I bind and cast you out, in the name of Jesus. Spirit of the living God, enter into my life and take over, in the name of Jesus. I break and lose my body, soul and spirit from satanic defilement, in the name of Jesus. Any evil spirit assigned to defile me, fail woefully, be bound and cast out of my life, in the name of Jesus. I break and loose myself from every evil relationship, in the name of Jesus. Let the purchasing power in the blood of Jesus repurchase me from every satanic captivity, in the name of Jesus. Any witchcraft animal in the garden of my life, your time is up, die, in the mighty name of Jesus. Almighty God, destroy the speed of my enemies and cripple every move against my life, in the name of Jesus. Any evil river, flowing into my life, your time is up, dry up, in the name of Jesus. Father Lord, take me far away from every demonic bondage, in the name of Jesus. Job 33:4; Matthew 10:20 … Almighty God, open my mouth in wisdom and speak mystery against satanic words militating against my destiny, in the name of Jesus. Let the cleansing power in the blood of Jesus sanctify my tongue and deliver me from every demonic pollution, in the name of Jesus. By the power in God's Spirit, I receive perfect deliverance from every work of the devil over my life, in the name of Jesus. Father Lord, command your breath to enter into every part of my life and take over, in the name of Jesus. Let the power of resurrection minister eternal life into every department of my life, in the name of Jesus. Every messenger of death in my life, I reject you and your message, in the name of Jesus. Father Lord, send your Spirit into my life and take over my speech, forever and ever, in the name of Jesus. Let every utterance from me be controlled by the Spirit of God, in the name of Jesus. Every evil spirit assigned to speak through me, I bind and cast you out, in the name of Jesus. Let the defiling anointing of the devil fail woefully before me forever, in the name of Jesus. Let every power of darkness that pollutes human tongues, avoid my tongue forever and ever, in the mighty name of Jesus. O Lord arise and deliver me from every negative speech, in the name of Jesus. Almighty God, deliver me from every satanic agent, in the name of Jesus. Father Lord, impart your wisdom, knowledge and understanding into my life, in the mighty name of Jesus. Every seed of foolishness planted into my life, be uprooted by the power of God, in the name of Jesus. Almighty God, deliver me from police case and court case, in the name of Jesus. Any arrow from the witchcraft kingdom, fired against my life, I fire you back, in the name of Jesus.

Every fire of witchcraft in my life, sent to torment me, go back to your sender, in the mighty name of Jesus. Every organized darkness militating against my divine assignment, be disorganized, in the name of Jesus. I dismantle every satanic plantation in every area of my life, in the name of Jesus. O Lord arise, fight my battles and give me victory, in the name of Jesus. Any satanic program going on against my life, be terminated, in the name of Jesus.

> "But if I cast out devils by the Spirit of God, then the kingdom of God is come unto you."
>
> — MATTHEW 12:28

> "And these signs shall follow them that believe; In my name shall they cast out devils; they shall speak with new tongues; they shall take up serpents; and if they drink any deadly thing, it shall not hurt them; they shall lay hands on the sick, and they shall recover."
>
> — MARK 16:17, 18

By the power in the Spirit of God, I cast out every demonic spirit militating against my destiny, in the name of Jesus. Father Lord, by your Spirit, I set every area of my life free from satanic attack, in the mighty name of Jesus. Any part of my life possessed by the devil, receive deliverance by the power of the Holy Spirit, in the name of Jesus. Almighty God, send your Spirit into every organ of my life and heal me from diseases, in the name of Jesus. Every defect in my body, soul and spirit, receive the touch of the Holy Spirit, in the name of Jesus. Father Lord, deliver me from every spiritual and physical sickness, in the name of Jesus. I break and loose myself from every demonic captivity, in the name of Jesus. Father Lord, by your anointing that breaks every yoke, break the yoke of suffering, hardship and poverty in my life, in the name of Jesus. I command the spirit of Beelzebub to be bound and cast out of my life, in the name of Jesus. Every evil thought and desire against my life, be destroyed, in the name of Jesus. I scatter the kingdom of darkness against my life and render them impotent, in the name of Jesus. Any evil force fighting against my destiny from Beelzebub, the prince of the devils, scatter and fail woefully before me, in the name of Jesus. Let the dividing power of God divide my unrepentant enemies into pieces, in the name of Jesus. Every satanic embargo placed upon my life to waste my efforts in life, be lifted, in the name of Jesus. Spirit of the living God, empower me to cast out devils by your power, in the name of Jesus. Father Lord, command your signs to follow me everywhere I go in life, even while sleeping, in the name of Jesus. Every demonic spirit fighting to separate me from God, I bind and cast you out, in the name of Jesus. Almighty God, baptize me in your Spirit and fill me to speak in tongues, in the mighty name of Jesus. I present the name of Jesus against every evil spirit hiding in any part of my life, in the name of Jesus. Any evil presentation against the plan of God for my life, I reject you forever, in the name of Jesus. I refuse to yield to sin for any reason, in the name of Jesus. Any evil hand planting evil in my life, wither by fire, in the name of Jesus. I cut every serpent and scorpion, living in the garden of my life, into pieces, in the name of Jesus. Almighty God, neutralize every poison prepared to harm me for any reason, in the name of Jesus. Let the gathering of the devil and his agents against my life, now, tomorrow and in the future scatter and fail woefully, in the name of Jesus. Father Lord, by your mercy, bless my food and drinks forever, in the name of Jesus. Any evil arrangement against my life, scatter and be burnt to ashes, in the name of Jesus. Every evil movement against my destiny among the creation, be demobilized to death, in the name of Jesus. Let the fighting spirit of the devil and his agents against my life be punctured to nothing, in the name of Jesus. Father Lord, empower me to overcome every trial and temptation, in the name of Jesus. Spirit of the living God, begin to minister to me every day of my life, in the name of

Jesus. Every mountain standing before me, your time is up, disappear forever from my presence, in the name of Jesus. I command my heavens to open and remain open for the abundant supply of my needs, in the name of Jesus. Every evil gang up against my promotion and prosperity, scatter in defeat, in the name of Jesus. Any evil call to my name from any satanic kingdom, blood of Jesus, answer for me, in the name of Jesus. Almighty God, take me higher above the reach of the devil, his agents and my unrepentant enemies, in the name of Jesus. I command all the answers to my prayers to begin to manifest without delay, in the name of Jesus. Any evil force prepared to destroy my faith in Christ, scatter and perish, in the name of Jesus. Anointing to preach the word of God rightly without compromise and sin, possess me, in the name of Jesus. Father Lord, deliver me by your Spirit wherever I need deliverance, in the name of Jesus. Every arrow of fear fired against my life, go back to your sender, in the name of Jesus. Almighty God, deliver me by your Almightiness from every organized darkness, in the name of Jesus. I break and loose myself from every demonic contact and relationship, in the name of Jesus. Every yoke placed upon my destiny by marine spirits, be broken to pieces, in the name of Jesus. O Lord arise and take me to my place of service to you, in the name of Jesus. Father Lord, arise and take me far away from every demonic manipulation, in the name of Jesus. Every demonic journey taken to terminate my journey with Christ, fail woefully, in the name of Jesus. I destroy every witchcraft attack against my relationship with God, in the name of Jesus. Every satanic captivity designed to waste my life, be terminated immediately, in the name of Jesus. Any satanic mark in any part of my life, your time is up, be cleansed by the cleansing power in the blood of Jesus. Father Lord, use the blood of your son, Jesus Christ, to quench every strange fire burning in my life, in the name of Jesus.

TWENTY

UNKNOWN POWERS IN THE NAME OF JESUS

DECREE WITH JESUS NAME

(Exodus 3:13-15, Genesis 22:13, 14, Judges 6:23, 24, Jeremiah 23:6, Exodus 15:26, Exodus 17:8-15, Ezekiel 48:35, Exodus 23:17, Isaiah 10:16, 33, Proverbs 18:10, Acts 19:13-16, Philippians 2:9-11, Acts 3:1-8, John 14:12-14)

Day 1

Expectations:

1. **Commanding every name among God's creation fighting you to fail**
2. **Total deliverance from every evil name keeping you in bondage**
3. **Commanding every satanic incantation and enchantment assigned to weaken you to be neutralized**
4. **The destruction of the powers or forces backing every evil name assigned to torment you**

Every name on earth and among the creations, fighting against the name of God in my life, fail woefully, in the name of Jesus. Let the name of God called I AM THAT I AM destroy every evil name militating against my destiny, in the name of Jesus. By the name, The LORD God of your fathers, the God of Abraham, the God of Isaac and Jacob, I frustrate every evil name keeping me in bondage, in the name of Jesus.

"And Moses said unto God, Behold, when I come unto the children of Israel, and shall say unto them, The God of your fathers hath sent me unto you; and they shall say to me, what is his name? what shall I say unto them? And God said unto Moses, I AM THAT I AM: and he said, thus shalt thou say unto the children of Israel, I AM hath sent me unto you. And God said moreover unto Moses, thus shalt thou say unto the children of Israel, The LORD God of your fathers, the God of Abraham, the God of Isaac, and the God of Jacob, hath sent me unto you: this is my name for ever, and this is my memorial unto all generations."

— EXODUS 3:13-15

Every satanic incantation and enchantment assigned to weaken my life, be neutralized, in the name of Jesus. Almighty God, neutralize and equip me with the powers in your name to confront and conquer every demonic strength attached to any evil name, in the name of Jesus. Let the whole earth open and swallow the strength in any evil name militating against my destiny, in the mighty name of Jesus. Any evil personality asking me who my God is, receive destruction, in the name of Jesus. Father Lord, by your power, I disable the powers and authority backing any evil name assigned to torment my destiny, in the name of Jesus. Any evil name holding me and my people in bondage, I break your backbone, in the name of Jesus. I command every Pharoah-like personality, reigning over me to be dethroned and disgraced, in the name of Jesus. Let the disappointing power of God disappoint every enemy of God's name in my life, in the name of Jesus. I break and loose myself from the bondage of the Egyptian Pharaoh, in the name of Jesus. I command any evil personality contending against the voice of God in my life to be silenced, in the name of Jesus. Every negative voice speaking against the rulership and the reign of God's name in my life, be silenced by the speaking blood of Jesus. By the power in the name of God in my life, I break every satanic bondage in my life, in the name of Jesus. Any satanic contention against the commandment of God's name, be frustrated, in the name of Jesus. Any hindrance to my journey out of bondage to freedom, be removed without delay, in the name of Jesus. Any demonic office assigned to put me into suffering, your time is up, be destroyed, in the mighty name of Jesus. Almighty God, deliver me from every satanic burden and the wicked taskmasters, in the mighty name of Jesus. I break and loose myself from the yokes of Egyptian taskmasters of my time, in the mighty name of Jesus. Father Lord, by your diminishing power, I bring to an end every demonic assignment and daily target designed to destroy me, in the name of Jesus. Almighty God, by your strong hand, take me far away from the reach of my enemies, in the name of Jesus. Father

LORD, arise in your anger, without mercy, and show every unrepentant personality that you are God and no-one else, in the name of Jesus. Let the remembering power in the name of God Almighty and Jehovah remember me and come to my rescue, in the name of Jesus. Heavenly father, appear in the battle field of my life by your name of Almighty and JEHOVAH, in the name of Jesus. Let the establishing anointing of God ALMIGHTY appear before me and establish his supremacy in every part of my life, in the name of Jesus. Let the fighting strength of my enemies be intimidated and be destroyed by the name of God ALMIGHTY and JEHOVAH, in the name of Jesus. Father Lord, by your name Almighty and Jehovah, take me far away from every bondage of this life, in the name of Jesus. Any evil inherited covenant militating against my freedom, be broken to pieces by the name Almighty God, in the name of Jesus. Father Lord, by your name Jehovah, rid me out of every bondage of the devil and his agents, in the name of Jesus. Let the redeeming anointing in the name of Jehovah take me far away from every evil situation, in the name of Jesus. Almighty God, in your Almightiness, stretch out your arm with great judgment against unrepentant enemies in my life, in the name of Jesus. Father Lord, come out with your power in full force and take me away from all evil, in the name of Jesus. Let the promises of God's deliverance begin to manifest in my life with full force, in the name of Jesus. Heavenly father, show my enemies that you are the only LORD of all, in the mighty name of Jesus. Any evil appearance against me in the battlefield, I cut you off without delay, in the name of Jesus. By the power of God's LORDSHIP over my life, I dethrone every problem in my life, in the name of Jesus.

"And Abraham lifted up his eyes, and looked, and behold behind him a ram caught in a thicket by his horns: and Abraham went and took the ram, and offered him up for a burnt offering in the stead of his son. And Abraham called the name of that place Jehovah-jireh: as it is said to this day, In the mount of the LORD it shall be seen."

— GENESIS 22:13, 14

By the name of God JEHOVAH-JIREH, I receive abundant blessings from God to please Him all the days of my life, in the name of Jesus. Almighty God, confront and conquer anything here on earth standing in your place in my life, in the name of Jesus. I receive everything given to me by God to serve Him, please Him and fulfill my destiny here on earth, in the name of Jesus. Almighty God, open my eyes to see your provisions for my life and the people around me on daily bases, in the name of Jesus. Everything I ever need in life to serve God with no sin attached, wherever you are, begin to manifest, in the name of Jesus. Anointing to please God with all that I have, fall upon me, in the name of Jesus. Let the provisions of God Almighty be made available to me without delay, in the mighty name of Jesus.

"And the LORD said unto him, Peace be unto thee; fear not: thou shalt not die. Then Gideon built an altar there unto the LORD, and called it Jehovah-shalom: unto this day it is yet in Ophrah of the Abi-ezrites."

— JUDGES 6:23, 24

I command my presence everywhere to attract God and to be dominated with his righteousness, in the name of Jesus. By the power in the name JEHOVAH-SHALOM, I forbid every evil presence in my life, in the name of Jesus. Almighty God, empower me to honor you without negotiation under any situation, in the name of Jesus. Any evil force influencing me to commit sin against my God, scatter and perish forever, in the name of Jesus. Let the prevailing power attached to sin fail woefully in my life, in the name of Jesus. Any satanic structure in any area of my life, catch fire, be uprooted and burn to ashes, in the name of Jesus. Anything in my life under satanic attack from satanic kingdom, receive deliverance, in the mighty name of Jesus. Any evil altar ministering against my destiny, be roasted by the fire of God, in the name of Jesus. I command all the destroyers of my increase from God in life to be destroyed, in the name of Jesus. By the power of God's sustaining ability of good things, I receive the reward of my labor, in the mighty name of Jesus. Every demonic grasshopper, spiritually and physically assigned to waste my life, be wasted, in the name of Jesus. Any stranger in the garden of my life, your time is up, be destroyed, in the name of Jesus. Let the anointing of God enter into my life and waste every satanic investment in my life, in the name of Jesus. Any evil spirit that has impoverished my destiny, your time is up, receive destruction, in the name of Jesus. Let my cry reach to the throne of God for immediate deliverance, in the name of Jesus. Almighty God, by your mercy, send my destiny helpers and move them to help me in life, in the mighty name of Jesus. I break and loose myself from every demonic bondage assigned to keep me in captivity, in the name of Jesus. Almighty God, deliver me from every spiritual and physical oppressor, in the name of Jesus. I break and loose myself from the fear of the devil and the kingdom of darkness, in the name of Jesus. Almighty God, command your angels to appear before me, in the battle field, and deliver me from my enemies, in the name of Jesus.

Day 2

Expectations:

1. The destruction of every arrow of death fired against your life and destiny.
2. The termination of every evil that has befallen you and your family.
3. Commanding the removal of every evil hand resting on your life.
4. Commanding divine motivated prosperity to spring up in your life.
5. The destruction of every yoke of falsehood affecting you.

Every arrow of death, fired against my life and destiny, I fire you back, in the name of Jesus. Almighty God, increase your presence in my life without measure, in the name of Jesus. Any evil that has befallen me, my family and people, be terminated, in the mighty name of Jesus. Almighty God, please don't forsake me for any reason, appear and fight for me, in the name of Jesus. Any evil hand resting upon my life, your time is up, expire and dry up, in the mighty name of Jesus. Father Lord, increase your might upon my life and empower me to receive victory, in the name of Jesus. Father Lord, remove my limitations and replace it with your sufficient and sustaining grace, in the name of Jesus. Blood of Jesus, enter into the land of the living and the dead and speak me out of every trouble, in the name of Jesus. Let the touching power of God be extended to me to touch every part of my life, in the name of Jesus. Father Lord, multiply your boldness without fear in every area of my life, in the mighty name of Jesus.

"In his days Judah shall be saved, and Israel shall dwell safely: and this is his name whereby he shall be called, THE Lord OUR RIGHTEOUSNESS."

— JEREMIAH 23:6

"And said, if thou wilt diligently hearken to the voice of the LORD thy God, and wilt do that which is right in his sight, and wilt give ear to his commandments, and keep all his statutes, I will put none of these diseases upon thee, which I have brought upon the Egyptians: for I am the LORD that healeth thee."

— EXODUS 15:26

Almighty God, use my family and children to raise righteousness in every generation, in the mighty name of Jesus. Let divine motivated prosperity spring up through me and spread as a branch all over the world, in the name of Jesus. Almighty God, use me to execute judgment and justice here on earth without partiality, in the name of Jesus. Let the revival of salvation and the demonstration of God's power begin to manifest in my life and ministry, in the name of Jesus. Almighty God, arise by your mercy and use me as a vessel to bring liberation, in the name of Jesus. Let the RIGHTEOUSNESS OF GOD take over my activities here on earth, in the mighty name of Jesus. Father Lord, command my righteousness to be like yours, "THE LORD OUR RIGHTEOUSNESS", in the name of Jesus. Every righteousness in me standing against the RIGHTEOUSNESS OF OUR LORD, perish, in the name of Jesus. Father Lord, deliver me and take me far away from every fake unrighteousness, in the name of Jesus. Every yoke of falsehood in my life, your time is up, break to pieces, in the mighty name of Jesus. Father Lord, empower me with greater grace to diligently hear your voice and do exactly your wish without negotiation, in the name of Jesus. Anointing to stand on the truth and do what is right at all times, possess me, in the mighty name of Jesus. Almighty God, move me to the right direction, empower me to give ear to your commandments, in the name of Jesus. I command every power of sickness, disease and all the consequences of sin to avoid my life, forever, in the name of Jesus. By the power of God's deliverance and healing anointing, I command every problem in my life to perish, in the name of Jesus.

"Then came Amalek, and fought with Israel in Rephidim. And Moses said unto Joshua, choose us out men, and go out, fight with Amalek: tomorrow I will stand on the top of the hill with the rod of God in my hand. So Joshua did as Moses had said to him, and fought with Amalek: and Moses, Aaron, and Hur went up to the top of the hill. And it came to pass, when Moses held up his hand, that Israel prevailed: and when he let down his hand, Amalek prevailed. But Moses' hands were heavy; and they took a stone, and put it under him, and he sat thereon; and Aaron and Hur stayed up his hands, the one on the one side, and the other on the other side; and his hands were steady until the going down of the sun. And Joshua discomfited Amalek and his people with the edge of the sword. And the LORD said unto Moses, Write this for a memorial in a book, and rehearse it in the ears of Joshua: for I will utterly put out the remembrance of Amalek from under heaven. And Moses built an altar, and called the name of its Jehovah-nisei:"

— EXODUS 17:8-15

Father Lord, take me to your presence, the source of the waters of life, and establish me there, in the name of Jesus. Any evil congregation, assigned to distract my focus to God's eternal benefits, scatter in shame, in the name of Jesus. Blood of Jesus, quench my thirst and deliver me from every lack, in the mighty name of Jesus. Let my cries and earnest prayers reach the throne of God and attract divine intervention, in the name of Jesus. Father Lord, command the waters of life to flow into my life and to kill every seed of death in any area of my life, in the name of Jesus. Father Lord, empower me with your fighting ability to overcome every enemy in the battle field of my life, in the name of Jesus. Almighty God, choose men and women of integrity to support and sponsor your ministry, in the name of Jesus. I break the fighting spirit of the devil and his agents against my life to pieces, in the name of Jesus. Let holy men and women, and angels of the living God, hold my hand until my enemies are subdued, in the name of Jesus. By this time tomorrow, I decree that all my enemies shall bow and surrender to my God, in the mighty name of Jesus. Every weakness in any part of my life, your time is up, be replaced with divine strength, in the mighty name of Jesus.

"It was round about eighteen thousand measures: and the name of the city from that day shall be, The LORD is there."

— EZEKIEL 48:35

"Three times in the year all thy males shall appear before the Lord GOD."

— EXODUS 23:17

Almighty God, convert my life, family and ministry to prove that THE LORD IS THERE without a trace of the devil and his agents, in the name of Jesus. I command every part of my body, soul and spirit to appear before the LORD and remain with Him forever, in the name of Jesus. Every demonic appearance in any area of my life, your time is up, disappear, in the mighty name of Jesus. Every spiritual and physical evil attachment in my life, catch fire and burn to ashes, in the name of Jesus. I command the separating power of the devil and his agents to fail woefully, in the name of Jesus. Father Lord, help me to abide in you and never depart from your presence, in the name of Jesus. By the power in the linking anointing of the Almighty God, I connect my body, soul and spirit to God forever, in the name of Jesus.

"Behold, the Lord, the LORD of hosts, shall lop the bough with terror: and the high ones of stature shall be hewn down, and the haughty shall be humbled."

— ISAIAH 10:16, 33

Father Lord, reduce the presence of the devil and his agents in my life to zero, in the mighty name of Jesus. By the power of the LORD of host, I disengage myself from every connection to Satan, sin and its consequences, in the name of Jesus. Let the glory of God be multiplied in every area of my life, forever and ever, in the mighty name of Jesus. Father Lord, release your burning fire to burn forever until every trace of the devil and his works are burnt to ashes and removed far away from me, in the name of Jesus. Let the burning fire of God be spread into every part of my life and burn to ashes every satanic presence, in the name of Jesus. Father Lord, by your mercy, get angry at the works of the devil in my life and destroy them, in the name of Jesus. I release divine indignation against every satanic program in my life, in the mighty name of Jesus. Almighty God, deliver me from hypocrisy and every evil character prospering in my life, in the name of Jesus. Any evil movement towards my destiny, be diverted to the camp of the devil, in the name of Jesus. I break and loose myself from the destabilizing power of the devil and his agents, in the name of Jesus. Every demonic egg, laid against me among the creations, break to pieces, in the name of Jesus. Let the boasting power of the devil and his agents against my life be crippled unto death, in the name of Jesus. Almighty God, by your magnifying ability, magnify your righteousness in my life without any trace of sin, in the name of Jesus.

Day 3

Expectations:

1. **Commanding the sustaining grace of God to sustain your relationship with him**

2. **The destruction of every hindrance to the manifestation of God's righteousness in you**

3. **Commanding every enemy that wants to remove you from God's righteousness and protection to fail.**

4. **Commanding every evil movement in the waters against you to be frustrated.**

Let the sustaining grace of God sustain my relationship with Him forever, without a trace of sin, in the name of Jesus. Anointing to be identified with the name of the LORD, fall upon me and begin to manifest, in the name of Jesus. Almighty God, input your complete righteousness in me, without measure, in the mighty name of Jesus. Every hindrance to the manifestation of God's righteousness in my life, be exposed and be disgraced, in the name of Jesus. Let the name of God conquer every other name within and around me, in the name of Jesus. Father Lord, bring me into your perfect righteousness, in the name of Jesus. I command everything on earth and among the creations to bring me into God's righteousness, in the name of Jesus. Any evil force hindering me from running into the name of the LORD, scatter and perish, in the name of Jesus. Almighty God, bring me into the righteousness and the safety that is in your name, in the name of Jesus. Let the rushing power in the name of the LORD rush me into the divine presence of God, in the name of Jesus. Every enemy that does not want me to remain in God's righteousness and protection, fail woefully and be frustrated, in the name of Jesus.

"The name of the LORD is a strong tower: The righteous runneth into it, and is safe."

— PROVERBS 18:10

Father Lord, arise in your power and disgrace every enemy of Christ (vagabonds and exorcists) using your name negatively, in the name of Jesus. Any evil personality, using the name of God wrongly, be exposed and disgraced, in the name of Jesus. Almighty God, frustrate every evil minister using the name of Jesus in vain, in the name of Jesus. I destroy every occultic person that wants to use my name against me, in the name of Jesus. Any evil personality in covenant with evil spirits to use the name of Jesus to promote evil, be exposed and disgraced, in the name of Jesus. I command evil spirits to turn around and disgrace one another, in the name of Jesus.

"Then certain of the vagabond Jews, exorcists, took upon them to call over them which had evil spirits the name of the Lord Jesus, saying, we adjure you by Jesus whom Paul preacheth. And there were seven sons of one Sceva, a Jew, and chief of the priests, which did so. And the evil spirit answered and said, Jesus I know, and Paul I know; but who are ye? And the man in whom the evil spirit was leaped on them, and overcame them, and prevailed against them, so that they fled out of that house naked and wounded."

— ACTS 19:13-16

Any evil movement in the waters, against my life, be demobilized unto death, in the name of Jesus. I command the whole creation to rise and defend my faith in Christ, in the name of Jesus. Father Lord, stretch your holy hand and wipe away every tear on my face forever, in the name of Jesus. Every demonic judgment passed against my life, be reversed by God's reversing power, in the name of Jesus. I command the hosts of darkness, militating against my life, to tremble and perish, in the name of Jesus. By the power of divine infinity, I search the universe and command every hidden enemy of my life to be exposed and disgraced, in the name of Jesus. I command the uprising of my enemies to be exposed and disgraced, in the name of Jesus. I darken every understanding my enemy has of my destiny, in the name of Jesus. Almighty God, clear my path and remove every stumbling block that is standing on my way, in the mighty name of Jesus. Every evil tongue speaking against my destiny, be silenced by the speaking blood of Jesus, in the name of Jesus. Let my front and back be covered by divine presence, in the name of Jesus. Almighty God, empower me to attain to divine knowledge and understanding, in the mighty name of Jesus. Let the Spirit of God possess me and take me far away from every danger, in the name of Jesus. Almighty God, open my heaven and shower your blessings into my life without measure, in the name of Jesus. Let my laying down, standing, walking and running on daily basis be blessed mightily by the Spirit of God, in the name of Jesus. Any part of my life captured by the devil and his agents, be released by force, in the name of Jesus. Almighty God, create spiritual wings in me; help me to fly out from every satanic captivity, in the name of Jesus. Let the holding and restraining power of God hold me back and restrain me from every sin and danger, in the name of Jesus (Psalm 139:7-12). I command every creature to cease from rest, day and night, until every enemy of my life is incapacitated, in the name of Jesus. Anointing to give glory, praises and worship unto God, without ceasing, fall upon me, in the name of Jesus. Any evil throne standing against the manifestation of God in my life, be dethroned, in the name of Jesus. Almighty God, make me worthy to see you and to live with you forever and ever in heaven, in the mighty name of Jesus. By the power in God's wisdom, I receive the wisdom to cripple every satanic movement against my life, in the name of Jesus. Father Lord, fill me with your wisdom to overcome every satanic wisdom assigned to confuse me, in the name of Jesus. Let my life attract divine wisdom against the devil and his agents, in the name of Jesus. Father Lord, release your riches into my life by your wisdom, in the mighty name of Jesus. By the power of the Omnipotent anointing of God, I command every power attached to the devil and his agents against me to be frustrated, in the name of Jesus. Almighty God, bring me into perfection and empower me to live a holy life, in the name of Jesus. By the power in the name of the LORD, I discover and destroy every problem in my life, in the name of Jesus. Almighty God, perfect your knowledge and use me to disgrace every satanic knowledge militating against my destiny, in the name of Jesus. Father Lord, sanctify and render me holy by your holy nature, in the name of Jesus. Ancient of days, command your faithfulness to manifest in my life and make me faithful forever, in the name of Jesus. I break every yoke of being unfaithful to God to pieces, in the name of Jesus. Let the love of God begin to rule and reign in every area of my life, in the name of Jesus. By the power of God's mercy, I command every good thing to start taking place in every area of my life, in the name of Jesus.

"Wherefore God also hath highly exalted him, and given him a name which is above every name: that at the name of Jesus every knee should bow, of things in heaven, and things in earth, and things under the earth; and that every tongue should confess that Jesus Christ is Lord, to the glory of God the Father."

— PHILIPPIANS 2:9-11

Let the mind that is in Jesus Christ be duplicated in my life, in the name of Jesus. Any demonic plantation in my life, be uprooted by the power in the blood of Jesus, in the mighty name of Jesus. By the decree of the Almighty God, I decree that every divine investment that the Lord has apportioned for me shall locate me in the name of Jesus. By the power that is in the exalted name of Jesus, I rise above every problem militating against my life, in the name of Jesus. Any name from anywhere fighting against the reign of Jesus in my life, be destroyed, in the mighty name of Jesus. Every satanic embargo placed against the manifestation of Jesus in my life, be lifted, in the name of Jesus. I dethrone every name that is not of God in my life, in the name of Jesus. I command every knee and evil force in any area of my life to surrender to the supremacy of the name of Jesus, in the name of Jesus. Let everything in the heavens and in the earth bow and perish before the name of Jesus in my life, in the name of Jesus. Any evil mouth, wicked tongue that will ever speak against my life, be silenced forever, in the name of Jesus. Every tongue and creature that has refused to confess that Jesus Christ is Lord, to the glory of God the father, perish, in the name of Jesus. Every evil deposit in my life through dreams of the night, receive death without life, in the name of Jesus. I command the helpers of my enemies to withdraw their help and support, in the name of Jesus. Let the whole creation withdraw their services to every unrepentant enemy of my life, in the name of Jesus.

"Now Peter and John went up together into the temple at the hour of prayer, being the ninth hour. And a certain man lame from his mother's womb was carried, whom they laid daily at the gate of the temple which is called Beautiful, to ask alms of them that entered into the temple; who seeing Peter and John about to go into the temple asked an alms. And Peter, fastening his eyes upon him with John, said, Look on us. And he gave heed unto them, expecting to receive something of them. Then Peter said, Silver and gold have I none; but such as I have give I thee: In the name of Jesus Christ of Nazareth rise up and walk. And he took him by the right hand, and lifted him up: and immediately his feet and ankle bones received strength. And he leaping up stood, and walked, and entered with them into the temple, walking, and leaping, and praising God."

— ACTS 3:1-8

Almighty God, by the power you invested in the name of Jesus Christ, deliver me from every satanic captivity, in the name of Jesus. Father Lord, use me to silence the powers of darkness in the temple without negotiation, in the name of Jesus. Every inherited problem from my place of birth, your time is up, be terminated by the speaking blood of Jesus. Let the power in the name of Jesus cripple every problem that has entered into my life from my mother's womb, in the name of Jesus. Any evil name that wants to limit my progress in life, be destroyed by the power in the name of Jesus, in the mighty name of Jesus. Every yoke of impossibility in my life, your time is up, break to pieces, in the name of Jesus. Any problem that has defiled every solution in my life, I terminate your assignment, in the mighty name of Jesus. Father Lord, send your deliverance power into every part of my body, soul and spirit, in the name of Jesus. Every witchcraft achievement in any area of my life, receive full destruction, in the name of Jesus. Let the killing power of God kill every satanic problem in my life, in the name of Jesus. Almighty God, feed me with the food of champions, in the name of Jesus.

"Verily, verily, I say unto you, He that believeth on me, the works that I do shall he do also; and greater works than these shall he do; because I go unto my Father. And whatsoever ye shall ask in my name, that will I do, that the Father may be glorified in the Son. If ye shall ask any thing in my name, I will do it."

— JOHN 14:12-14

I scatter every evil force troubling my heart, in the mighty name of Jesus. Almighty God, with the power in the name of Jesus, I increase my power to receive answers to prayers, in the mighty name of Jesus. Father Lord, empower me to believe in your promises, in the name of Jesus, in the mighty name of Jesus. Almighty God, by the power in the name of Jesus, I destroy every work of the devil in my life, in the name of Jesus. Father Lord, help me to do greater works, more than Jesus did, in the name of Jesus. Every evil arrow ever fired against me by anyone living or dead, go back to your base, in the name of Jesus. I command every evil development in my life to be terminated and destroyed, in the name of Jesus. Every satanic embargo working in my life, be lifted, in the name of Jesus. Father Lord, guide me into every truth and bless me beyond my imaginations, in the name of Jesus.

THANK YOU!

I'd like to use this time to thank you for purchasing my books and helping my ministry and work. Any copy of my book you buy helps to fund my ministry and family, as well as offering much-needed inspiration to keep writing. My family and I are very thankful, and we take your assistance very seriously.

You have already accomplished so much, but I would appreciate an honest review of some of my books through the link below. This is critical since reviews reflect how much an author's work is respected.

Please [click here] to leave a review on Amazon. If you're viewing from a printed version, please visit amazon.com/review/create-review?asin=B0CZV3WR19 to leave a review.

Please be aware that I read and value all comments and reviews. You can always post a review even though you haven't finished the book yet, and then edit your reviews later.

Thank you so much as you spare a precious moment of your time and may God bless you and meet you at the very point of your need.

You can also send me an email to hello@madueke.com if you encounter any difficulty while writing your review.

PRAYER M. MADUEKE'S BESTSELLING BOOKS

Click on any of the [Buy Now] buttons to view or purchase them on my website. If you're viewing from a printed version, please visit madueke.com and search for these books.

1. Dictionary of Demons & Complete Deliverance   [Buy Now]

2. Monitoring Spirits   [Buy Now]

3. Praying with The Blood of Jesus   [Buy Now]

4. The Power of Speaking in Tongues   [Buy Now]

5. Speaking Things into Existence by Faith   [Buy Now]

6. Discerning and Defeating the Ahab & Jezebel Spirit   [Buy Now]

7. Defeating the Python Spirit   [Buy Now]

8. 35 Special Dangerous Decrees   [Buy Now]

9. 21/40 Nights of Decrees and Your Enemies Will Surrender   [Buy Now]

10. Command the Morning, Day and Night   [Buy Now]

11. Evil Summon   [Buy Now]

12. Overcoming & Destroying the Spirit of Rejection & Hatred   [Buy Now]

13. Queen of Heaven: Wife of Satan   [Buy Now]

14. The False Prophet   [**Buy Now**]

15. Dominion Over Sickness & Disease   [**Buy Now**]

16. The Battle Plan for Destroying Foundational Witchcraft   [**Buy Now**]

17. The Queen of the Coast   [**Buy Now**]

18. Dictionary of Unmerited Favor   [**Buy Now**]

19. Prayers for Breakthrough in your Business   [**Buy Now**]

20. A Jump From Evil Altar   [**Buy Now**]

21. 100 Days Prayers to Wake Up Your Lazarus   [**Buy Now**]

22. Breaking Evil Yokes   [**Buy Now**]

23. When Evil Altars are Multiplied   [**Buy Now**]

24. The Battle Plan for Destroying Foundational Occultism   [**Buy Now**]

25. Prayers for Protection   [**Buy Now**]

26. Prayers for Academic Success   [**Buy Now**]

27. Your Dream Directory   [**Buy Now**]

28. Prayers for Financial Breakthrough   [**Buy Now**]

29. Destiny and Star Hunters   [**Buy Now**]

30. Prayers to Pray during Courtship   [**Buy Now**]

31. 91 Days Decrees to Takeover the Year   [**Buy Now**]

4 Free Ebooks

In order to say a 'Thank You' for purchasing *Battleground Prayers and Decrees*, I offer these books to you in appreciation. Click or type **madueke.com/free-gift** in your browser.

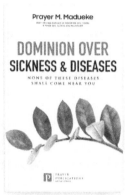
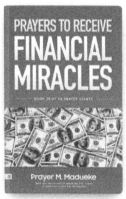

Message from the Author

I want to see you succeed, grow, and break free from negativity and obstacles. My hope is for you to thrive, unaffected by negative influences and challenging situations. Because of that, please permit me to introduce two courses that I believe passionately will help you:

1. To break the evil altars and powers of your father's house, The role of altars in the realm of existence is very key because altars are meeting places between the physical and the spiritual, between the visible and the invisible.

   Unless a man cuts off the evil flow from the power of his father's house, he will not fulfil his destiny. Click here to learn more about my course on how to tear down unholy altars and close the enemy's entryways into your life!

2. To help you seamlessly break iron-like problems, illness, delayed marriage, poverty, or any long-standing battle.

   Discover the transformative power of Christian fasting and prayer. Remember, Matthew 17:21 teaches us, *"But this kind of demon does not go out except by prayer and fasting."* Ready to overcome your struggles? Click here to learn more about this course.

Embrace the journey ahead with faith, for through prayer, fasting, and the dismantling of evil altars, you shall unlock the doors to spiritual liberation and divine breakthrough. May your path be illuminated by His grace as you walk towards a life free from bondage.

If you're seeing this from the physical copy, type the link: madueke.com/courses in your browser to view all the courses on my website.

Christian Counselling

We were created for a greater purpose than only survival and God wants us to live a full life.

If you need prayer or counselling, or if you have any other inquiries, please visit the counselling page on my website to know when I will be available for a phone call.

Click or type **links.madueke.com/counselling** in your browser.

Let's Connect on Youtube ▶

Join me on my YouTube channel, "Prayer M. Madueke," where I share powerful insights, guidance, and prayers for spiritual breakthroughs.

Subscribe today to unlock the secrets of the Kingdom and embrace an abundant life. Let's grow together!

Click or type **links.madueke.com/youtube** in your browser.

An Invitation to Become a Ministry Partner

I appreciate the support and inquiries I have received regarding collaboration with my ministry. Your prayers and dedication to the work of the Kingdom are highly valued.

You can also visit the donation page on my website if you would like to contribute or learn more about supporting my ministry: madueke.com/donate.

Thank you for your continued support and faithfulness in Christ Jesus.

Made in the USA
Las Vegas, NV
11 July 2024

92171947R00267